A Luxury of the Understanding

A Luxury of the Understanding

On the Value of True Belief

Allan Hazlett

OXFORD

UNIVERSITY PRESS

OXFORD

UNIVERSITY PRESS

Great Clarendon Street, Oxford, OX2 6DP,
United Kingdom

Oxford University Press is a department of the University of Oxford.
It furthers the University's objective of excellence in research, scholarship,
and education by publishing worldwide. Oxford is a registered trade mark of
Oxford University Press in the UK and in certain other countries

First Edition published in 2013

Impression: 2

Published in the United States of America by Oxford University Press
198 Madison Avenue, New York, NY 10016, United States of America

British Library Cataloguing in Publication Data
Data available

Library of Congress Control Number: 2013938358

ISBN 978–0–19–967480–0

Printed and bound in Great Britain by
CPI Group, (UK) Ltd, Croydon, CR0 4YY

I wasn't sure whether to go back to that, whether, if I insisted, he'd end up telling me what had happened or what he'd found out, I knew he would tell me something, however partial or erroneous, but it's easy to want to know nothing when you still don't know, once you do, you've no choice, he was right, it's better to know about things, but only once you do know them (and I still didn't).

—Javier Marias, A Heart So White

Acknowledgements

Even the sympathetic reader will note that this book leaves myriad questions unanswered, even unconsidered; and most of you will have many other complaints. Revisions, amendments, corrections, additions, codas, qualifications, and clarifications could have gone on indefinitely. There are some vexing omissions: a discussion of contemporary accounts of intellectual virtue would have been appealing; an historical genealogy of the idea of the value of truth would have been illuminating; an inquiry into the nature of belief would have been another book. In any event, before acknowledging my numerous debts to others, I should like to acknowledge these failures (among others) of my own.

I developed the approach to philosophy applied in this book, and the broader ethical picture that it supports and with which it coheres, with Simon Feldman, over the last decade. For being a great interlocutor and friend, I owe him thanks.

The Epistemology Reading Group at the University of Edinburgh read a manuscript of this book in the Fall of 2012. The feedback I received from members of that Group has saved me from many errors; for their help I am most grateful.

I should like to thank, for conversations and valuable feedback: Mark James Adams, Cathy Bach, Anne Baril, Tim Bates, Michael Brady, Evan Butts, Dave Chambers, Matthew Chrisman, Bryan Frances, John Greco, Stephen Grimm, Brian Hazlett, Daniel Howard-Snyder, Xingming Hu, Sebastian Köhler, Michael Lynch, Robin McKenna, Duncan Pritchard, Mike Ridge, Bill Rowley, Nishi Shah, Ted Sider, Ernie Sosa, Asbjørn Steglich-Petersen, Valerie Tiberius, Nick Treanor, Lani Watson, Ralph Wedgwood, Lee Whittington, and Jared Woodard, as well as Peter Momtchiloff and my readers at Oxford University Press. I'll also include here the Graduate Center Bar, in Providence, and the Brass Monkey, in Edinburgh.

In May 2008 research for this book was supported by a Faculty Research Grant from Fordham University (who provided cash) and by the Arché Centre at the University of St. Andrews (who provided an office), and in April 2012 by a Small Research Grant from the British Academy.

I presented material for this book in 2008 at the APA Central Division meeting in Chicago, at the Arché Centre in St. Andrews, at Durham University, and at the University of Arizona; in 2009 at a conference on *Epistemic Goodness* at the University of Oklahoma, and at a workshop on *The Normativity of Belief and Epistemic Agency* at the Instituto de Investigaciones Filosóficas at the Universidad Nacional Autónoma de México; in 2010 at the University of Edinburgh, at the University of Glasgow, at Rochester University, and at East Carolina University; in 2011 at the winter meeting of the Scots Philosophical Association, in Edinburgh; and in 2012 at Edinburgh's Departmental Symposium. My sincere thanks to all those audiences for their questions and objections, and for their hospitality.

AH

Edinburgh, December 2012

Prologue

Before making any move … he threw back his head and gave a long trombone-blast of anarchistic laughter. It was all so wonderful, even if it did go wrong, and it wouldn't.

—Kingsley Amis, *Lucky Jim*

Imagine that you have just fallen in love. Your love is extraordinary. It's come unexpectedly and without warning, but it's the most brilliantly dizzying feeling you've ever experienced. You've been transformed, but more than that: your world has been transformed, for now everything seems different. Things, places, events, ideas—their existence, their very nature, is colored by their relationship to you and your beloved. You look at each other, embarrassed, and the meaning of the song playing on the radio changes forever. You'll never visit Logan Airport again without thinking of her, the way her eyes lit up when she came into the arrivals hall. The significance of entire cities shifts: he was born in Lexington, went to college in Chicago, and fell in love with you in Baton Rouge. But more than this: you've not only been transformed, you've been transubstantiated: you aren't just yourself in a new relationship, you're a new self, essentially defined by that relationship. You've become a relational being. Unused to this existence, you imagine that it's not really happening. Your feet feel light and the sidewalk feels elastic. Can other people tell how strange you've become? Your behavior must give you away: you drive from one coast to another for a surprise rendezvous that is both spontaneous and inevitable; you cringe at a cynical joke that you would have loved—before your strange metamorphosis. You don't know who you are; your beliefs and values seem up for grabs: you're a vegetarian but her roasted beef ribs somehow seem appealing; you've never liked pets but you find yourself wanting to play with his dog. You're in love, and you realize that the supreme good in the entire universe is your beloved's smile. You keep saying to yourself: don't let this end, don't let this end, don't let this miraculous, incredible, perfect state of affairs ever come to an end.

But your love is ordinary. Like most loves, it will probably come to an end. Your beloved will stop loving you, and you will stop loving your beloved. And your relationship with your beloved will probably be severed along the way. It might be an amicable and mutually agreeable breakup; it might be a messy divorce. Someone will cheat on someone—you hope it doesn't come to that, but it probably will. You do some research on other people's relationships, hoping that it's some alien demographic that's driving the divorce rate up. Imagine that it isn't: you learn that most romantic relationships, of the sort that you are in, are impermanent. This seems like good evidence that your relationship is likely to end; suppose that's right. And now imagine further that your relationship *is* likely to end—in whatever sense future events are likely or unlikely.

What should you believe, when it comes to the proposition that your relationship is likely to end? We stipulated that that proposition is true, and that you have good evidence that it is true. You hope that your relationship won't end; you want nothing more than for it not to end; you *need* it not to end. But the question remains: what should you believe?

This book is motivated by that question. It won't answer it, and indeed it won't address it directly. A more basic question needs to be addressed first, a question about the value of true belief, and that question will be the topic of most of what follows. But I hope most of all to convince you that the answer to the present question—about what you should believe, when you're in love—is not at all obvious. It's profoundly un-obvious what you should believe, in the situation described above.

You might think it's obvious that you *should not* believe that your relationship is likely to end. One reason you might think this would be that you think something like this: in the situation described, you have evidence that you and your beloved are an exception to the statistical regularities that you researched. In effect, on this proposal, you don't have reason to think that most romantic relationships, of the sort that you are in, are impermanent, because there is something exceptional about the relationship you are in—it's not actually of the relevant "sort." There is something right about this idea. When you are in love, it sometimes seems like your relationship will never end—it can be hard, or impossible, to imagine such a thing. Inconceivability is a kind of evidence for impossibility, so perhaps the lover's inability to imagine her relationship ending is a kind of evidence that it won't. But this seems like a bad argument. For presumably all relationships feel this way at first, including those that end, and which comprise the majority of relationships. Better: presumably there is no reliable connection between the feeling of romantic necessity, as we might call it, and actual relationship success. Perhaps this is wrong, but it seems plausible, and you've been given no reason to think that it's true, in the situation described above. If this is right, then the present proposal, in defense of the view that you obviously should not believe that your relationship is likely to end, won't work.

A different kind of reason that you might think it's obvious that you should not believe that your relationship is likely to end is that you think such a belief would be really unpleasant, in the situation described, and that you should therefore avoid forming such a belief, either by suspending judgment or by believing that your relationship is not likely to end. There is something right about this idea, too. But as articulated, this proposal won't work either. The reason is that it seems to rely on the principle that you should never do something that will be really unpleasant. But this is implausible, since there are lots of situations in which the best thing to do is really unpleasant. Health-preserving medical treatments can be really unpleasant, for example, but we should not conclude, from that fact alone, that you should not undergo health-preserving medical treatments. Romantic relationships, to take another example, can be really unpleasant, but we should not conclude, from that fact alone, that you should avoid romantic relationships. So the present proposal, as articulated, won't work.

You might reply that the relevant belief—that your relationship is likely to end— isn't merely really unpleasant, but is also bad vis-à-vis its potential consequences on the relationship, and so (plausibly) on your general wellbeing. This idea is important, and we'll be looking closely at the relationship between true belief and wellbeing in what follows. But, as we'll see, that relationship is fantastically complicated, and far too complicated for it to be *obvious* that you should not believe that your relationship is likely to end, in the situation described above.

You might think it's obvious that you *should* believe that your relationship is likely to end. One reason you might think this would be that you think that not believing this truth is likely to have detrimental consequences on your relationship, and so (plausibly) on your general wellbeing. Again, we'll be looking closely at the relationship between true belief and wellbeing below, but the relationship is too complicated for anything about it to be obvious.

A different kind of reason that you might think it's obvious that you should believe that your relationship is likely to end is that you think that true belief is valuable for its own sake. The truth—that your relationship is likely to end—is staring you in the face; you've got very good evidence in favor of this proposition. You should therefore believe that proposition, so the argument goes, and neither suspend judgment nor believe its negation. There is something right about this idea, as well, but what exactly is right about it is difficult to articulate. This is why we'll soon turn our attention to the question of the value of true belief.

In what follows I'll argue for two theses. The first is that true belief is at most *sometimes* valuable vis-à-vis the wellbeing of the believer. The second is that, although true belief is always "epistemically" valuable, this is a trivial consequence of the definition of "epistemic," and we should be anti-realists about "epistemic normativity." The best way to capture the stance towards the value of true belief that is adopted in this book is to say that it is a *skeptical* stance. It is most certainly skeptical of the idea that the value of true belief is *obvious*.

In my view, true belief is valuable only to the extent that, and in the sense that, some people value true belief. Our love of truth—the contingent fact that some people love true belief—is all there is to the value of true belief. I won't be able to provide a comprehensive defense of this view here, but I will try to convince you that some common and initially plausible positions, which favor the value of true belief, should be rejected. This should at least make plain the appeal of the view just mentioned.

Contents

1

Two Ancient Ideas

Methinks I am like a man, who having struck on many shoals, and having narrowly escap'd ship-wreck in passing a small firth, has yet the temerity to put out to sea in the same leaky weather-beaten vessel, and even carries his ambition so far as to think of compassing the globe under these disadvantageous circumstances.

—Hume, *Treatise of Human Nature*

This book is a critical study of the value of true belief, an examination of the idea that true belief has value.[1] This chapter will introduce two ideas that will be with us throughout. The first idea, which is evaluative, is that true belief is better than false belief. The second idea, which is metaphysical, is that there is something in the nature or essence of human beings, or in the nature or essence of our beliefs, that makes us, or our beliefs, directed at truth.

Although a few important conclusions will be drawn in this chapter, most big issues will be introduced here and examined in detail in later chapters, which are divided into two parts: Part I concerns what I will call the "eudaimonic" value of true belief (Chapters 2–4); Part II concerns the "epistemic" value of true belief (Chapters 5–9). Our task in this chapter will be to get a sense of the issues that are at stake in those later chapters, and to draw some distinctions that will prove essential later on.

The philosophical questions at stake here are complex and not well understood. It would be insensible for anyone to claim to know their answers. My aim is to establish the virtues and vices of various views, which is not to say that my approach isn't partisan: I argue for a particular answer to the question of the value of true belief. On my view, although it's plausible that true belief is sometimes valuable, it's not the case that true belief is always valuable (Chapter 4), nor is it the case that true belief is normally valuable (Chapters 2–3). And I shall defend anti-realism about the "epistemic" value of true belief (Chapter 9). Overall, these views are best described as a form of skepticism about the value of true belief. But all my arguments are based on assumptions; your

---

[1] On the title of the book, see the Epilogue. "The understanding" refers to the intellectual faculty (as in: "a heart unfortified, a mind impatient, an understanding simple and unschool'd"), not to the species of knowledge (as in: "give it an understanding, but no tongue").

assumptions might be different and you might come to different conclusions. When we have finished, however, we will be able to see various assumptions in play, and we will be able to see the motivations for, and commitments of, the various views from which we can choose.

If we can say anything about philosophers in general, it's that they love truth. Someone who purported to be a philosopher, but lacked a passion for truth, would be a fraud. If a philosopher defends either of the two ideas mentioned above, therefore, we should be suspicious, just as we are always rightly suspicious when someone from some particular group insists that anyone outside that group is not "really" happy, or not doing what "nature" intended, or whatever. There is a temptation for human beings to want to say that their way of life, at least if they are happy with it, is the *only* way of life that could make anyone happy. David Hume describes this tendency in his essay of 1741 on "The Sceptic":

Almost every one has a predominant inclination, to which his other desires and affections submit, and which governs him, though, perhaps, with some intervals, through the whole course of his life. It is difficult for him to apprehend, that any thing, which appears totally indifferent to him, can ever give enjoyment to any person, or can possess charms, which altogether escape his observation. His own pursuits are always, in his account, the most engaging: The objects of his passion, the most valuable: And the road, which he pursues, the only one that leads to happiness. (Hume 1985, p. 160)

But, as Hume observes, such thinking, though common even among philosophers, is absurd. It forgets the "vast variety of inclinations and pursuits among our species" (ibid.). That the two ideas we'll discuss exhibit this common pattern may explain their popularity, but it only diminishes their credibility. Hume's skeptical interest in individual differences was not new—such interest can be traced back to the Ancient skeptics, who marveled at the diversity of human opinions, values and preferences, practices, laws, and customs, and whose work inspired a renaissance of skeptical thinking in the Early Modern period[2]—and my inquiry in this book, which is skeptical of the value of true belief, similarly emphasizes difference as against universality.

1.1 The eudaimonic value of knowledge

We shall begin by asking after the value of knowledge, which we'll first articulate as "eudaimonic"—i.e. value vis-à-vis wellbeing.

1.1.1 Socrates on the unexamined life

Among the most well-known slogans in the history of philosophy is "The unexamined life is not worth living," articulated by Socrates in Plato's *Apology* (38a).[3] Socrates

---

[2] See, for example, Sextus Empiricus, *Outlines of Pyrrhonism*, Book I, 79–90 and 145–61, or Book III, section xxiii, and Michel de Montaigne, "An Apology for Raymond Sebond."

[3] For English quotations from Plato I am using G.M.A. Grube's translations of the *Apology*, *Meno*, and *Republic*, in Plato 1997.

has been asked to defend his philosophical practice against the charge that it's impious and socially corrupting. He responds by maintaining that philosophy is "the greatest good for a man," and that "the unexamined life is not worth living for men." Call this the **Socratic maxim**.

Life is said to be not worth living if one fails to *exetazein* life; the word means to examine well or to inquire into. Inquiry is intentional activity with a certain goal: knowledge about the thing examined. Someone who inquires about x seeks knowledge about x. Why should we think, then, that intentional activity aimed at knowledge of life (setting aside for the moment what knowledge "of life" amounts to) is so valuable that life is not worth living without it?

The Socratic maxim suggests that knowledge (of life) is extremely valuable. This suggestion is based on the idea that inquiry about x is valuable only if knowledge about x is valuable. And this idea, in turn, seems well supported on the assumption that aiming at x is valuable only if x is valuable. But this is not always the case. Suppose my physician prescribes the following regimen: I shall stretch the muscles in my lower back by trying to touch the floor while standing up. Aiming at touching the floor is good, since it leads me to stretch, but touching the floor (we can easily imagine) is not good. We can even imagine a variant on this case in which aiming at x is valuable while x is disvaluable: if my physician gets me to stretch by placing an appealing cupcake on the floor, which cupcake would actually be quite unhealthy for me were I to get my hands on it. Aiming at acquiring the cupcake is good, but acquiring the cupcake is bad. These cases show not only that aiming at x can be valuable while x is not valuable, but also that the value of aiming at x need not be explained in terms of the value of x. The goodness of touching the floor is not what explains the goodness of trying to touch the floor; it's the goodness of stretching that explains the goodness of trying to touch the floor.

It's possible that the relationship between inquiry and knowledge, when it comes to their value, is akin to the relationship between trying to touch the floor and touching the floor, when it comes to their value. But note well that this conclusion is not implied by the skeptical thought that inquiry will never terminate with the acquisition of knowledge. That is consistent with knowledge being valuable, and with the value of knowledge explaining the value of inquiry. There are at least two (compatible) possibilities here. The first is that inquiry is good because it gets us *closer* to knowledge, which is good. So even though knowledge cannot be acquired, the value of knowledge explains why seeking knowledge is valuable. The second is that inquiry is good because it *represents* knowledge, which is good, as being good. Even though knowledge cannot be acquired, by seeking knowledge the inquirer treats knowledge as something valuable, and since knowledge is valuable, inquiry is therefore valuable in the sense that it is an apt response to the value of knowledge.

And for this reason, saying that the value of knowledge explains the value of inquiry does not imply that inquiry is merely of instrumental value. Something has **instrumental value** iff it is valuable for the sake of something else, i.e. if it is valuable as a means to some (wholly distinct) end;[4] something has **final value** iff it is valuable for its own sake. The value of knowledge could explain the value of inquiry, even if inquiry never leads to knowledge (because knowledge is impossible), and therefore even if inquiry has no instrumental value, because it is not a means to the end of knowledge.

Here I'll pursue the idea that the Socratic maxim suggests that knowledge (of life) is extremely valuable, noting only that this does not imply that knowledge (of life) is possible nor that inquiry is merely instrumentally valuable. But you may opt for an alternative interpretation, on which the relationship between inquiry and knowledge, when it comes to their value, is akin to the relationship between trying to touch the floor and touching the floor, when it comes to their value.

So the Socratic maxim suggests that knowledge (of life) is extremely valuable. On the most obvious reading of this, the value in question here is value vis-à-vis wellbeing. It's the value of knowledge vis-à-vis wellbeing that explains why the unexamined life is not worth living (or "not to be lived," an equally good translation). This sort of value— which we'll call **eudaimonic value**[5]—will be our concern in Part I of this book. Eudaimonic value, for S, is value vis-à-vis the wellbeing of S. Eudaimonic value, for a person, concerns what is good and bad for that person, i.e. her wellbeing. "**Wellbeing**" is used here in a broad sense, such that it is a name for welfare, the good life (on one disambiguation, see below), quality of life, happiness—in the sense of a happy life, rather than the feeling of being happy (Kraut 1979, p. 179), and not necessarily in the sense of a life of "contentment, enjoyment, or pleasure" (Foot 2001, p. 85)—or for "living well and faring well" (Aristotle, *Nicomachean Ethics*, 1095a15).[6] Just as "everything" is the uninformative answer to the question of what there is, "wellbeing" is the uninformative answer to the question "What makes someone's life go best?" (Parfit 1984, pp. 493–502), or, more exactly, "What makes a life a good one for the person who lives it?" (Scanlon 1993, p. 185) Given this broad sense of "wellbeing," there are various theories of wellbeing, including hedonist theories, desire-fulfillment theories, life-satisfaction theories, and essentialist theories—more on which below (§1.1.6). "Eudaimonic value," therefore, does not necessarily refer to value vis-à-vis Aristotelian *eudaimonia*, nor to value vis-à-vis *eudaimonia* according to any particular theory, nor to value vis-a-vis wellbeing, on an essentialist theory of wellbeing. "Eudaimonic value"

---

[4] Note the requirement that the end be wholly distinct from the means. What I will call "constitutive value" (§1.1.5) is a species of final value, but some would call it instrumental value where the means is "internal" to the end.

[5] From the Greek word *eudaimonia*: "prosperity, happiness" (Liddell and Scott, *Greek-English Lexicon*, abridged). This terminology reflects consideration. "Wellbeing" doesn't work grammatically: there's no adjectival and adverbial forms. Eudaimonic value is the same as what some would call "prudential value," but "prudential" suggests expediency and self-interest, which we should not build in to our conception of wellbeing. "Ethical value" captures the idea that we are concerned here with the question of how to live a good life, but is too suggestive of morality, or of the view that we ought to pursue or promote (our own or others') wellbeing (on which we'll remain neutral). "Pragmatic value" suggests philosophical pragmatism, and, again, expediency and self-interest.

[6] For English quotations from Aristotle I am using W.D. Ross' translations of the *Nicomachean Ethics* and the *Metaphysics* in Aristotle 1984.

refers, by definition, to value vis-a-vis wellbeing, whatever wellbeing is. In other words, "eudaimonic" is to be understood formally, not materially.[7]

Wellbeing is the uninformative, i.e. trivial, answer to the question of what makes someone's life go best for her. It is *not* a trivial answer to the **ethical** question of what she ought to pursue or promote (cf. Sumner 2002, pp. 33–4, Tiberius 2008, pp. 9–15), although one might defend that non-trivial ethical view.

Furthermore, eudaimonic value is conceptually distinct from **moral** value, moral virtue, and from other moral notions (cf. Sumner 1996, pp. 24–5). Eudaimonic value concerns the wellbeing of a person, and the concept leaves open the possibility that something might be morally good for a person but eudaimonically bad for her. This possibility is plausibly realized in cases of morally virtuous self-sacrifice. However, the concept also leaves open the possibility of causal and constitutive connections between morality and wellbeing. This possibility is plausibly realized in as much as moral virtue is a constituent of wellbeing. The view that morality is among the constituents of wellbeing represents an appealing *via media* between, on the one hand, the view that being moral is irrelevant to a person's wellbeing, and, on the other hand, the view that being moral never involves a sacrifice of wellbeing. In what follows I will assume that falling short of moral virtue is sometimes better for a person than not (§2.9.1), but that moral virtue is partially constitutive of wellbeing (§3.3.2). We'll look at the social value of true belief, below (§4.4).

I assume no particular theory of wellbeing. I will, however, make some controversial assumptions about wellbeing. When I say that I assume no particular theory of wellbeing, I don't mean that what I'll say will be compatible with any theory of wellbeing. You might object that little can be said about wellbeing without first settling on a theory of wellbeing. I disagree. It's wrong, in general, that particular claims about x can't be evaluated until a philosophical account of x has been given. There are two reasons for this. First, so long as a concept is one that we already possess, prior to philosophical theorizing, then however vague, ambiguous, and in need of clarification that concept is, there will still often be claims, employing that concept, that are obviously true. You don't need to settle on a theory of wellbeing to know that your life would go worse if, while everything else remains the same, you were to be tortured every day for the rest of your life. Second, and more importantly, we must consider how the imagined methodology would go. How shall we evaluate, for example, various theories of wellbeing? The only possible way to do this is to consider their particular implications about wellbeing, and to consider the plausibility of those particular implications. But

---

[7] This usage is appealing, in part, because it easily allows us to give a natural interpretation of the disagreement between (for example) defenders of desire-fulfillment theories of wellbeing and Aristotelian essentialists: the two camps are disagreeing about the nature of wellbeing (cf. Kraut 1979, and also MacIntyre 2007, p. 181–2, on "virtue"). This isn't to say that there aren't other ways to articulate the disagreement (e.g. we might treat both camps as agreeing that wellbeing is desire-fulfillment, but disagreeing about whether wellbeing is to be pursued). But understanding this as a disagreement about wellbeing is the most natural interpretation of the debate.

this means that, in at least one sense, we can evaluate particular claims about wellbeing without having antecedently settled on a theory of wellbeing. This is not to say that we might not learn something about particular cases by seeing what our preferred theory says about them. But this means that it's not misguided to consider particular claims about wellbeing without first adopting a specific theory of wellbeing. (Compare other areas of philosophy.)

Our discussion of the eudaimonic value of knowledge, and later true belief, will require a modal notion of eudaimonic betterness:

> **Definition:** The proposition that p is better for S than the proposition that q iff either p and were it the case that q then S would be worse off, or q and were it the case that p then S would be better off.

To say that the proposition that p is better for S than the proposition that q is to say that the fact that p makes (or would make) S's life go better than it would go were it the case that q (or better than it actually goes given the fact that q). To say that the proposition that p is better for S than the proposition that q is a way of saying that the proposition that p is good for S, that the proposition that p contributes to S's wellbeing, at least compared to the proposition that q, and that the proposition that q is bad for S, that the proposition that q detracts from S's wellbeing, at least compared to the proposition that p. This is what I shall mean below when I speak of one thing being "better" than another; I'll not mention the subject S when she is implied by the context.

Returning to the Socratic maxim: why should we think that knowledge of life has eudaimonic value? Is it the case, for example, that knowledge of life is better than ignorance of life? Here we must make a decision: does the eudaimonic value of knowledge of life derive from the eudaimonic value of knowledge in general, or from something about knowledge of life in particular?

It seems clear, at least when it comes to the idea that the unexamined life is not worth living, that Socrates holds the latter view. Examination of life seeks a particular species of knowledge, and it's the pursuit of this particular species of knowledge that Socrates maintains is necessary for life being worth living. For it's the practice of *philosophical* examination that is at issue in the *Apology*. What Socrates defiantly refuses to give up is inquiry into philosophical questions in ethics and metaphysics—the subject matter of his inquiries as depicted in Plato's dialogues. Knowledge about these matters, therefore, is eudaimonically valuable, in such a way that examination of these matters is necessary for one's life being worth living. Consider the maxim in context:

[I]f I say that it is the greatest good for a man to discuss virtue every day and those other things about which you hear me conversing and testing myself and others, for the unexamined life is not worth living, you will believe me even less. (op. cit.)

The Socratic maxim, on this interpretation, says that knowledge of answers to philosophical questions in ethics and metaphysics, which we might call "wisdom" (although this is out of step with contemporary usage), is eudaimonically valuable such that life is not worth living unless one seeks it. Is this plausible?

I do not think it is, but because my primary concern is with the value of knowledge in general, I will be brief here. The idea that the lives of non-philosophers are not worth living (whether this is down to their lack of eudaimonic value, or whether it's down to something else) seems both elitist, in condemning the great majority of human lives to "not worth living" status, and suspiciously self-serving, in as much as this idea about the worthlessness of non-philosophical lives is put forward exclusively by philosophers. Even granting that philosophical inquiry is eudaimonically valuable, the Socratic maxim seems to ignore all the other eudaimonically valuable things that might make a life go well enough to be worth living: scientific inquiry, the appreciation or pursuit of athletic excellence, friendship, living with a family, the appreciation or creation of music, literature, cuisine, and the other forms of art, romantic relationships, the pleasures of drink and sex, and so on. Even this list seems rarefied; where are the suburban values of owning a home and having a career? If Aaron and Maria excel at their well-paying and interesting jobs, maintain a pleasant house where they raise their happy and precocious children, enjoy home-cooked food and going out to minor-league baseball games with the kids, but never give a moment's thought to the big philosophical questions, could anyone in good faith say that their lives are not worth living?

It will not help to say that Socrates is employing an ancient conception of wellbeing, one that is foreign to contemporary common sense, unless this is just to offer an historical explanation of why he got things wrong. Nor will it help to say that Socrates is appealing to a notion of perfect human excellence that is a rare and elite thing, acquired only by a select few. Consider the context of the *Apology*: Socrates has been threatened with death, and in the passage in question he is explaining why he would not cease to practice philosophy even if ordered to do so by the law, on pain of death. Socrates effectively says to the jury, "Give me philosophy, or give me death!" and the jury chooses to give him the latter. In the context of that story, the Socratic maxim is most naturally interpreted as meaning that death is superior to a life without philosophical examination, i.e. that the unexamined life is not worth living, not (merely) that the unexamined life falls short of perfect human excellence.[8]

Socrates defends his maxim on the grounds that philosophy is "the greatest good for men." If not for this fact, we might interpret his claim in a relative way, on which Socrates is saying that, given *his own* commitment to philosophy, he would rather die than give up the pursuit of wisdom. In other words, we might interpret him as saying that the unexamined life is not worth living *for Socrates*. On this reading, Socrates would be heroically affirming his love of wisdom, without making any claim about the value of philosophy for human beings in general. It can certainly be the case that someone cares about something so much that she would rather die than give up its pursuit, and we should have no objection to caring about wisdom in that way, nor to Plato's depicting his teacher as caring about wisdom in that way.

---

[8] Cf. the distinction between flourishing and excellence (§1.1.6).

1.1.2 The eudaimonic ideal of knowledge, implausibly formulated

Let's turn our attention to the idea that knowledge in general is eudaimonically valuable. When we speak of the eudaimonic value of knowledge (or true belief), we'll mean the value of knowledge vis-à-vis the wellbeing of the knower (or believer). Let's say that **S knows whether p** iff either p and S knows that p or ~p and S knows that ~p. We'll take **ignorance about whether p** to be the logical negation of knowing whether p. Consider the following thesis, which affirms the eudaimonic value of knowledge in general:

> **Implausibly formulated eudaimonic ideal of knowledge:** For any subject S and proposition that p, knowing whether p is better for S than being ignorant about whether p.

In other words, for any subject S and proposition that p, either S knows whether p and were she ignorant about whether p she'd be worse off, or S is ignorant about whether p and were she to know whether p she'd be better off.[9] As the name suggests, this claim is not plausible:

Karen is scheduled to compete in a tennis match against an opponent that, unbeknownst to her, is very much her superior on the court. Given an anxious disposition, she will perform terribly and almost certainly lose if she is made aware of her opponent's talent. Karen's coach has seen the opposing player in practice, but knows that Karen stands a chance only if she believes that she and her opponent are evenly matched. So he tells Karen that she and her opponent are evenly matched, and she believes this. She begins the match confident and optimistic.

Karen would *not* be better off were she knowledgeable about whether her opponent is vastly superior to her, so knowing is *not* better for her than being ignorant.[10] So the implausibly formulated eudaimonic ideal of knowledge is false.

I'll have much more to say in defense of the existence of species of eudaimonically valuable false belief. We'll consider evidence from social psychology that supports the idea that false beliefs, resulting from "self-enhancement bias," are often eudaimonically valuable (Chapter 2), and I'll argue that false beliefs about other people are often eudaimonically valuable (Chapter 3). And we'll consider some other candidates for "functional false belief," below (§7.4.1).

There is an important objection to our counterexample that can be addressed here. You might argue that Karen is irrational or vicious in some way, and that this is what puts her in the unfortunate position where ignorance is better for her than knowledge. What would be best for Karen, so the argument goes, is not to falsely believe that she

---

[9] As formulated the eudaimonic ideal of knowledge leaves open the question of whether ignorance in the form of false belief is worse than ignorance in the form of lack of belief, or ignorance in the form of suspended judgment. Few would want to say that a lack of true belief about uninteresting or insignificant truths is disvaluable, vis-à-vis wellbeing (cf. §§4.2–4.3). My focus in this book will be on ignorance in the form of false belief.

[10] Note that this doesn't imply that Karen's coach is morally justified in lying to Karen.

is evenly matched with her opponent, but to abandon her nervous disposition, and develop the strength of character needed to perform well despite knowing that she is the inferior player. But given our modal definition of betterness (§1.1.1), this objection is a non sequitur. The implausibly formulated eudaimonic ideal of knowledge entails that, when you are ignorant, you would be better off were you knowledgeable. It does not merely entail that, when you are ignorant *and* you are perfectly rational or perfectly virtuous, then you would be better off were you knowledgeable.

The eudaimonic ideal might be reformulated, with a restriction placed on the domain of quantification, such that it applies only to the perfectly rational or perfectly virtuous. This might yield what Gavin Lawrence (1993) calls an "ideally circumstanced...ideal" or a **utopian ideal** (p. 8). We won't consider that idea further. One reason why such a reformulation will be set aside is that we seek to articulate principles of wellbeing that might provide a certain kind of **guidance** for living well that applies to us, as we actually and presently are. If I know that the proposition that p would be better for me than the alternatives, then I've got a nice bit of advice: try to make it the case that p. But if all I know is that the proposition that p would be better for my perfectly rational or perfectly virtuous counterpart, then I've got nothing to go on, given the fact that I know I'm neither perfectly rational (nor even especially rational) nor perfectly virtuous (nor even especially virtuous).[11]

This is not to say that a utopian ideal cannot provide guidance of a different kind. A description of my perfectly rational or perfectly virtuous counterpart would provide me with something to aspire to and work towards. Guidance would come in the form of the injunction to try to make myself like my perfectly rational or perfectly virtuous counterpart as possible. But I will require a different sort of guidance so long as my efforts to become perfectly rational or perfectly virtuous are not immediately successful. Imagine that I suffer from intemperance, and that I am on my way home for Thanksgiving dinner, when I realize that I ought to stop at the pub to wish some old friends a happy holiday. However, I have excellent reason to think that entering the pub will precipitate a bender that will land me in the drunk tank and ruin Thanksgiving for my family. I should obviously not go to the pub. But my perfectly virtuous counterpart would be better off going to the pub, to say hello and have a quick pint, before temperately heading home. I, however, am too intemperate to have any use for the advice "do what your perfectly virtuous counterpart would do."

Ideals should provide guidance. But does that mean that the eudaimonic ideal of knowledge commits us to the view that we can *choose* whether or not we are knowledgeable or ignorant about some question? That suggests a kind of voluntary control over our beliefs that many have thought impossible (cf. §8.4.1). But we are not committed to this by insisting that the eudaimonic ideal of knowledge provide guidance. The eudaimonic ideal of knowledge tells us what is, or would, be good for us.

---

[11] As Valerie Tiberius (2008) puts a related point, "[g]iven that we are not, nor ever will be, ideally or perfectly rational, it is not obviously helpful to be told that we should choose whatever we would choose if we were" (p. 7).

Guidance will be implied by the ideal in the form of the injunction to try to make it the case that p, when the proposition that p is better for me than the alternatives. How might you be guided by the eudaimonic ideal of knowledge? The implied injunction is to make it the case that you are knowledgeable. How can you be guided by this? By inquiring carefully, by reflecting critically, by engaging in the practices of the intellectually virtuous with an aim to habitually acquiring those virtues yourself, by being vigilant when it comes to your own prejudices and biases, by keeping company with the intellectually virtuous and avoiding the unreliable and the incurious, and so on.

There are other objections you might have to the putative counterexample. These will be addressed below (see, in particular, §§2.9.3–2.9.4 and §§2.10.6–2.10.7). For now, we'll reformulate the eudaimonic ideal of knowledge so as to avoid it.

1.1.3 The eudaimonic ideal of knowledge

If you are sympathetic with the eudaimonic value of knowledge, how might you respond to the putative counterexample (§1.1.2)? First, you might say that knowledge always has **prima facie** eudaimonic value (Lynch 2004, pp. 46–57, 2009a, pp. 225–8, cf. Kvanvig 2003, p. 93). "Prima facie" means something like "at first glance" or "on its face." Something that is prima facie valuable may turn out to have no value at all, if that's what further examination reveals. Knowledge doesn't *always* have prima facie value—that's just what the counterexample shows. So perhaps knowledge has prima facie value, in the sense that our default assumption is that knowledge has eudaimonic value. This claim is quite weak. Knowledge might have prima facie eudaimonic value, in this sense, but rarely turn out to be valuable, since appearances might be misleading. Fool's gold, for example, always has prima facie economic value. The philosopher sympathetic to the eudaimonic value of knowledge should not be satisfied by this. But those who say "prima facie" often mean "pro tanto"; we'll return to that more promising idea below (§1.1.4).

Second, you might say that knowledge is better than ignorance "**other things being equal**" (Finnis 1980, p. 72, Lynch 2004, p. 47, p. 54, p. 144). This claim is also weak. The eudaimonic ideal might be true, other things being equal, and yet it might turn out as a matter of fact that things are rarely equal. Imagine that I defend the eudaimonic value of taking cocaine on the grounds that, other things being equal, it's always better to take cocaine. You can't object to this that cocaine is unhealthy, or that cocaine is addictive, or that it destroys you psychologically, since I only claim that cocaine is good *other things being equal*. What I claim is that if you have two people who are the *same* in terms of health, addiction, and so on, then the one who takes cocaine is better off than the one who doesn't. This is clearly an inadequate defense of the eudaimonic value of taking cocaine. Or, at best, it shows us very little about the eudaimonic value of taking cocaine. The philosopher sympathetic to the eudaimonic ideal of knowledge should not be satisfied by this.[12]

---

[12] The idea that x is good, other things being equal, might be offered by way of articulating the idea that x has *intrinsic* value; the idea being that the goodness of x does not depend on anything other than x itself. So

Third, you might say that:

- Knowledge is **normally** better than ignorance.
- Knowledge is **generally** better than ignorance.
- Knowledge is **typically** better than ignorance.
- **For the most part**, knowledge is better than ignorance.[13]
- Knowledge is better than ignorance, save in **exceptional** cases.

Thus Michael Lynch (2004) says that cases of bad true belief are "exceptions that prove the rule" (p. 46), namely, the "general rule that it is good to believe what is true and only what is true" (p. 48). Linda Zagzebski says that knowing the truth is valuable "most of the time (1996, p. 200)", that "true belief is usually good for us" (2003b, p. 23), and that "sometimes caring about knowledge…can be over-ridden by other things that we care about, but my conjecture is that this does not happen very often among self-reflective persons" (2004, p. 372), and Richard Foley (1987) says that false belief is practically rational only in "funny" situations, but not in "relatively normal situations," and that while there are "exceptions," it is "highly improbable that this will happen frequently" (p. 224; see also Foley 1993, p. 27).

Claims about what is normal can be tricky to evaluate. Part of the reason is that our judgments about what is normal tend to manifest our normative commitments, even when there is agreement about statistics. Suppose that 1% of offshore oil drilling operations result in oil spillage. Oil company executives will insist that this is simply the "exception that proves the rule," namely, the rule that offshore drilling is generally safe. Environmentalists will vehemently object to this characterization; the spills are "all too typical" of offshore drilling. What the fan calls exceptions are just what the critic calls counterexamples. The oil companies call oil spills "exceptions to the rule" because they support continued offshore drilling, and the environmentalists call them "all too typical" because they oppose continued offshore drilling. Our normative commitments, therefore, can influence what cases we take to be normal. Defenders of the eudaimonic value of knowledge often appeal to perception of our immediate environment in defense of their view, where ignorance is presumed to be fantastically dangerous. In my critique of the eudaimonic value of knowledge I'll appeal to cases involving other species of ignorance: ignorance of self (Chapter 2) and ignorance of other people (Chapter 3). If perception is taken to be the normal case, then these counterexamples will appear abnormal, mere "exceptions to the rule." But this is special pleading, on behalf of the cases that support the eudaimonic value of knowledge, at the expense of the cases that threaten it. There is a worry here, that when we describe cases in which ignorance is better than knowledge as abnormal we may be doing nothing more than emphasizing our commitment to the eudaimonic value of knowledge.

you might say that knowledge has intrinsic value. We'll consider the idea that true belief has intrinsic value, below (§1.5).

[13] Cf. Aristotle: "We must be content…to indicate the truth roughly and in outline, and in speaking about things which are only for the most part true" (1094b19–23).

Someone skeptical about the eudaimonic value of knowledge, who wanted to get to the bottom of things, should be worried about all this. And if there is genuine controversy about the eudaimonic value of knowledge, little progress will be made by trading intuitions about what is, or isn't, abnormal.

Despite these worries, we'll employ an articulation of the eudaimonic value of knowledge in these terms. I'll borrow some language from Rosalind Hursthouse (1999), who articulates the idea that "the virtues, for the most part, benefit the possessor" (p. 173). On her view, this is falsified neither by cases of virtuous people faring badly nor by cases of wicked people flourishing. The claim that the virtues benefit the possessor is the claim that the virtues are "one's only reliable bet as far as a flourishing life is concerned" (p. 174). Hursthouse's claim is that no "regimen," other than virtue, "will serve one better" (p. 174), which leaves open the possibility that the "regimen" is not an especially reliable bet, just the most reliable of the options. (Consider here Hursthouse's comparison of the virtue theorist's "regimen" with a doctor's prescription: a medical treatment might be the best option, and still likely, perhaps even almost certain, to fail.) This would be falsified only by a "clearly identifiable pattern" of wicked people flourishing (pp. 173–4) or by a "clearly identifiable pattern" of virtuous people faring badly. All cases in which wicked people flourish or in which virtuous people fare badly, however, must be seen as abnormal, on this view.

Given our comparative notion of betterness (§1.1.1), we'll adopt a comparative version of Hursthouse's idea. Consider:

> **Eudaimonic ideal of knowledge:** For any subject S and proposition that p, knowing whether p is normally better for S than being ignorant about whether p. In other words, there is no clearly identifiable pattern of cases in which ignorance is better than knowledge. Thus, for any subject S and proposition that p, knowing whether p is a more reliable bet, when it comes to wellbeing, than being ignorant about whether p.

So the basic idea is that knowledge is normally better than ignorance, and what we mean by that is that there is no clearly identifiable pattern of cases in which ignorance is better than knowledge, and we take this to imply that knowledge is a more reliable bet, when it comes to wellbeing, than ignorance. (The formulation is neutral as to whether the claim is necessary or contingent.) This isn't falsified merely by cases in which ignorance is better than knowledge, as those cases can, and must, be seen as abnormal: as exceptions to the rule, as strange or one-off cases. Take, for example, Foley's (1987) "extreme example" in which believing some falsehood is necessary to save the world. Such cases are familiar in epistemology. The eudaimonic ideal of knowledge is not falsified by "extreme" cases in which ignorance is better than knowledge; it is only falsified by a clearly identifiable pattern of cases in which ignorance is better than knowledge (cf. McKay and Dennett 2009, p. 498).[14]

---

[14] Compare Linda Zagzebski's (1996) approach to the value of the virtues (which she does not take to be eudaimonic value, p. 82). "[T]he sense in which virtue makes its possessor good," for Zagzebski, is that

Our worries, articulated above, remain. As Hursthouse (1999) points out, controversy about whether the virtues benefit their possessors is controversy over "beliefs…about…human nature and the way human life works," and such beliefs are not straightforwardly beliefs about "empirical facts…accessible from 'the neutral point of view'," nor are they straightforwardly "evaluative beliefs" (p. 189). They are, she concludes, "ethical but non-evaluative beliefs about human nature and how human life goes" (ibid.). The idea that knowledge is normally better than ignorance is of exactly the same kind; and controversy about it is likewise problematic.

However, we can assume from the start that the eudaimonic ideal of knowledge is not verified if it turns out that in the statistical majority of cases, knowledge is better than ignorance (whatever exactly it would mean for there to be a statistical majority of "cases of knowledge"). On the statistical majority of roads, the more reliable bet, when it comes to avoiding a crash, is to drive on the right. But we should not say that, for all roads, driving on the right is the more reliable bet, when it comes to avoiding a crash, than driving on the left. The right thing to say is that *sometimes* driving on the right is the more reliable bet, and *sometimes* driving on the left is the more reliable bet. When you're in the UK, for example, driving on the left is the more reliable bet. There are exceptions to this rule, as when another car has stopped in the left lane and you need to swerve into the right lane to avoid it. *That* is an abnormal circumstance. But the whole business of driving in the UK is not an abnormal circumstance. It is a clearly identifiable pattern of cases in which driving on the left is the more reliable bet, when it comes to avoiding a crash.

Our counterexample (§1.1.2) didn't suggest that knowledge is never better than ignorance (cf. Lynch 2004, pp. 46–51). Below (Chapters 2 and 3), I'll describe species of eudaimonically valuable false belief. I'll argue that these constitute clearly identifiable patterns of cases in which false belief is better than true belief. By appealing to empirical psychology (Chapter 2), we'll be able to move beyond the assessment of "ethical but non-evaluative beliefs," which exist somewhere between the empirical and the non-empirical, in the direction of the empirical. And this is the best we can

"[a]nyone who has it is closer to reaching a high level of excellence than one who lacks it, other things being equal" (p. 95). Virtue in combination with vice can make someone less excellent; for all Zagzebski says, this may even be typical of virtue, when combined with vice. The sense in which it is good to possess some particular virtue, even when this makes you less excellent than you would otherwise be (because of some vice that you possess), is that possession of that virtue is an essential constituent of "a high level of excellence," and in that sense possessing the virtue makes you "closer" to "a high level of excellence." For this reason "virtue…invariably makes its possessor closer to a high level of admirability" (p. 101). My worry about this approach is that the supposed value of the virtues does not seem to be a value worth seeking. Suppose that a cheeseburger with ketchup would be the best meal for me to eat, but that I can only afford soup. It would not be good, in any way, to add ketchup to my soup, even though ketchup is an essential constituent of the best meal for me to eat, and in that sense adding ketchup will make my soup "closer" to the best meal. Note that Zagzebski also maintains something analogous to Hursthouse's claim about the eudaimomic value of the virtues: being virtuous "*usually* results in an actual increase in a person's overall moral worth" (p. 95, my emphasis) and "nothing is a virtue unless it benefits both the possessor and others in the *typical* case" (p. 100, my emphasis).

do, if we want to make progress. Our best bet for identifying patterns, when it comes to "how human life works," is empirical psychology.

1.1.4 The pro tanto eudaimonic value of knowledge

There is an alternative, and more modest, way of articulating the eudaimonic value of knowledge. Rather than saying that knowledge is *normally* better than ignorance, we might say that knowledge *always* has pro tanto eudaimonic value (DePaul 2010, p. 114). Something valuable *x* has **pro tanto** value iff the value of *x* can be trumped by other values. On the present proposal, although knowledge always has eudaimonic value, its eudaimonic value can be trumped by the value of other things. This claim is relatively weak, in the sense that it might turn out that cases in which knowledge is better than ignorance are few and far between, since its eudaimonic value might be trumped more often than not. Below (Chapter 4) we'll consider the idea that true belief always has pro tanto eudaimonic value.

We can now distinguish between two ways of articulating the idea that *x* has eudaimonic value. On the view that *x* is a **eudaimonic ideal**, *x* is normally better than alternatives. On the view that *x* is a **non-ideal eudaimonic good**, *x* is (sometimes or always) eudaimonically valuable, but *x* is not a eudaimonic ideal. One natural way of articulating the idea that knowledge is a non-ideal eudaimonic good is by saying that knowledge always has pro tanto eudaimonic value. An **ideal approach to the eudaimonic value of *x*** is one that maintains that *x* is a eudaimonic ideal; a **non-ideal approach to the eudaimonic value of *x*** is one that maintains that *x* is a non-ideal eudaimonic good.

1.1.5 Instrumental vs. constitutive eudaimonic value

Consider the idea that the only reliable way for someone to get what she wants is to make informed, in other words knowledgeable, decisions. You might defend the eudaimonic value of knowledge by appeal to this. This would be an **instrumental value approach** to the eudaimonic value of knowledge, on which knowledge is said to have **instrumental eudaimonic value.**

On such an approach, knowledge and wellbeing are conceived of as distinct (though causally connected) entities. One might argue, by contrast, that knowledge and wellbeing are not wholly distinct, as knowledge partially constitutes wellbeing. Some necessary connections are constitutive connections, when it is a necessary truth that all *F*s are *G* because being *G* (at least) partially constitutes being *F*, i.e. because (at least) part of what it is to be *F* is to be *G*. And some valuable things seems valuable in virtue of being parts of valuable wholes. Consider the aesthetic value of the parts of an aesthetically valuable painting. The aesthetic value of the painting depends, at least in part, on its beauty, and the painting's parts do not cause the painting to be beautiful, but rather constitute its beauty. Because of this, they are (so the argument might go) valuable in virtue of being parts of a valuable whole, namely, the painting. Something similar is often said of friendship: friendship does not merely cause a person's life to go well, but rather, or in addition, partially constitutes her good life. We have the following notion of a certain species of value:

Definition: Something x has **constitutive value** when x has final value in virtue of the fact that x (at least) partially constitutes some finally valuable whole.[15,16]

Given this, we can articulate a notion of final eudaimonic value, namely, constitutive eudaimonic value:

Definition: Something x has **constitutive eudaimonic value** when x has final eudaimonic value in virtue of the fact that x (at least) partially constitutes wellbeing.

Moral virtue, friendship, and knowledge have all been said to have constitutive eudaimonic value. In the sequel, I'll use "constitutive value" to mean constitutive eudaimonic value. Something has constitutive value when it is eudaimonically valuable **in virtue of** being (at least) partially constitutive of wellbeing. Given this, I shall assume that something has constitutive value only if it **contributes** to the goodness of the whole of which it is a part, by partially **explaining** the goodness of the whole of which it is a part. There may be things that are, in some sense, parts of my life, and that life may be a good human life, but those things make no contribution to the goodness of my life.

Given this conception of constitutive value, you might propose a **constitutive value approach** to the eudaimonic value of knowledge, on which knowledge (sometimes or always) has constitutive value. Constitutive value is a species of final eudaimonic value, although it may not be the only species of final eudaimonic value; here it will be treated as the alternative to instrumental eudaimonic value. (On the intrinsic value of knowledge, see §1.5.) The constitutive value of knowledge is suggested by the familiar Aristotelian idea that human beings are essentially rational beings. Thus knowledge is said to be a "basic form of good" (Finnis 1980, p. 65), "being able to…think, and reason" is described as a "central human functional capability" (Nussbaum 2000, p. 78), "intelligence" is said to be a "primary good" (Rawls 1971, p. 62), and "the pursuit of knowledge" is said to be a "human good," suited "for an important if not a central place in our life" (ibid. p. 425).

If knowledge has constitutive value, it's because knowledge is *partially* constitutive of wellbeing. Being knowledgeable is not all there is to living well. Consider someone

---

[15] Although we define constitutive value as a species of final value, this assumption won't make a difference for what follows. You might object to this definition, on the grounds that constitutive value is conditional and extrinsic value; cf. our definitions of final and instrumental value (§ 1.1.1). Cf. Kvanvig's (2003) distinction between the "external" and "internal" value of knowledge.

[16] The notion of constitutive value is not to be confused with the notion of a constitutive standard of correctness (§8.1.2).

knowledgeable to the highest possible degree whose life consists in nothing more than being pointlessly tortured all day, every day. Such a life, given some obvious assumptions about the story, goes poorly, at least to some extent, and therefore there is more to wellbeing than knowledge.

Can we say more about the specifics of the constitutive connection between knowledge and wellbeing? For example, might this idea be used to defend the eudaimonic ideal of knowledge?

A difficulty arises here because the claim that knowledge has constitutive value is ambiguous. Consider the fact that something might be partially constitutive of wellbeing, in one sense, even though that thing rarely has eudaimonic value. This is because of the nature of constitution. Think of the way in which eggs partially constitute Hollandaise sauce. It's only under certain idiosyncratic conditions that a given egg is part of some portion of Hollandaise sauce. The great majority of eggs are not part of any portion of Hollandaise sauce. For all we have said, knowledge may partially constitute wellbeing in a formally analogous way: only under certain uncommon conditions does a given piece of knowledge have any eudaimonic value at all.[17] Alternatively, one might take the claim that knowledge partially constitutes wellbeing to mean that knowledge per se has eudaimonic value.[18] But this too is compatible with rejecting the eudaimonic ideal of knowledge. For one might think that the value of knowledge, although present in every case of knowledge, is not strong enough (as it were) to make it the case that knowledge is always better than ignorance. Indeed, even if knowledge per se has constitutive value, it might turn out that knowledge is better than ignorance only under certain idiosyncratic conditions.

We can now articulate an important distinction between constitutive value approaches to the eudaimonic value of knowledge (cf. §1.1.4). **Ideal constitutive value approaches** maintain that, in virtue of the constitutive value of knowledge, knowledge is normally better than ignorance. **Non-ideal constitutive value approaches** maintain that knowledge (sometimes or always) has constitutive value, but that it's not the case that knowledge is normally better than ignorance.

Saying that knowledge (always) has constitutive value does not force us to look at our counterexample to the implausibly formulated eudaimonic ideal of knowledge any differently than we were originally inclined to look at it (§1.1.2). That original thought was something like: ignorance is better for Karen than knowledge. That

---

[17] This just raises the question of *how* knowledge constitutes wellbeing. Is it like eggs and Hollandaise sauce (a necessary ingredient, in the right proportion), or is it like walnuts and bran muffins (not an essential ingredient, but constitutive in some cases); is it like mass and weight (adding more mass gets you more weight), but not like eggs and Hollandaise (adding more eggs won't get you more Hollandaise)? Some of these issues are explored below (§4.3).

[18] Things that are F are **per se** valuable iff things that are F are valuable "as such" or in virtue of being instances of F. A corollary of this is that if things that are F are per se valuable then things that are F are always valuable: if instances of F are per se valuable, then all instances of F must be valuable, since if they weren't, it couldn't be the case that instances of F are valuable in virtue of being instances of F—their being instances of *x* wouldn't explain their having value. Note that to say that things that are F are per se valuable is not the same as to say that things that are F have final value (Sosa 2001, p. 51).

knowledge has constitutive value is orthogonal to the question of whether or not that thought is correct. Likewise, that knowledge has constitutive value does not conflict with denying the eudaimonic ideal of knowledge (§1.1.3).

However, one might understand the appeal to constitutive value in this way: that we were right in our treatment of the counterexample, in as much as we were right that ignorance can sometimes have good consequences vis-à-vis wellbeing, and that knowledge can sometimes have bad consequences vis-à-vis wellbeing. What we were wrong about, so the argument goes, was the thought that this is enough to show that ignorance is sometimes better than knowledge. Our description of the case was fine; it was our evaluation that was flawed. The constitutive value of knowledge is such that, even though Karen will likely lose her match a result of knowing about her chances, this would be better for her than to live in ignorance. After all, the unexamined life is not worth living! So the argument goes, we mistakenly took Karen to be better off ignorant than she would be were she knowledgeable because we mistakenly ignored the constitutive value of knowledge, focusing on the eudaimonic value of success in one's projects. Expanding our conception of wellbeing so as to include knowledge as a constituent allows us to see that Karen would be better off were she to possess the knowledge that she lacks.

There is a fair and important point being made here, which is that the critic of the eudaimonic value of knowledge should not confine her attention to instrumental value approaches. It's possible that knowledge has final eudaimonic value, in virtue of being partially constitutive of wellbeing. My point is only that one could embrace this idea while rejecting (either formulation of) the eudaimonic ideal of knowledge. Recognizing the constitutive value of knowledge does not make it any more plausible that Karen would be better off knowledgeable. There may be situations in which one suffers on account of knowing something, but where knowledgeable suffering is intuitively better than ignorant bliss. Karen's case isn't like that: knowledge of her opponent's superiority doesn't seem valuable enough to trump the value of (potentially) winning. Better: Karen's case doesn't need to be imagined like that. For example, we can imagine that Karen cares deeply about winning and cares not a whit for knowledge of her opponent's relative abilities. That knowledge has constitutive value doesn't yet tell us anything about the strength (as it were) of the eudaimonic value of knowledge compared to other eudaimonic goods. So to recognize the constitutive value of knowledge does not require that we rethink what we said about Karen's case. Our examination of the eudaimonic ideal of knowledge continues.

1.1.6 Desire-fulfillment vs. desire-independent theories of wellbeing

How can we adjudicate the dispute between someone who maintains that knowledge has constitutive value and someone who maintains that knowledge doesn't have constitutive value? And how can we adjudicate disputes about the relative strength (as it were) of the constitutive value of knowledge? Imagine a follower of Hippias (Plato, *Hippias Major*, 289e) who maintains that *owning gold* has constitutive value, and who maintains furthermore that the constitutive value of gold is such that it would be better to die than to live with less than 10 ounces of gold. How can we argue against this view? What sort of considerations can we adduce in our critique? What can we say to convince the defender of the constitutive value of owning gold that she is wrong? And, on the other side, what can the defender of the constitutive value of owning gold say by way of argument for her position?[19]

We can identify an important division among theories of wellbeing by considering their attitude towards the connection between a person's wellbeing and her desires (broadly understood). According to what Derek Parfit (1984), in his influential discussion (pp. 492–502), calls "objective list theories," "certain things are good or bad for us, whether or not we want to have the good things, or to avoid the bad things" (1984, p. 493). These are **desire-independent theories of wellbeing**.[20] They make no essential reference to individual desires (broadly understood) in their account of individual wellbeing. Consider Parfit's sketch of such a theory:

The good things might include moral goodness, rational activity, the development of one's abilities, having children and being a good parent, knowledge, and the awareness of true beauty. The bad things might include being betrayed, manipulated, slandered, deceived, being deprived of liberty or dignity, and enjoying either sadistic pleasure, or aesthetic pleasure in what is in fact ugly. (p. 499)

Seeking or acquiring these things, then, is what makes our lives go well, regardless of our desires. As Thomas Hurka (2001) argues, "[k]nowledge and achievement…make a person's life go better regardless of how much she enjoys or wants them, and their absence impoverishes her life even if it does not cause regret" (p. 7), or as John Finnis (1980) argues, being well-informed is better than being ignorant "whether I like it or not" (p. 72).

The most influential species of desire-independent theories of wellbeing are **essentialist theories of wellbeing** (Aristotle, *Nicomachean Ethics*, Finnis 1980, Nussbaum 1993, 1995, 2000, Brink 1989, pp. 231–38, Foot 2001, Chapter 6, Kraut 2007; cf. Kraut 1979, pp. 180–3), according to which the extent to which a person's life goes well or badly is principally a matter of her flourishing vis-à-vis standards that flow from the essential nature of the kind of being that she is (e.g. a human being).[21]

---

[19] We'll look at these questions as they arise in connection with final value claims below (§1.5).

[20] Cf. "objective theories" (Hurka 2001, p. 7, Sumner 1996, Chapter 3) and "substantive good theories" (Scanlon 1993, p. 189–91).

[21] However, **hedonist theories of wellbeing** (Feldman 2004; cf. Parfit 1984, pp. 493–4, Sumner 1996, Chapter 4, Heathwood 2010, pp. 648–50), on which the extent to which a person's life goes well or badly is principally a matter of the pleasure and pain experienced by that person, are also desire-independent theories. We can therefore divide desire-independent theories of wellbeing into two groups: **Pluralistic desire-independent theories of wellbeing** propose a plurality of eudaimonic goods. These might be "human goods," as for the essentialist, but need not be understood as such. Parfit's "objective list" makes no implication about human nature. **Monistic desire-independent theories** propose a single eudaimonic good (cf. Scanlon 1993, p. 189). This division is artificial, to the extent that the individuation of eudaimonic goods is artificial. The hedonist might call herself a pluralist on the grounds that there are many species of pleasure; the essentialist might call herself a monist on the grounds that human flourishing is ultimately the only eudaimonic good.

Other theories of wellbeing make essential reference to individual desires (broadly understood) in their accounts of individual wellbeing. These are **desire-fulfillment theories of wellbeing** (cf. Kraut 1979, pp. 177–80, Parfit 1984, pp. 493–9, Sumner 1996, Chapter 5, Heathwood 2010, pp. 650–2), on which the extent to which a person's life goes well or badly is principally a matter of the extent to which her desires (broadly understood) are satisfied. On the simplest version of such a view:

Simple desire-fulfillment theory: What is best for someone is what would fulfill all of her desires, throughout her life (Parfit 1984, p. 494).

Other desire-fulfillment theories can be understood as placing a restriction on the relevant desires. We might say that what is best for someone is what would fulfill her fully informed desires, or that what is best for someone is what would fulfill her authentic or wholehearted desires. We can understand **life-satisfaction theories of wellbeing** (Sumner 1996, Tiberius 2008, Tiberius and Plakias 2010) as species of desire-fulfillment theories of wellbeing. On these views, the extent to which a person's life goes well or badly is principally a matter of the extent to which she appraises or evaluates her life positively (perhaps along some specific dimension). "Desire" is here understood broadly, so that the state of being satisfied with one's life is understood as a species of desire-fulfillment.

Desire-fulfillment theories take wellbeing to consist in a person's getting what she wants (broadly understood); desire-independent theories take wellbeing to consist in a person's acquiring goods other than getting what she wants. **Hybrid theories of wellbeing** (cf. Parfit 1984, pp. 501–2, Heathwood 2010, pp. 652–3) are therefore possible, on which the extent to which a person's life goes well or badly is principally a matter of the extent to which her appropriate desires (broadly understood) are satisfied, where appropriate desires are desires for "objective" goods.

The distinction between desire-independent theories and desire-fulfillment theories does not seem to be sharp. John Rawls (1971) argues that happiness is the successful execution of a rational life plan (p. 409), which suggests a sophisticated desire-fulfillment theory, but certain "human goods" are said to have "an important if not central place in our life," including "personal affection and friendship, meaningful work and social cooperation, the pursuit of knowledge, and the fashioning and contemplation of beautiful objects" (p. 425), which suggests an essentialist theory of wellbeing.

The distinction between desire-independent theories and desire-fulfillment theories is orthogonal to a distinction between **relativist** and **absolutist** theories of wellbeing. Essentialists about wellbeing, for example, may offer a list of human goods (Finnis 1980, Nussbaum 2000, Foot 2001), or they may propose different, non-intersecting lists of eudaimonic goods for different people, or for different groups of people. Given the diversity of human desires (broadly understood), desire-fulfillment theories will be relativistic: anything that is eudaimonically valuable for one person may not be eudaimonically valuable for someone else, and vice versa.

Desire-fulfillment and desire-independent theories will tend to disagree about cases in which "someone's fully informed preferences would be bizarre," like a man "who wants to spend his life counting the number of blades of grass in different lawns" (Parfit 1984, p. 499–500). They will also disagree about cases in which someone bizarrely *lacks* some desire. But they will also disagree about cases that aren't bizarre, such as cases of incuriosity, more on which below (§1.2).

We can distinguish (Ackrill 1973, p. 20, Urmson 1988, p. 20, Zagzebski 1996, pp. 89–90, Lawrence 2009; cf. Swanton 2003, Chapter 3, Heathwood 2010, pp. 653–4) between two notions of "the good life" (and perhaps between two notions of "eudaimonia"):

- **Flourishing**, i.e. what is *good for* an individual (of a particular kind). In this sense, the good human life is essentially a life that is good *for* a human being.
- **Excellence**, i.e. the state or activity of being *good as* an individual (of a particular kind) or that which is the *good of* an individual (of a particular kind). In this sense, the good human life is essentially a life that is good *as* a human life.

Excellence is at least conceptually distinct from flourishing. "Flourishing" is synonymous with "wellbeing," in our sense, and is sometimes understood in terms of what is **desirable**; "excellence" is sometimes understood in terms of what is **admirable**. Among other things, this yields a division of essentialisms: essentialist theories of human wellbeing will offer an account of human flourishing in terms of human nature; other essentialist theories (Hurka 1993) will offer an account of human excellence in terms of human nature. Others (Baehr 2011) offer accounts of personal excellence that make no appeal to human nature (pp. 95–100). Given our focus on eudaimonic value, we shall set aside questions about excellence, although I'll offer two comments. First, I think that my conclusions about the eudaimonic value of true belief (Part I), apply, mutatis mutandis, to the **arêtic value** of true belief, i.e. the value of true belief vis-à-vis excellence. Second, the idea that knowledge has arêtic value could naturally be understood as the claim that knowledge is "epistemically" valuable (cf. Baehr 2011, pp. 107–8), more on which below (§1.3, Part II).

For desire-independent theories of wellbeing there is a **basic methodological difficulty** in evaluating claims about eudaimonic value.[22] This difficulty arises both for claims to the effect that something (e.g. knowledge) has eudaimonic value and for claims to the effect that something has more or less eudaimonic value than something else (e.g. that the unexamined life is not worth living). What sorts of considerations can one bring to bear in favor of such a claim? Against such a claim? If it seems to you that a life without gold is not worth living, while it seems to me that gold is worthless, how are we to find out which of us is right? Compare the desire-fulfillment theorist's elegant solution: gold is good for you, but not for me.

What I am calling a difficulty for pluralistic desire-independent theories is embraced by some defenders of such theories: Finnis (1980), for example, argues that there is a

---

[22] Compare Sumner's (1996, pp. 45–6) complaint that "objective theories" of wellbeing don't explain what unites the members of the "objective list" of goods.

"sense in which…basic values are obvious ('self-evident') and even unquestionable" (p. 59). Thus "[t]he good of knowledge is self-evident. It cannot be demonstrated, but equally it needs no demonstration" (pp. 64–5). And evidently Finnis intends not only that basic values can't be demonstrated, but that no argument can be given in their defense. This is the upshot of his comparison of basic values to "principles of logic" (pp. 68–9). Less drastically, for T.M. Scanlon (1993), a theory on which "certain diverse goods make a life better…will be prepared to defend this claim by offering reasons (possibly different in each case) about why these things are desirable," although "it may offer no unified account of what makes things good" (p. 191).

It seems to me that, if desire-independent theories are right, the best we can do when evaluating claims about eudaimonic value is to appeal to our **reflective and empirically informed intuitions**. As Finnis might put it, we must be content to embrace what is obvious and self-evident to us. If, after careful and empirically informed reflection, gold seems worthless to me, I should conclude that gold has no eudaimonic value. If, after careful and empirically informed reflection, it seems possible to live a good life without gold, then I should reject the claim that the life without gold is not worth living. Our reflective and empirically informed intuitions about eudaimonic value are what we have to go on when it comes to evaluating theories of wellbeing, if desire-independent theories of wellbeing are right (cf. Brink 1989, p. 218, Tiberius 2008, pp. 9–15).

Our discussion of the eudaimonic value of knowledge will be neutral, to the extent that this is possible, as between desire-fulfillment and desire-independent theories of wellbeing. But we will sometimes assume the correctness of one sort of theory for the sake of argument (e.g. Chapter 3).

1.2 The allure of knowledge

Desire-fulfillment theories seem to imply that desire-fulfillment, and desire-fulfillment alone, constitutes wellbeing. But not so fast. We could say that x partially constitutes wellbeing, for those who want x, and thus say that knowledge partially constitutes wellbeing, for those who want knowledge. But could we say anything absolute about the eudaimonic value of knowledge? We could, given a universal human desire for knowledge. We could say that knowledge is partially constitutive of wellbeing, for everyone, if we said that everyone wants knowledge.

1.2.1 Aristotle on curiosity

Aristotle begins his *Metaphysics* with a claim that is sometimes appealed to in discussions of the value of knowledge: "All men by nature desire to know" (980a20).[23]

---

[23] Alvin Goldman (1999, p. 3) and William Alston (2005, p. 31) explicitly appeal to Aristotle's claim; see also Zagzebski (1996, p. 203). Lynch (2004, pp. 15–19) and Philip Kitcher (2004, p. 216) appeal to curiosity in connection with the value of true belief. For critical discussion of such appeals, see Finnis 1980, pp. 66–7, Grimm 2008, pp. 726–30, 2009, pp. 247–51, and Brady 2010.

What does this claim mean? What could it mean? And in what sense or senses, if any, is it true?

Let's call this claim, that everyone naturally wants knowledge, Aristotle's **principle of curiosity**. What Aristotle says everyone naturally wants is *to eidenai*, which means to see or to know. This makes sense of the passage that follows:

An indication of this is the delight we take in our senses; for even apart from their usefulness they are loved for themselves; and above all others the sense of sight. (980a20–22)

There are a number of Greek words that can (at least sometimes) be translated with "knowledge," including *to eidenai*, *epistêmê* (from which we get "epistemology"), and *gnôsis* (from which we get "knowledge"). Aristotle here claims that a desire for knowledge is natural, but what sort of knowledge does he mean? Although the word Aristotle uses is *to eidenai*, it becomes clear, from the passages that follow his statement of the principle of curiosity (982a1), that he is not interested in knowledge in general, nor in perceptual knowledge, but rather in a species of *epistêmê*, which he calls *sophia* (from which we get "philosophy"), and in particular in an understanding of fundamental causes or principles in metaphysics.

It's not obvious how to translate these words into English. Nor is the relationship between these various notions clear. Let's use "understanding" to translate *epistêmê* and "wisdom" to translate *sophia*. And let's (following Aristotle) treat wisdom as a species of understanding, and understanding as a species of knowledge.[24] Understanding can be distinguished from mere knowledge by its content. Understanding is knowledge of causes and principles. As Aristotle explains it, the senses (which yield *to eidenai*) "do not tell us the 'why' of anything—e.g. why fire is hot, they only say that it is hot" (981b11–12). We can have mere knowledge that a certain proposition is true, but we can also have knowledge of the causes and principles that explain the truth of that proposition, i.e. understanding. And wisdom can be distinguished from mere understanding by its content. Wisdom is understanding of fundamental causes and principles. This is why Aristotle says that everyone naturally wants knowledge to open the *Metaphysics*—by way of justifying his inquiry into philosophical questions in metaphysics. What do we do when we seek wisdom? We ask basic questions about reality, the existence of God, the fundamental structure of the world, and so on.

If we add to this list some other philosophical questions that are not obviously metaphysical, in particular questions about ethics, the good life, virtue, and so on, then we

---

[24] These moves won't matter below, where our focus will be on the value of true belief. On the relationship between knowledge and understanding, see Grimm 2006, forthcoming. Many contemporary epistemologists argue that understanding is not a species of propositional knowledge (Zagzebski 2001, Kvanvig 2003, p. 196–200, Elgin 2009, Pritchard 2010, pp. 78–81). This leaves open whether it is a species of non-propositional knowledge. There seem to be several senses of "wisdom" at play in contemporary discussions (see, e.g. Ryan 1999, Tiberius 2008). Part of the difficulty here arises from the fact that "wisdom" can translate two important words employed by Aristotle, *sophia* and *phronêsis*. The latter isn't a species of propositional knowledge, but rather a species of practical knowledge or ability. Compare also Plato, *Theatetus*, 146e.

would arrive at the same conception of wisdom arrived at above (§1.1.1): knowledge of answers to philosophical questions in ethics and metaphysics.

As I said, Aristotle's reason for saying that everyone naturally wants knowledge (*to eidenai*) is to justify his pursuit of wisdom (*sophia*) in the rest of the *Metaphysics*. So the most charitable way to interpret his principle of curiosity is to take it to mean that everyone naturally wants wisdom. This, in any event, is the claim that Aristotle seems to want by way of justifying his inquiry. But he says more than this. The rhetorical upshot of this part of the *Metaphysics* (Book I, Parts 1–2) is to justify philosophical interest in metaphysics by appeal to some more general claim about human curiosity.

1.2.2 Descriptive interpretations of the principle of curiosity

Aristotle claims that we want knowledge *phusei*—naturally or by nature. On one way of understanding the principle of curiosity, when Aristotle says that everyone naturally wants knowledge, he is saying that everyone wants knowledge, and also telling us why they want knowledge, namely, because it's natural, i.e. because it's natural for humans to do so, i.e. because it's part of their human nature. This corresponds to one way of understanding claims about what is "natural," where such claims are conjunctions: they tell us something about what is the case and also offer an explanation of why it is the case. Recall the second idea mentioned above: that there is something in the nature or essence of human beings, or in the nature or essence of our beliefs, that makes us, or our beliefs, directed at the truth. One form this idea might take is the claim that everyone wants knowledge, as a consequence of human nature. This is a **descriptive interpretation** of the principle of curiosity, on which everyone wants knowledge. This is precisely the kind of interpretation we presently seek, since we sought some way for desire-fulfillment theories of wellbeing to say that knowledge is partially constitutive of wellbeing, for everybody.

Consider just the first conjunct of the descriptive interpretation. We might understand this as:

Unrestricted descriptive principle of curiosity: For any subject S and proposition that p, S wants to know whether p.

This is subject to two kinds of counterexample. First, cases of apathetic incuriosity (Kitcher 1993, p. 94, Sosa 2001, p. 49, 2003, p. 156, Kelly 2003, p. 625, Grimm 2008, p. 726, 2009, p, 247): I do not want to know whether there are an even number of grains of sand on the beach at Coney Island. I just do not care about that. Ignorance is no more or less appealing than knowledge. Second, cases of positive incuriosity (Kelly 2003, p. 626): I do not want to know whether Gordon Brown looks good with his shirt off. And it's not just that I don't want to know that, I positively want *not* to know that. I strongly prefer ignorance to knowledge.

Clearly a descriptive interpretation of the principle of curiosity needs to be restricted. Supposing we still seek some claim that applies to everyone, the restriction must be placed on the questions to which everyone is said to want to know the answer. One possibility would be to go with Aristotle, and restrict ourselves to some absolute subset of questions:

Restricted descriptive principle of curiosity—significant: For any subject S, and for any proposition that p that answers a philosophical question in ethics and metaphysics, S wants to know whether p.

But this, too, is not plausible. Many people are abjectly incurious about these and other topics that seem to be deeply significant (Baril 2010, p. 221). There are individual differences when it comes to curiosity about such things: some people find these questions fascinating and yearn to answer them, and others could care less.

Alternatively, we might make our restriction relative to individuals:

Restricted descriptive principle of curiosity—interesting:[25] For any subject S, and for any proposition that p that answers a question that interests S, S wants to know whether p.[26]

But this is trivial: for the proposition that p to answer a question that interests S *just is* for S to want to know whether p. Consider William Alston's (2005) gloss on Aristotle's principle: "Members of our species seem to have a built-in drive to get the truth about things that pique their curiosity" (p. 31). But what is "curiosity," other than a drive to get the truth about some question? As Ernest Sosa (2003) puts it:

[O]ur desire for truths is largely coordinate with our desire for answers to our various questions. [...] We may want true beliefs, in this sense: that *if*, for whatever reason, we are interested in a certain question, we would prefer to believe a correct rather than an incorrect answer to that question[.] In so far as we seek to answer questions of interest to us, we of course aim at truth, *trivially so*, as we have seen. (p. 157–8, my emphasis)

To put this another way, to restrict the principle of curiosity to interesting questions is to reduce the principle to the following triviality: we want to know the answers to questions to which we want to know the answers. Interest in a question *just is* curiosity about its answer. Any creature that is curious about the question of whether p wants the truth about whether p; this isn't the result of a "built-in drive"; it's a trivial necessary truth. No member of any species could be curious without wanting the truth.

But not so fast. Something can be of interest to me, in at least one sense, without my realizing it. I can have an interest in the answer to a question, even if I am unaware of it. The question of whether my wife poisoned this glass of bourbon is of interest to me, in the present sense, given that I am presently taking drinks from it, even though

---

[25] On the distinction between the interesting and the significant, see §4.3.3.

[26] These formulations are neutral as to whether the curiosity in question consists in an instrumental or a non-instrumental desire to know whether p. Bernard Williams (2002) calls the later "pure curiosity," and rightly points out that the fact that what I am "purely" curious about depends on my "background, temperament, and experience" does not mean that my seemingly non-instrumental desire to know is actually an instrumental desire in disguise (p. 66). Finnis (1980) distinguishes "curiosity, or the pure desire to know" from an instrumental desire for knowledge (p. 60).

I'm not curious about the question of whether she poisoned it, because I'm not suspicious of her. But if that is how we understand a question's being interesting, then the principle seems false. For someone might be quite unaware that the question of whether p is of interest to her, in this sense, and on account of this not want to know whether p. She "wants to know it," in the sense that it's in her best interest to know it, perhaps; but this kind of "wanting to know" is not a kind of curiosity. What seems unfortunate about such a person is precisely that she is *incurious* in a situation where being curious would be in her best interest.[27]

We'll return to these issues below (§6.3). We'll consider several views that might capture the idea that we have a "truth goal." For now I provisionally conclude that a descriptive interpretation of the principle of curiosity is false (or trivial). We'll consider the consequences of this when it comes to the eudaimonic value of true belief, below (§4.3.3).

1.2.3 Prescriptive interpretations of the principle of curiosity

Some people are incurious; therefore descriptive interpretations of the principle of curiosity are false. We should now consider an alternative conception of the "natural," on which actual cases of incuriosity are not counterexamples to the claim that everyone is naturally curious. Recall the second idea mentioned above. On the present interpretation, human beings are directed at knowledge not in the sense that they all actually want knowledge, but rather in the sense that those who want knowledge are doing what they ought, or what is good for them, or what is proper for them, or some such prescriptive claim.

So perhaps everyone *ought* to want knowledge (Lynch 2009a, pp. 225–6), or everyone *rational* ought to want knowledge (cf. Sosa 2001, p. 49), or everyone *intellectually virtuous* wants knowledge (Zagzebski 1996, pp. 168–76, Baehr 2011, pp. 100–2). But what explains these facts? It is natural to appeal here to the value of knowledge (Baehr Zoll, p. 101–2, p. 136–7), but then we have made little progress towards understanding or explaining the value of knowledge. Alternatively, you might think that the fact that we ought to want knowledge is simply obvious, and not to be explained by appeal to the value of knowledge (Zagzebski 1996, p. 83, p. 203). In that case, the value of knowledge again remains unexplained.

We might understand the "natural" in terms of the essential nature of human beings (which seems to be what Aristotle had in mind; cf. essentialist theories of wellbeing, §1.1.6). Just as the nature of a tree is to grow in such-and-such a way (even if this particular tree, or even most trees, fail to grow in that way), perhaps the nature of a human being is to be curious (even if this particular human being, or even most

---

[27] Note that curiosity about matters of interest to me, in the present sense, cannot be what Aristotle has in mind: "not only with a view to action, but even when we are not going to do anything, we prefer sight to almost everything else" (980a25–6).

human beings, are incurious). Just as it's in the essence of this particular tree, in virtue of being a tree, to grow in such-and-such a way, such that it is a good tree only if it grows in that way, so it's in the essence of each individual human being, in virtue of being a human being, to be curious, such that she is a good human only if she is curious.

Such appeals to human nature have a rich history in philosophical ethics, which can be traced from Aristotle through Medieval Christianity to contemporary neo-Aristotelian virtue ethics and theories of natural law. But secular and naturalistic philosophers have generally resisted them, on three fronts. First, there is a strain of skeptical thought, tracing from to the Academics and the Pyrrhonians, that rejects the idea of natural human goodness, on the grounds that human beings are too diverse for there to be universal human goods. Second, there is a strain of thought that traces from Hume's rejection of deriving an "ought" from an "is" (*Treatise of Human Nature*, III.i.1) through to G.E. Moore's rejection of the "naturalistic fallacy" (*Principia Ethica*, §§27–35). Third, there is a metaphysical thought that traces from medieval nominalism through to the joint rejection of essentialism by both French existentialists, such as Simone de Beauvoir and Jean-Paul Sartre, and American naturalists, including W.V.O. Quine and David Lewis, in the 20th century. For our purposes here, we can simply note the anthropological and metaphysical commitments that anyone takes on who wishes to defend a prescriptive version of the principle of curiosity on essentialist grounds. Below (Chapter 7) we'll consider versions of Aristotelian functionalism based on the theory of evolution by natural selection. These views are empirically supported, scientifically credible inheritors of Aristotelian functionalism. A key theme there will be that claims about the function of human cognition are a posteriori, empirical claims about the genetics and natural history of human beings. And elsewhere (Chapters 6 and 8) we will consider two other views which seek to explain the value of true belief by appeal to essentialist ideas.

We should reflect on what is really meant by appeals to our "natural" or "human" curiosity (Aristotle, op. cit., Kitcher 2001, p. 81, 2004, p. 216, Alston 2005, p. 31, cf. Grimm 2008, p. 739). Someone who is curious about some question will benefit, in a straightforward way, by coming to know its answer: she will get what she wants. What more is being suggested if we imagine that her curiosity is "natural" or "human"? Some of my desires, perhaps, are "natural" or "human"—my hunger and thirst, my libido, and (Aristotle seems to want to say) my metaphysical curiosity. The upshot of this is unclear. Should I give the objects of such "natural" or "human" desires pride of place in my deliberations about what to do, think, and feel? Should I pursue these objects with more tenacity than other things that I desire, in virtue of their being the objects of my "natural" or "human" desires? Are these objects good, in some special sense, in virtue of being objects of my "natural" or "human" desires? These questions don't have obvious answers.

1.3 On the very idea of the "epistemic"

Many epistemologists will have been squirming through all of this, for it is often argued that the value of knowledge needs to be understood from the perspective of a sui generis domain of "epistemic" value, distinct from the domain of eudaimonic value. "Epistemic" value will be the subject of Part II (Chapters 5–9) of this book. We'll therefore take a brief look at the notion of the "epistemic" here, with a promise of further scrutiny to come.

Our search for the eudaimonic value of knowledge will seem misguided to fans of the "epistemic" because that notion is typically characterized by contrasting it with the eudaimonic. Consider a case from Richard Feldman (1988a):

Jones…is about to take an oral exam. [...] Apparently the teacher's evaluations are improved by sincere manifestations of confidence. [...] Since he wants to pass and knows that the best way to increase his chances is to believe that he'll pass, he should believe that he'll pass. (p. 236)

So far, this is in all relevant respects the same as the case of Karen (§1.1.2), except that Jones is his own coach. Feldman writes:

The inclination to say that Jones ought to believe that he'll pass concerns a *practical* or *prudential* sense of obligation. Sometimes it makes sense to treat beliefs like other actions and to evaluate their practical or prudential merit. [...] The contrary intuition concerns *epistemic* obligation. The peculiarly epistemic judgment concerns not these practical merits but rather the propriety of a disinterested believer in Jones' situation having that belief. [...] Epistemic obligation, then, concerns obligations to believe to which the practical benefits of beliefs are not relevant. (Ibid.)

Even if Jones' optimism is "practically or prudentially" merited, it's "epistemically" unjustified. This is a first step towards characterizing the "epistemic."[28]

Before turning to a closer examination of this idea of the "epistemic," some terminology needs to be sorted out. We should not speak of the "practical" here—not as interchangeable with "prudential," and not as essentially contrasting with the "epistemic."[29] We should define the domain of the **practical** as the domain of action (from *praxis*, "activity"), and a **practical reason** as a reason for action. By contrast, the domain of the **theoretical** is the domain of belief, or cognition, or intellection (from *theoria*, "contemplation, speculation, theory"); a **theoretical reason** is a reason for belief.

We should not (from the start) identify the "epistemic" with the theoretical, nor with the intellectual, nor with the cognitive, nor with the **doxastic**, which means

---

[28] See also Alston 1985, p. 83. On the idea of "purely epistemic" or "purely intellectual" curiosity, see Grimm 2008, pp. 726–30, Brady 2010, p. 270. That "epistemic" derives from *epistêmê* is no help here.

[29] I will not speak of the "prudential" in this book. On one way of using the word (cf. Sumner 1997, pp. 24–4), the prudential is the same as the eudaimonic; on another it essentially contrasts with the moral. In one sense, "prudence" implies a kind of expediency, practicality, or financial wisdom; on another, it translates *phronêsis*. A similarly ambiguous word is "pragmatic," which is also sometimes employed by way of contrast with the "epistemic."

"of or concerning belief" (from *dokeõ*: "to think, suppose, expect, or imagine"). The reason this would be a mistake is that the questions we have been considering so far are in the most straightforward sense questions about belief—they are questions about what beliefs would be good vis-à-vis wellbeing. They are not questions about what actions would be good. But—and this is an important assumption—we were not discussing those questions from the "epistemic" point of view (hence the squirming of the epistemologists). This is just Feldman's point: talking about what to believe with a view to impressing a teacher with one's self-confidence is *not* talking about what to believe from the "epistemic" point of view. We'll examine this point in more detail, below (§5.2.4).

I have characterized the domain of eudaimonic value as the domain that takes the good to be a person's wellbeing. We can make Feldman's point by noting that the "epistemic" is conceptually distinct from the eudaimonic. Some considerations—that believing that p will be pleasurable, that believing that p will make me confident—are "non-epistemic" considerations. But this leaves the notion of the "epistemic" unarticulated. Can we say anything positive about it?

Unfortunately, any positive claim about the nature of the "epistemic" would be controversial. (If this makes you suspicious of the notion, good.) However, epistemologists standardly say that the "epistemic" fundamentally has something to do with treating truth as a good, or end, or goal (§5.1). We can see more clearly now why Feldman was right to say that Jones' optimism was "epistemically" unjustified. For Jones' optimism was not responsive to considerations indicative of the truth of the proposition believed (that he would do well on the test), such as evidence that he would do well on the test. Nor was his belief responsive to considerations indicative of the falsity of the proposition believed, such as evidence that he was not well prepared. Rather, it was responsive to considerations indicative of the fact that so believing would be in his best interest.

Above (§1.1) we attempted to capture the value of knowledge in eudaimonic terms. We sought some plausible connection between knowledge and wellbeing. There we spoke of a person's life going well or badly in an unqualified way. Perhaps we should speak of a person's life going well or badly *with respect of knowledge*.[30] This qualification would allow us to concede that Karen is better off ignorant, while maintaining that her life goes badly in one respect. But what does it mean for one's life to go well or badly "with respect of knowledge"? This is where we are inclined to appeal to the notion of the "epistemic." Ignorance is always "epistemically" disvaluable, even if it is sometimes eudaimonically valuable. The ignorant would always be "epistemically better off" were they knowledgeable, even if not better off. As mentioned above (§1.2.3), perhaps we should say that everyone naturally wants knowledge, in the sense that everyone "epistemically" ought to want knowledge (Lynch 2009a, pp. 224–5).[31] We'll return to the "epistemic" below (Part II), where I'll propose a definition of "epistemic" (§9.3).

---

[30] For example, Baehr (2011), although his primary concern is with excellence rather than flourishing (p. 96n), speaks of "epistemic well-being" and "epistemic flourishing" (p. 111 and passim).

[31] Note the fruitfulness of *not* equating the "epistemic" with the theoretical: we can speak of what I "epistemically" ought to *want*.

1.4 From the eudaimonic ideal of knowledge to the eudaimonic ideal of true belief

Epistemologists have often inquired after the value of knowledge, as opposed to mere true belief (§5.1). They are concerned with cases in which mere true belief seems just as good as knowledge: someone who has a true belief about the way to Larissa will get there just as fast as someone who knows the way to Larissa. This book is about the value of knowledge, as opposed to ignorance—but not the ignorance of mere true belief. The cases we are concerned with are cases in which false belief seems better than knowledge. The central question here is not whether, and in what way, knowledge is more valuable than mere true belief, but rather the question of whether, and in what way, knowledge is more valuable than false belief. So we will be examining the value of true belief, rather than the value of knowledge.[32]

We'll say that **S has a true belief about whether p** iff either p and S believes p or ~p and S believes that ~p, and that **S has a false belief about whether p** iff either p and S believes that ~p or ~p and S believes p. Consider:

Eudaimonic ideal of true belief: For any subject S and proposition that p, having a true belief about whether p is normally better for S than having a false belief about whether p. In other words, there is no clearly identifiable pattern of cases in which false belief is better than true belief. Thus, for any subject S and proposition that p, having a true belief about whether p is a more reliable bet, when it comes to wellbeing, than having a false belief about whether p.

Everything we have said so far about the eudaimonic ideal of knowledge, and the eudaimonic value of knowledge, applies, mutatis mutandis, to the eudaimonic ideal of true belief, and to the eudaimonic value of true belief. Recall, in particular, that this claim concerns us, not (merely) our perfectly rational or perfectly virtuous counterparts (§1.1.2).

You might think that the plausibility of the eudaimonic ideal of knowledge (and of the eudaimonic value of knowledge more generally) depends on the plausibility of the eudaimonic ideal of true belief (or at least on the eudaimonic value of true belief more generally). If the eudaimonic ideal of true belief isn't defensible, then it's hard to see how the eudaimonic ideal of knowledge could be defensible. In this sense, the eudaimonic ideal of true belief seems weaker, a less controversial and risky claim, than the eudaimonic ideal of knowledge (although cf. Zagzebski 2004, p. 354).

However, the eudaimonic ideal of knowledge doesn't entail the eudaimonic ideal of true belief. There are counterexamples to the eudaimonic ideal of true belief that may not be counterexamples to the eudaimonic ideal of knowledge; we'll examine them below (Chapter 2). The reason for this is that the eudaimonic ideal of true belief says that true belief is better than false belief; not that true belief is better than the

---

[32] From here we therefore set aside non-propositional species of knowledge.

negation of true belief; the eudaimonic ideal of knowledge says that knowledge is better than its negation. What we'll see below are cases in which false belief is better than true belief, but I'll leave open the question of whether these are cases in which false belief is better than knowledge. Later on (Chapter 3) we'll examine kinds of cases in which false belief is better than knowledge. However, our focus shall be on the eudaimonic ideal of true belief, and more generally on the eudaimonic value of true belief, including the pro tanto eudaimonic value of true belief (Chapter 4).

You might think that the eudaimonic ideal of true belief is obviously false. Why then should we expend any effort criticizing it?

First, it's better to have an argument than to rest with what seems obvious. Our case of eudaimonically valuable false belief (§1.1.2) was based on our intuitions and assumptions about contingent human psychology. We should shore up such intuitions and assumptions with empirical evidence, since folk intuitions and assumptions about these matters are sometimes unreliable. A review of empirical research that is relevant to the eudaimonic ideal of true belief will allow us to advance an argument against the eudaimonic ideal of true belief (Chapter 2). This is important because the falsity of the eudaimonic ideal of true belief actually hinges on some complex contingencies of human psychology. For example, you might worry (as Descartes does in the Seventh Replies to the *Meditations*) that false belief will always "spread," resulting in massive error. That false belief does not "spread" in this way is a contingent feature of human cognition, and only a study of empirical research can provide support for this (§2.9.7).

Second, our critique of the eudaimonic ideal of true belief will allow us to see the scope of the eudaimonic value of true belief. Think of our strategy like this: we will assume the eudaimonic ideal of true belief, and in seeing where it fails, we will be able to see those species of belief such that true belief is normally better than false belief, and those species of belief such that it is not the case that true belief is normally better than false belief. Thus we will be able to come to better understand the eudaimonic value of true belief.

Third, many philosophers are reluctant to admit the eudaimonic value of false belief. I base this conclusion in part on some philosophers' appeal to the normatively loaded notion of "exceptions that prove the rule" in connection with eudaimonically valuable false belief (§1.1.3), but also on anecdotal evidence: many philosophers I have met are repulsed by the idea (for example) that overestimating your abilities can be eudaimonically valuable. And some have criticized this idea in print (Badhwar 2008).

1.5 The "intrinsic value of truth"

A popular idea in ethics is that knowledge is intrinsically valuable (Ross 1930, pp. 138–9, Finnis 1980, p. 62, Hurka 2001, pp. 12–13). Some epistemologists (Greco 2010, p. 99, Zagzebski 2003b, pp. 24–5) maintain that knowledge has both constitutive value

(§1.1.5) and intrinsic value. Truth is also said to have intrinsic value (Zagzebski 2003b, p. 24, Kvanvig 2003, p. 42), and that claim is obviously relevant to our inquiry into the value, whether eudaimonic or "epistemic," of true belief. Is this claim plausible? And what exactly does it mean?

First, the correct formulation of this claim is that true belief has intrinsic value, not that truth has intrinsic value. Truth itself is neither good nor bad. Some truths are good (that no one was hurt in the plane crash) and others are bad (that the Lakers won in the NBA Finals). If there is anything right about the claim that "truth has intrinsic value," it's that true belief has intrinsic value (Zagzebski 2003a, p. 135). Consider the fact that there is nothing especially good, in general, about my getting at the truth via some propositional attitude or other. If I imagine that p, where it is true that p, this is no better than if I imagine that some false proposition is true. But the "intrinsic value of truth" would be present in my imagining that p just as much as it would be present in my believing that p. So it's not the value of truth that we are after, but the value of true belief.

Second, we should speak of final value here, rather than intrinsic value (cf. Pritchard 2010, pp. 29–30n, Korsgaard 1983, Langton 2007). Recall that something has final value iff it is valuable for its own sake, and instrumental value iff it is valuable for the sake of something else. Those who say that true belief has intrinsic value (Kvanvig 2003, DePaul 2010) often say this by way of denying that true belief merely has instrumental value. Thus they are best interpreted as claiming that true belief has final value (cf. Hurka 2001, pp. 12–13). Note that constitutive value (§1.1.5) is not a species of intrinsic value: when something has constitutive value, it is valuable not in virtue of its intrinsic properties, but in virtue of its relation to the valuable whole of which it is part.

Something valuable has **intrinsic value** iff the fact that it is valuable supervenes on its intrinsic properties; otherwise it has **extrinsic value**. The standard example philosophers offer of something that has intrinsic value is pleasure. It's hard to see how this helps us understand the value of true belief. Pleasure, so the argument must go, has an intrinsic qualitative nature such that anyone acquainted with that nature can recognize the intrinsic value of pleasure. But true belief does not seem to have an intrinsic *qualitative* nature. All this favors our consideration of the claim that true belief has final value, rather than the claim that true belief has intrinsic value.

Third, the claim that true belief has final value is ambiguous. On the one hand, you might understand this claim as an alternative to the idea that true belief is merely useful, i.e. that true belief merely has instrumental eudaimonic value. But this claim is sometimes presented as an alternative to approaches that understand the value of true belief in eudaimonic terms. Thus Kvanvig (2003) writes that "obtaining the truth is valuable in itself, apart from any contribution it makes to our well-being" (p. 41). So we must distinguish the claim that true belief has final eudaimonic value (e.g. the claim that true belief has constitutive value) from the claim that true belief has final non-eudaimonic value. The latter is what some have in mind when they say that true belief has "epistemic" value, and this may be what many intend by appealing to the "intrinsic value of truth."

This brings us to a fourth point. As we saw above concerning constitutive value claims (§1.1.6), we face a methodological difficulty when it comes to final value claims. Several questions arise. How are final value claims to be defended? How are they to be criticized? How might disputes about them be adjudicated? Absent some explanation or account of the final value of true belief, the defender of the final value of true belief is in the same dialectical position as the philosopher who maintains, without argument, the final value of gold. (And the situation would only be made worse if the final value of gold were said to derive from a sui generis, non-eudaimonic domain of "auric" value!)

Kvanvig (2003) responds to this worry:

When we find something of intrinsic value and attempt to explain its value, we are forced to resort to explanations that are apparently circular. For example, many take pain to be disvaluable. When questioned concerning its disvalue, it is hard to cite any explanation of its disvalue other than the fact that pain hurts. This is no explanation, however. Instead, what it indicates is an inability to explain the disvalue of pain in any other terms, indicating an account of the disvalue of pain on which pain is disvalued intrinsically. The same should be said about true belief. When we attempt to explain its [value], we do so in hopelessly circular fashion. (p. 154)

And Lynch (2004) claims that "appeals to intrinsic value are conversation stoppers" (p. 127). So is it true that intrinsic value claims cannot be defended without hopeless circularity? And is the same thesis true, mutatis mutandis, when it comes to final value claims?

First, it's not true of intrinsic value claims. Consider this formally beautiful painting. It is (among other things) intrinsically valuable, in virtue of its aesthetic properties: the beauty and elegance of the composition, the graceful lines, the use of color, and so on. Already, it seems, we are explaining the intrinsic value of the painting. But we can say more. If someone challenges our evaluation, we can engage her in critical discussion: we can draw her attention to this or that part of the canvas, we can note relations between parts of the canvas, we can describe in more detail the painting's formal properties, and so on. Therefore, defenses of intrinsic value claims are not always hopelessly circular (cf. Horwich 1998, pp. 62–3, DePaul 2010, p. 132).

Second, Kvanvig's thesis is not true, mutatis mutandis, when it comes to final value claims. Consider this pistol, a relic of the Klondike Gold Rush. Its final value supervenes on its history, and if someone challenges the claim that it's valuable, we can point to facts about its history in support of our claim.

What Kvanvig may be right about is that the intrinsic value (or disvalue) of certain qualitative properties is inexplicable. But it's not easy to come up with examples of such properties other than that of being pleased (or in pain). The fact that the value of pleasure is inexplicable has much more to do with the fact that said value supervenes on the qualitative nature of the property of being pleased, than with the fact that being pleased is an intrinsic property, or the fact that the value in question is final value. Since true belief does not have a qualitative nature, the door is open for a critical discussion of the claim that true belief has final value.

The final value of truth is sometimes defended by appeal to "our" interest in the truth for its own sake (Zagzebski 1996, p. 206, Kvanvig 2003, pp. 40–1, Lynch 2004, p. 17, Alston 2005, p. 31). For one thing, this is curious, since it seems like something can be worthless and yet prized by many, just as something can be valuable and yet prized by few, or even none (Finnis 1980, p. 66, Brady 2010, pp. 266–71). For another, the failure of descriptive interpretations of the principle of curiosity (§1.2.2) problematizes the idea that "we" are interested in the truth (whether for its own sake, or for some other reason).

We have at least some commonsensical grasp of the notion of wellbeing, and have defined eudaimonic value in terms of wellbeing. Things are different when it comes to the (as yet undefined) notion of "epistemic" value. This is one reason why we should seek an explanation or account of the "epistemic" value of true belief. Philosophers have offered accounts of belief that, if true, would yield explanations of the value of true belief. We'll examine those accounts below (Chapters 6–8).

1.6 What is true belief?

This book is about the value of true belief. It assumes that there is, or could be, such a thing as true belief, and asks after its value. Someone skeptical about the very idea of truth, or about the very idea of belief (cf. §8.7), may be unable to engage with the question that I am asking. The discussion in what follows makes some modest assumptions about truth and belief, which I'll make explicit here.

1.6.1 What is truth?

A belief is true when its propositional content is true. What then is it for a proposition to be true? Our inquiry about the value of true belief needn't make many controversial assumptions about the answer to this question. I'll proceed on the assumption that Aristotle (*Metaphysics*, 1011b25) is basically right when he writes that

To say of what is that it is not, or of what is not that it is, is false, while to say of what is that it is, and of what is not that it is not, is true.

Subsequent theories of truth have not improved substantially on this explanation. We will remain neutral, at least, between minimalist, deflationist, correspondence, and other "realist" theories of truth.

There are three approaches to truth that we must reject if the following inquiry is to make sense. First, we must reject any view on which false belief is impossible. According to a certain kind of extreme relativism, no proposition is merely true or false, but is always true or false for a particular person. And one way of cashing out what it means for a proposition to be true or false "for a person" is to say that a proposition is true for a person iff she believes it, and false for a person iff she believes its negation. On this view false belief is impossible; our inquiry will assume the possibility of false belief. Second, we must reject any view on which the truth and falsity of propositions is only a matter of community agreement or executive decision. On such a view, the value of true belief may be obvious: believing the truth will put you in solidarity with your community, make you a good citizen or neighbor, or protect you from the danger of falling out with the Orwellian truth-makers. Third, we must leave open the question of the correctness of any view on which the value of true belief is a trivial consequence of the essential nature of truth (cf. §8.1.2). For the value of true belief is the subject of our inquiry, and must not be assumed from the start.

1.6.2 What is belief?

Although it may be that belief is not always a propositional attitude (e.g. believing in someone), true belief is necessarily a propositional attitude: again, a belief is true when its propositional content is true. The question of the nature of belief is a matter of much controversy in contemporary philosophy. As with the question of the nature of truth, we should try to remain as neutral as possible in our inquiry. We'll encounter a number of conceptions of belief later on (Chapters 6–8). But I will make some modest, but not uncontroversial, assumptions about the criteria for belief attribution.

I'll assume that belief has a **characteristic functional profile**, such that someone who believes that p is disposed to act, think, and emote in ways characteristic of believing that p. In line with my neutrality on theories of belief, however, I do not assume that this profile exhausts or is part of the essential nature of belief. The functional profile of belief indicates that belief will manifest itself in action, thought, and emotion in various characteristic ways, depending (at least in some cases) on the other mental states of the believer. Thus, to take a simple and familiar case, someone who believes that she will avoid being run over by a bus if and only if she jumps out of the way, and who desires that she avoid being run over by a bus, may manifest her belief by jumping out of the way. Alternatively, to take a case not involving desire (and thus a more controversial case), someone who believes that if she eats what is on her plate she will eat some bread, and who believes that bread is what she should eat, may manifest her belief by eating what is on her plate. You might think that some beliefs have characteristic manifestations, regardless of the other mental states of the believer, e.g. beliefs about what duty requires.

John Locke (*Essay concerning Human Understanding*, I.iii.6) suggests that the functional profile characteristic of belief might be exhausted by the believer's dispositions to perform non-verbal actions. He writes, of supposedly innate principles, that "the outward acknowledgement Men pay to them in their Words, proves not that they are innate Principles[,] Since we find that self-interest and the Conveniences of Life, make many Men, own an outward Profession and Approbation of them, whose Actions sufficiently prove" that they do not really endorse the principles in question. Thus, Locke concludes, we should "think their Actions to be the Interpreters of their Thoughts."

This conclusion—if taken to mean that the functional profile characteristic of belief is exhausted by the believer's dispositions to perform non-verbal actions—is too hasty. Locke's premise is that people often assert that p, and with good reason, even though they do not believe that p. This is right, and is reason to reject the sufficiency of asserting that p for believing that p. However, people often act as if p, or as though they believed that p, and with good reason, even though they do not believe that p. Just as self-interest and convenience might lead you to *say* that your boss is competent, they also might lead you to (non-verbally) *act* as though your boss is competent, or as though you think that your boss is competent. You might, for example, spend the day working on a senseless project that your boss suggested, so that you can impress her and get a promotion. The point here is that both verbal and non-verbal actions are criteria for belief attribution; both verbal and non-verbal actions can be the "interpreters" of our thoughts. But careful interpretation is required. In Locke's example of the person who professes principles that she does not endorse, we can already see that verbal action manifests belief (even when such manifestation is not straightforward): in this case, the belief manifested is the belief that it will be more convenient to profess such-and-such principle than to reveal that one does not endorse it. All this doesn't contradict Ruth Millikan's (1990) apt point that non-verbal behavior counts as an indicator and as a counterindicator of belief (1990, p. 138); as she notes, "speech acts are *among* the acts which may and often do manifest a belief" (p. 141, her emphasis). So I conclude that it's a mistake to privilege non-verbal behavior to the exclusion of verbal behavior, when it comes to belief attribution, as Locke seems to suggest we should.

It would also be a mistake to confine our attention to practical dispositions. Cognitive dispositions are also criteria of belief. Believing other propositions on the basis of the premise that p is characteristic of believing that p, although as with the practical criteria, we should be open to the possibility of someone who believes that p but fails to believe other propositions on the basis of the premise that p.

Finally, affective dispositions are criteria of belief. This often goes unmentioned in discussions of the functional profile of belief. In the *Lives of Eminent Philosophers*, Diogenes Laertius relates a story about the skeptic Pyrrho:

When his fellow-passengers on board a ship were all unnerved by a storm, he kept calm and confident, pointing to a little pig in the ship that went on eating, and telling them that such was the unperturbed state in which the wise man should keep himself.[33]

What explained the affective difference between Pyrrho (and the pig) and the other passengers? So the story goes, this was down to their cognitive difference: Pyrrho (and the pig) lacked beliefs to the effect that going down with the ship would be bad, while the other passengers held this opinion, and so were terrified. Pyrrho's tranquility was a manifestation of his lack of belief. Once we think about it, it's obvious that affective dispositions are criteria of belief. Your delight when your team wins the Championship manifests your belief that they won; your heartache over lost love manifests your belief

---

[33] From R.D. Hicks' translation in *Lives of Eminent Philosophers* (William Heinemann, 1925), p. 481.

that love was lost. It might be pointed out that an emotional state like fear is partly a cognitive state, but this doesn't threaten the point, it just requires that we isolate the non-cognitive element in such emotional states, and make the point thus: such non-cognitive elements of emotional states are criteria of belief.

To sum up, then: I shall assume that someone who believes that p is disposed to act, think, and emote in ways characteristic of believing that p. This is compatible with a plurality of theories of the essential nature of belief, and part of what we'll be doing below (Chapters 6–8) is critically examining some of those theories.

1.7 Conclusion

In this chapter I introduced two ideas. The first was the idea that true belief is better than false belief (§1.1); the value of true belief has been a mainstay of philosophical thinking since Socrates said that the unexamined life is not worth living. The second was the idea that human beings are naturally directed towards truth (§1.2); this thought was well articulated by Aristotle when he said that everyone naturally wants knowledge. In this book I give an extended argument for a kind of skepticism about the value of true belief. And below (Chapters 6–8), I'll target the idea that beliefs are essentially directed towards truth.

We've introduced two species of value. The first is eudaimonic value, i.e. value vis-à-vis wellbeing. This will be the subject of Part I (Chapters 2–4). The second is "epistemic" value. This will be the subject of Part II (Chapters 5–9).

There are three species of value that we have encountered, but which will not be discussed (in any detail) in the sequel. They are:

- Moral value
- Arêtic value
- Intrinsic value

Let be briefly recapitulate what I said about these three other species of value. On the moral value of true belief, I will discuss the idea that true belief has social value (§4.4). On the arêtic value of true belief, I offered a promissory note that what I'll say about eudaimonic value would apply to arêtic value, mutatis mutandis (see especially Chapter 4), and said that the arêtic value of true belief may be what people are talking about when they talk about the "epistemic" value of true belief (on which see Part II). And on the intrinsic value of true belief, I maintain that when people speak of the intrinsic value of true belief they mean either its final eudaimonic value (see especially Chapter 4) or its "epistemic" value (on which see Part II).

PART I

The Eudaimonic Value of True Belief

2

Greatness of Mind

When in his heightened self-criticism he describes himself as petty, egoistic, dishonest, lacking in independence, one whose sole aim has been to hide the weakness of his own nature, it may be, so far as we know, that he has come pretty near to understanding himself.

—Freud, "Mourning and Melancholia"

We are interested here in the eudaimonic value of true belief (§1.1.1), i.e. the value of true belief vis-à-vis the wellbeing of the believer, where "wellbeing" is a name for welfare, the good life, quality of life, happiness, living well or faring well, or for what makes someone's life go best. We'll first look at the eudaimonic ideal of true belief (§1.4). This chapter presents an argument against the eudaimonic ideal of true belief, based on research in social psychology on "self-enhancement bias." Later on (Chapter 3), I'll present non-empirical arguments against the eudaimonic ideal, which appeal to "partiality bias" and "charitable bias." I'll argue that cases of these three species of bias constitute normal cases in which false belief is better, for a person, than true belief. Finally, (Chapter 4), we'll consider the pro tanto eudaimonic value of true belief.

This chapter proceeds as follows: first we'll consider the history of the idea that self-knowledge is eudaimonically valuable (§2.1) and look at Hume's remarks on pride (§2.2), before turning to (empirical) evidence that "self-enhancement bias" is ubiquitous (§2.3). We'll then look at (empirical) evidence that self-enhancement bias is correlated with nondepression and high self-esteem (§2.4), and clarify this claim with some distinctions (§2.5). We'll then turn to the eudaimonic ideal of true belief. What is required, to criticize the eudaimonic ideal of true belief, are normal cases in which false belief is better, for a person, than true belief. I'll argue that many people's beliefs that manifest self-enhancement bias are cases of this kind. I'll first propose some explanations of the correlations between self-enhancement bias and nondepression (§2.6) and explore what I'll call the "selectivity" of self-enhancement bias (§2.7), before presenting the (non-empirical, philosophical) argument against the eudaimonic ideal of true belief (§2.8). Finally, we'll look at some objections to my argument (§§2.9–2.10).

The argument presented here is not novel; versions of it have been articulated by social psychologists (Tesser and Campbell 1983, Alloy and Abramson 1988, Taylor and

Brown 1988, 1994, Taylor 1989, Brown 1993, Brown and Dutton 1995, Brown 1998, Armor and Taylor 2002; cf. McKay and Dennett 2009). But its conclusion is controversial in contemporary psychology. So my argument in this chapter is not an appeal to the authority of psychological orthodoxy. My argument in this chapter is a philosophical argument, and can be evaluated as such.

2.1   The eudaimonic value of self-knowledge

There is a tradition in philosophy and psychology that prizes self-knowledge. Consider the Delphic motto, "Know Thyself," often cited by philosophers. Indeed, one might interpret the Socratic maxim (§1.1.1) as maintaining the eudaimonic value of self-knowledge, with "examination of life" referring to examination of one's own life: to reflective, introspective examination of oneself. Socrates sympathetically cites the Delphic motto in the *Philebus* (48c–d), calling ignorance an "evil" and self-ignorance "ridiculous." The idea of the eudaimonic value of self-knowledge appears throughout Western intellectual history. An influential tradition in ethics, going back at least to Aquinas and Avicenna, conceives of self-awareness of one's conscience, or of innate natural law, as a necessary precondition of moral action. Ignatius of Loyola proposed rigorous self-examination as part of his spiritual exercises, and the meditations of Descartes (who was educated by the Jesuits) are a self-directed inquiry, concerned fundamentally with knowing the truth about one's own nature. Rousseau took self-knowledge to be a crucial part of natural and authentic human development. The Romantics (and, later, 20th-century popular psychologists) recommended knowledge of one's true self, as an essential step on the path to authenticity. Ralph Waldo Emerson's ideal of self-reliance was constituted in part by self-awareness. Existentialist philosophers railed against the willful self-ignorance of those in bad faith. In the 20th century psychologists developed an emphasis on realistic self-acceptance; Abraham Maslow (1950) writes that "healthy individuals find it possible to accept themselves and their own nature without chagrin or complaint," and that "they can take the frailties and sins, weaknesses and evils of human nature in the same unquestioning spirit that one takes or accepts the characteristics of nature" (p. 54). Summing up this contemporary view, Charles Taylor (1989) writes that "the ideally strong character...would be able to face unflinchingly the truth about himself or herself" (p. 33).

So we must keep these traditions in the background as we critically consider the eudaimonic value of true belief about oneself, in no small part because we should be wary of our intuitions about accuracy of self-conception, given the rich history in our culture of seeing self-knowledge as especially valuable.

2.2   Hume on pride

In the *Treatise of Human Nature* (III.iii.2), Hume writes that "[w]e have, all of us, a wonderful partiality for ourselves," but that this tendency is not a bad thing:

[N]othing is more useful to us in the conduct of life, than a due degree of pride, which makes us sensible of our own merit, and gives us a confidence and assurance in all our projects and enterprizes. [...] Fortune commonly favours the bold and enterprizing; and nothing inspires us with more boldness than a good opinion of ourselves. Add to this, that tho' pride, or self-applause, be sometimes disagreeable to others, 'tis always agreeable to ourselves[.] Thus self-satisfaction and vanity may not only be allowable, but requisite in a character. (1978, pp. 596–7)

Hume concludes that "a genuine and hearty pride or self-esteem ... is essential to the character of a man of honor" (ibid. p. 600). A good opinion of oneself Hume calls "greatness of mind" (a literal translation of the Greek *megalopsychia* and the Latin *magnanimitas*, from which we get "magnanimity").

Hume, for his part, does not suggest that virtuous pride speaks against the eudaimonic ideal of true belief. He calls "impertinent" that "almost universal propensity of men to over-value themselves" (ibid.), and says that "nothing can be more laudable, than to have a value for ourselves," but only "where we really have the qualities that are valuable" (ibid.). Thus, on his view, pride is virtuous only when accurate.

What is of interest here is the fact that Hume's defense of pride appeals not to its positive "epistemic" traits, like its truth, but to its positive eudaimonic traits: "the merit of ... self-esteem is deriv'd from two circumstances, *viz.* its utility and its agreeableness to ourselves" (ibid.). When it comes to utility, pride "capacitates us for business" (ibid.), i.e. pride puts us in a state of mind conducive to successful action; when it comes to agreeableness, pride "gives us an immediate satisfaction" (ibid.), i.e. it simply feels good to think well of oneself. In principle at least, these two merits might be enjoyed by false beliefs. Hume's insight in his discussion of pride is to draw attention to the fact that living well depends in part on how one thinks, and in particular on how one thinks about oneself: beliefs, or belief-forming faculties or practices, may have "merit" in virtue of their contribution to the quality of one's life, i.e. they may have eudaimonic merit, and this form of merit is conceptually distinct from "epistemic" merit. Hume's defense of pride anticipates Valerie Tiberius' (2008) defense of the virtue of "realistic optimism," which disposes one towards a "positive appraisal of human nature" (p. 150): "if you choose the optimistic strategy, you will be more likely to be satisfied with your life upon reflection" (p. 153). The value of "realistic optimism" is eudaimonic.

In this chapter I'll argue that Hume was right about the eudaimonic merits of pride, but not in his suggestion that pride only has eudaimonic value when accurate.

2.3 The ubiquity of self-enhancement bias

A **doxastic bias** is a species of unreliable doxastic practice. A **doxastic practice** is a way of forming, sustaining, and revising one's beliefs. This section presents evidence that most people manifest "self-enhancement bias"—a species of doxastic bias—in their beliefs about themselves. This claim is relatively uncontroversial in social psychology, and there are some good reviews of the evidence for it (Taylor and Brown 1988,

Kunda 1990, Brown and Dutton 1995, Brown 1998, Armor and Taylor 2002, Sedikides and Gregg 2003, 2008, Dunning 2005, Leary 2007, Vazire and Carlson 2010).

2.3.1 The self-enhancement "motive"

Social psychologists argue that most people's beliefs about themselves—their self-conceptions—manifest bias in favor of a positive self-conception. We'll call such bias **self-enhancement bias**. So social psychologists argue that most people's beliefs manifest self-enhancement bias, i.e. that self-enhancement bias is ubiquitous.[1]

Self-enhancement bias, in our sense, may be caused, at least in part, by the use of "judgmental heuristics" (Kahneman et al. 1982, Nisbett and Ross 1980, Gilovich et al. 2002), or by "cognitive dissonance" (Aronson 1969). As Lauren Alloy and Lyn Abramson (1988) argue, "self-enhancing biases...may be multiply determined and result from a number of motivational and cognitive mechanisms, perhaps with different mechanisms operating in different situations" (p. 247, and see §2.3.4).

Self-enhancement bias, in our sense, can occur without a (psychologically real) desire to believe that which favors a positive self-conception.[2] Social psychologists (Wills 1987, Tesser 1988, Kunda 1990, Heckhausen and Krueger 1993, Taylor et al. 1995, Sedikides and Strube 1995, Leary 2007, Sedikides and Gregg 2003, 2008, Fiske and Taylor 2008, pp. 121–30) posit a plurality of "motives" in belief-formation including "self-assessment" (aimed at achieving certainty in self-conception)[3], self-enhancement (aimed at maintaining a positive self-conception, avoiding a negative self-conception, maintaining a sense of self-worth), and "self-verification" (aimed at maintaining a consistent self-conception over time). But the existence of these "motives" does not depend on the desires or intentions of the believer, concerning her self-conception.

We must distinguish between **belief at will**, in which I believe that p (partially) as a result of desiring or intending to believe that p, and **wishful thinking**, in which

---

[1] Psychologists sometimes distinguish between self-enhancement and self-defense, and some research is more suggestive of ubiquitous self-defensive bias than of ubiquitous self-enhancement bias (Brown 1986, Ingram 1989, Buunk et al. 1990, Brown 1993, Trafimow et al. 2004). But this would not threaten my argument; and nothing speaks against adopting a broad sense of "self-enhancement," covering both "self-promotion" (or "self-advancement") and "self-protection" (Sedikides and Gregg 2003, 2008). Furthermore, the goals of self-enhancement (narrowly construed) and self-defense are mutually supporting (Buunk 1990).

[2] The ubiquity of self-enhancement bias is also orthogonal to the question of "motivated reasoning" (Kunda 1990). Some psychologists use the cognitive/affective or cognitive/motivational distinction to contrast unbiased (cognitive) with biased (affective or motivational) reasoning processes. Others use the cognitive/motivational distinction to contrast one set of biases (cognitive biases) without another set of biases (motivational biases). In this connection, "cold" information processing is contrasted with "hot" motivated belief-formation. Because of my views about the term "cognitive" (§1.4), I'll steer clear of this terminology. Our interest, given our inquiry into the eudaimonic value of true belief, concerns unreliable bias, whether "motivated" or "cognitive."

[3] The "self-assessment" motive is sometimes described as aimed at self-knowledge: but "knows" is being used non-factively; self-assessment seeks self-knowledge in the sense that it seeks certainty about the self (Sedikides 1993).

I believe that p (partially) as a result of desiring that p (cf. Mele 1997, Lazar 1999). Self-enhancement bias may often involve wishful thinking: I want to be good, in various ways, and this desire to be good influences my self-evaluations, resulting in an overly positive self-conception, i.e. beliefs to the effect that I am good, in those ways. Whether it ever involves belief at will is orthogonal to everything I'll say here.

The most natural interpretation of psychologists' talk of "motives" in self-evaluation is that they are not committed to belief at will (cf. Sedikides and Gregg 2008, Wilson and Dunn 2004). For example, Mark Leary (2007) defines a "self-motive" as "an *inclination* that is *focused on* establishing or maintaining a particular state of self-awareness, self-representation, or self-evaluation" (p. 319, my emphasis). A "self-motive" exists, in this sense, when someone is *disposed* to maintain a particular state of self-evaluation, or when she *tends* to maintain such a state. Alternatively, we could also think of the "motive" of maintaining a positive self-conception as analogous to a biological "need": we could say that the process of digestion is motivated by the need to extract nutrients from the food that one has eaten, but this does not require that the one who digests has a psychologically real motive or desire to extract nutrients from the food she has eaten. Neither does it require that the process of digestion is voluntary or under one's control. We could think of self-enhancement bias as "motivated" in a similar way: motivated by the need to maintain a positive self-conception (cf. Kunda 1990 on "the need for specific conclusions or structures" p. 483).

All this matters because philosophers tend to think that belief at will is impossible or at best very difficult. William Alston (1988) writes:

Sometimes people succeed in getting themselves to believe (disbelieve) something. But I doubt that the success rate is substantial. To my knowledge there are no statistics on this, but I would be very much surprised if attempts of this sort bore fruit in more than a small proportion of cases. [W]e are considering cases in which the subject is swimming against either a preponderance of contrary evidence or a lack of evidence either way. S is fighting very strong tendencies to believe when and only when something seems true to one. Some of these tendencies are probably innate and some engendered or reinforced by socialization; in any event they are deeply rooted and of great strength. To combat or circumvent them one must exercise considerable ingenuity[.] This is a tricky operation, requiring constant vigilance as well as considerable skill, and it would be very surprising if it were successful in a significant proportion of cases. (p. 276)

Now, on the one hand, Alston may be making a very simple point here: that someone believes that p only if it seems true to her that p. This is obviously right, in some sense (cf. §8.5.4). Moreover, Alston's remarks here may have no bearing on the ubiquity of self-enhancement bias, because the ubiquity of self-enhancement bias does not require the ubiquity of belief at will. However, on the other hand, there are some problems with this reasoning that need to be corrected before we can proceed. First, Alston ignores the possibility of unconscious intentions to believe—which could be what psychologists are talking about when they talk about "motives" in self-evaluation.

Second, Alston imagines two situations: one in which there is a preponderance of evidence that p is false, and another in which there is no evidence about whether p. But this ignores a number of possible situations, including those in which there is significant, but not a preponderance of, evidence that p is false, and those in which there is significant, but not conclusive, evidence that p. We will see below (§2.7) that self-enhancement bias manifests itself in these kinds of situations, not in situations where there is conclusive evidence that some proposition is true or false. Third, social psychologists have done a lot of empirical work on self-enhancement bias. So there are "statistics" on self-enhancement bias, at least. We do not have to satisfy ourselves merely with what seems to be the case, or with what seems surprising to us. As we will see, self-enhancement bias is in some ways a "tricky operation" that requires "considerable skill"—but, as it turns out, most of us have the skills required, and manage the operation with relative ease.

2.3.2 Overly positive self-evaluation

Let's take **self-evaluation** to consist in the formation of beliefs about oneself in terms of properties (traits, abilities) that have a positive or negative valence (e.g. physical attractiveness, intelligence, athletic ability, leadership ability, social competence, as well as more specific personality traits such as being sincere, being considerate, being rude, being superficial, etc.), as opposed to mere description of oneself in terms of more-or-less evaluatively neutral properties (e.g. hair color, city of birth). A property might be positively valenced either because the term for that property has valence built into its meaning, or because that property is perceived as important or desirable. Studies found that most people consider themselves "above average" or "better than most other people" when it comes to positive traits and abilities (Larwood and Whittaker 1977, Alicke 1985, Brown 1986, Dunning et al. 1989, Brown and Gallagher 1992, Helgeson and Taylor 1993, Sedikides 1993, Krueger 1998, Krueger and Dunning 1999, Trafimow et al. 2004).[4] Others found that most people's self-evaluations did not correspond with the evaluations of others (Lewinsohn et al. 1980, Gosling et al. 1998), with the evaluations of experts (Helgeson and Taylor 1993), or with objective measures (Borkenau and Liebler 1993, Krueger and Dunning 1999, Vazire 2010). For example, Jonathon Brown (1986) compared people's self-evaluations with their evaluations of their friends and their evaluations of "most other people," in terms of a list of obviously positive (e.g. "dependable," "considerate") and obviously negative (e.g. "spiteful," "superficial") trait adjectives. To a significant degree, subjects rated themselves more positively, and less negatively, than they rated both their friends and "most other people." Other studies made similar findings (Alicke 1985, Campbell 1986, Frey and Stahlberg 1986, Ingram 1989, Dunning 1995, Krueger 1998, Trafimow et al. 2004). One conclusion that can

---

[4] Something similar, mutatis mutandis, was found for negative traits and abilities. I'll focus on positive traits and abilities here and in what follows.

be drawn from all this is that most people are overly positive in their self-evaluations.[5] Their self-conceptions manifest self-enhancement bias.[6]

The case for the ubiquity of self-enhancement bias can be strengthened by looking at the psychological mechanisms (processes, strategies) that explain why most people make overly positive self-evaluations. In the most general terms, the mechanisms of self-enhancement bias are summed up well by Bram Buunk and his colleagues (1990): "there are cognitive filters of selective attention, representation, and recall that help people maintain positive beliefs" (p. 1246; see also Sedikides and Gregg 2008, Brown 1998, pp. 70-8).

These "filters" (as the name suggests) will not generate beliefs on their own (cf. Kunda 1990), but will interact with other doxastic practices of the believer. For example, self-enhancement bias in some cases is correlated with "metacognitive" deficiencies that accompany first-order inability (Krueger and Dunning 1999; see also Dunning 2005, Chapter 2). As Constantine Sedikides and Aiden Gregg (2008) argue, "when reasoning is impaired...self-enhancement is let loose" (p. 108). Similarly, Emily Pronin and her colleagues (2002) found that self-enhancement was facilitated by the "availability heuristic," and concluded that "a combination of—or even an interplay between—low cognitive ability and perceived negativity plays a role in creating and perpetuating the invidious self-other distinction" (p. 374; see also Pronin et al. 2004, Epley and Dunning 2006).

Overly positive self-conception can be maintained by taking responsibility for your successes but not for your failures. Such *self-serving causal attributions* seem to be ubiquitous (Snyder et al. 1976, Zuckerman 1979, Kunda 1987, Brown and Rogers

---

[5] You might object that this isn't necessarily so, since it's possible for the majority of people to be above average (Colvin and Block 1994, Krueger 1998, Badhwar 2008). Note, first, that this leaves untouched the argument based on studies that compared people's self-evaluations with those of observers, experts, objective measures, and the argument based on studies that found people describing themselves as "better than most" (as it really is impossible for most people to be better than most). Second, it's strange to attribute to the naïve respondents in these studies the sophisticated idea required for this objection to work. What people are thinking, when they think of themselves as above average, seems clearly to be something that isn't true of the majority of them. We can imagine asking one of these subjects: "When you say you're of above-average intelligence, do you mean to say that you're more intelligent than most people?" We'd be shocked to find anyone saying: "Of course not; I've above-average intelligence only because there are a few extremely low-intelligence individuals such that mean intelligence is quite low." Third, granting the objection, the question of the accuracy of people's beliefs, to the effect that they are above average when it comes to some trait or ability, depends now on the actual distribution of those traits and abilities in the population subjects are asked to compare themselves to. So, for example, it turns out that most people are above average when it comes to whether they drive safely—average driving ability is low because of a few bad eggs (Gigerenzer 2008, p. 15, Cokely and Feitz 2009). There is no evidence that intelligence or athletic ability, for example, are distributed in that way.

[6] There is an interesting question of how a person ought to respond to this conclusion (cf. Elga 2005). Anecdotally, most professional philosophers I've talked to about this respond by saying: "What morons ordinary people are! Thank goodness I'm not prone to their weak-minded irrationality." (Some, conceding that self-enhancement bias is correlated with nondepression, gleefully purport to be depressed.) Two things to keep in mind here. First, studies suggest (Cross 1977) that the self-conceptions of college teachers manifest self-enhancement bias. Second, researchers have found (Pronin et al. 2002) that people tend to overestimate their immunity to self-enhancement bias: when surveyed and then informed that most people's survey responses were biased, 63% of people said that their responses were not biased, and a brave 13% even concluded that their responses had been overly modest.

1991; see Bradley 1978, Abramson and Alloy 1981, Pyszczynski and Greenberg 1987a for reviews, and Dunning 1995, p. 77, Fiske and Taylor 2008, pp. 159–63, for overviews). Professional academics looking for work are familiar with this bias: when you fail to get a job, you attribute it to the randomness of the job market, or to some contingency outside of your control (e.g. embarrassing ripped pants during interview, spilled linguini with clams on self during lunch at the Faculty Club, unexpected hangover), or to some institutional prejudice against you (e.g. racism, sexism, affirmative action, your degree from an obscure university). As Jonathon Brown (1993) argues, "[m]ost events in life are ambiguous and admit of multiple interpretations. Some of these interpretations will be more congenial to the individual's sense of self-worth than will others" (p. 33).

Overly positive self-conception can be maintained by careful *interpretation of the importance of different traits*. Most people tend to think of themselves as better than others when it comes to positive traits they consider important or desirable but not when it comes to other positive traits (Alicke 1985, Campbell 1986, Krueger 1998, Brown 1986, Ingram 1989, Sedikides 1993, Dunning 1995; see also Frey and Stahlberg 1986). On a related point, William James writes, in the *Principles of Psychology* (1890):

I, who…have staked my all on being a psychologist, am mortified if others know much more psychology than I. But I am contented to wallow in the grossest ignorance of Greek. My deficiencies there give me no sense of personal humiliation at all. Had I "pretensions" to be a linguist, it would have been just the reverse. (James 1950, p. 310)

Studies (Sedikides 1993; see also Kunda 1990, and Tesser and Campbell 1983, Tesser 1988 for reviews) suggest that people tend to rate themselves as better than others, but only when it comes to positive traits that they see as "central," self-definitional, or reflective of their "true self."

Overly positive self-conception can be maintained by *selective inquiry*: seeking out positive information, and avoiding negative information, about oneself. Studies suggest that such selective inquiry is common, especially when self-esteem is threatened (Frey and Stahlberg 1986, Brown 1990, Sedikides 1993, Dunning 1995; see also Dunning 2005, pp. 73–4). Overly positive self-conception can also be maintained by *selective attention to evidence*: dwelling on evidence that reflects well on you, and attending little to evidence that reflects badly on you (cf. Mele 2001, pp. 25–49).

Self-enhancement bias varies depending on the ambiguity of the terms involved. Some trait terms (e.g. "sensitive," "sophisticated," "idealistic," "impractical," "naïve," "insecure") are more ambiguous than others (e.g. "well-read," "thrifty," "athletic," "sarcastic," "clumsy," "gullible"). David Dunning and his colleagues (1989) found that self-enhancement bias was diminished when questions were asked using unambiguous trait terms. Dunning and his colleagues argue that people adopt *self-serving criteria or standards of evaluation*, which is easier to do for ambiguous trait terms than for unambiguous trait terms. An academically incompetent athlete might consider herself "more intelligent than most" on the basis of her high "basketball IQ"; a clumsy nerd might consider herself "more athletic than most" on the basis of her juggling skills (cf. Brown 1993).[7]

Overly positive self-conception can be maintained through *biased social comparisons*. A person's self-conception is fundamentally relational, consisting crucially of beliefs about how she compares to other people (Mead 1934, Festinger 1954, Sartre 1956, Brown 1986). More simply, social comparisons can have a significant impact on how we feel. Hume observed in the *Treatise* (III.iii.2) that:

The direct survey of another's pleasure naturally gives us pleasure; and therefore produces pain, when compar'd with our own. His pain, consider'd in itself, is painful; but augments the idea of our own happiness, and gives us pleasure. (1978, p. 594)

And people's social comparisons tend to be biased in favor of a positive self-conception. In one study (Hackmiller 1966), subjects who had been told they'd done poorly on a test made significantly more "downward" social comparisons (comparisons to worse-off others) than did subjects who'd been told they'd done well, suggesting that downward comparisons were used to cope with information that threatened people's positive self-conceptions. Other studies came to the same conclusion (see Wills 1987 and Taylor and Lobel 1989 for reviews). Much of this work has focused on individuals facing negative life events, and has defended the idea that social comparisons are a common and effective strategy for coping with negative life events (Wills 1987, Taylor et al. 1983, Taylor and Lobel 1989, Helgeson and Taylor 1993; see also Taylor et al. 1983, pp. 29–30, Taylor and Brown 1994, p. 22). Shelly Taylor and her colleagues (1986) found that 96% of cancer patients said they were in better health than other cancer patients, while other researchers found that both downward and "upward" comparisons are employed in the service of a positive view of one's own situation (Buunk et al. 1990).

Finally, studies have found that most people enjoy *differential processing and recall speeds* for positive and negative information: they recall and process positive information about themselves more rapidly than negative information about themselves (see Kuiper et al. 1983 for a review; see also Greenberg and Alloy 1989, Sedikides and Green 2000).

2.3.3 Unrealistic optimism

Social psychologists argue that most people have overly optimistic views about their futures. This bias can be seen both by looking at people's beliefs about their own futures as compared to other people's futures (e.g. most people think they are less likely than others to experience negative life events, and more likely than others to experience positive life events) and by looking at the correlation between predictive beliefs and

---

[7] Critics argue that "the self-selection of dimensions of comparison can provide a reasonable explanation for much of the better off than most effect" (Colvin and Block 1994, pp. 14–15; cf. Dunning et al. 1989). But the selection of self-serving criteria or standards of evaluation is consistent with the existence of self-enhancement bias; indeed, the former explains the latter. As Shelly Taylor and Jonathon Brown (1994) argue, "people are highly resourceful when it comes to promoting positive views of themselves. However, these are demonstrations of the ways in which people develop and maintain illusions rather than counter-explanations or exceptions to the effect" (p. 22; see also Sedikides et al. 2002).

the desirability of future events (e.g. most people's expectations about the likelihood of future events correlates with how desirable they take those events to be). Early work on expectations found that people manifested bias in their expectations, tending to over-estimate their chances of success (Marks 1951, Irwin 1953, Crandall et al. 1955). Neil Weinstein (1980) found that subjects' comparative estimates of their chances of experiencing future life events were strongly correlated with the valence (positive or negative) of the event in question. For example, on average these college-aged subjects estimated that their chances of owning a home were 44% higher than "the average chances of their classmates," and on average subjects estimated their chances of being divorced were 48% lower than average. Differences in comparative judgments were not significantly correlated with the perceived general probability of the event in question or with the subject's personal experience with the type of event in question. These studies, and others (Robertson 1977, Brickman et al. 1978, Larwood 1978, Weinstein 1987, Brinthaupt et al. 1991, Heckhausen and Krueger 1993, Regan et al. 1995, Epley and Dunning 2006), suggest that most people are unrealistically optimistic about their own futures.

There may be a plurality of mechanisms that explain the phenomenon of unrealistic optimism. People may make biased causal attributions and conclude that their abilities are superior to those of other people, and thus appear to themselves to be less susceptible to problems that befall other people, and more likely to do well. Or they may be biased in the dimensions along which they choose to compare themselves to other people, or they may choose to make upward social comparisons from which they draw inspiration. Alternatively, given relative familiarity with themselves, and thus the availability of more evidence about themselves than about other people, "they may conclude incorrectly that their chances differ from those of other people" (Weinstein 1980, p. 807). (Notice how the self-enhancement "motive" interacts here with the "availability heuristic.") People may process and recall positive information more rapidly than negative information; this may lend credibility to their positive perceptions of the future. Alternatively, it may be easier for most people to visualize or imagine a positive future for themselves; this ease of imagination may bias their beliefs about the likelihood of various future events (Pietromonaco and Markus 1985).

2.3.4 Illusion of control

Most people's beliefs appear to manifest biases in their perceptions of their degree of control over events in the world. Certain situations in particular tend to cause people to overestimate their degree of control over events. Ellen Langer and Jane Roth (1975) asked people, who had just predicted the outcome of a series of coin tosses, to estimate their ability to predict the outcomes of coin tosses and to indicate the degree to which they felt their ability to predict said outcomes could be improved with practice. Subjects' perceived performance predicting coin tosses was manipulated, so that some saw themselves as initially successful (but later unsuccessful), others saw themselves as initially unsuccessful (but later successful), and others as neither of these. All subjects were "correct" in their predictions 50% of the time. Subjects in the initial success condition rated themselves significantly better at predicting coin tosses than did subjects in the other two conditions, and subjects in the initial failure condition were significantly more likely to say that the ability to predict coin tosses could not be improved with practice. Across all three conditions, 25% of people reported that their ability to predict the outcomes of coin tosses would be hampered by distractions, and 40% felt that their ability could be improved with practice. Langer (1975) also found evidence of an illusion of control manifested in people's betting behavior. The illusion of control bias is clearly a close cousin of self-serving causal attributions (§2.3.2).

An illusion of control is ubiquitous in the sense that most people appear prone to overestimate their degree of control in certain situations. But it's hard to imagine our dispositions to overestimate our degrees of control only manifest themselves in outré circumstances. Consider, again, the job-seeker's post hoc evaluation of her success or failure (§2.3.2). In success we are likely to see the task we succeeded at as something we could control; in failure we are likely to see the task we failed at as something we could not control—or, more exactly, we are likely to exaggerate the degree of control we had over our successes, and underestimate the degree of control we had over our failures.

2.4 Individual differences in self-enhancement bias: depression and self-esteem

My aim is to evaluate the eudaimonic ideal of true belief. But you might think that the ubiquity of self-enhancement bias, in the form of the ubiquity of people's overly positive self-conceptions, is completely irrelevant to the eudaimonic ideal of true belief. For you might think that most people's lives are going quite poorly. Plato and Aristotle, for example, would probably be fine with admitting that most people do not live especially good lives, and so it's no surprise that most have many false beliefs about themselves. Or, more modestly, you might simply argue that most people's false beliefs about themselves make their lives go worse, even if their lives are not all that bad, overall. However, in this section we will begin to see that even this modest claim is not plausible.

Most people's beliefs manifest self-enhancement bias (§2.3). But there are individual differences in the extent to which people's beliefs manifest self-enhancement bias. In particular, there are correlations between self-enhancement bias, depression, and self-esteem. In particular, there is evidence that self-enhancement bias is correlated with nondepression and high self-esteem (for reviews see Taylor and Brown 1988, Alloy and Abramson 1988; see also Taylor 1989, Brown 1998, pp. 274–81).

A brief comment on terminology. **Depression** (cf. Beck and Alford 2009) is understood to include a variety of emotional (dejected mood, self-dislike, loss of gratification), cognitive (negative self-evaluation, negative expectation), motivational (loss of motivation, suicidal wishes), and somatic (loss of appetite, loss of libido) symptoms. **Self-esteem** is understood as a matter of a person's evaluation or appraisal of herself; it is a function of her evaluation or appraisal of her quality or self-worth. Both "depression" and "self-esteem" are here used to refer to factors that vary along a continuum. Self-esteem ranges from high to low; depression ranges from nondepression to mild, moderate, and severe depression. The correlations between self-enhancement bias, depression, and self-esteem, with which we are concerned here, are for the most part correlations established by studying non-clinical populations.

2.4.1 Overly positive self-evaluation

Overly positive self-evaluation is correlated with nondepression and high self-esteem. Brown (1986) found that the discrepancy between people's evaluations of themselves and their evaluations of other people was significantly higher in subjects with high self-esteem (upper tertile) as compared to those with low self-esteem (bottom tertile), and high self-esteem was significantly correlated with biased evaluations of self as compared to most other people. Peter Lewinsohn and his colleagues (1980) made a similar finding with respect to depression, and found that self-enhancement bias increased with outpatient treatment for depression. These and other studies (Greenberg and Alloy 1989, Ingram 1989, Brown and Gallagher 1992, Brown 1993) suggest that self-enhancement bias is correlated with nondepression and high self-esteem.

Other studies found correlations between biased social comparisons and both positive affect (Buunk et al. 1990) and lack of psychological distress (Helgeson and Taylor 1993, see also Crocker et al. 1987), between self-serving causal attributions and nondepression (Kuiper 1978, Seligman et al. 1979), and between nondepression and the "false consensus effect" (Campbell 1986). Studies suggest (Greenberg and Alloy 1989; for reviews see Kuiper et al. 1983, Blaney 1986) that nondepressed people recall and process positive information more rapidly than they recall and process negative information about themselves, as opposed to depressed people whose recall and processing speeds are similar for positive and negative content; nondepressed people recall negative information about themselves more slowly than do depressed people.[8,9]

---

[8] Note the diversity of these studies. Bias was tested for by comparing self-evaluations with observers' evaluations (Lewinsohn et al. 1980), by comparing self-evaluations with subjects' evaluations of others (Brown 1986, Greenberg and Alloy 1989, Brown and Gallagher 1992, Brown 1993), and by asking subjects whether they endorsed self-evaluations that were "personally favorable but unlikely for most people" (Ingram 1989). Critics of these studies (Colvin and Block 1994, cf. Coyne and Gotlib 1993, Helweg-Larsen and Shepperd 2001) argue that bias cannot be established without objective measures against which to compare people's beliefs about themselves. But to avoid the conclusion that nondepressed people's beliefs manifest bias, we would need to say that nondepressed people tend to be more intelligent, attractive, kind, and so on, than depressed people, and that nondepressed people tend to be less prone to divorce, car accidents, serious illness, and so on. There's nothing especially implausible about the idea that someone with high self-esteem and a positive outlook would make a better leader, for example, or that depression interferes with relationships, making divorce more likely. But there is no evidence that nondepressed people are more physically attractive than depressed people, or that their homes are less likely to be damaged by earthquakes.

[9] Critics of these studies sometimes point out that they use college students as their subjects. This, of course, is true of much of contemporary empirical psychology. There might be two worries here. The first is that college students really are better than most people. Randall Colvin and Jack Block (1994) argue that "undergraduates from an elite university ... could be expected, realistically, to themselves be higher—and to know they were higher—than a vaguely identifiable, generalized other on the traits on which they were asked to rate themselves and others (e.g., bright, responsible, interesting, friendly, loyal, and humorous)" (p. 7; see also p. 15, Krueger 1998). Three replies to this. First, self-enhancement bias, and its correlation with nondepression and high-self esteem, has been studied in non-college populations (Langer 1975, Langer and Roth 1975, Cross 1977, Robertson 1977, Golin et al. 1979, Lewinsohn et al. 1980, Buunk et al. 1990, Taylor et al. 1991, Heckhausen and Krueger 1993, Helgeson and Taylor 1993, Borkenau and Liebler 1993, Krueger

This suggests that depression and low self-esteem are correlated with different doxastic practices than are non-depression and high self-esteem. More specifically, it suggests that nondepression and high self-esteem are correlated with self-enhancement bias.

2.4.2 Unrealistic optimism

Unrealistic optimism is correlated with nondepression and high self-esteem. Lauren Alloy and Anthony Ahrens (1987) asked subjects to estimate students' chances for academic success or failure given several relevant "cues" (SAT scores, illness, hours spent studying, difficulty of course schedule), as well as to estimate their own chances of success (having specified their own "cues"), and found that nondepressed subjects' predictions of their own chances of success were higher than those of depressed subjects, and their predictions of their chances of failure were lower. This was true even when the effect of "cues" was removed: nondepressed subjects' estimates of their own chances of success and failure were more positive than those of depressed subjects *who gave the same estimates of their SAT scores*. As the experimenters put it, "when confronted with identical information with which to make forecasts...depressed individuals' predictions of the likelihood of future outcomes [are] more negative than those of nondepressed individuals" (1987, p. 366). Other studies (Pietromonaco and Markus 1985, Pyszczysnki et al. 1989, Helweg-Larsen and Shepperd 2001) concluded that the predictive beliefs of nondepressed people are more unrealistic—biased in favor of optimism—than those of depressed people. Finally, Taylor and her colleagues (1991) argue that, among people who are HIV positive, unrealistic optimism is both ubiquitous and correlated with positive mood, coping, and diminished anxiety.

2.4.3 Illusion of control

Illusion of control is correlated with nondepression. Significant differences were found (Alloy and Abramson 1979, 1982) between depressed and nondepressed subjects when asked to estimate their degree of control over turning on a light by pressing a button. Nondepressed subjects tended to overestimate their degree of control; depressed subjects were significantly more accurate in their estimates. Other studies made similar findings (Golin et al. 1977, Golin et al. 1979). Other studies suggest that perceived

and Dunning 1999; on this point see Dunning 2005, p. 8, Brown 1998, pp. 64, 269). Second, a number of studies involving college students asked subjects to compare themselves to the "average" college student, or to compare themselves to "most other" college students (Alicke 1985, Boyd-Wilson et al. 2004), or to compare themselves to the "average" student at their particular college, or to compare themselves with "most other students" at their college (Larwood and Whittaker 1977, Weinstein 1980, Campbell 1986, Dunning et al. 1989, Krueger and Dunning 1999). Therefore, Colvin and Block's hypothesis, that elite college students accurately perceive their superiority to non-college populations, does not explain what needs to be explained. Third, and finally, it is extremely hard—it borders on the morally repugnant—to imagine that elite college students are superior to people who don't go to college, in the ways that Colvin and Block suggest. As Taylor and Brown (1994) write, "in what sense are university students warranted in believing they are kinder, warmer, and more sincere than the average person?" (1994, p. 22). The second worry about the use of college students is that college students are not representative of people in general, as their "youth and inexperience" makes them "particularly susceptible to the illusion of control and to exaggerated optimism" (Badhwar 2008, p. 95). But my first reply to Colvin and Block is also a reply to this objection.

control is correlated with psychological adjustment to negative life events (Buunk et al. 1990, Reed at al. 1993; see Taylor et al. 1991 for a review).

2.4.4 Self-focused attention

Depressed and nondepressed individuals have been found to differ significantly in the degree to which their thoughts are focused on themselves. Using a standard measure of "private self-consciousness," which measures the degree to which someone is attending to her "inner thoughts and feelings," significant correlations have been found between self-focused attention and low self-esteem (Turner et al. 1978) and between self-focused attention and depression (Smith and Greenberg 1981, Ingram and Smith 1984, Smith et al. 1985). Depressed subjects were more disposed to think about themselves than were nondepressed subjects; to put this another way, subjects more disposed to think about themselves were more likely to be depressed than were subjects less disposed to think about themselves. Timothy Smith and his colleagues (1985) propose that these differences in self-focused attention at least partially explain many of the other cognitive differences found between depressed and nondepressed people. They found, for example, that private self-consciousness was correlated with more accurate self-descriptions, confirming findings from previous work (Pryor et al. 1977, Gibbons 1983). Thomas Pyszczynski and his colleagues (1989) found that self-focused attention is crucial to negative memory bias, which is common for depressed people. Depressed subjects were found to recall significantly more negative events than were nondepressed subjects, but when subjects' attention was manipulated so as to be focused either on the self or on others, depressed subjects who were not self-focused did not differ significantly from nondepressed subjects in the positivity of their recall. Conversely, nondepressed subjects who were self-focused tended to be significantly more negative in their recall of events. Pyszczynski and Greenberg (1987b) propose that depression involves a "depressive self-focusing style," manifested in depressed people's tendency to focus on themselves following failures, but not following successes. This contrasts with nondepressed people, who exhibit the oppose pattern: focusing on themselves following successes, but not following failures. (This fact, Pyszczynski and Greenberg argue, may explain the correlation between nondepression and self-serving causal attributions.) Putting all this together, we have reason to think that increased focus on the self, and in particular a negatively biased focus on the self, is characteristic of depression, whereas less focus on the self, and a positively biased focus on the self, is characteristic of nondepression.

2.5 Two distinctions

Although there is clearly a lot going on here, some conclusions can be drawn. Self-enhancement bias—which can be manifested in various ways, including overly positive self-evaluation, unrealistic optimism, illusions of control, self-serving causal attributions, valence biases in recall and processing speeds, biased attention to evidence, biased self-focused attention, and so on—is both ubiquitous as well as positively correlated with nondepression and high self-esteem. This, I'll argue, threatens the eudaimonic ideal of true belief, and the eudaimonic value of self-knowledge in particular (§2.1). Self-ignorance, in the form of biased self-conceptions, is eudaimonically valuable, given its role in sustaining nondepression and high self-esteem. Before articulating that argument, however, we'll need to draw two distinctions.

2.5.1 Depressive realism vs. nondepressive unrealism

The research canvassed above has suggested to some the thesis of **depressive realism**, according to which "depressed people's perceptions and inferences are often more accurate or realistic than those of nondepressed people" (Alloy and Abramson 1988, p. 223). Whether this is true depends crucially on two things. First, it depends on whether there is a significant correlation between having accurate beliefs and being depressed. Second, it depends on what is meant by "being realistic."

According to certain cognitive theories of depression (Brown 1998, Chapter 9, Beck and Alford 2009) and some critics of depressive realism (Colvin and Block 1994), depressed people's beliefs about themselves tend not to be accurate but rather to be overly negative. Depressed people, for example, may manifest an illusion of control bias for negative outcomes (Vazquez 1987) and a self-derogating causal attribution bias (Sackheim and Wegner 1986). A negative recall bias in depression—e.g. more rapid and frequent recall of negative as opposed to positive information—is supported by a number of studies (see Kuiper et al. 1983 for a review). Many of the studies cited above (§2.4) suggest merely that depressed individuals' beliefs about themselves are *more* accurate than those of nondepressed individuals, and not that depressed individuals are unbiased or accurate in their beliefs about themselves (e.g. Lewinsohn 1980, Alloy and Abramson 1979; see also Brown 1993, p. 38). Jennifer Campbell (1986), for example, concluded that her results were "consistent with previous evidence that low self-esteem and depressed subjects are more evenhanded or less self-serving in their perceptions of social reality…but not with the hypothesis that they are generally more accurate in perceiving social reality (they are simply less biased in the direction of inaccuracies)" (p. 290). So one possibility is that depression and low self-esteem are correlated with *less* self-enhancement bias, not with the absence of self-enhancement bias. Another, mentioned above, is that depression and low self-esteem are correlated with bias in favor of a *negative* self-conception. More on this below.

Compare the thesis of depressive realism with that of **nondepressive unrealism**, on which nondepressed people's beliefs about themselves tend to be inaccurate and manifest self-enhancement bias. Nondepressive unrealism is independent of depressive realism. As Taylor and Brown (1994) argue:

Most healthy adults are positively biased in their self-perceptions. This fundamental fact is not altered by evidence that depressed people often bias information in a negative direction. Evidence that the perceptions of depressed people are just as distorted as those of healthy adults can hardly be taken as supporting the traditional view that mental health demands accuracy. (p. 22; see also Brown 1998, pp. 273–4)

In my view, there is good empirical support for nondepressive unrealism. For depressive realism this is less clear.[10]

This brings us to our second issue: the meaning of "being realistic." There are weak and strong senses of "being realistic." In the weak sense, this can be used "to refer to the degree of accuracy of people's judgments and perceptions" (Alloy and Abramson 1988 pp. 226–7). In the strong sense, "being realistic" requires more than mere accuracy—it requires reliability, or responsiveness to evidence, or objective, unbiased inquiry. The difference between the weak and strong senses of "being realistic" corresponds to the difference between mere true belief and knowledge. Suppose, for example, that because I am filled with self-loathing I believe that my colleagues constantly make fun of me behind my back. I have no evidence that they do so, and I'm not an especially ridiculous person, so there's no objective reason to suspect that they make fun of me. But, as it turns out, my colleagues do constantly make fun of me behind my back. On traditional accounts of knowledge, my belief that my colleagues make fun of me does not amount to knowledge. For knowledge that my colleagues make fun of me, I'd need some evidence that they do, or to have arrived at that conclusion by using some reliable method of inquiry, or something of that kind. My belief—based in self-loathing—does not have the right kind of basis to count as knowledge. My belief is realistic, in the weak sense, but not in the strong sense.

Given this distinction, we can consider a weak and a strong version of depressive realism. The **weak version** maintains a correlation between depression and accurate beliefs about oneself. The **strong version** maintains a correlation between depression and knowledge (as traditionally conceived) of self. Whatever evidence there is for depressive realism is evidence only for the weak version. As well, some evidence speaks against the strong version. For example, even though depressed individuals appear to be for the most part unbiased in their beliefs about themselves, they seem to manifest a positive bias in their beliefs about others. For example, depressed subjects have been shown to overestimate other people's control over events (Martin et al. 1984) and to be overly optimistic about other people's futures (Sacco and Hokanson 1978). Combined with the evidence canvassed above, suggestive of self-derogating biases in depression (Vazquez 1987, Sackheim and Wegner 1986, Kuiper et al. 1983), what emerges is a picture of depressive cognition as biased and unreliable. Even if depressed individuals tend to have accurate self-conceptions, their self-conceptions hardly amount to self-knowledge.

To sum up, nondepressive unrealism is well-supported, and the jury is still out on depressive realism. Furthermore, weak depressive realism is more plausible than strong depressive realism. In what follows I'll further defend nondepressive unrealism, and appeal to this view in arguing against the eudaimonic ideal of true belief. Depressive realism will not be assumed.

---

[10] In criticism of the view that "positive illusions" are correlated with mental health (Taylor and Brown 1988), some writers (Colvin and Block 1994, pp. 6–14, Badhwar 2008, p. 97) target the thesis of depressive realism. Colvin and Block's (1994) complaints about the empirical support for depressive realism do not apply to the empirical support for nondepressive unrealism. For their part, defenders of "positive illusions" back away from depressive realism when pressed, since their "concern is with mental health, not depression" (Taylor and Brown 1994, p. 22).

Finally, note well that nondepressive unrealism does not imply that self-enhancement bias is necessary for nondepression. The basis for nondepressive unrealism is a set of empirically supported *correlations* between nondepression and various species of self-enhancement bias. But it's compatible with the reality of these correlations that there might be people who are not depressed and are highly accurate in their self-conceptions. As Taylor and Brown (1994) put it, "[a]n argument that illusions promote mental health does not imply that they are a necessary condition for mental health" (p. 25; see also Brown 1998, p. 274).

2.5.2 *Illusion vs. delusion*

Taylor (1989) distinguishes between illusions and delusions:

[U]nrealistic optimism about the future is highly and appropriately responsive to objective qualities of events ... People are less unrealistically optimistic about their chances of experiencing common events like divorce or chronic illness than they are about less frequent events, such as being the victim of a flood or fire. [...] When people receive objective evidence about the likelihood of risks, they change their estimates accordingly. These qualities most clearly distinguish illusion from delusion. Delusions are false beliefs that persist despite the facts. Illusions accommodate them, though perhaps reluctantly. [In unrealistic optimism p]ositive events are simply regarded as somewhat more likely and negative events as somewhat less likely to occur than is actually the case. (p. 36)

There are two essential differences between illusions and delusions, in Taylor's sense. First, illusions are beliefs that are to some degree responsive to evidence. As Bernard Williams (2002) writes, "wishful thinking has to do its work in the densely covered ground of the merely factual" (p. 139). Imagine that I think that I'm a better teacher than most academics. Imagine further that I am contacted by the chair of my department: it has been decided, on the basis of several observations of my teaching as well as numerous complaints from students, that I am to be suspended from teaching indefinitely while I attend teaching workshops and a seminar on anger management. My inflated sense of my ability is an illusion, in Taylor's sense, if my response to this is to rethink my view of my abilities, to admit that I have been doing poorly and that I should rethink aspects of my teaching style; perhaps at this point I engage in some creative self-re-definition, realizing that I'm really more of a researcher than a teacher. On the other hand, my inflated sense of my ability is a delusion, in her sense, if my response to the sanctions is to conclude that the CIA must have infiltrated the department, turned my colleagues against me, and forged the negative student evaluations. It's consistent with the idea that some illusions are hallmarks of normal psychology and good mental health (as some maintain) that delusions are hallmarks of abnormal psychology and mental illness (Brown 1998, p. 274). The false beliefs said to be normal and healthy are said also to be "tethered to reality" (Vazire and Carlson 2010, p. 610). Studies suggest (Sedikides et al. 2002; see Kunda 1990, p. 481, for a review) that cognitive biases can sometimes be reduced when people are motivated for accuracy—when they expect to have to justify their judgments, for example, or simply when told that accuracy is important, although this is not always the case (Sedikides 1993). Ordinary, ubiquitous self-enhancement bias is sensitive to prior self-knowledge (see Kunda 1990, p. 485, for a review). In one study, both extroverted and introverted subjects' judgments of their own degree of extroversion depended significantly on whether they had been told that extroversion was correlated with academic success. But extroverted and intro-verted subjects differed significantly in terms of their judgments. When motivated to believe that they were extroverted, subjects did not uniformly believe that they were extroverted. Rather, they tended uniformly to believe they were more extroverted than they actually were. Sensitive to the facts, subjects modified what they knew in the direction of a positive self-conception. They did not spin a delusory self-conception out of thin air. Nondepressed people's self-conceptions tend to track their actual traits and abilities—but to track them in a systematically overestimating way (Taylor et al. 1989, p. 121). People with high self-esteem are responsive to negative evidence about themselves; but there is a difference in their degree of responsiveness, when compared to people with low self-esteem (Sanbonmatsu et al. 1994).[11]

Second, delusions can be distinguished from illusions in terms of their degree of inac-curacy. Overly positive self-evaluation, for example, involves overestimating the degree to which one possesses a certain trait or ability *that one actually possesses to some degree* (intelligence, social competence, attractiveness). As just suggested, self-enhancement bias involves augmenting an existing quality, rather than believing in a non-existent one (cf. Taylor and Brown 1994, pp. 23–4). Consider the illusion of control. To believe that you are responsible for the movement of the planets is a psychotic delusion; to believe that you are responsible for the academic job you landed is a comfortable bit of wishful thinking.

For these reasons, defenders of the thesis that "positive illusions" are correlated with mental health posit an **"optimal margin of illusion"** (Baumeister 1989, Taylor and Brown 1994, Boyd-Wilson et al. 2004; see also Dunning 2005, pp. 175–6, Epley and Dunning 2006, Sedikides and Gregg 2008, Tiberius 2008, Chapter 5, Brown 2009). "Slight" or "small" or "mild" exaggeration of one's positive traits and abilities (for example) is praised, while more severe inaccuracy is rejected as dangerous and unhealthy. **Moderate bias** is said to be beneficial; **excessive bias** is correlated with bad outcomes (Brown 1998, pp. 282–6). According to Roy Baumeister (1989), the "optimal margin" lies between com-plete accuracy (correlated with depression) and delusional inaccuracy (which is assumed to lead to dangerously imprudent behavior), balancing the twin (and sometimes con-flicting) goals of self-enhancement and prudent action. The reality of self-enhancement bias, and its correlation with nondepression and high self-esteem, does not mean that people's self-conceptions are constructed for the purposes of self-enhancement alone. Self-conceptions are the result of a plurality of "motives" (§2.3.1). One thing we can say about nondepressed, high self-esteem people's self-conceptions is that they tend to mani-fest a moderate, but significant, degree of self-enhancement bias.

[11] As well, because "positive illusions" can in some cases be corrected, it's preferable to speak of "bias" (as I've done), rather than "illusion" (Krueger 1998).

Our evidence (§2.4) suggests a correlation between illusion and nondepression and high self-esteem, not between delusion and nondepression and high self-esteem. The doxastic practices that appear to be correlated with nondepression and high self-esteem involve relatively slight, but significant, overestimations of one's positive traits and abilities (for example), which are responsive to evidence and prior knowledge. The relative mildness and evidence-responsiveness of self-enhancement bias explains how it's possible for such a doxastic practice to be ubiquitous. Below (§2.7) we'll explore several ways in which self-enhancement bias is "selective," involving inaccuracy only about certain domains and only in certain contexts, which further demystifies how inaccurate belief could be systematic and common.

Philosophers sometimes defend the eudaimonic disvalue of false belief by appeal to scenarios involving extremely high degrees of inaccuracy or comprehensive error, involving most or all of a person's beliefs, or both. For example, Michael Lynch (2004) writes:

> [I]magine what would happen if I were to *constantly* form false beliefs in the real world. Walking out my door, I would fall down ... I might put my car in drive when I meant for it to reverse ... or think safe food was poisonous and poisonous food safe. (p. 48, cf. Alston 2005, p. 30)

This point may be effective against Lynch's target (the view that in general true belief "has no value"), but we should exercise caution in bringing such scenarios to mind. The drastic consequences of false belief can easily be overestimated when false belief is imagined in extreme abundance. This is like assessing the prudence of drinking beer by considering the most vicious cases of overconsumption. Why are we inclined to appeal to these disaster scenarios when the specter of eudaimonically valuable false belief presents itself? Consider Robert Nozick's "experience machine" thought experiment, sometimes appealed to in defense of the value of knowledge (Finnis 1980, pp. 95–7, Brink 1989, pp. 223–4). We can learn something from this thought experiment—that many of us value knowledge such that we would not choose to do entirely without it, even if great amounts of pleasure were our reward for ignorance—but this actually tells us very little. It tells us that we would not trade all our knowledge away, in exchange for pleasure and massive error. But what about some portion of our knowledge, in exchange for happiness and moderate bias? What if our ignorance were not so severe as in the "experience machine"? More subtle questions are obscured if we treat the question of the value of true belief as a question of choosing between utter delusion and perfect "epistemic" virtue. What empirical psychology suggests is that most people have ended up somewhere between these two extremes.

2.6 Explaining the correlation between bias and depression

Self-enhancement bias is correlated with nondepression. I propose three (related) explanations of this correlation: a subjective wellbeing explanation (§2.6.1), a motivational explanation (§2.6.2), and a coping explanation (2.6.3).

Some aspects of the correlation between self-enhancement bias and nondepression require no explanation, in virtue of how nondepression is defined. For example, positive self-conception is partially constitutive of nondepression, according to the cognitive theory of depression (Beck and Alford 2009), and is standardly taken to be partially constitutive of mental health (Taylor and Brown 1988, pp. 197–8). It's therefore obvious why self-enhancement bias would correlate with nondepression and mental health, since self-enhancement bias is bias in favor of a positive self-conception.[12] Therefore, in these respects, the correlation between bias and nondepression stands in no need of explanation. But more can be said here, and in particular we can examine the connections between bias and several non-cognitive aspects of nondepression.

In this section, and below (§2.8), I'll focus on nondepression, setting aside self-esteem. It is worth noting that some argue that the value of high self-esteem has been overestimated (Baumeister et al. 2003): high self-esteem is correlated with none of the following: academic achievement, job performance, successful interpersonal relationships, and leadership ability. (Nor is low self-esteem correlated with: violence, anti-social behavior, intemperance, promiscuity, and gluttony.) So we should not expect self-enhancement bias (which is correlated with high self-esteem) to be correlated with academic achievement (cf. Robins and Beer 2001), job performance, successful interpersonal relationships, and leadership ability. In spite of this, high self-esteem does seem to be correlated with happiness (subjective wellbeing) and coping ability (Baumeister et al. 2003). High self-esteem, though overrated, "strongly and consistently" predicts "self-reported life satisfaction and assorted measures of happiness," and predicts against anxiety, depression, and hopelessness (Sedikides and Gregg 2008, p. 120).

2.6.1 The subjective wellbeing explanation

Recall Hume's account of "the merit of self-esteem" (§2.2). Hume maintains that pride ("greatness of mind," "self-esteem," "self-applause") derives its merit from "two circumstances," namely, "its utility and its agreeableness to ourselves" (1978, p. 600). Let's consider Hume's second point first. He writes that pride "gives us an immediate satisfaction" (ibid.), while "modesty, tho' it give pleasure to every one who observes it, produces often uneasiness in the person endow'd with it" (p. 597). This suggests an account of the correlation between self-enhancement bias and nondepression. Self-enhancement bias leads people to have overly positive self-conceptions, to be unrealistically optimistic about their futures, and to overestimate their degree of control over the world. These beliefs (and this is Hume's point) are pleasant, they give an "immediate satisfaction" to the believer. Such beliefs elevate one's mood, produce positive affect, and in short enhance one's subjective wellbeing.

---

[12] Self-esteem, as well, is partially cognitive—and high self-esteem is partially constituted by a positive view of oneself. As Brown (1993) argues, the maintenance of high self-esteem requires the protection of one's sense of self-worth, a function that positive beliefs about the self constitutively serve (cf. Tesser 1988).

Empirical work supports a causal connection between self-enhancement bias and subjective wellbeing (see Scheier and Carver 1992 for a review). In one study, subjects' mood states varied depending on whether they engaged in self-serving causal attributions after performing a task (McFarland and Ross 1982); in another, subjects' levels of optimism predicted their levels of postpartum depression (Carver and Gaines 1987); in a third, depressed subjects' moods could be improved by engaging in positively biased social comparisons (Gibbons 1986; see also Lewinsohn 1980, but also Alloy et al. 1981).

Depression is partially constituted by affective states like mood and subjective wellbeing (Beck and Alford 2009, pp. 17–22). An essential element of nondepression is subjective wellbeing, feeling good about oneself, or simply not being in pain, not being sad or "depressed" in the colloquial sense. Given a causal connection between self-enhancement bias and subjective wellbeing, we should expect a correlation between self-enhancement bias and nondepression.

2.6.2 The motivational explanation

Let us now turn to Hume's other argument in defense of "greatness of mind." Pride, Hume maintains, "gives us a confidence and assurance in all our projects and enterprizes" (1978, p. 597), "capacitates us for business" (p. 600), and "secretly animates our conduct" (ibid.). "Fortune commonly favours the bold and enterprizing," Hume argues, "and nothing inspires us with more boldness than a good opinion of ourselves" (p. 597).

Empirical work supports Hume's argument (see Taylor and Brown 1988 and Bandura 1977 for a review). Subjects with a positive self-image worked harder and longer on tasks (Felson 1984), people's beliefs in their "personal efficacy" were correlated with their ability to complete tasks (Bandura 1977) and with "behavioral persistence" (Greenwald 1980), and "mastery-oriented" optimism was correlated with constructive thinking (Epstein and Meier 1989). Kate Sweeny and her colleagues (2006) argue that optimism "serves the goal of preparedness by organizing thoughts and activity around goal pursuit and persistence and the acquisition of opportunities and resources" (p. 302). You might think that optimism and other positive views about oneself would lead to diminished motivation, on the assumption that someone who believes she will succeed will have no reason to try especially hard to bring success about, but the studies mentioned here suggest that this prediction turns out to be false.

It remains puzzling how self-enhancement bias fails to interfere with self-improvement. More recent empirical work may have solved this puzzle: self-enhancement bias manifests itself when people are working on a task, but does not manifest itself when people are deliberating about what is to be done (§2.7). Self-enhancement bias, as it is manifested in most people, appears to be fine-tuned to the goal of increasing motivation: bias manifests itself when motivation and self-esteem are needed, and conspicuously drops out of the picture when accurate information is needed for planning and self-assessment.

An important symptom of depression is a lack of motivation (Beck and Alford 2009, pp. 27–30). If Hume and these contemporary psychologists are right, the correlation between self-enhancement bias and nondepression is partially explained by the fact that self-enhancement bias causally sustains motivation. Belief in one's competence, success, and control, whether true or false, will promote one's motivation to work hard and persist in one's efforts, which explains why self-enhancement bias is correlated with nondepression.

2.6.3 The coping explanation

To these two Humean explanations I'll add a third. Psychologists have proposed and tested the hypothesis that various doxastic biases can serve as effective coping mechanisms when a person is confronted with a negative life event, such as serious illness, victimization, the death of a friend or spouse, or divorce. Their research found that biased social comparisons (Taylor et al. 1983, Taylor and Lobel 1989, Buunk et al. 1990, Collins et al. 1990, Helgeson and Taylor 1993; see Wills 1987 for a review) and illusions of control (Taylor et al. 1984, Reed et al. 1993, Thompson et al. 1993; see Thompson 1981 for a review) were correlated with effective coping, i.e. diminished distress, anxiety, hopelessness, low self-esteem, and depression, in response to negative life events (Taylor 1991, Brown 1998, pp. 276–81).

It's not hard to imagine why this would be so. As Ronnie Janoff-Bulman (1989) argues, ordinary nondepressed people make some basic assumptions about the world that are undermined by negative life events: that one is not likely to experience negative life events (Weinstein 1980), that the world is meaningful and at some basic level "makes sense," and that the self has worth (Tesser 1988). This picture of the world is maintained, I propose, by biases that are ubiquitous in ordinary, nondepressed cognition. Unless the impact of a negative life event can be mitigated in some way, depression and anxiety threaten. In such situations, as noted above, successful coping involves managing negative information in a biased way: someone with a serious illness might focus her attention on others whose illness is worse (Taylor et al. 1983, Taylor and Lobel 1989), or overestimate her degree of control of the illness' progress (Reed et al. 1993). Such biased thinking serves to protect one's sense of the world as meaningful and safe. So, as Valerie Tiberius (2008) argues, "a lack of self-knowledge can benefit us" because "self-deception looks to be a necessary coping mechanism" (p. 115).

You might think that all this isn't relevant to explaining the correlation between self-enhancement bias and nondepression, because this connection between bias and coping is confined to people who are dealing with negative life events. As Tiberius (2008) argues, cases of coping with negative life events "are cases of extreme circumstances, in which one might just say that ordinary imperatives of virtue do not apply" (p. 127; see also Dunning 2009). How does the fact that effectively coping with negative life events involves bias bear on the question of why nondepression and high self-esteem, outside the context of negative life events, are correlated with bias?

Taylor and her colleagues (1991) argue that the kinds of bias typical of successful coping with negative life events are just extensions of the ubiquitous and everyday "positive illusions" we described above (§2.3). They propose a continuum of biased responses, from responses to relatively serious and threatening negative life events to the events of everyday life (p. 240). But we can reverse this argument: given the utility of biases as means of coping with serious negative life events, we should predict that similar, though less extreme, biases are useful as means of coping with the events of everyday life. What this argument requires, of course, is the premise that everyday life is something to be coped with, something that requires or calls for coping ability. I leave this as an assumption of the argument, but it is motivated by the following thought: ordinary human existence is full of frustration and indignity, annoyance and insult. It *is* something with which we need to cope. If so, we should expect (unless we have some reason to think otherwise) that the same coping mechanisms that are effective in extraordinary cases would be effective in ordinary cases. This expectation is supported by recent work on self-enhancement bias and coping. Taylor and her colleagues (2003) found that self-enhancement bias was correlated with lower blood pressure, lower heart rate, and lower HPA (hypothalamic-pituitary-adrenocortical) levels, in response to stress—where the stressful situation was not a dramatic negative life event but rather having to count backwards by 7s from 9,095.

Epistemologists standardly acknowledge the potential utility of false belief in response to negative life events; a familiar example is the sick person whose chances of recovery are improved by optimism. But if the utility of false belief in such extraordinary cases of coping is conceded, then there is no good reason not to extend the idea to the ordinary case of coping with everyday life. Coping with negative life events is just a special case of coping, in general; the various cases involve the same mechanisms and biases, manifested to differing degrees, depending on the severity of the case.

If self-enhancement bias is an effective means of coping with negative life events and with everyday life, then we should expect a correlation between self-enhancement bias and nondepression. This for two reasons. First, serious depression is often triggered by negative life events (e.g. the death of a child, divorce, victimization), and thus we should expect a correlation between ability to cope with negative life events and nondepression. Second, if I am right that ordinary life is something that requires some degree of coping, we should expect a correlation between ability to cope, which is sustained by self-enhancement bias, and psychological health.

2.7 The selectivity of self-enhancement bias

The thesis that self-enhancement bias is correlated with nondepression and high self-esteem suggests to some the idea that "ignorance is bliss" and that true belief is eudaimonically worthless. I repudiated that idea above (§2.5.2). In this section we'll see that self-enhancement bias is highly "selective," both in the contents of biased beliefs and in the contexts in which said bias manifests itself. The upshot is to reject the picture of nondepressed, high self-esteem people as deluded or biased in *all* their thinking. Rather, nondepressed, high self-esteem people are biased about specific subject matters and in specific contexts and circumstances. This idea has been advanced by many theorists of self-enhancement bias (Brown 1998, Armor and Taylor 2002, Haselton and Nettle 2006, Sedikides and Gregg 2008; cf. Tiberius 2008, p. 128).[13]

Self-enhancement bias favors a positive view of oneself, not a positive view of others, in general, nor of the world, in general. Most people are unrealistically optimistic about their own futures, but not about other people's futures (Regan et al. 1995), and overly positive in their evaluations of themselves, but not in their evaluations of other people (Sedikides 1993; see also Alicke 1985, Brown 1986, Dunning et al. 1989).

Self-enhancement bias manifests itself to a greater degree in beliefs about subject matters that are "subjective," in the sense of not admitting of easy verification or falsification (cf. McKay and Dennett 2009, p. 508). There is no evidence that nondepressed people tend to have inaccurate beliefs about, for example, their height, or what city they live in. Self-enhancement bias tends to be manifested in people's beliefs about "low observability" traits (e.g. intelligence), rather than in their beliefs about "high observability" traits (e.g. behavior indicative of extroversion) (Vazire 2010), when questions employ ambiguous trait terms (Dunning et al. 1989), and when it comes to general claims ("the world is meaningful") as opposed to specifics ("I have just been hit by a bus") (Janoff-Bulmanf 1989; cf. Collins et al. 1990).

Elderly people and children seem to engage in greater levels of self-enhancement than do people in the 20s and 30s (Heckhausen and Krueger 1993; *pace* Badhwar 2008, p. 95). Researchers explain this in terms of utility: college-aged populations need a more accurate view of their futures for the purposes of effective decision-making; elderly people and children have less at stake in their decisions, and so are free to promote their feelings of self-worth through self-enhancement bias.

Social comparison activity seems to manifest a pattern of selective self-enhancement. Studies of people with serious illnesses (Buunk et al. 1990, Reed et al. 1993, Taylor and Lobel 1989, Helgeson and Taylor 1993, Taylor et al. 1995) suggest that those who cope well with their illness often seek out downward social comparisons (comparisons with worse-off others) for purposes of self-enhancement, but seek out upward social comparisons (comparisons with better-off others) for the purposes of acquiring accurate information (on how to become less ill), as well as for inspiration or to foster optimism. The picture that emerges from all this is that of a variety of affective, cognitive, and informational functions being performed through social comparisons, with biases appearing in certain contexts and not in others.

Finally, and most importantly, the manifestation of self-enhancement bias depends in part on a person's "mindset" at a given time. Peter Gollwitzer and Ronald Kinney

---

[13] It's worth comparing selective self-enhancement bias with "optimism" or "positivity," in their ordinary senses. As we will see below, the selectivity of self-enhancement bias makes it different from ordinary optimism or positivity.

(1989) tested illusions of control using a standard method (Langer 1975, Langer and Roth 1975): subjects were told to turn on a light, using a switch, which (to varying degrees) actually corresponded with the light turning on. In one experiment, some subjects were put into a "deliberative mindset" by being told that their task was to find out which of two lights they had more control over, while others were put into an "implemental mindset" by being told that their task was to turn on the light (on a machine of their choosing) as often as possible. Subjects in the "implemental mindset" condition overestimated their degrees of control to a significantly higher degree than did subjects in the "deliberative mindset" condition. In another experiment, "delibera-tive mindset" was induced by asking subjects (before working on the light apparatus) to reflect on solving a personal problem, while "implemental mindset" was induced by asking subjects to work on planning the implementation of some goal they had already decided upon. Similar effects on illusion of control were found. Gollwitzer and Kinney concluded from this that "illusionary optimism (in estimating personal control) promotes effective goal striving, whereas a realistic perspective is beneficial to sound decision-making" (p. 531). The basic idea that unrealistic optimism and illu-sions of control are manifested to a greater degree in situations of implementation and action than in situations of deliberation and decision-making, is supported by a grow-ing body of research (Taylor and Gollwitzer 1995, Thompson et al. 1993, Armor and Taylor 2002, Armor and Taylor 2003, Kurman 2006, Sweeny et al. 2006).

2.8 Against the eudaimonic ideal of true belief

Recall the eudaimonic ideal of true belief:

> **Eudaimonic ideal of true belief:** For any subject S and proposition that p, hav-ing a true belief about whether p is normally better for S than having a false belief about whether p. In other words, there is no clearly identifiable pattern of cases in which false belief is better than true belief. Thus, for any subject S and proposition that p, having a true belief about whether p is a more reliable bet, when it comes to wellbeing, than having a false belief about whether p.

In this section I'll argue against this, by appeal to my proposed explanations (§2.6) of the correlation between self-enhancement bias and nondepression. What we require, to falsify the eudaimonic ideal of true belief, is a clearly identifiable pattern of cases in which false belief is better for a person than true belief. I shall argue that some people's biased self-conceptions provide such cases.

Suppose that my self-conception manifests self-enhancement bias. Given this sup-position, I assume that many (or most, or even all) of my biased beliefs are false, and that were my self-conception accurate, my beliefs about myself would not manifest self-enhancement bias. My argument will have three steps. First (§2.8.1), I'll argue that, were my self-conception accurate, I'd be more depressed. Second, (§2.8.2), I'll argue that in that situation I'd be worse off than I actually am, and conclude that were my self-conception accurate, I'd be worse off than I actually am. Third (§2.8.3), I'll argue that this case is an instance of a clearly identifiable pattern, and thus a counterexample to the eudaimonic ideal of true belief.

2.8.1 From true belief to depression

It's tempting to appeal here to the thesis of depressive realism (§2.5.2), and in addition to the idea that self-knowledge causes depression. This is sometimes suggested by those in the depressive realism camp (Abramson and Alloy 1981, p. 442). However, the evidence for depressive realism is ambiguous. But there is good empirical support for nondepressive unrealism; and it's uncontroversial that depression is sometimes brought on by negative life events, so there is clearly some causation in the direction from cognition to depression. We have developed three explanations of the correlation between self-enhancement bias and nondepression (§2.6), on which beliefs that manifest self-enhancement bias are partial causes of nondepression. Were my self-conception accurate, these partial causes would be absent, and thus I would be more depressed. This is the first step in my argument against the eudaimonic ideal of true belief.

Does this commit me to the view that having a biased self-conception causes nondepression? Is there empirical support for that causal claim? I assume (cf. Beck and Alford 2009) that nondepression is a complex and interconnected set of cognitive, affective, and behavioral dispositions, that is (at least in many cases) partially constituted by certain forms of false belief (overly positive self-evaluation, unrealistic optimism, illusions of control), in which positive affective and behavioral dispositions are causally sustained by those forms of false belief, and in which positive affective states are partial causes of the self-enhancement bias that sustains those false beliefs. The right model, in other words, is one on which biased beliefs are partially constitutive of nondepression, and where, importantly, causation goes both ways between the affective and motivational elements of nondepression, on the one hand, and the cognitive elements, on the other.

Figure Constitutive and causal relations between the elements of nondepression. Dotted arrows are constitution relations; filled arrows are causal relations. Compare Beck and Alford 2009, on the constitution and causation of depression.[14]

---

[14] N.b. that the proposed model is consistent with the idea that the underlying causal explanation of nondepression is neurological or genetic.

Consider the causal relationship between the affective state of liking yourself (self-esteem, self-worth) and your cognitive self-conception, consisting of biased beliefs about your traits and abilities. Does self-love cause bias, which in turn causes overly positive self-evaluation? Or does bias cause overly positive self-evaluation, which in turn causes self-love? We should see this question as pushing a false dichotomy. A more plausible picture is one on which self-love and self-enhancement bias are mutually reinforcing, on which they are both partial causes of each other. That we like ourselves is part of the reason why we exhibit a "wonderful partiality for ourselves," which in turn is part of the reason why we overestimate our positive traits and abilities, which in turn is part of the reason why we like ourselves.

We have reason to think, therefore, that were my self-conception accurate, I would be more depressed. This is because, were my beliefs about myself not to manifest self-enhancement bias, I would be more depressed. The only way this could turn out to be completely wrong is if the causal arrow goes in one direction only, from nondepression to bias, in which case my lacking biased beliefs would not involve any change in my level of depression. But as we have seen, this simple picture is not plausible. Biased beliefs both causally and constitutively sustain nondepression; therefore, without those beliefs, a biased person's level of nondepression would be lower.

2.8.2 From depression to faring worse

My first step was factual; it defended a counterfactual connection between bias and nondepression. My second step is evaluative: here I'll argue that, were I more depressed, while enjoying an accurate self-conception, I'd be worse off than I actually am. To evaluate this, we will need to examine the eudaimonic value of the constituents and consequences of nondepression. In particular, consider those goods discussed above (§2.6):

- Subjective wellbeing
- Motivation
- Coping ability

I argued that self-enhancement bias is a partial cause of people's possession of these goods. My claim here is that I'm better off with these goods, while suffering from a biased self-conception, than I would be were my self-conception accurate—since were my self-conception accurate, I'd miss out on the share of these goods that I currently enjoy as a result of my biased self-conception. In other words, in the present case, the eudaimonic value of subjective wellbeing, motivation, and coping ability trumps the eudaimonic value of:

- Having an accurate self-conception

To evaluate this, we must consider the relative eudaimonic value of these various goods. And to do this, we will need to divide our discussion, addressing things from the perspective of our three main species of theories of wellbeing (§1.1.6): desire-fulfillment theories, desire-independent theories, and hybrid theories.

Desire-fulfillment theories of wellbeing If a simple desire-fulfillment theory of wellbeing is right, then it's easy to imagine that I would be worse off were I more depressed, while enjoying an accurate self-conception: all we need to imagine is that I do not want to have an accurate self-conception, but do want subjective wellbeing, motivation, and coping ability. Less severely, we can simply imagine that I prefer my actual share of subjective wellbeing, motivation, and coping ability to having an accurate self-conception. Recall our imaginary athlete, Karen (§1.1.2); it's easy to imagine that she prefers defeating her opponent to having an accurate self-conception.

What about other desire-fulfillment theories? What needs to be appreciated here is that a person's preference for subjective wellbeing, motivation, and coping ability (or for that which they bring, e.g. winning tennis matches), over having an accurate self-conception, need not be a "mere" preference or "shallow" desire. Subjective wellbeing, motivation, and coping ability might be what I *authentically* or *wholeheartedly* prefer, or what I would prefer were I *fully informed*. I might *care* about these goods more than I care about self-knowledge; I might care about these goods, but not care about self-knowledge at all. Consider, again, Karen's desire to win: her athletic pursuit might be what Williams (1976, p. 12) calls a "ground project"—that which gives her life meaning—while accuracy of self-conception does not enjoy, for her, "ground project" status. Compare Socrates (§1.1.1) for whom self-examination is plausibly a "ground project." Desire-fulfillment theories derive their appeal from Hume's observation that desire-independent theories seem to ignore the "vast variety of inclinations and pursuits among our species" (1985, p. 160). Among our species there is a vast variety of inclinations, in particular, with respect to accuracy of self-conception, and so, if such a theory is right, there will be individual differences in the eudaimonic value of accuracy of self-conception. This applies not only to "mere" desires, but to cares, loves, "ground projects," and so on.

For this reason, we should expect individual differences in what yields life-satisfaction. Tiberius (2008) argues that "[a] well-lived life is a life we endorse or approve of upon reflection" (p. 12). Someone whose ruling passion is self-knowledge will require an accurate self-conception in order for her life to merit endorsement upon her reflective survey, but someone whose passion for self-knowledge is minute by comparison with her passion for subjective wellbeing, motivation, and coping ability, or for that which they bring, will not require this. For this reason, defenders of life-satisfaction theories of wellbeing should agree that it's easy to imagine that I would be worse off were I more depressed, while enjoying an accurate self-conception.

Given a desire-fulfillment theory of wellbeing, to evaluate the claim that S would be worse off were she more depressed, while enjoying an accurate self-conception, we need to know more about S. In particular, we need to know about S's desires, her authentic or wholehearted desires, her fully informed desires, what she cares about, her values, her "ground projects," or her "predominant inclination" (depending on the particular desire-fulfillment theory in question), and where subjective wellbeing, motivation, coping ability, and accuracy of self-conception rank among them. How do we find that out? This will depend on how you think about desires, values, "ground projects," and so on. You might think that the fact that most people's beliefs manifest self-enhancement bias itself betrays that they care more for subjective wellbeing, motivation, and coping ability, than for accuracy of self-conception; just as you can infer, from the fact that someone avoids eating steak, that she prefers (for whatever reason) not to eat steak, you can infer, from the fact that someone avoids accuracy of self-conception, that she prefers (for whatever reason) not to have an accurate self-conception. Alternatively, you might think that preferences and values are best determined by simply asking a person: what do you care more about, this or that? Finally, you might think that someone's "real" values are revealed only in certain idealized, non-actual conditions, like what she would prefer under rational reflection with full information.

Desire-independent theories of wellbeing As I argued above (§1.1.6), if desire-independent theories of wellbeing are right, reflective and empirically informed intuition is our best guide when evaluating claims about wellbeing. What is needed, to make a case against the eudaimonic ideal of true belief, based on the premise (§2.8.1) that were my self-conception accurate, I would be more depressed, is the premise that I would be worse off in that situation.

For my part, this seems right, when it comes to my biased self-conception: the "epistemic" cost is relatively low, given that the inaccuracy with which we are concerned is moderate (§2.5.2), and the payoff vis-à-vis subjective wellbeing, motivation, and coping ability is relatively high. This intuition is compatible with the eudaimonic value of true belief; the thought is that such value is trumped in this case by the eudaimonic value of subjective wellbeing, motivation, and coping ability. I am inspired here by John Rawls' (1971) idea that "self-respect and a sure confidence in the sense of one's worth is perhaps the most important primary good" (p. 396)—so even if true belief is a "primary good" as well, self-esteem is more important than this.

You might not share this intuition, or you might object to it on theoretical grounds. There are two ways to go here. First, you could reject the eudaimonic value of subjective wellbeing, motivation, and coping ability. It seems obvious to me that these things are eudaimonically valuable, but it might not seem obvious to you, or you might favor a theory on which these things aren't eudaimonically valuable. My argument assumes that, intuitively, they are.

Second, you could reject my claim about the *relative* eudaimonic value of true belief: you might argue that the eudaimonic value of true belief is not trumped in this case. It seems obvious to me that it is, but it might not seem obvious to you, or you might have a theory that says otherwise. My argument assumes that, in the present case, intuitively, the eudaimonic value of true belief is trumped in this case.

My sympathies lie not with desire-independent theories of wellbeing, but with desire-fulfillment theories. You might think that trading subjective wellbeing, motivation, and coping ability for an accurate self-conception sounds like the deal of the century, or you might think it sounds like a total rip-off. Which of these "views" is right? Who has it right about what "really" matters, and about how much it "really" matters? I favor the desire-fulfillment theorist's elegant answer: that eudaimonic value is relative to the individual. However, *even if* desire-independent theories are right, we should conclude that I would be worse off were I more depressed, while enjoying an accurate self-conception—at least to the extent that our guide for evaluating claims about wellbeing is our reflective and empirically informed intuitions.

Hybrid theories of wellbeing Recall that, on hybrid theories of wellbeing, the extent to which a person's life goes well or badly is principally a matter of the extent to which her *appropriate* desires are satisfied. Just as the desire-independent theorist should concede that subjective wellbeing, motivation, and coping ability are eudaimonically valuable, the hybrid theorist should concede that it's appropriate to desire subjective wellbeing, motivation, and coping ability. And just as the desire-independent theorist should concede that the eudaimonic value of subjective wellbeing, motivation, and coping ability sometimes trumps the eudaimonic value of having an accurate self-conception, the hybrid theorist should concede that it's sometimes appropriate to prefer subjective wellbeing, motivation, and coping ability to having an accurate self-conception. Suppose that my desires are, in this respect, in line with what is appropriate: that I appropriately prefer subjective wellbeing, motivation, and coping ability to having an accurate self-conception, in the present case. Would I be better off, were I more depressed, while enjoying an accurate self-conception? I would be worse off, because said desires would in that case be frustrated; by contrast those desires are actually satisfied. So the hybrid theorist should also agree that I would be worse off were I more depressed, while enjoying an accurate self-conception.

Conclusion We can put our first two steps together now.

1. Were my self-conception accurate, I'd be more depressed (and in particular I'd enjoy a lesser share of subjective wellbeing, motivation, and coping ability).
2. Were I more depressed (and to enjoy a lesser share of subjective wellbeing, motivation, and coping ability), while enjoying an accurate self-conception, I'd be worse off.
3. Therefore, were my self-conception accurate, I'd be worse off.[15]

We have a case, therefore, in which false belief is better than true belief. It remains to argue that this case is normal, i.e. that it is an instance of a clearly identifiable pattern.

---

[15] I favor a view of subjunctive conditionals on which their truth-conditions are context-sensitive. We evaluate the truth of "If it were the case that p, then it would be the case that q" by going to the nearest possible worlds in which p, and asking whether the proposition that q is true at those worlds. But which

2.8.3 The clearly identifiable pattern

Have we found a clearly identifiable pattern of cases in which false belief is better than true belief? Note well that we might identify such a pattern, while conceding that true belief is better than false belief *most of the time*, where this refers to the statistical majority of cases. Driving on the right is safer on most roads, but there is a clearly identifiable pattern of cases in which it is unsafe (§1.1.3). There are two reasons to think that we have found a clearly identifiable pattern of cases in which false belief is better than true belief.

First, we have identified the correlation between self-enhancement bias and non-depression and high self-esteem (§2.4) as a (partial) explanation of the existence of those cases in which false belief is better than true belief. The pattern these cases conform to is explained by people's need for a positive self-conception, which provides a sense of self-worth, and which serves to partially causally sustain their good mood, happiness (in the subjective sense), motivation, and ability to cope with the world. Moderate (§2.5.2) and selective (§2.7) self-enhancement bias satisfies this need, without substantial eudaimonic cost.

Second, suppose desire-fulfillment theories of wellbeing are right. I assume that a great many people care more for subjective wellbeing, motivation, and coping ability than they do for accuracy of self-conception. It would be quite wrong to say that *no one* cares more for these things than for accuracy of self-conception. It would be equally wrong to say that *everyone* cares more for these things than for accuracy of self-conception. Many people care more for subjective wellbeing, motivation, and

worlds are the "nearest" worlds? The evaluation of a counterfactual as true or false will depend crucially on which worlds we take to be "nearest." But there is no objective fact of the matter about that; the "nearness" of possible worlds is a matter determined by context. Our argument exploits the context-sensitivity of counterfactuals in four ways. First, in assessing what would be the case were my self-conception accurate, I suggested we look to a world in which I am generally unbiased in my beliefs about myself. This was a natural place to look, in the context of a discussion of the eudaimonic value of true belief. Our question is one about the relative goodness of different types of lives: self-knowledgeable lives versus lives involving bias and certain kinds of self-ignorance. Second, note that the eudaimonic ideal of true belief entails that someone who believes falsely about whether p would normally be better off were she to believe the truth about whether p. This can suggest the idea that such a person would normally be better off were she *to become* a true believer with respect of p. But this is not quite right, as the contextually determined nearest q-worlds might be worlds in which it was always the case that q, rather than worlds in which it becomes the case that q. Again, in the context of our discussion of the eudaimonic value of true belief it was appropriate for us not to consider worlds in which I go from having false beliefs about myself to having true beliefs about myself, but rather to consider worlds in which I am and have been generally unbiased in my beliefs about myself, and in which therefore I have and have had a generally accurate self-conception. Third, when we evaluated the claim that I would be better off if I had an accurate self-conception, we took the "nearest" world in which I have an accurate self-conception to be a world in which I fit the statistical pattern of correlation between self-enhancement bias and nondepression. We did not assume that there is not a possible world in which I am both nondepressed and self-knowledgeable. To say that were I unbiased I'd be more depressed is to treat worlds in which I fit the statistical pattern as "nearer" than worlds in which I don't. Finally, we asked, above, whether I would be better off with an accurate self-conception; in evaluating this claim we looked at worlds in which my self-conception was brought into conformity with the truth, and not at worlds in which the world was brought into conformity with my self-conception.

coping ability than they do for accuracy of self-conception. Our identification of this category of people constitutes our identification of a pattern that (partially) explains the existence of those cases in which false belief is better than true belief.

Note that, regardless of our theory of wellbeing, our conclusion here—that the eudaimonic ideal of true belief is false—commits us to *no absolute claim* about the eudaimonic value of bias.[16] Our conclusion is not that, for all S, having a biased self-conception is better for S than having an accurate self-conception. Our conclusion is that it is *not* the case that, for all S, true belief is normally better than false belief. This is consistent with the view that false belief, manifesting self-enhancement bias, is better for some people, but not for all—and that is all I've argued for here.[17] Thus our conclusion does not entail that "epistemically" virtuous philosophers would be better off were they less "epistemically" virtuous (*pace* Badhwar 2008, pp. 102–3; cf. Brown 2009, p. 514).

Does my argument beg the question against defenders of the intrinsic value of knowledge and true belief (§1.5)? There are two reasons to think not. First, the argument is compatible with both the (pro tanto) intrinsic value of knowledge and the (pro tanto) intrinsic value of true belief, as well as with the constitutive value of knowledge and true belief (§1.1.5). We'll return to the pro tanto eudaimonic value of true belief (§1.1.4) below (Chapter 5). Second, whatever the plausibility of the idea that knowledge or true belief is intrinsically valuable, it's no less plausible that subjective wellbeing is intrinsically valuable. My argument has not, therefore, criticized the value of true belief by appeal to some good—subjective wellbeing—that defenders of the intrinsic value of knowledge and true belief can sensibly reject as worthless. What some fans of both knowledge (or true belief) and subjective wellbeing may have assumed is that the value of knowledge (or true belief) does not normally conflict with the value of subjective wellbeing. In my view, the connections between nondepression and self-enhancement bias show that this is not the case.

2.9 Objections to the value of self-enhancement bias

I have argued (§2.8) that there are normal cases in which false belief, in the form of an inaccurate self-conception resulting from self-enhancement bias, is better than true belief. I have appealed, in this argument, to the premise that self-enhancement bias is ubiquitous (§2.3) and correlated with nondepression (§2.4). Here I'll consider two types of objection to my argument. The first type of objection (considered in this section) challenges the value of self-enhancement bias by arguing that I have not taken

---

[16] This is important, in part, given cultural differences in self-enhancement bias (cf. §7.4.3).

[17] Cf. Roy Baumeister and his colleagues (2003): "As scientists, we are inclined to favor the pursuit of truth above all else, but we can recognize that some people might prefer self-flattering illusions over accurate knowledge" (p. 38).

account of its eudaimonically disvaluable consequences. The second type (§2.10) challenges the ubiquity of self-enhancement bias.

I have argued that the eudaimonic cost of self-enhancement bias—having an inaccurate self-conception—is worth paying, given the benefits—subjective wellbeing, motivation, and coping ability. The first type of objection suggests that when additional costs are taken into account, this is not plausible: the costs are not worth paying. My general strategy in response will be to argue that the alleged additional costs are either illusory, or still worth paying. The motivating idea behind my response to these objections is the premise that self-enhancement bias is ubiquitous. The eudaimonic costs of self-enhancement bias are costs that most people pay, and therefore these costs are not so great as to tip the balance in favor of having an accurate self-conception. This thought, in turn, is motivated by a certain **egalitarian** intuition, on which the good life is not restricted to an elite minority: it's not the case that most ordinary people—and in particular, the relatively rich people, living in liberal societies, who were the subjects of most of the empirical work described above (§2.3)—are living especially bad lives. You might reject this intuition. It seems to me that disagreement about this question, about the quality of ordinary life, is the source of many other disagreements about wellbeing.

2.9.1 The objection from narcissism

Self-enhancement bias is correlated with narcissism (John and Robins 1994, Gosling et al. 1998, Paulhus 1998, Robins and Beer 2001; see also Sedikides et al. 2004 on self-esteem). Does this threaten my argument? Three reasons to think that it doesn't.

First, narcissism is defined as "self-admiration that is characterized by tendencies towards grandiose ideas, fantasized talents, exhibitionism, and defensiveness in response to criticism; and by interpersonal relations characterized by feelings of entitlement, exploitativeness, and lack of empathy" (John and Robins 1994, p. 210). It's unsurprising, however, that self-enhancement bias is correlated with "grandiose ideas" and "fantasized talents"—i.e. inaccurate beliefs, and in particular inaccurate beliefs about the self. The correlation between self-enhancement bias and narcissism, therefore, may not tell us anything substantial.

Second, it's not obvious that the criteria of narcissism are eudaimonically disvaluable. Whether it would be better for a person not to have "grandiose ideas" and "fantasized talents" just is the question of the eudaimonic value of true belief. So despite the fact that "narcissism" is a pejorative, we should consider the possibility that narcissism isn't eudaimonically disvaluable.

Exploitativeness and lack of empathy, we can assume, are moral vices. Given the assumption that moral virtue is partially constitutive of wellbeing (§1.1.1), we should conclude that narcissism is eudaimonically disvaluable, to the extent that it involves exploitativeness and lack of empathy. But this leaves the relative eudaimonic disvalue of narcissism open. We must now weigh the benefits of self-enhancement bias not only against its cost vis-à-vis true belief, but also against its moral cost. But it's unclear whether the moral cost is not worth paying. You might think it's better for a person to fall short of perfect moral virtue. And it seems clear that whether the moral cost of self-enhancement bias is worth paying depends on the severity of the narcissism involved.

So, third, and most importantly, we should welcome the idea that moderate narcissism is psychologically healthy, given its correlation with subjective wellbeing, nondepression, lack of loneliness, lack of anxiety, and non-neuroticism (Sedikides et al. 2004), despite its interpersonal costs. As Brown (1998) argues, "a moderate degree of narcissism is considered to be a component of a healthy personality" (p. 283). In this connection our distinction between moderate and excessive self-enhancement bias (§2.5.2) is crucial: our conclusion is that moderate self-enhancement bias, with the moderate narcissism that it brings, is eudaimonically valuable; this is consistent with a rejection of excessive self-enhancement bias, with the more extreme narcissism that it brings, as eudaimonically disvaluable. This explains why even those who argue that "self-enhancers tended to be narcissistic" conclude that their findings "support claims made about the psychological benefits of positive illusions" (Robins and Beer 2001, p. 344).

The fact that self-enhancement bias is correlated with narcissism is less of a threat to the eudaimomic value of biased beliefs when we consider the relatively uncontroversial fact that moderate self-enhancement bias is ubiquitous (§2.3). So, therefore, is moderate narcissism. The sort of narcissism associated with moderate self-enhancement bias is something that most people suffer from—which should make egalitarians wonder if they are in fact suffering all that much for it.

2.9.2 The objection from being disliked

Studies have suggested that self-enhancement bias is correlated with being disliked by other people, especially in long-term social interaction (Colvin et al. 1995, Paulhus 1998). A closer look at these studies will show that they do not threaten my argument.

Randall Colvin and his colleagues (1995) found that overly positive self-evaluations are correlated with various "negative personality traits" (as evaluated by observers). However, there is little evidence against the eudaimonic value of biased self-conceptions here. Among the supposedly "negative" personality traits, found to be correlated with self-enhancement bias, are the following, for male subjects: "has fluctuating moods," "evaluates motivations of others," "is unpredictable," "pushes and tries to stretch limits," "tends to be rebellious, non-conforming," "is sensitive to demands," and "thinks and associates ideas in unusual ways." For female subjects, the list of "negative" traits includes: "sex-typed," "regards self as physically attractive," "expresses self through action," "power oriented," "interested in opposite sex," "values own independence," and "is sensitive to demands." For my part, I can't find a consistent way of understanding these traits as "negative"; among them are traits that I would say are downright positive. This is not to deny that some of the traits found to be correlated with self-enhancement bias seem to be unambiguously negative ("hostile towards others," "is self-defeating," "keeps people at a distance"). These results do not suggest a correlation between self-enhancement bias and "negative" personality traits, but rather between self-enhancement bias and a range of traits, some "negative," some "positive," and others more or less neutral ("concerned with functioning of own body").

The endorsement of conformity with traditional gender roles here is perhaps most troubling.[18] Female subjects with high levels of self-enhancement were described as sexually aggressive, independent, and "emotionally bland," which suggests that these subjects were perceived negatively in virtue of their violating a certain gender stereotype (of a sensitive, submissive, emotional woman with low sex drive). Male subjects with high levels of self-enhancement were described as moody, defensive, and highly concerned with other people; this suggests that these subjects were perceived as violating a certain gender stereotype (of a rational, unemotional, autonomous man). There is obviously a sense in which conformity with traditional gender roles can be beneficial for a person. But you might think that personalities that violate traditional gender roles should, at the very least, be seen as "neutral," if not "positive" in their refusal to conform to harmful stereotypes.

Colvin and his colleagues (1995) argue that

[While] "sex-typed" and "regards self as physically attractive" ... are not inherently negative in tone ... they connote a rigid, narcissistic style when combined with ... other qualities, such as being thin-skinned, self-defensive, and denying of unpleasant thoughts and conflicts. (p. 1155)

In other words, they suggest giving a "negative" interpretation of these personality traits, given the other traits they were associated with in women with high levels of self-enhancement bias. But this is a mistake, as one might just as easily give a "positive" interpretation of various so-called "negative" traits. Consider being "power oriented"—this seems "negative" if we imagine Mu'ammer Qaddafi, but quite "positive" when we imagine an aspiring manager, determined to become her company's first female CEO. An "emotionally bland" woman might simply be a cool-headed person who fails to conform to the stereotype of women as highly emotive, unpredictable, and flighty.

Delroy Paulhus (1998) found that although self-enhancement was correlated with "positive reactions" from others after the first meeting of a series of weekly discussion groups, it was correlated with "negative impressions" after the seventh meeting (p. 1206). Again, the evidence against the eudaimonic value of biased self-conceptions is unclear.

First, self-enhancing subjects were (significantly) more likely to be described by their peers as "arrogant," "tends to brag," "overestimates abilities," and "hostile," and (significantly) less likely to be described as "warm," but they were also more likely to

---

[18] Compare a study (Joiner et al. 2003) in which self-enhancing men were found to be disliked by their roommates, while self-enhancing women were found to be liked by their roommates; the experimenters concluded that "excessive self-enhancement does not have uniformly negative effects on relationships" (p. 27).

be described as "confident," (non-significantly) more likely to be described as "entertaining," and (non-significantly) less likely to be described as "boring." As with narcissism (§2.9.1), the correlation between self-enhancement bias and being perceived as overestimating one's abilities is non-substantial. More importantly, the picture that emerges is that of self-enhancement as a "mixed blessing" (as Paulhus puts it). This is consistent with my conclusion that, in many cases, for many people, having a biased self-conception is better than having an accurate self-conception.

Second, although Paulhus describes a "deteriorating pattern of interpersonal perceptions" (p. 1197), it's unclear whether the correlates of self-enhancement bias he found are especially eudaimonically disvaluable. It would be a mistake to assume that eudaimonically valuable interpersonal relationships require, or are exemplified by, being liked by other people. For example, Paulhus found that self-enhancement bias was negatively correlated with being described by others as "well-adjusted," but the eudaimonic value of being described by others as "well-adjusted" is unclear, as is, in general, the eudaimonic value of being liked by other people.

The egalitarian thought applies here: self-enhancement bias is correlated with being disliked, but moderate self-enhancement bias is ubiquitous, so it seems to follow that being moderately disliked is ubiquitous. This makes less plausible that idea that being moderately disliked is especially bad.

Hume recognized the interpersonal difficulties associated with "greatness of mind" (§2.2). He argues that pride is a virtue, but only "if well conceal'd" (1978, p. 598) and says that "the almost universal tendency of men to over-value themselves" has resulted in our generally condemning "self-applause," and that this fact partially explains why we may be reluctant to recognize pride as a virtue. "[G]ood breeding and decency," Hume maintains, require "humility," but this requirement does not "go beyond the outside"; there is no requirement of humility in our "inward sentiments" (ibid.). For this reason "the world esteems a well-regulated pride, which secretly animates our conduct, without breaking out into such indecent expressions of vanity, as may offend the vanity of others" (ibid. p. 600). Although pride is "always agreeable to ourselves," it is "sometimes disagreeable to others" (p. 597).

What Hume gives us here is a suggestion as to how we might negotiate the costs and benefits of self-enhancement bias: one might enjoy the eudaimonic value of self-enhancement bias (subjective wellbeing, motivation, coping ability) while avoiding its eudaimonic disvalue (arrogance, hostility, boasting). What is required for this is, on the one hand, a certain doxastic (self-enhancement bias) combined with a practical virtue (humility, modesty, politeness).

It might seem difficult or impossible to combine these in practice, but empirical research is suggestive of a solution to this dilemma. Brown and Gallagher (1992) found differences in self-enhancement bias, in subjects' evaluations of their performance on a test, depending on whether self-evaluations were "private" or "public": in one condition the experimenter, having told the subject that he or she was going to be paying close attention to the subject's responses, was seated behind the subject as he or she entered self-evaluations into a computer ("public" condition); in the other condition the experimenter was seated elsewhere, and emphasized the researcher's concern for privacy and the fact that all evaluations given were anonymous ("private" condition). Subjects' levels of self-enhancement (discrepancy between subjects' self-evaluations and other-evaluations) were significantly lower in the "public" condition than in the "private" condition (and in particular when responding to a perceived failure on the test). The researchers concluded that in general "people respond to public failure with relative modesty and humility" (p. 9), despite the ubiquity of self-enhancement bias. Similarly, Sedikides and her colleagues (2002) found that self-enhancement was diminished when subjects were told that they would have to justify their self-evaluations in person to someone else. This species of selectivity in self-enhancement bias (§2.7) suggests that Hume was not far off the mark in his description of how a virtuous person might combine private pride with public humility.

2.9.3 Self-enhancement threatens self-satisfaction and self-improvement

You might object that having an inaccurate self-conception will inevitably interfere with a person's ability to achieve her goals: how can someone get what she wants if she doesn't know what she wants? Alternatively, you might worry about interference with the ability to improve oneself: without accurate self-knowledge, how is it possible to know when one needs to improve?

First, we should distinguish between the inaccuracy of self-conception involved in self-enhancement bias and other failures of self-knowledge. We have considered a specific kind of inaccurate self-conception (§2.5.2, §2.7), and there's no reason to think that self-enhancement bias would involve or lead to a lack of knowledge of what one wants. Furthermore, as Brown and Dutton (1995) argue, "accurate self-knowledge is incidental to many life tasks," and "the domain of life in which inaccurate knowledge is as punishing and fatal as [people] have claimed is in fact quite small" (p. 1293).

Second, if self-enhancement bias is manifested when people are in an "implemental mindset," but not when in a "deliberative mindset" (§2.7), we shouldn't expect self-enhancement bias to be manifested by someone reflecting on whether she needs to improve. And we should keep in mind that the presence of a self-enhancement "motive" is compatible with the presence of other "motives" in self-evaluation (§2.3.1). Taylor and her colleagues (1989) describe a hypothetical case:

Consider, for example, a man who does poorly at his job but who fails to interpret negative feedback correctly as evidence that he is doing a poor job. Although his perceptions of himself as a capable worker persist, it cannot have escaped his attention that his work situation is not the most desirable one possible. He may come to feel that he does not like the job very much or that he does not particularly enjoy interacting with his boss or his coworkers. Consequently, he may leave his position, even though he has failed to correctly interpret the negative feedback as evidence that he is doing a poor job. (pp. 124–5)

Alternatively, he might conclude that although he is not doing a poor job, he could be doing a better job, and strive to perform better. There are any number of ways that he might resolve the situation, while maintaining a biased belief about his performance. If he does so, he will have managed a neat trick: he will have succeeded in solving his practical problem while maintaining his positive self-conception. Would it be better— would his life go better—if he were to solve his practical problem in a more straightforward way, by recognizing his poor performance as such, lowering his opinion of himself, and resolving to change? Two reasons to think that the answer to this question is: not necessarily. First, it may be the case, with this particular man, that were he to recognize his poor performance as such, and lower his opinion of himself, he would lack the motivation to do better (§2.6.2). His diminished self-esteem, it's easy to imagine, might make the difference between a successful resolution ("I'm good, but I can be great") and an unsuccessful resolution ("I'm bad, and I need to become adequate"). It may be the case that he is simply not capable of taking the "straightforward" route to a solution to his practical problem (cf. Arpaly 2003, Chapter 2). Second, why should we think that the "straightforward" route to a practical solution to his problem is superior, from the perspective of wellbeing, to the route we imagined above, involving biases and rationalizations? The "straightforward" route involves greater "epistemic" virtue, to be sure; but the alternative route involves greater subjective wellbeing (§2.6.1). Which route is better, the "epistemic" route or the pleasant route? If desire-fulfillment theories of wellbeing are right (§1.1.6), this will depend on the desires of the individual whose wellbeing we are concerned with. But even if desire-independent theories are right, it's not obvious that "epistemic" goods always trump the good of subjective wellbeing, such that "straightforward" self-improvement is always better.

Third, self-enhancement bias is not correlated with maladaptive behavior, as the objection suggests. In an early study of optimism (Robertson 1977), perceived vulnerability to being in an automobile accident was not correlated with willingness to buy insurance covering damage from an accident. Many people were optimistic about their chances of being in a crash, but this didn't have a significant effect on their willingness to pay for insurance coverage to protect against that eventuality. Similarly, Taylor and her colleagues (1991) found no significant correlation between unrealistic optimism about AIDS and safe-sex practices: most of the subjects interviewed had unrealistic views about their likelihood of developing AIDS, but such views were not correlated with, e.g., a lower rate of condom use.

Fourth, we should keep in mind that the falsity of the eudaimonic ideal of true belief doesn't imply that self-knowledge isn't often instrumentally eudaimonically valuable. So it's not a good objection to my argument that self-knowledge often has a great deal of instrumental value. Colvin and Block (1994) argue that "reality orientation" *is* an important component of mental health (p. 9) and that perceptions of control are sometimes "beneficial when they are reality based" (p. 11). Nothing I've said here implies that relative accuracy is worthless (cf. Taylor and Brown 1994, p. 25), nor that true belief isn't eudaimonically valuable (§2.8.3). My conclusion is compatible with Tiberius' (2008) view that "knowing the facts is a good thing, but we shouldn't go overboard" (p. 138). I would add that self-enhancement bias is a good thing, but we shouldn't go overboard (cf. §2.5.2).

Similarly, it's not a good objection that inaccurate views about yourself can be bad for you. The view defended here isn't that it's *always* better for a person to overestimate her positive traits and abilities. Nor does the view defended here imply that increased positivity in self-conception is always beneficial. As Taylor and Brown (1994) write, "[i]t is absolutely clear that certain illusions or distortions (e.g., delusions of grandeur, hallucinations, gross misperceptions of physical reality) are associated with mental illness" (p. 25). Beliefs that manifest self-enhancement bias are inaccurate, but not entirely divorced from the truth; people's inaccurate self-conceptions systematically track their actual traits and abilities (§2.5.2). As Taylor and her colleagues (1989) put it, even though such beliefs are false, they are "patterned realistically" (p. 121).

However, overconfidence may have other negative consequences. Baumeister and his colleagues (1993) found that people with high self-esteem were prone to overestimate their chances of success when faced with "ego threats" (challenges to their self-esteem), resulting in their placing unwise bets on themselves, as compared to people with low self-esteem, who did not respond in this way to "ego threats." But it's unclear whether this threatens my argument. Baumeister and his colleagues (1993) write that "[m]aximal rewards are typically obtained by selecting the highest goal that one can reach—and then succeeding" (p. 142). But while this is certainly true in a betting situation, where "maximal rewards" are defined as dollars earned, it's not at all clear that this is true when the "reward" one seeks is wellbeing. Baumeister's argument assumes substantial eudaimonic value for successfully reaching goals that one sets, and significant eudaimonic disvalue for failing to reach goals that one has set. But this assumption should be challenged. Compare two aspiring philosophers, both with papers they want to publish, who both put a lot of stock in having their work recognized. Cathy makes a list of five venues for submission: the *Distinguished Philosopher's Quarterly Review*, her top choice, along with four other well-regarded venues. Ingrid makes a list as well: the *Proceedings of the Paraguayan Philosophical Club (Eastern Division)*, her top choice, along with four other journals with bad reputations. How much wellbeing does Ingrid gain when she succeeds, when her paper is accepted by her top choice, and (more importantly) how much does Cathy lose when she fails, and her paper is accepted by some lesser journal on her list? Setting unrealistic goals and not meeting them is bad in gambling; but it's not obviously bad in life.

2.9.4 Self-enhancement bias leads to painful failures and joyless successes

You might object that self-enhancement bias will lead to painful discoveries of the truth. However, there is no evidence that this actually happens to people whose beliefs manifest moderate self-enhancement bias (§2.5.2). This may be the case because there are no recognized empirical tests for the traits and abilities in question (Brown 1993, p. 34) or because terms for those traits and abilities are ambiguous (cf. §2.7). People seem to be capable of painlessly incorporating evidence against their biased beliefs, both by being selective in the gathering and interpretation of evidence (§2.3.2), as well as by subtle revision of their illusory beliefs (Taylor and Brown 1988, pp. 201–3, Taylor et al. 1989, p. 125, Janoff-Bulman 1989).

Alternatively, you might object that self-enhancement bias will lead to diminished satisfaction upon success. One study (McGraw et al. 2004) found that overconfidence in a basketball shooting drill was correlated with diminished satisfaction with the outcome of the drill: overconfident players were less happy with the outcome of the drill than were players who were underconfident or who judged their shooting abilities accurately. Again, this may reveal further that biased beliefs have eudaimonic value only when they concern "subjective" matters (§2.7). When one predicts that one will make a shot in basketball, one's prediction is swiftly and decisively either confirmed or disconfirmed. In the case of an unexpected miss, there is no way a sane person can avoid knowing that she has failed. The biased beliefs involved in the sort of self-enhancement bias described above (§2.3), however, are for the most part unlike this: they are not subject to swift and decisive confirmation or disconfirmation.

We should keep the correlation between self-enhancement bias and nondepression (§2.4) in mind. This is compatible with the finding that self-enhancement bias is correlated with diminished pleasure in certain situations, "diminished" by contrast with what pleasure might have been had, *sans* bias. What we can conclude from these two findings is that nondepression is compatible with "diminished" pleasure in certain situations. An underconfident person will be more pleased with her success, but she will also be less motivated to work towards success (§2.6.2). An overconfident person enjoys such motivation, but is less pleased with her success. These complexities are what make theorizing about the good life interesting.

2.9.5 True belief is eudaimonically best

You might object that false beliefs aren't necessary for wellbeing, since it's easy to imagine a nondepressed person who has an accurate self-conception. Indeed, so the argument goes, accuracy of self-conception conjoined with nondepression would be eudaimonically best; it would be the combination we would expect in the best human life. However, these two points are consistent with my conclusion (cf. §1.1.2). I have not alleged (cf. §2.8.3) that false belief is necessary for wellbeing, nor that the best human life involves false belief.

2.9.6 Wellbeing isn't subjective

Neera Badhwar (2008) objects that, "as is standard in contemporary psychology, Taylor and Brown regard happiness as a purely subjective state" (p. 92). This is technically true of Taylor and Brown (1988), who identify happiness with "contentment" (p. 198). But Badhwar's objection is misleading, as Taylor and Brown are explicit that happiness is only one element of "mental health" (pp. 197–8)—and it is mental health that they maintain is promoted by "positive illusions." They are keen to point out (ibid.) the inadequacy of theories that identify mental health with the ability to be happy; on their view, mental health requires that ability, but also has a cognitive element (e.g. positive self-regard) as well as behavioral and practical elements (e.g. the ability to grow and develop, social mastery, autonomy). Badhwar misses this when she speaks of "mental health or happiness" (p. 92) in connection with Taylor and Brown's view.

Of particular importance, in response to Badhwar's objection, is the fact that Taylor and Brown (1988) maintain that "positive illusions" promote "the ability to care for and about others, and the capacity for productive and creative work" (p. 198). It is therefore wrong to cast Taylor and Brown's conception of happiness as "subjective" by comparison with Aristotelian "eudaimonia." Mental health, as Taylor and Brown define it, has both a subjective element (happiness, understood as contentment) as well as objective elements (capacity for work, social mastery, positive self-regard). Mental health, as Taylor and Brown describe it, thus has a similar structure to happiness on what Richard Kraut (1979) calls an "objective" conception of happiness, which he attributes to Aristotle. Moreover, it's not the case that most contemporary psychologists regard wellbeing (or mental health) as a subjective state. Many contemporary psychologists defend desire-independent, "eudaimonist" theories of wellbeing (cf. Tiberius 2006, p. 495, Tiberius and Plakias 2010, pp. 407–10). We should not stumble here on the ambiguity of the word "happiness," of which most contemporary speakers of English are aware. Badhwar is surely right that many contemporary authors—following perfectly ordinary English usage—use "happiness" to refer to a subjective state, or a feeling, specifically, a state or feeling of contentment or satisfaction. And some people, in addition to this, believe that wellbeing consists in this "subjective" state. But that view is not orthodox in contemporary psychology.

More importantly, I have been clear here about the supposed eudaimonic benefits of self-enhancement bias: subjective wellbeing, motivation, and coping ability (§2.8.2). And I tried to assume as little as possible about wellbeing; in particular I did not assume that wellbeing is a "subjective" state. In connection with desire-fulfillment theories of wellbeing, I assumed that many people want subjective wellbeing. And in connection with desire-independent theories of wellbeing, I assumed that subjective wellbeing was eudaimonically valuable. But nothing above assumed that wellbeing is a "subjective" state, nor that wellbeing is entirely constituted by subjective wellbeing.

It's worth distinguishing between two ways in which a belief might have eudaimonic value. On the one hand, it might be the case that having that belief makes the believer feel good, or comfortable, or happy, or satisfied. On the other hand, it might be the case that the believer is better off with the belief than she would be were she to lack it. A belief might be both of these things at once, but the two concepts are distinct. What I have argued is that there is a clearly identifiable pattern of cases in which people are better off with false beliefs than they would be with the corresponding true beliefs.

2.9.7 Self-enhancement bias threatens agency

Marcia Baron (1988) argues that "self-deception wrongs or harms the self in roughly the way that deception wrongs or harms others," and in particular that self-deception is wrong (to the extent that it is) because, when I deceive myself, I "undermine my own agency" because "I bring it about that I operate with inadequate information (i.e. less adequate than it would otherwise have been had I not deceived myself) or a warped view of circumstances" (p. 436). So "insofar as self-deception is wrong, it is wrong because it corrupts our belief-forming practices" (ibid. p. 438). This idea, it seems clear, applies not only to self-deception but to other unreliable doxastic practices (biases, wishful thinking, stereotypes), including self-enhancement bias. The idea is that unreliable doxastic practices are bad for me, in as much as they deprive me of information, or provide me with false information, because this undermines my agency, or my ability to act.

How does self-deception undermine agency, on Baron's view? Baron's argument has two stages. First, she argues that in certain cases self-deception "limits" or "cripples" one's agency. Second, she argues that self-deception "can become a habit, a strategy one falls back on too often" (ibid. p. 437), so that self-deception can be seen as wrong even in situations in which it fails to limit one's agency, because even then it threatens to "spread" and limit one's agency in other situations. Let's consider these two steps separately.

How does self-deception "limit" one's agency? Baron does not say more than what I've quoted above: as a result of self-deception, I operate with relatively limited or false information. But what is bad, when it is bad, about operating with relatively limited or false information? We can imagine three kinds of cases:

(i) I miss out on a preferable option, merely through ignorance that it was an option, e.g. I don't know that the McRib sandwich is available (for a limited time only), so I order something else, even though I would prefer the McRib to what I end up eating.

(ii) I act with bad consequences, as a result of having a false picture of what's going on, e.g. I go to Casablanca for the waters, having been misinformed about there being waters there, and I don't enjoy myself.

(iii) No bad consequences result, but my "action" is not fully an action, or not fully an intentional action, or not fully an autonomous action, in virtue of being based on a false belief, and in virtue of this my life goes worse, e.g. I order 66 fried potato balls, mistakenly thinking that "soixante-six" is French for "sixteen," but the balls are smaller than I thought, and I'm hungrier than I thought, so I enjoy eating them all.

In type-(i) and type-(ii) cases, it seems clear that true belief is better for me than false belief, and nothing we've said so far has suggested that cases like these aren't common. Biased self-conceptions don't have the kind of bad consequences found in type-(i) and type-(ii) cases, as Baron concedes (ibid. p. 437). The worry here comes from the second step in Baron's argument: the threat that self-deception will "spread" (more on which in a moment). But what about the kind of badness involved in type-(iii) cases? Doesn't that threaten with *any* false belief? I would suggest that we reject the species of eudaimonic badness supposedly found in type-(iii) cases. Not knowing the right word for "sixteen" in French is bad because someone ignorant of this runs the risk of bad consequences, but there is nothing bad, per se, about actions (or "actions") based on false beliefs. There is nothing eudaimonically valuable about performing actions, per se, or about performing fully autonomous actions, fully intentional actions, and so on.

Let's now consider the second step of Baron's argument. Baron makes two points: that self-deception can become a habit (i.e. one can condition oneself to employ self-deceptive strategies by repeatedly employing them), and that self-deception requires additional self-deception (e.g. as new evidence comes in against my self-deceptive belief, I must engage in additional self-deceptive maneuvering to preserve the credibility of that original belief). Both these points apply to self-enhancement bias, whether or not we choose to classify it as a form of, or as involving, self-deception. But the worry about "spread" can be alleviated by considering the selectivity of self-enhancement bias (§2.7). One might expect, a priori, that self-enhancement bias would lead to a more general species of biased belief formation, and perhaps eventually to a state of massive delusion about oneself, other people, and the world. This, given the principle that repetition of a doxastic practice habituates a person to it (Baron's first point) or the fact that sustaining a biased belief one has already formed will often require additional biased interpretation of evidence, selective attention to evidence, and so on (Baron's second point). It can seem obvious that bias will spread, given the principle that someone with one false belief will be rationally required to form other false beliefs, namely, beliefs whose contents follow from or rationally cohere with the content of the original false belief. But these a priori considerations are refuted if self-enhancement bias, but not massive delusion, is ubiquitous (§2.3). Self-enhancement bias does not, as a matter of fact, lead to massive delusion. People, as it turns out, are capable of **compartmentalizing** their biased self-conceptions (and the unreliable doxastic practices that those beliefs manifest), and of keeping them from "infecting" their other beliefs (and the relatively reliable doxastic practices that those beliefs manifest). The habits of one domain turn out, as a matter of fact, not to transfer to other domains. We shouldn't make the mistake of thinking that people will believe what rationality requires; indeed, the fact that people often don't has been one of our themes. If we were to implant a false belief into the mind of a fully rational believer, the falsity would surely spread. But most people are not fully rational believers, and our biased beliefs appear **insulated** from the rest of our "web of belief." So we should not agree a priori that "one who eschews self-criticism by telling himself that his problems are due to allergies thereby improves the climate for other self-deception," such as collective self-deception of the sort Baron associates with Germany under the Nazis and the United States under Ronald Regan (Baron 1988, p. 439). These are legitimate (if hyperbolic) concerns, but our approach to them should be empirical: if there is a correlation between self-enhancement bias and susceptibility to pernicious political ideologies, then presumably an experiment can be devised to reveal it.

2.9.8 Self-enhancement bias threatens authenticity

Michael Lynch (2004, pp. 120–8) defends the constitutive value of self-knowledge on the grounds that self-knowledge is partially constitutive of authenticity, which in turn is partially constitutive of wellbeing. If this is right, you might think that having a false self-conception is eudaimonically disvaluable because it's incompatible with authenticity.

Let's examine Lynch's argument. He begins by positing a particular species of self-knowledge with which he is concerned: knowledge of what you care about. Caring for something, on Lynch's view, requires both that my desire for that thing be sustained over a long period (cares, in this sense, cannot be "fleeting" or "momentary," p. 120) and that I want that thing for its own sake (so, in this sense, I cannot care about something instrumentally). Care, for Lynch, is sustained final valuation. He goes on to give an account of authenticity, identifying it with Frankfurtian "wholeheartedness," on which authenticity requires identifying "with those desires that effectively guide your action," where "[y]ou identify with a desire when it reflects the kind of person you wish to be, what you care about" (p. 125). Here, then, is the crux of Lynch's argument:

[A]uthenticity...requires...identifying with the desires that guide your action. What you identify with is determined by what you care about. Thus if you don't know what you care about...you don't know which of your first-order desires you identify with. If you don't know which of your possibly conflicting desires you identify with, you cannot be acting authentically. Consequently, knowing what matters to you is partially constitutive of authenticity. (p. 126)

And because authenticity "is an important part of happiness" (p. 125), knowing what you care about is partially constitutive of happiness.

The argument has two premises—that knowledge of what you care about is partially constitutive of authenticity, and that authenticity is partially constitutive of happiness—but the first premise should not be challenged: "authenticity" is an ambiguous word, at best, and so we should allow Lynch to define it however he likes.[19] Given this, two replies. First, in defense of the eudaimonic value of self-enhancement bias, it's not clear that self-enhancement bias, given its selectivity (§2.7), would tend to threaten a person's knowledge of what she cares about. Just as self-enhancement bias does not entail bias in beliefs other than those constituting a person's self-conception, it does not entail bias across the board in one's self-conception. Second, self-knowledge is not

---

[19] On the various senses of "authenticity," see Feldman and Hazlett 2012 and Feldman forthcoming, as well as Arpaly 2003, Chapter 4.

required for Frankfurtian wholeheartedness. What is required for wholeheartedness is that you are moved to act by what you care about, not that you are moved to act by what you *know* you care about. So we can grant the eudaimonic value of Frankfurtian wholeheartedness, without conceding the eudaimonic value of self-knowledge (cf. Feldman and Hazlett forthcoming).

2.10 Objections to the ubiquity of self-enhancement bias

This section considers objections to the premise that self-enhancement bias is ubiquitous (§2.3). These objections allege, for different reasons, that the phenomena that I said were manifestations of self-enhancement bias do not really involve bias, in the sense of an unreliable doxastic practice (cf. Flanagan 2009).

2.10.1 *"Biased" beliefs are responsive to evidence*

Beliefs that manifest self-enhancement bias are not unresponsive to evidence; this was the upshot of our discussion of the distinction between illusion and delusion (§2.5.2, cf. Colvin and Block 1994, p. 9, p. 11). Ziva Kunda (1990) argues, in defense of "motivated reasoning," that:

> People do not seem to be at liberty to conclude whatever they want to conclude merely because they want to. Rather,...people motivated to arrive at a particular conclusion attempt to be rational and to construct a justification of their desired conclusion that would persuade a dispassionate observer. They draw the desired conclusion only if they can muster up the evidence necessary to support it. In other words, they maintain an "illusion of objectivity" (pp. 482–3).

This description of "motivated reasoning" describes many paradigms of self-enhancement bias. Were we right to call such phenomena "biases"? There are three reasons to think so.

First, for the purposes of our examination of the eudaimonic ideal of true belief, we assumed that a "bias" is an unreliable doxastic practice (§2.3). The phenomena described above, and in general "motivated reasoning" that is driven by "motives" other than accuracy, are surely unreliable doxastic practices. So it matters not whether they are not "biases" in some more narrow sense.

Second, we should allow that some false beliefs are closer to the truth than others: if I falsely believe that I am an above-average teacher, my self-conception is closer to the truth than it would be were I to believe that I last year won my university's award for outstanding teaching. Given my evidence, the latter belief would be delusional; however, the former belief, although it is false and not justified given my evidence, is still better justified and closer to the truth than the belief that I won a teaching award last year. I have argued that having false beliefs that are relatively close to the truth can be better for people than having the corresponding true beliefs, but haven't said anything about whether false beliefs that are relatively far from the truth can be eudaimonically valuable.

Third, we should not adopt a narrow understanding of "bias," if we wish to say that bias threatens "epistemic" justification. Consider Katie, who very much wants civilians not to be injured by US military activities in Afghanistan, and who consequently tears out and discards any page of the newspaper that has a headline reporting civilian deaths in Afghanistan, apart from those published in the *American Patriot Review*, which reports that there have been a total of 14 civilian deaths as a result of US activity. As a result of this selective inquiry (§2.3.2), Katie has little evidence of civilian deaths caused by US military activity in Afghanistan. Suppose now that she believes, on the basis of what little evidence she has, that only 14 civilians have been killed as a result of US military activity. Her belief is "epistemically" unjustified, and it is "epistemically" unjustified because it manifests bias on her part. So even though, in some narrow sense, Katie's belief is not "biased," because it is a proper response to the evidence that she has, it is still biased, in the wider sense that precludes "epistemic" justification. The same applies, mutatis mutandis, when it comes to other mechanisms of self-enhancement.

2.10.2 *"Beliefs" that manifest self-enhancement bias don't affect behavior*

I assumed that belief has a characteristic functional profile (§1.6.2). If people's responses to questions about how likely they think they are to be involved in a car accident are unrelated to their willingness to buy car insurance (§2.9.3), isn't this reason to think that their responses to those questions aren't actually revealing their beliefs?

It seems to me that there are a number of reasonable interpretations available, when it comes to people whose verbal risk estimates do not correlate with their insurance purchases. We might say that some of the subjects' dispositions to purchase insurance are irrational, given their beliefs. We might say that they believe that it's irrational not to buy insurance, regardless of how likely one thinks an accident is. (Think here of the kind of reasoning you must go through when waiting for a red light in the dead of night, on an isolated road, when no one is around.) We might say that there is some inconsistency in their beliefs; we might say (in particular) that their "implicit" beliefs about the likelihood of a crash (manifested in their insurance purchases) are in tension with their "explicit" beliefs about the likelihood of a crash (manifested in their verbal risk estimates). We might say that people have different thresholds for outright belief (which accounts for their different verbal risk estimates), but that they all have more or less the same credence with respect to the proposition that they'll be in an accident (which accounts for their similar insurance purchases). Finally, we might say that people's verbal risk estimates don't reveal their beliefs.

That last interpretation—the only interpretation on which self-enhancement bias isn't a doxastic practice—might be appropriate if non-verbal actions were the sole criteria for belief attribution. But I've assumed a broader conception of the criteria for belief attribution (§1.6.2), on which these include not practical dispositions, both verbal and non-verbal, but also cognitive and affective dispositions (cf. McKay and Dennett 2009, p. 508). Self-enhancement bias is correlated with verbal practical dispositions, in the form of people's responses to questions about their traits, abilities, futures, and degrees of control over events, with affective dispositions for nondepression and high self-esteem, and with non-verbal practical dispositions for persistence (§2.8.2) and arrogance (§2.9.2). Once we allow a broader conception of the criteria for belief attribution, we have ample reason to attribute belief in the relevant cases. Someone who believes that she is attractive and intelligent will, other things being equal, feel good about herself. This is the case, even if her belief fails to manifest itself in non-verbal action. Likewise, someone who believes that her chances of being in a car accident are low will, other things being equal, not be anxious about being in a car accident, regardless of whether her belief reveals itself in non-verbal action.

Supposing that people's verbal risk estimates are sincere, but that they don't reveal their beliefs, is to attribute to them ignorance of their own beliefs. Nothing speaks against this a priori, but it's not obvious that the attribution of such ignorance is more charitable than the attribution of irrationality in the form of inconsistent beliefs (e.g. between "implicit" and "explicit" beliefs) or akrasia (e.g. buying insurance in spite of one's judgment that insurance is unnecessary).

Social psychologists' conclusions about people's beliefs, in the self-enhancement literature, are based on a relatively uncontroversial inference rule: if someone sincerely asserts that p, assume (other things being equal) that she believes that p. Importantly, their conclusions are not based on a more controversial inference rule: if someone sincerely asserts that she believes that p, assume (other things being equal) that she believes that p. The assumption is that assertion reveals belief, not that belief is transparent to consciousness or that people's reports about their own mental states are reliable.

2.10.3 "Beliefs" that manifest self-enhancement bias are unstable

Alternatively, the selectivity of self-enhancement bias (§2.7) might make you suspicious that self-enhancement bias isn't a doxastic practice. If people's assessments of their degree of control over events change depending on whether they're in a "deliberative mindset" or an "implemental mindset," isn't this reason to think that those assessments aren't really revealing their beliefs?

However, we should not require, as part of the nature of belief, that belief is stable across situations. If Gollwitzer and Kinney (1989) are right, people are disposed to have positive beliefs about themselves when working towards completing a task, to a greater degree than they are when they're deliberating about how to complete a task. There isn't compelling reason to deny them this conclusion, on the grounds that beliefs, by their very nature, cannot be so fleeting.

Compare Hume's descriptions of the psychology of his skeptical inquiry in the *Treatise* (I.iv.2), which center on what can seem like a contradiction. On the one hand, Hume suggests that when he is seriously engaged in philosophical reflection, he becomes completely agnostic about the existence of material things—in a moment of such reflection he writes:

> [W]e ought to have an implicit faith in our senses…But to be ingenuous, I feel myself *at present* of a quite contrary sentiment, and am more incline'd to repose no faith at all in my senses. (1978, p. 217)

Hume thus suggests that, when engaged in such serious reflection, he suspends judgment about the existence of material things. On the other hand:

> [W]hatever may be the reader's opinion at this present moment…an hour hence he will be persuaded that there is both an external and internal world. (Ibid. p. 218)

In other words, as soon as serious reflection ceases, we believe once again in the existence of material things. This is prima facie reason not to require that beliefs be stable across contexts and situations.

2.11   Conclusion

I've presented (§2.8) and defended (§§2.9–2.10) an argument against the eudaimonic ideal of true belief, based on the premise that moderate (§2.5.2) and selective (§2.7) self-enhancement bias causally sustains nondepression (§2.6). On my view, many people have false beliefs about themselves which contribute to their wellbeing. In the next chapter, we'll turn to beliefs about other people, and I'll argue that here too there can be eudaimonically valuable false beliefs.

3

Partiality and Charity

No whit worse than a brother is a comrade who has an understanding heart.
—Odysseus, according to Homer's *Odyssey*

I've argued (Chapter 2) that false belief sometimes has eudaimonic value, and that cases in which false belief is better than true belief instantiate a clearly identifiable pattern. If so, the eudaimonic ideal of true belief (§1.4) is false.

If one adopts a desire-fulfillment theory of wellbeing, then *some* people are such that false belief is sometimes better for them than true belief. This claim follows from three assumptions: (i) that people care about things other than true belief (call these "non-alethic goods"), (ii) that cases can easily arise in which a person has a false belief about whether p while enjoying a greater share of non-alethic goods than she would were she to believe the truth about whether p, and (iii) that in some such cases, people care more about said non-alethic goods than they do about believing the truth about whether p. The details of these assumptions would have to be modified to suit the particular desire-fulfillment theory in question. But for any plausible desire fulfillment theory, these three assumptions, mutatis mutandis, can be made. Such cases instantiate a clearly identifiable pattern of cases in which false belief is better than true belief. And so the eudaimonic ideal of true belief is false, if one adopts a desire-fulfillment theory of wellbeing.

So in this chapter, which further examines the plausibility of the eudaimonic ideal of true belief, I will assume that desire-independent theories of wellbeing are right. I'll again argue for cases in which false belief is better than true belief. But my argument here will have an important feature that distinguishes it from the argument from self-enhancement bias: in this chapter I will not appeal to empirical psychology.

I'll argue that certain biases (unreliable doxastic practices) are partially constitutive of wellbeing. I'll argue (§3.1) that some friendships are partially constituted by (being disposed towards) an unreliable doxastic practice that I'll call "partiality bias." Then I'll argue (§3.2) that (being disposed towards) an unreliable doxastic practice, which I'll call "charitable bias," is a moral virtue. Finally (§3.3), I'll argue against the eudaimonic ideal of true belief, on the ground that friendship and moral virtue are partially constitutive of wellbeing.

3.1 Partiality bias

In this section I'll argue that partiality in action and motivation is partially constitutive of some friendships (§3.1.1), that "partiality bias" is partially constitutive of
some friendships (§3.1.2), and that "partiality bias" is an unreliable doxastic practice
(§§3.1.3–3.1.4).

3.1.1 Partiality and friendship

Our focus will be on friendship, in the contemporary, everyday sense, but what I'll
say about friendship could be said, mutatis mutandis, about romantic relationships and
familial relationships. It seems that at least some friendships are partially constituted by
various species of **partiality**—the disposition to treat (in a broad sense) one's friends
differently than strangers (non-friends). The most obvious species of such partiality is
partiality in action. For example:

- A friend asks that I buy her a drink, on account of her not being able to afford
  it. I'm more inclined to do so than I would be were the request coming from a
  stranger.
- A friend and a stranger are in distress. I'm disposed to give help to my friend first,
  and only then assist the stranger.
- A friend asks me to donate money to some non-profit organization. I'm more
  inclined to do so than I would be were the request coming from a stranger.
- A friend of mine is being ridiculed behind her back. I'm more inclined to object
  to the ridicule than I would be were it directed at someone unknown to me.
  (Stroud 2006, p. 503)

What does it mean to say that some (or all) friendships are partially constituted by
partiality in action? It means at least this much: that in (at least some) friendships, we
expect our friends to be disposed towards partiality in action; we think that friends
ought to be so disposed; we think that failure to be so disposed is evidence of someone's not being a genuine, true, or real friend.[1] In this sense, (at least some) friendships
require (a disposition towards) partiality in action.

Do all friendships require a disposition towards partiality in action? The counterexample to this that I have in mind is a friendship between moral saints, whose love is
conditional on a mutual respect and admiration for the other's impartiality. Supposing
that Gandhi and Peter Singer were to become close friends, we can imagine that they
might not expect partial treatment from each other: on their trips to the pub, they
wouldn't buy drinks for each other, but for needy strangers. The claim that (a disposition towards) partiality in action is partially constitutive of some friendships is sensitive

---

[1] I'll follow at least some aspects of ordinary language in understanding "friend" and "friendship" such
that the conditions for being a true, genuine, or real friend are the conditions for being a good friend. Thus,
in some sense, there are no bad friends—a bad friend turns out to be no friend at all.

to the possibility of individual differences in friendship. However, for us non-saints, it seems that our friendships are partially constituted by (a disposition towards) partiality in action.

The requirements of partiality in such friendships, however, extend beyond the realm of action. At least some friendships are partially constituted by (a disposition towards) **partiality in motivation.** This is Michael Stocker (1976, p. 462) and Bernard Williams' (1976, p. 18) point about the motivations of a genuine friend:

- When I visit a friend in the hospital, I do so because I'm concerned for her well-being, not because doing so is required by the categorical imperative, or because doing so will maximize happiness in general.
- When I help a friend in distress, at the expense of a stranger, I give preference to my friend simply because she's my friend, and not because impartial moral principle says that I'm permitted to give her preference.

For Stocker and Williams, partiality in motivation has both a positive and a negative component. On the positive side, the partial actions of a genuine friend are motivated by non-instrumental concern for the wellbeing of the beloved. On the negative side, said actions are not motivated by impartial principles or rules. As Williams argues, even if impartial moral theories are able to say that partiality in action is morally permissible or even morally required, the genuine friend is not motivated by *that* kind of consideration when she behaves partially. If my friend discovers that the reason I visited her in the hospital is that I felt it was my impartial duty, or if she discovers that the reason I gave her preference was that I felt that impartial morality required it, then she could rightly accuse me of not being a genuine friend. Stocker and Williams' insight, as Sarah Stroud (2006) points out, is that "a proper analysis of friendship should not neglect to look inside, at the motivational and affective states of the good friend" (p. 501). More generally, "there is a distinctive moral psychology associated with friendship" (ibid.). The requirements of (some) friendships extend beyond the realm of action, and into the realm of thought.

3.1.2 *Partiality bias is partially constitutive of some friendships*

I'll argue that (a disposition towards) a species of unreliable doxastic practice, which I'll call "partiality bias," is partially constitutive of some friendships, in the same way that (dispositions towards) partiality in action and partiality in motivation are partially constitutive of some friendships. This thesis has been defended by a number of contemporary philosophers (Baker 1987, Morton 1988, Baron 1991, Keller 2004, Stroud 2006; see also Price 1954, pp. 13–14, Feldman 1988a, p. 236, Pace 2011, p. 258).

What do we mean by "partiality bias"? Recall our conception of partiality (§3.1.1) as the disposition to treat one's friends differently than strangers. Partiality bias, then, will be understood as differential *doxastic* treatment. More specifically, **partiality bias** is manifested when someone's beliefs about her friend are different from those of a neutral (impartial, non-friend) party, in possession of the same evidence (or different from those that a neutral party would form). More specifically still, partiality bias is bias in favor of a positive conception of one's friends.

Let's consider a case of partiality bias (cf. Morton 1988, p. 177, Keller 2004, pp. 332–3, Stroud 2006, pp. 504–6):

Someone has been stealing pens from the faculty resource room and selling them on the black market. A committee is established to determine the guilty party, and after investigating the matter, they announce their findings: there is strong, if inconclusive, evidence that your best friend, Dr Birosniper, stole the pens.

What should you believe on the basis of the committee's testimony? If you are disposed towards partiality bias, then the idea is that your doxastic attitude about whether Dr Birosniper stole the pens will differ from that of a neutral party, e.g. one of your colleagues who is not friends with Dr Birosniper, and in particular (assuming being a pen thief is a bad thing) your credence that Dr Birosniper stole the pens will be lower than the credence of a neutral party. In short, if you are disposed towards partiality bias, you will not believe the committee's accusation, in a situation where a neutral party will believe the committee's accusation.

Why think that some friendships require (a disposition towards) partiality bias?[2] Following Stroud (2006, pp. 501–2), the way to proceed here is to ask why we think that (dispositions towards) partiality in action and motivation are required for (some) friendships (§3.1.1). The answer is that we think that someone who did not exhibit partiality in action or partiality in motivation would not be a genuine, true, or real friend. The argument is based on our intuitions about cases. When it comes to partiality in motivation, Stocker and Williams evoke these intuitions by asking us to adopt the perspective of the other. If your "friend" came to see you in the hospital, but admitted that she did so out of duty, how would *you* feel? If your "friend" saved your life, but then admitted that she did so only after consulting the principles of impartial morality to see if it was permitted, how would *you* feel? In both cases the answer is obvious: we would feel that our "friend" was, at least in this respect, not a genuine friend.

The same argument can be mustered in defense of the requirement of partiality bias. Suppose *you* were accused of stealing the pens. After the faculty meeting, you ask your best friend and colleague whether she believes the accusation. If your friend were to admit that she believes the accusation, you would feel that she was not, in this respect, a genuine friend. Just as failures of partiality in action and motivation strike us, intuitively, as betrayals of friendship, so do failures of partiality in belief. We expect our friends to think well of us, we think that they ought to think well of us, and to the extent that they fail to do so, they strike us as less than genuine friends.

---

[2] Since we seek to proceed without empirical premises, we shall set aside empirical evidence for the ubiquity of partiality bias (e.g. Brown 1986, Murray and Holmes 1993, 1997; cf. McKay and Dennett 2009, p. 506).

There are three important qualifications to this argument that must be made. First, just as we admitted the possibility of an impartial friendship between moral saints (§3.1.1), we should admit the possibility of an unbiased friendship between "epistemic saints." We imagined that Gandhi and Singer's friendship is based on a shared commitment to impartial morality; imagine now a friendship based on a shared commitment to "epistemic" virtue, including a commitment to impartiality in belief, freedom from bias, and the like. Imagine, perhaps, the kind of friendship that Aristotle praises in Book X of the *Ethics*, based on a shared love of wisdom, inquiry, and contemplation. It's not plausible that a friendship of that kind requires (a disposition towards) partiality bias. As Simon Keller (2004) argues, "some of the best and strongest friendships are grounded in the friends' regarding each other with an uncompromising lack of prejudice" (p. 334).[3] But many friendships are not like that. So we can imagine that your friendship with Dr Birosniper is not like that.

Second, recall the assumption that being a pen thief is a bad thing. You might object that friendship is compatible with believing your friend is a pen thief. As Judith Baker (1987) points out, "[t]here may be friends one does not trust in certain areas" (p. 3), but they are no less friends for that. But what this point reveals is not that partiality bias isn't required by some friendships, but that we'll not be able to specify universal content for the beliefs involved in partiality bias. Different friends, and different friendships, will require partiality bias in different situations, and involve beliefs about different things. Consider a friendship between two career criminals, based on mutual respect and admiration for the other's skills as a thief. If you and Dr Birosniper have a friendship like that, then we would expect you to be *more* willing to believe the accusation, compared to a neutral party. Partiality bias is manifested when we think well of our friends, and think better of them than would an impartial stranger. But what "thinking well" of someone amounts to cannot be specified in absolute terms. Within the context of specific people and relationships, however, it will be obvious what it amounts to. In any event, we can imagine that your friendship with Dr Birosniper is not based on a shared love of criminality. Indeed, we can strengthen the argument by imagining that your friendship is based on a shared moral sensibility and an aversion to dishonesty.

Third, recall the distinction between illusion and delusion (§2.5.2). Just as we understood self-enhancement bias as manifested in illusions about oneself, as opposed to delusions, we should understand partiality bias as manifested in illusions about one's friends, as opposed to delusions. Thus I have claimed that your friendship may require you to refuse to believe that Dr Birosniper stole the pens, on the basis of testimony to the effect that there is strong but inconclusive evidence that she stole the pens. I do not claim that friendship would ever require you to refuse to believe that Dr Birosniper stole the pens, having seen Dr Birosniper stealing the pens, or having heard

---

[3] Cf. his distinction between the virtues of a "philosophical colleague" as opposed to those of a "coach" (pp. 338–40).

Dr Birosniper confess to the theft. Partiality bias, we can assume, manifests itself only when you have inconclusive evidence, never when you have conclusive evidence.

There's an important objection to all this. You might object that all that is required, in these cases, is not partiality bias, but mere partiality in action: you ought to speak up on Dr Birosniper's behalf at the faculty meeting, but you ought not doubt the accusation. Thus friendship need not require any false beliefs.

But friendship, on this proposal, seems to require an unappealing kind of insincerity. As Keller (2004) argues, "this kind of pretend approval is [not] what we really want in a good friend" (p. 335), and as Stroud (2006) argues, "[a] good friend does not defend her friend outwardly…while inwardly believing the worst" (p. 505).[4] Compare the Austenian contrast between "agreeableness" and "amiability," where the latter requires "a certain real affection for people as such," while the former is "only the simulacrum of a genuine virtue" (MacIntyre 2007, p. 183). If we reject the idea that friendship ever requires this kind of insincerity, then we should conclude that (some) friendships really do require (a disposition towards) partiality bias.

We should examine the kind of insincerity that might be involved here. You might think that you ought to *deny* the accusation against Dr Birosniper—"I know her; she didn't steal those pens." If you believe that Dr Birosniper stole the pens and say that she didn't steal the pens, then you are being insincere in the most straightforward way: you are asserting that p whilst not believing that p. When it comes to assertion, we cannot separate the practical from the doxastic, on pain of insincerity. Might we say that, although you ought not *deny* the accusation against Dr Birosniper, you ought to speak up on her behalf in some other way? For example, perhaps you ought merely to point out that the evidence against her is inconclusive. It seems to me that some friendships will not tolerate this degree of impartiality. What you ought to say, on the present proposal, is something like: "I agree that Dr Birosniper stole the pens. But I must point out that the evidence is inconclusive." It indeed seems required, at least in some friendships, to point out that the evidence is inconclusive, in cases in which a neutral party might be inclined not to do so. However, in some friendships, your friend can expect you to go further: she can expect you to deny the accusation as well.

We can offer some explanations of *why* partiality bias is required for friendship. Adam Morton (1988, p. 176) and Stroud (2006, pp. 511–12) argue that friendship involves a commitment to a person, which in turn involves a desire to "think well of" him, to find him to have a decent character, to have "esteem for his merits." Baker (1987) argues that friendship involves intimacy, which in turn requires trust:

[T]o think of someone as a friend is to expect her to have one's interests at heart, to act on one's behalf, to take one's part, and to take one at one's word. […] If one thinks that one cannot…form such expectations…it is hard to believe that the intimacy of friendship could be preserved. (p. 10)

---

[4] Contrast this point with cases of unproblematic insincerity described by H.H. Price (1954, p. 12).

And Keller (2004) argues that friendship involves "two people's...opening themselves up to each other's influence" (p. 340), which leads to shared interests, projects, and values, and this in turn will lead you to see things in the way that your friend sees things (p. 344). The value of friendship is on display here; and as Keller argues, the value of partiality bias itself can be appreciated: "even if you know that your friends' beliefs on the relevant matter are affected by bias...there's something nice about having friends who won't believe" the worst of you (p. 340). (In this respect, our desire for partiality bias in our friends is distinct from our desire to think well of ourselves.)

Partial love seems to require various kinds of **differential treatment**. This is how partial love is distinguished from impartial love: friends get different treatment than strangers. Given this, we should not be surprised if we find that friends get different doxastic treatment. This is just a specific instance of a more general phenomenon. And this suggests a stronger line of reasoning: partial love requires partiality in action and in motivation; but there is no principled way to concede that while denying that partial love requires partiality in belief. For what makes the domain of belief special, that would insulate it from the kinds of partiality that seem required in the domains of action and motivation? Why would we expect it to be special, in this way? There is no reason to expect that. So partial love requires partiality in belief.

If Williams and Stocker are right, there is a deep divide between partial and impartial perspectives. Partial love for a person is in tension with cleaving to impartial principles in your dealings with that person. However, "epistemic" principles are impartial principles (§9.3). Such principles forbid self-deception and wishful thinking. The doxastic practices involved in partiality bias, selective attention to evidence, differential interpretive charity towards friends, and the like, violate these impartial rules. As Morton suggests (1988, p. 176), the basic principle operative in partiality bias is wishful thinking: I want my friend to be worthy of my esteem, and this leads me to think of her as worthy of my esteem. This is a basic violation of impartial "epistemic" principles. So if Williams and Stocker are right that partiality conflicts with impartiality, then we should expect partiality to conflict with the "epistemic" as well, since "epistemic" principles are impartial principles.

3.1.3 Mechanisms of partiality bias

The underlying phenomenon behind partiality bias, I propose, is wishful thinking: we desire that our friends have positive characteristics, and such desire surreptitiously influences our beliefs. Desire can influence belief in several ways. First, it can lead to selective attention to evidence (cf. §2.3.2), as when I attend to evidence that supports positive views about my friend, and give said evidence greater weight than I give to less favorable evidence. This is how H.H. Price (1954) imagines that "Victorian ladies" might shore up their faith in the virtue of their husbands and fiancés:

"Being loyal to him in one's innermost thoughts" consisted, I suggest, in a habit of directing one's attention appropriately, by attending carefully and repeatedly to all the evidence which is creditable to X, and averting one's attention from all the evidence which is discreditable to him. (p. 18; see also Mele 2001, pp. 25–49)

This is what we might expect you to do when the evidence against Dr Birosniper is revealed: to dwell on the evidence that she is a good person and not a thief, that she would not do a thing like that, and to avert one's attention from the evidence that she stole the pens. Here is Stroud's (2006) description of a similar case:

> Suppose...that a third party reports that your friend Sam recently slept with someone and then cruelly never returned any of that person's calls, knowingly breaking that person's heart. Importantly...this story is not something you know to be false. [A]s a good friend, you ought to react differently to this information than you otherwise would, or than a detached observer would. [W]e tend to devote more energy to defeating or minimizing the impact of unfavorable data than we otherwise would. To start with, we are more liable to scrutinize and to question the evidence being presented than we otherwise would be. (pp. 504–5)

Second, wishful thinking about our friends can lead us to engage in biased interpretation of the evidence (cf. §2.3.2). Morton (1988) writes:

> There are reliable reports that your loved one voted Tory, or stole from a famine collection box. The reports are reliable enough that were you uncommitted you would be justified simply in believing that he or she is a rotten person. But given your commitment you will not be pushed so quickly to that conclusion. Your commitment commits you to resist it. There may be alternative explanations of the action consistent with the loved one's being the kind of person you wanted them to be. Perhaps it was tactical voting, designed to elect someone so terrible he would utterly discredit the party. Perhaps the collection box was fraudulently labeled, and after the theft the money was donated to famine relief. Another strategy would be to accept the facts at face value and to revise your conception of the kind of virtue the loved one possesses. Perhaps the loved one is politically naïve because all their good sense goes into work and into care for friends. Perhaps the loved one's devotion to friends is so touchingly, if foolishly, great that they will steal from the starving—no doubt intending to repay it—in order to buy a present. (p. 177)

And Stroud (2006) argues that

> [W]e will go to greater lengths in the case of a friend to construct and to entertain alternative and less damning interpretations of the reported conduct than we would for a nonfriend. [W]e draw different conclusions and make different inferences than we otherwise would (or than a detached observer would). [A]t the end of the day we are simply less likely to conclude that our friend acted disreputably, or that he is a bad person, than we would be in the case of a nonfriend. (pp. 504–6)

And Keller (2004) argues that, even though Eric "has no familiarity with her work...[a]s Rebecca's friend, he should listen to her poetry in a way that makes him more likely to emerge with the belief that her poetry is of high quality"; he will "actively seek out its strengths, and play down its weaknesses; he'll be disposed to interpret it in ways that make it look like a stronger piece of work" (pp. 332–3).

Biased interpretation of evidence that speaks against a friend will involve, in some respects, believing what a neutral party would. Above we imagined that you would reject the accusation against your friend. In the case of Dr Birosniper, we imagined that you would refuse to believe that Dr Birosniper stole the pens, on the grounds that she wouldn't do such a thing. Here we are imagining that you accept the accusation, but only up to a point. Perhaps, as in Morton's case, you accept that she stole the pens, but refuse to believe that she sold them for profit, on the grounds that she must have had a good reason to steal the pens. This is just as much an example of partiality bias, so long as there is a difference between your conclusions and those of a neutral party. But that is precisely what Stroud and Morton and Keller describe: the idea that your friend stole from the collection box for the sake of famine relief, or to buy a present with the intention of repaying, or that Sam is not a bad person, or that your friend's poetry is of high quality, are not conclusions that a neutral party could sensibly draw.

This connects up with the idea that partiality bias manifests itself in illusions rather than delusions (§3.1.2). As Stroud (2006) argues, partiality bias need not involve "deny-ing…base-level facts and events," but will involve "interpreting the reported actions and placing them in perspective" (p. 507). Partiality "need not be a matter of flatly denying the obvious"; it is a matter of your beliefs about your friends being "slanted in their favor in various respects" (p. 507). Similarly, as Keller (2004) notes, the require-ment of partiality bias need not be understood to imply "that good friends provide each other with slavish, unconditional affirmation" (p. 334).

3.1.4 The objection from insider evidence

I have argued that (a disposition towards) partiality bias is partially constitutive of some friendships. The most important objection to this conclusion is that the doxastic practices required for such friendships are not unreliable, and therefore do not con-stitute a bias, properly so called. Friendship requires that my doxastic treatment of my friends will differ from that of a neutral party, you might concede, while maintaining that there is nothing unreliable about this doxastic practice, since it's merely a proper response to the different *evidence* I have about my friends, as opposed to strangers (cf. Baker 1987, p. 4). Call this the **objection from insider evidence**.

Consider Morton's case of the accusation of voting Tory. Imagine that I refuse to believe that my friend Lilian voted Tory, on the grounds that *I know she's not a Tory*. The accuser says he looked over her shoulder at the polls. Well, maybe he misread her ballot. Maybe he mistook someone else for her. Maybe he's slandering her intention-ally. Any of these seems more likely than that Lilian voted Tory. This isn't bias at work, but good, old-fashioned, unbiased inference to the best explanation, based on a body of evidence larger than that available to the accuser. I know Lilian well, I know her politics, she loathes the Tories, and so on. My access to this additional information doesn't make me biased; on the contrary, it puts me in an evidential position superior to that of the accuser.

We could take a closer look at the motivations involved in partiality bias (cf. Stroud 2006, pp. 513–18, Baker 1987, p. 5). The "epistemically" virtuous person is moved to believe that p by the preponderance of evidence that p; the "epistemically" vicious person is moved to believe that p by other factors, such as her friendship with someone upon whom the fact that p would reflect well, along with whatever evidence she possesses. We said above that someone might refuse to believe an accusation about her friend. The difference between an "epistemically" virtuous and an "epistemically" vicious refusal to believe is one of motivation. Price (1954) writes:

When a man says "I cannot believe p," "nothing would induce me to believe it," what prevents him from believing it, very often, is not that he has strong evidence against the proposition…but just some emotion or desire which he has. He cannot believe the proposition because he so much *wants* it to be false, or because the situation would be so upsetting or shocking or terrifying if the proposition were true. (p. 6)

The difference between a reasonable refusal to believe and an unreasonable refusal to believe, Price maintains, is the motivation behind the refusal. But even if we were to argue, along the lines of Williams and Stocker, that partiality bias, of the sort partially constitutive of partial love, requires a partial motivation (e.g. love for one's friend), and *not* an "epistemically" virtuous motivation (e.g. support by evidence), this might not guarantee that partiality bias is unreliable, which is what we set out to show. Reliability, we may suppose, is a necessary condition on a doxastic practice being "epistemically" virtuous. But we should not assume that "epistemically" vicious practices are always unreliable.

What we need to consider are cases in which you and the neutral party have the same, or equally good, evidence, relevant to the proposition in question. If some friendships require differential doxastic treatment even in cases like that, then we can reject the objection from insider evidence.

Consider your disagreement with the committee over Dr Birosniper's alleged conduct. Is this down to a difference in evidence, or in quality of evidence, between you and the committee? Suppose that the strong but inconclusive evidence is revealed: footage of Dr Birosniper's car entering the parking lot behind Staples late at night, when the black-market pen sales take place. Now you and the committee both have the same incriminating evidence. We imagined that your friendship with Dr Birosniper was based on a shared moral sensibility and an aversion to dishonesty. Is that sufficient evidence to warrant disagreeing with the committee? Suppose you share this evidence with the committee—you tell them all you know about Dr Birosniper. Would we expect the committee to change its mind? It seems that we can expect the disagreement to remain, even after all the relevant evidence has been shared.[5] Think of

---

[5] Might there be insider evidence that can't be shared, akin to the "private insights" discussed in the epistemological literature on disagreement (cf. Feldman 2006, pp. 222–4, Bergmann, 2009 pp. 238–40)? Perhaps, but the existence of "private insights" into our friend's moral virtue strikes me as evidence that we are biased in favor of our friends

how things might go at Dr Birosniper's criminal trial, where all the relevant evidence is revealed and recorded. The prosecution reveals to everyone the evidence that Dr Birosniper stole the pens (e.g. the footage of her car); the defense reveals to everyone the evidence that Dr Birosniper didn't steal the pens (e.g. your testimony as a character witness). Even after this, we would still expect your doxastic attitude to differ from that of a neutral party.

Friendship seems to require differential doxastic treatment even when there is no difference in evidence, or in quality of evidence. Consider Keller's (2004) case of the poetry reading, in which Eric has no prior familiarity with Rebecca's work (p. 332), and his point that "[f]riendships need not be predicated upon anything that makes the friends especially likely to be talented poets, and we did not need to stipulate that Eric's friendship with Rebecca *does* have such a basis in order to have the example make sense" (pp. 336–7). Friendship may give one insider evidence about one's friends' voting habits, but partiality bias seems required even in cases where no insider evidence is available.

So: there are cases in which you and a neutral party have the same evidence, or the same quality of evidence, but in which your friendship requires a difference in doxastic attitude. I propose concluding, from this, that friendship requires (being disposed towards) an unreliable doxastic practice, namely, what I have called "partiality bias." One possibility remains: that in such cases it is not you whose practice is unreliable, but the neutral party. Rather than saying that people are biased in favor of a positive conception of their friends, perhaps we should say that people are biased in favor of a negative conception of strangers. Which of these options we should choose seems to depend, among other things, on the question of whether negative accusations tend, in general, to be true, or whether they tend, in general, to be false. The former strikes me as more plausible, but I will defer discussion of this question, to which we'll return below (§3.2.3).

3.2 Charitable bias

I have argued (§3.1) that we owe it to our friends to think well of them. In this section I'll argue that we owe everyone a degree of charity in our thinking about them. We'll begin with a description of "charitable bias" (§3.2.1), and I'll then argue that charitable bias is a moral virtue (§3.2.2) and an unreliable doxastic practice (§3.2.3).

3.2.1 Everyday charity

We described partiality bias (§3.1.2) as bias in favor of a positive conception of one's friends. **Charitable bias** is bias in favor of a positive conception of people in general. It is manifested by seeing people in general—strangers—in a more positive light than the evidence warrants (cf. §3.2.3). Julia Driver (1989, 2001) calls this the virtue "blind charity," which is "charity in thought rather than charity in deed" (1989, p. 381, 2001, p. 28). Just as the "principle of charity" enjoins us to interpret other people's utterances or beliefs in a positive way, "blind charity" requires interpreting other people, in general, in a positive way (1989, p. 381, 2001, p. 28).[6] And Valerie Tiberius (2008) defends the virtue of "realistic optimism," which is characterized as "being disposed to look for…evidence [of] the goodness of human nature…and to make generalizations about human potential that are positive" (p. 151). Finally, Michael Pace (2011) writes that:

> [T]hinking charitably of others…may in fact be a *prima facie* moral obligation…regarding all people. The disposition to think charitably of others is often considered a moral and intellectual virtue. Doing so arguably involves requiring less evidence to think well of them and requiring more evidence before one thinks ill of them. (p. 258)

This description shows the sense in which charitable bias is a doxastic practice: someone disposed toward charitable bias will end up with different beliefs (or credences) than someone not so disposed. Someone who has higher evidential standards for propositions that reflect negatively on people, and lower evidential standards for propositions that reflect well on people, will end up with different beliefs than someone with equal standards for both types of proposition.

What will charitable bias look like in practice? David Foster Wallace (2009) provides a nice description; he begins with a sketch of an "average day":

> [Y]ou get up in the morning, go to your challenging job, and you work hard for nine or ten hours, and at the end of the day you're tired, and you're stressed out…But then you remember there's no food at home…and so now, after work, you have to get in your car and drive to the supermarket. It's the end of the workday, and the traffic's very bad, so getting to the store takes way longer than it should, and when you finally get there the supermarket is very crowded…and the store's hideously, fluorescently lit, and infused with soul-killing Muzak or corporate pop, and it's pretty much the last place you want to be…[Y]ou have to manoeuvre your junky cart through all these other tired, hurried people with carts, and of course there are also the glacially slow old people and the spacey people and the kids who all block the aisle and you have to grit your teeth and try to be polite as you ask them to let you by, and eventually, finally, you get all your supper supplies, except now it turns out there aren't enough checkout lanes open even though it's the end-of-the-day rush, so the checkout line is incredibly long, which is stupid and infuriating, but you can't take your fury out on the frantic lady working the register. (pp. 67–71)

Our ordinary lives are filled with this "petty, frustrating crap" (p. 76), and a lot of the frustration comes from interactions with other people, people who are strangers to us: the other drivers stuck in traffic, the other people in the supermarket, the clerk working the register, and so on. Indeed, ordinary life can be so petty and frustrating that you can find yourself *hating* everyone else:

> [It can] seem, for all the world, like everybody else is just in my way, and who are all these people in my way? And look at how repulsive most of them are and how stupid and cow-like

---

[6] Driver's other "virtues of ignorance" (1989, 2001, Chapter 2) don't involve false belief, in my view. Modesty is manifested in a lack of belief (or suspension of judgment) about one's own worth, not (as Driver maintains) in underestimation of one's own worth. See her 1989, p. 377, 2001, p. 20.

and dead-eyed and nonhuman they seem here in the checkout line, or at how annoying and rude it is that people are talking loudly on cell phones in the middle of the line [...] Or...I can spend time in the end-of-the-day traffic jam being angry and disgusted at all the huge, stupid, lane-blocking SUVs and Hummers and V12 pickup trucks burning their wasteful, selfish, 40-gallon tanks of gas, and I can dwell on the fact that the patriotic or religious bumper stickers always seem to be on the biggest, most disgustingly selfish vehicles driven by the ugliest, most inconsiderate and aggressive drivers, who are usually talking on cell phones as they cut people off in order to get just twenty stupid feet ahead in a traffic jam[.] (pp. 77–9)

However:

[I]t's not impossible that some of these people in SUVs have been in horrible car accidents in the past and now find driving so traumatic that their therapist has all but ordered them to get a huge, heavy SUV so they can feel safe enough to drive; or that the Hummer that just cut me off is maybe being driven by a father whose little child is hurt or sick in the seat next to him, and he's trying to rush to the hospital, and he's in a much bigger, more legitimate hurry than I am— it is actually I who am in his way [...] [Y]ou can choose to look differently at this fat, dead-eyed, over-made lady who just screamed at her little child in the checkout line—maybe she's not usually like this; maybe she's been up three straight nights holding the hand of her husband who's dying of bone cancer, or maybe this very lady is the low-wage clerk at the Motor Vehicles Dept. who just yesterday helped your spouse through some small act of kindness. (pp. 85–9)

This is charitable bias at work.

Just as partiality bias was understood as manifested in illusions about one's friends, rather than delusions about one's friends (§3.1.2), charitable bias should be understood as manifested in illusions about other people in general, rather than delusions about other people in general. Suppose someone cuts you off on the freeway: it's charitable to think that she may have good reason for her reckless driving; it's delusional to think that the other driver was a figment of your imagination. Suppose you hear a news report that 70% of parents do not read to their children: it's charitable to think that some of these parents are probably overwhelmed by their jobs; it's delusional to think that the report was a fabrication.

You might think that what Wallace describes isn't a doxastic practice, since what he describes is just a different way of *imagining* people, not a different way of forming beliefs about them. After all, he merely says that his charitable interpretations are "not impossible." Three reasons to think that what Wallace describes is, in fact, a doxastic practice.

First, to say that it's possible that (for example) the other driver has good cause for her recklessness is ambiguous: it could mean that it is logically or metaphysically possible that the other driver has good cause for her recklessness, but it could also mean that it is epistemically possible that the other driver has good cause for her recklessness. The practice of conceding the logical or metaphysical possibility of charitable interpretations may not be a doxastic practice, but the practice of conceding the epistemic possibility of charitable interpretations is. And it seems to me that an epistemic reading of "possible," when it comes to Wallace's claim, is the more natural reading. What we are doing, if and when we engage in the kind of charity that Wallace describes, is lowering our credences in propositions the truth of which reflects negatively on the people involved. I'm fairly certain that the guy who just cut me off is *not* rushing to the hospital. What Wallace is proposing, in asking me to imagine that he is rushing to the hospital, is that I raise my credence in that possibility, if only slightly, and lower my credence in the proposition that the other driver is an irredeemable asshole.

Second, what we imagine can effect what we believe (cf. Walton 1994). The habit of imagining that other drivers have good cause for their recklessness will tend to raise my credence in the proposition that other drivers have good cause for their recklessness. So the practice of imagining the truth of charitable interpretations is a doxastic practice, in as much as this practice will tend to have an effect on one's beliefs.

Third, we should bear in mind the characteristic functional profile of belief (§1.6.2). What we imagine, when we compare someone who is charitable in her thinking about other people with someone who is not charitable in her thinking about other people, is a difference not only in thought, but in practice and in affect as well. The actions and emotions of someone who is charitable in her thinking about other people will be different from the actions and emotions of someone who is not charitable in her thinking about other people. Think of the situation Wallace describes in the check out line. The uncharitable person feels awful, despises the other people in the line, frowns at them, and hands her money over mechanically to the clerk. The charitable person feels a bit better, feels no animus towards the other shoppers, smiles at them, and says "hello" to the clerk.

3.2.2 Charitable bias is a moral virtue

Wallace (2009) doesn't propose charity as a way of getting at the truth about other people. "Of course," he says, "none of this is likely, but it's also not impossible—it just depends on what you want to consider" (p. 90). Rather, he proposes charitable bias as a way of dealing with the petty frustrations of ordinary life, as a way "to stay conscious and alive," which "is unimaginably hard to do" (p. 135). In a similar spirit, Tiberius (2008) argues that "if you choose the optimistic strategy, you will be more likely to be satisfied with your life upon reflection" (p. 153). So both defend the eudaimonic value of charitable bias (although Tiberius, at least, would not classify the relevant doxastic practice as a bias, see §3.2.3). Without challenging these accounts, I'll argue that (being disposed towards) charitable bias is a moral virtue. We ought to try to think well of people, not just for our own sake, but because thinking well of them is what they deserve.

Why think that (being disposed towards) charitable bias is a moral virtue? For Driver (2001), "moral virtue contributes to the flourishing of others" (p. 38), and the question of whether a particular disposition is or is not a virtue is determined by its consequences vis-à-vis other people's flourishing. For her, "[l]ike deception itself, self-deception may be considered good and valued, depending upon the ends" (1999, p. 830). But the appeal of charitable bias need not be wedded to her consequentialist account.

We might appeal to the idea we owe a similar kind of charity to our friends and family (Feldman 1988a, p. 236, Pace 2011, p. 258), and argue by structural analogy with other obligations: what I owe to everyone is often less of the same of what I owe to my friends and family. I ought to give a friend $5 if she wants to buy a piece of chocolate cake; I ought to give a stranger $5 if she needs to buy a sandwich to survive. This kind of reasoning seems cogent when it comes to the domain of action, so we might extend it to the domain of belief. I ought to be biased in favor of my friends to such-and-such a degree; thus, I ought to be biased in favor of strangers to a lesser degree.

We can also advance a version of the argument from sincerity (§3.1.2) here. For virtue seems to require charitable treatment of other people. Picture yourself in one of Wallace's everyday situations, and ask yourself how the virtuous person would act in such a case. The virtuous person is polite and civil towards the frustratingly inept grocery clerk; but to be polite and civil towards someone while inwardly despising her requires an unappealing insincerity. To be sure, interior hostility combined with outward civility is to be preferred to interior hostility that is manifested in outward hostility. The clerk ought not to be strangled for the sake of authenticity. But all these possibilities are inferior to treating the clerk well *both* in action *and* in thought.

The method presupposed here, for determining whether a disposition is or is not a moral virtue, is one that relies principally on intuitions about particular cases. The idea that it's morally virtuous to be biased in your thinking about other people may seem counterintuitive to many. But we should consider particular cases here. When we do, what we discover is that our intuitive conception of virtue involves thinking well of others. This is effectively Wallace's point: it's obvious what it would be best to do, when faced with everyday petty frustration: it would be best to try to see things in a more charitable way. But this is just to say that what would be best, in such situations, is to manifest charitable bias in your thinking about other people.

Although we need not think of the morality of charitable bias in terms of moral obligation, I find it plausible that the reason a morally virtuous person manifests charitable bias in her thinking about other people is that this is what she *owes them*, in the sense that this is *what they deserve*. We should not construe morality narrowly so that it pertains only to our actions. There are myriad situations in which people deserve sympathy, others in which they deserve disapprobation; there are people who deserve our admiration, and others who deserve our condemnation. If this is right, people can deserve certain emotional responses, i.e. we can owe it to them to feel about them in certain ways. If so, there's no reason we shouldn't think that people can deserve certain doxastic responses, i.e. that we can owe it to them to think about them in certain ways.

3.2.3 The objection from optimism

However, you might object that what we have called charitable "bias" is no bias at all. Wallace says that none of the things that he asks us to imagine are "likely," but does insist that they are "not impossible." Might the practice of thinking well of people, of interpreting their behavior charitably, of being more willing to believe positive things about them, as opposed to negative things, be what people deserve simply because it yields mostly true beliefs about them?

When it comes to some of the doxastic practices described above, the answer is clearly "No." At least *some* of the drivers who cut me off *are* irredeemable assholes. In fact, aren't most of them? When I lower my credence in that negative belief, and raise my credence in some alternative explanation of their offensive behavior, I'm going to end up getting things wrong more often than I otherwise would. It's true that some people scream at their kids just because of the stress of an uncommonly horrible situation. But most people scream at their kids without any good excuse. To think otherwise is compassionate and appealing, but not a reliable way to form one's beliefs about other people.

When it comes to other charitable doxastic practices, the question of reliability is less easy to answer. Suppose I have higher evidential standards for negative beliefs about people than I do for positive beliefs about people. Is this practice unreliable? This seems to depend on whether some platitudinous generality like "people are good" is true. How can we evaluate such a claim?

As Stroud (2006) points out, "most people act very badly from time to time, and have some more or less serious character flaws" (p. 513). If so, then charitable bias is going to lead us seriously astray at least some of the time. Charitable bias is therefore an *unsafe* doxastic practice, in the sense that it could easily yield false beliefs. In this sense, at least, charitable bias is unreliable.

In defense of "realistic optimism," Tiberius (2008) criticizes "cynicism," which is "the disposition to judge that human beings are bad and therefore worthy of scorn or disdain" (p. 140). The cynic, on Tiberius' view, is "epistemically" vicious: "she tends to ignore evidence of goodness in others, to look for the bad and dwell on it, and to interpret evidence so that it supports her negative conclusions" (p. 141). Cynics are pessimists, and "[p]essimists have no positive illusions—in fact, they have negative illusions" (p. 144). The reason for thinking this, however, is just that "the pessimist judges things to be worse than the facts warrant" (p. 151), and so "cynicism is an attitude that is sustained by disputable beliefs (beliefs that are not warranted by the facts)" (p. 154). However, Tiberius' critique is *not* that cynicism is a vice because it involves unreliable belief-formation; "positive illusions" are virtuous, on her view (p. 144). Cynicism is a vice, on her view, because it is "morally bad" (p. 142), tends to erode one's motivation and commitments (pp. 142–3), precludes genuine friendship (pp. 145–6), and ultimately makes one unable to reflectively endorse one's life (p. 153).

What of my claim that charitable bias is unreliable? This was based, it seems fair to concede, on the premise that "human beings are bad"—thus the unreliability of a disposition in favor of thinking well of them—which is what Tiberius calls "pessimism." I see no easy way to argue for or against this claim, but two comments should make pessimism more plausible. First, pessimism does not entail that human beings are worthy of scorn or disdain. Tiberius argues that "it is reasonable to anticipate that pessimism will devolve into cynicism," since "it will seem to [the pessimist] that she has grounds for condemning human beings" (p. 149). Now, on the one hand, it does not speak against the truth of pessimism that it threatens to lead to cynicism. And, on the other, we should resist the idea that the badness of human beings is prima facie ground for scorn and disdain. Second, pessimism does not contradict "hope," which "is not a belief" but "is a positive attitude that includes an element of judgment—a positive appraisal of human nature" (p. 150). Because hope is not a belief, it need not conflict with a negative doxastic appraisal of human beings. So we can agree with Tiberius about the eudaimonic value of hope, and about the viciousness of scorn and disdain for other human beings, without conceding that pessimism is false.

You might object that interpreting people charitably is what they *deserve*. But this is in fact the very point I am urging: they deserve to be interpreted charitably, but not because charitable thinking is likely to yield correct interpretations of their behavior. In fact, I want to suggest, charitable thinking is likely to yield incorrect interpretations of people's behavior much of the time. But it's morally virtuous to interpret people charitably, in spite of this.

3.3 Against the eudaimonic ideal of true belief

In this section I'll argue against the eudaimonic ideal of true belief (§1.4), by appeal to the eudaimonic value of (being disposed towards) partiality bias (§3.3.1) and the eudaimonic value of (being disposed towards) charitable bias (§3.3.2).

3.3.1 The eudaimonic value of partiality bias

There's a rich tradition defending the eudaimonic value of friendship, beginning with Aristotle's account of friendship in Books XIII and IX of the *Nicomachean Ethics*, where he maintains that "[w]ithout friends no one would choose to live, though he had all other goods" (1155a5). This conception of the value of friendship is rooted in the conviction that human beings are essentially social animals, which finds alternative expression in the Early Modern sentimentalist conviction that human nature is essentially sympathetic (articulated by Hume in his *Treatise* and the *Enquiry concerning the Principles of Morals*, and by Adam Smith in his *Theory of Moral Sentiments*), as well as in the 20th-century conception of the self as socially constructed or socially embedded (articulated by Herbert Mead, Jean-Paul Sartre, and others). In contemporary philosophy, friendship appears on many lists of human goods (§1.1.6). John Finnis

(1980), for example, argues that "[t]o be in a relationship of friendship with at least one other person is a fundamental form of good" (p. 88), and Philippa Foot (2001) writes that "friendship [is] basic in human life" and therefore among "possible objects of deep happiness" (p. 88). Martha Nussbaum (2000) includes "affiliation" on her list of "central human functional capacities," arguing that a person's quality of life depends on her "[b]eing able to live with and towards others, to recognize and show concern for other human beings, to engage in various forms of social interaction," and in general "to have the capacity for both justice and friendship" (p. 79). That friendship is a human good is evinced by our horror at the hermetic Cyclops (Nussbaum 1995, p. 97), who we immediately recognize as monstrous and decidedly not human.

The eudaimonic value of friendship could be, and to a limited extent has been, challenged. Consider champions of autonomy, solitude, and isolation, such as Ralph Waldo Emerson in "Self-Reliance," or Henry David Thoreau in *Walden*, who extol the virtues of self-sufficiency and independence from other people. But even these thinkers would not have rejected Aristotle's idea. (We should remember that Thoreau's "life in the woods" involved weekends at his parents' house.)

In any event, my argument for the **eudaimonic value of partiality bias** goes like this: (being disposed towards) partiality bias is partially constitutive of (at least some) friendships; friendship is partially constitutive of wellbeing; therefore, (being disposed towards) partiality bias is partially constitutive of (some people's) wellbeing.[7] It's beyond the scope of this inquiry to give a substantial defense of the second premise, beyond appealing to the intuition that friendship seems like a valuable part of the best human lives. But this is an assumption that defenders of desire-independent theories of wellbeing will grant. I conclude, given this assumption, that (being disposed towards) partiality bias is partially constitutive of (some people's) wellbeing. (Being disposed towards) partiality bias (at least sometimes) has constitutive value (§1.1.5). And I will assume, on this basis, that (at least some) biased false beliefs about our friends, beliefs that manifest partiality bias, have constitutive value.

How does this threaten the eudaimonic ideal of true belief (§1.4)? It does not entail that the eudaimonic ideal of true belief is false, for it might be the case that the eudaimonic value of friendship is always, save in abnormal cases, trumped by the eudaimonic value of true belief, such that having a biased false belief about a friend is never better than having the corresponding true belief, save in abnormal cases. But given what we've said about partiality bias and friendship, this isn't plausible. There

---

[7] The argument assumes that constitution is transitive. You might think that constitution isn't transitive; cake is made of flour, flour is made of hydrogen, but it sounds strange to say that cake is made of hydrogen. However, the ancestral of constitution, constitution★, is transitive, and the modified conclusion of the argument—that (being disposed towards) partiality bias is partially constitutive★ of (some people's) wellbeing—poses the same problem for the eudaimonic ideal of true belief as does our original conclusion, because it is equally suggestive of the eudaimonic value of (being disposed towards) partiality bias. What threatens the eudaimonic ideal of true belief is the idea of a necessary connection between bias and wellbeing. The same, mutatis mutandis, when it comes to charitable bias.

are cases in which a biased false belief about a friend is better than the corresponding true belief, and moreover these cases instantiate a clearly identifiable pattern of cases in which biased false belief about a friend is better than the corresponding true belief, as in the cases described above (§3.1.2). That pattern is explained by the constitutive value of friendship, along with the fact that (being disposed towards) partiality bias is partially constitutive of (at least some) friendships. Such cases are not abnormal, but are a pervasive aspect of ordinary friendship.[8]

There are, however, some ways of thinking about friendship in which friendship does not require (being disposed towards) partiality bias. We should consider them briefly, with the aim of getting an idea of what sorts of assumption I've made here about friendship. First, consider Aristotle's conception of friendship. Aristotle maintains that the truest and most genuine friendships are friendships between men with the highest levels of virtue and excellence. Nothing I've said here implies that partiality bias would be involved in *this* kind of friendship. My argument for the idea that partiality bias is required for friendship essentially relied on our imagining ordinary friendships, between ordinary people: flawed and significantly vicious, middle-of-the-road and falling short of excellence. Second, consider a certain kind of Stoic conception of friendship, not requiring partiality in thought. The Stoic might resolve to give her friends their due in her actions, but vow not to get emotionally attached.

3.3.2 The eudaimonic value of charitable bias

The eudaimonic value of moral virtue is more controversial in the history of ideas than is the eudaimonic value of friendship: Plato's *Republic* opens with an uncourteous row over the benefits of virtue for the virtuous person. The Socratic position, that virtue benefits the virtuous person, finds its best expression in Aristotle's *Ethics* and in various inheritors of Aristotle's picture, and in the proverb "virtue is its own reward" (which may or may not be understood to mean that virtue is pleasant for the virtuous person). The Thrasymachian position, that virtue does not benefit the virtuous person, finds its best expression in the Christian conception of morality as self-sacrifice and service for others, as well as in the ideal of mortification. Morality, too, is part of contemporary conceptions of the human goods. In his description of "sociability," Finnis (1980) writes that sociability "in its weakest form is realized by a minimum of peace and harmony amongst men" (p. 88) and Nussbaum (2000) includes under the capacity for affiliation the ability "to imagine the situation of another and to have compassion for that situation" (p. 79) and, as mentioned, the capacity for affiliation includes the capacity for "justice."

---

[8] This doesn't mean that there aren't conflicting patterns when it comes to the eudaimonic value of unbiased evaluations of one's friends. An unbiased friend, for example, could benefit one by providing accurate information vis-à-vis self-improvement (cf. 2.9.3), and so a lack of partiality bias could have eudaimonic value. What I insist on is that such eudaimonic value is not such that *all* cases of eudaimonically superior partiality bias are abnormal.

My argument for the **eudaimonic value of charitable bias** mirrors my argument for the eudaimonic value of partiality bias: (being disposed towards) charitable bias is a moral virtue; being morally virtuous is partially constitutive of wellbeing; therefore, (being disposed towards) charitable bias is partially constitutive of wellbeing. As above, it's beyond the scope of this inquiry to give a substantial defense of the second premise. But this is an assumption that defenders of desire-independent theories of wellbeing will grant. Indeed, the main objection that is standardly leveled against desire-fulfillment theories of wellbeing (§1.1.6) is that they appear to entail that a deeply immoral person might live a good life: imagine someone who wants nothing more than to cause pain to other people, and who succeeds in doing so. Such a person surely doesn't live well, so the argument goes, so desire-fulfillment theories must be on the wrong track. Desire-independent theories of wellbeing are motivated by the thought that this consequence of desire-fulfillment theories is unacceptable. But if the defender of desire-independent theories motivates her view in this way, then she is committed to the eudaimonic value of moral virtue, and the most natural way to articulate such value will be to say that moral virtue is partially constitutive of wellbeing. In any event, I assume that moral virtue is partially constitutive of wellbeing, and conclude, given this assumption, that (being disposed towards) charitable bias is partially constitutive of wellbeing. Such a disposition, therefore, has final eudaimonic value. And I will assume, on this basis, that biased false beliefs about other people, beliefs that manifest charitable bias, have constitutive value.

This does not entail that the eudaimonic ideal of true belief is false, but given what we've said about charitable bias and moral virtue, the eudaimonic ideal of true belief is implausible. The moral requirement of charity is pervasive in everyday life (§3.2.1); and in such cases charitable bias will often yield false beliefs about other people. Such cases instantiate a clearly identifiable pattern of cases in which false belief is better than true belief. That pattern is explained by the eudaimonic value of moral virtue, along with the fact that (being disposed towards) charitable bias is a moral virtue; because of this, cases in which biased false belief is better than true belief are not abnormal.

3.3.3 Bias and wellbeing

These arguments are motivated by relatively simple ideas: that just as friendship demands partiality in action, it requires partiality in thought, and that just as morality demands charity in action, it requires charity in thought. These ideas, combined with the thought that partiality and charity in thought require bias, have led to the idea that (being disposed towards) partiality bias and (being disposed towards) charitable bias (sometimes) have constitutive value—a species of final, eudaimonic value. This, in turn, has led to the suggestion that biased false beliefs, which manifest partiality bias and charitable bias, themselves have constitutive value.

Do our two conclusions—that partiality bias (sometimes) has constitutive value and that charitable bias has constitutive value—conflict? Partiality bias requires that we give our friends differential doxastic treatment; charitable bias seems to require that we extend that treatment to everyone. Now, on the one hand, this is just the doxastic version of a familiar conflict between what I owe to my friends and what I owe to strangers. Shall I buy my friend an expensive birthday present or donate my money to Oxfam? We expect the good life to involve conflicts between partial and impartial concerns; given the conclusions of this chapter, we should expect those conflicts to exist at the level of cognition as well. To say that two goods, x and y, are both partially constitutive of wellbeing (i.e. that they both have constitutive value) need not be taken to mean that conflicts, between the pursuit of x and the pursuit of y, never arise, or that they never arise for the person who lives well. Such conflicts seem possible, indeed plausible, so long as we think of neither x nor y as eudaimonic ideals (§1.1.4).

As with the argument from self-enhancement bias (§2.8), my conclusion here is compatible with both the intrinsic value of knowledge and the intrinsic value of true belief (§1.5) as well as with the constitutive value of knowledge and true belief (§1.1.5). Again, we'll return to the pro tanto eudaimonic value of true belief (§1.1.4) below (Chapter 4).

The idea that false belief can have *final* eudaimonic value may strike you as counter-intuitive. In my view, this possibility is the result of the fact that "epistemic" and eudaimonic value can come into conflict: something "epistemically" bad, like biased belief, can be eudaimonically good, in virtue of its constitutive relationship with wellbeing. One reason that the idea that false belief can have final eudaimonic value is surprising is that we may have expected that these values would not come into conflict, or that they would come into conflict only in abnormal cases (as when a villain threatens some atrocity unless I believe against my evidence; cf. §1.1.3). This expectation is behind some people's confidence that false belief must, after all, in the end, lead to disappointment and disaster (again, save in abnormal cases). What I have been arguing here (and in Chapter 2) is that the conflict between "epistemic" and eudaimoninc value is a pervasive feature of ordinary human life, and that, both for empirical and philosophical reasons, false belief can easily *not* lead to disappointment and disaster. We should ask ourselves why we expected, in the first place, that "epistemic" and eudaimonic value would not come into conflict. Why would we have thought, or why are we tempted to think, that true belief and wellbeing must, at least normally, come together? We should be suspicious of uncritical acceptance of a certain picture of human happiness as contented integration, an ideal of authentic self-acceptance that we have inherited from sources as diverse as Ancient philosophy and 20th-century popular psychology. As Keller (2004) argues:

Thinking…about what motivates us to have friends—what we look for in a friendship, and why it's frightening to contemplate a life without it—well, the reinforcement of our epistemic integrity doesn't seem to have much to do with it. Why should there be any guarantee that a really good friend will never depart from epistemic norms? If epistemic norms always *were* consistent with the norms of friendship, wouldn't that be kind of surprising? (p. 343)

In general we should ask these questions about the possibility of conflict between "epistemic" value and other things that we care about. We should not allow ourselves to be misled by a conviction that "epistemic" value *must* be compatible with all else that we care about. The consistency of what we care about is something that we may legitimately *hope* to be so, but it's not something that we have any reason to *believe* to be so.

3.4 Conclusion

I've offered two arguments (§3.3), consistent with desire-independent theories of wellbeing, against the eudaimonic ideal of true belief. But this does not threaten the view that true belief is a non-ideal eudaimonic good—to which we turn in the next chapter.

4

True Belief as a Non-Ideal Good

Someone who loves learning must strive for every kind of truth.

—Socrates, according to Plato's *Republic*

I have argued against the eudaimonic ideal of true belief (Chapters 2 and 3). These arguments did not, however, speak against the idea that true belief is a non-ideal eudaimonic good (§1.1.4). This chapter examines that idea. We'll first distinguish between "strong" and "weak" approaches to the eudaimonic value of true belief (§4.1). I'll argue in this chapter that only a "weak" approach to the eudaimonic value of true belief is plausible. I'll defend this claim vis-à-vis the instrumental value of true belief (§4.2), before turning to the constitutive value of true belief (§4.3). Then I'll discuss the social value of true belief (§4.4). Finally, we'll look at the idea that true belief is, in some sense, "necessary" for wellbeing (§4.5).

4.1 Strong and weak approaches to the eudaimonic value of true belief

We distinguished above (§1.1.4) between ideal and non-ideal approaches to the eudaimonic value of *x*. We require another distinction to proceed. **Weak approaches to the eudaimonic value of *x*** maintain that *x* only sometimes has eudaimonic value. **Strong approaches to the eudaimonic value of *x*** maintain that *x* always has eudaimonic value.[1]

Strong approaches to the eudaimonic value of *x* can maintain that *x* always has pro tanto eudaimonic value, whereas weak versions can only maintain that *x* sometimes has pro tanto eudaimonic value, although perhaps they can say that *x* always has prima facie eudaimonic value. A strong approach might explain the fact that *x* is a non-ideal eudaimonic good, and not an ideal, by saying that in some normal cases the pro

---

[1] This is a corollary of the claim that *x* per se has eudaimonic value (§1.1.5), so to defend the per se eudaimonic value of *x* is to defend a strong approach to the eudaimonic value of *x*. See the quotation from DePaul, below.

tanto eudaimonic value of x is trumped by other pro tanto eudaimonic goods. And a weak approach will maintain that in some cases x has no pro tanto eudaimonic value at all.

For any given approach to the eudaimonic value of x, therefore, we have four possibilities:

- **Strong ideal approaches to the eudaimonic value of x**, on which x always has eudaimonic value and on which x is a eudaimonic ideal.
- **Weak ideal approaches to the eudaimonic value of x**, on which x is a eudaimonic ideal, but on which x does not always have eudaimonic value.
- **Strong non-ideal approaches to the eudaimonic value of x**, on which x always has eudaimonic value, but on which x is a non-ideal eudaimonic good.
- **Weak non-ideal approaches to the eudaimonic value of x**, on which x is a non-ideal eudaimonic good and on which x does not always have eudaimonic value.

I criticized ideal approaches to the eudaimonic value of true belief, above (Chapters 2 and 3). Here we will focus on strong and weak non-ideal approaches. Michael DePaul (2010) suggests a strong approach to the value of knowledge:

I understand the question of whether knowledge is valuable to ask whether items of knowledge have some value as, or in virtue of being, items of knowledge, or, to put it another way, whether items of knowledge are valuable as such. Similarly for other claims regarding value: that truth is valuable, or that true belief is valuable, or that gold is valuable. (pp. 113–14)

Here I'll argue against strong approaches to the eudaimonic value of true belief, and thus (given my rejection of true belief as a eudaimonic ideal), I'll conclude that the only plausible approach to the eudaimonic value of true belief is a weak non-ideal approach.

4.2 The instrumental eudaimonic value of true belief

Something has instrumental value (§1.1.1) when it is valuable as a means to some (wholly distinct) end; something has instrumental eudaimonic value when it is valuable as a means to some (wholly distinct) eudaimonically valuable end.[2] This section considers the instrumental eudaimonic value (hereafter "instrumental value") of true belief, and argues that only a weak non-ideal instrumental-value approach to the value of true belief (§1.1.5) is plausible.

---

[2] Instrumental eudaimonic value is sometimes called "practical" or "prudential" value. See Chapter 1, footnotes 5 and 29.

4.2.1 Instrumental value approaches

True belief is often said to have instrumental value, since having true beliefs will enable you to satisfy your desires (Foley 1987, p. 210, pp. 222–6, 1993, pp. 16–17, Craig 1990, pp. 132–3, Kornblith 1993, p. 371, Haack 1993, p. 200, Papineau 1999, p. 26, 1993, Chapter 3, Kvanvig 2003, p. 2, Alston 2005, p. 31, Horwich 2006, p. 350, 1998, pp. 44–6, pp. 139–41; cf. Zagzebski 2004). Note well that to say that true belief has instrumental value is not to say that true belief has *only* instrumental value. Thus Bernard Williams (2002) supplements his account of the instrumental value of true belief, on which said value is "explained in terms of other goods, and in particular the value of getting what one wants, avoiding danger, mastering the environment, and so on" (p. 58), with an account of why we should value true belief finally. To affirm the instrumental value of true belief is not to deny its constitutive value or its intrinsic value (cf. Kitcher 2004).

Williams and other social epistemologists (§4.4), who appeal to a collective need for information, may be committed to the instrumental value of true belief. One might jettison this commitment and appeal only to the constitutive value of true belief. But the story that social epistemologists typically tell reveals a commitment to the instrumental value of true belief, e.g. if the value of true belief is understood in terms of the satisfaction of our "basic human needs" (Williams 2002, p. 38).

The thought at the heart of all this is that it is good for someone to get what she wants; compare our discussion of desire-fulfillment theories of wellbeing (§1.1.6). If true beliefs lead, or tend to lead, to our getting what we want, then they will have, or tend to have, instrumental value.

4.2.2 Against ideal instrumental value approaches

I argued against ideal approaches to the eudaimonic value of true belief, above (Chapters 2 and 3), and these arguments apply against ideal instrumental value approaches. As Paul Horwich (2006) argues, the value of true belief is sometimes "outweighed by more important considerations," such that "in many circumstances, the value of finding out the truth, or falsity, of a given proposition will be less than the costs of doing so" (2006, p. 348; see also Papineau 1999, p. 24, Horwich 1998, p. 45; cf. Lynch 2004, p. 55). So two possibilities remain: strong non-ideal instrumental-value approaches and weak non-ideal instrumental-value approaches.

4.2.3 Against strong non-ideal instrumental value approaches

Strong non-ideal instrumental value approaches maintain that true belief always has pro tanto eudaimonic value. **Useless true beliefs** provide counterexamples to this. Consider the prospect of having a true belief about whether the number of grains of sand on the beach at Coney Island is even. Knowing the way to Larissa seems instrumentally valuable in all sorts of ways: if you want to go to Larissa, knowing the way will help you get there; if Larissa is objectively worth visiting (even absent your desire to go there), knowing the way will help you get there; if you meet someone on the road who needs to know the way to Larissa, knowing the way will help you tell her how to get there (cf. §4.4); and so on. But knowing whether the number of grains of sand on the beach at Coney Island is even will not help you do *anything*.

You might object that knowing whether the number of grains of sand on the beach at Coney Island is even is useful to someone who is curious about whether the number of grains of sand on the beach at Coney Island is even. That seems right. The curious person's true belief about that question seems to have some kind of eudaimonic value—perhaps constitutive value, if getting what you want is partially constitutive of wellbeing. But for the incurious person, such a belief seems utterly worthless.

You might object that knowing whether the number of grains of sand on the beach at Coney Island is even is useful because it does have unlikely possible uses: you might, for all you know, end up on a quiz show where the million-dollar question concerns whether the number of grains of sand on the beach at Coney Island is even. Given this potential for benefit, however unlikely, said true belief does have some instrumental value, however small an amount.

Let us grant that this objection is sound. We have found, however, that all true beliefs are not created equal when it comes to instrumental value. Some, like a true belief about the way to Larissa, have more instrumental value than others, like a true belief about whether the number of grains of sand on the beach at Coney Island is even. The instrumental value of true belief varies depending on the believer and on her situation. (Note that this seems clear, even if we have not found reason to reject a strong non-ideal instrumental value approach.)

However, the instrumental value of true belief really does appear to be nonexistent in some cases:

[There are] areas of inquiry in which the results have little bearing on everyday concerns, fields like cosmology and paleontology. (Kitcher 2001, p. 65)

The dinosaur extinction fascinates us, although knowing its cause would have no material impact on our lives. (Goldman 2002, p. 3)

[There are] fields of inquiry such as ancient history, metaphysics, and esoteric areas of mathematics…that may not be expected to have any pragmatic payoff. (Horwich 2006, p. 351)

The significance of [knowing that] Van Gogh's *Irises* expresses the looming, threatening nature of the world, as it appears to someone in the grip of loneliness…does not arise from its subjective practical value[; this knowledge] won't help me reach any of my aims, or satisfy any of my desires. (Baril 2010, pp. 219–220)

Could there be a chance, however small, that true beliefs such as these might benefit me in securing that which I desire? Could this chance be high enough so that said true beliefs could be seen to have instrumental value? Might knowledge of the dinosaur extinction be useful in combating contemporary existential threats? We can imagine paleontologists *saying* that in their grant applications, but our question is whether such utility really exists. In many cases, the chance of usefulness seems vanishingly small.

Above, we imagined that the possibility of a quiz show might ground the usefulness of seemingly useless true belief. But what if I am inquiring into previously uncharted territory in my own idiosyncratic branch of esoteric mathematics, where there will be no quiz, since I am the only one who will ever know the truths that I seek? Here the chance of usefulness is again vanishingly small.

The upshot of this is that there are cases in which I know that true belief won't be useful. And there are cases of worthwhile inquiry such that the knowledge I seek won't have any practical payoff. Some inquiries, perhaps, have value in virtue of satisfying our curiosity. But imagine someone incurious who comes to believe (through hypnosis, say) some useless true belief. Such a belief seems utterly worthless, from the perspective of instrumental value (Horwich 2006, p. 351, Baril 2010, pp. 219–20). Therefore, we should adopt a weak non-ideal instrumental value approach to the eudaimonic value of true belief.

You might object that seemingly useless true beliefs might end up impacting future deliberation via conclusions derived from them. For many defenders of the instrumental value of true belief (Papineau 1999, Horwich 2006), it is true means–ends beliefs (e.g. those in propositions of the form *that by Φing, I will Ψ*) that are fundamentally instrumentally valuable. Horwich (2006) argues that the instrumental value of other beliefs is derivative on this fundamental instrumental value:

> [Means–ends beliefs] are the result of inferences that tend to preserve truth; so it will benefit me for the *premises* of those inferences to be true. And there is no proposition that might not someday serve as a premise. Therefore it will indeed be good for me...if I believe every true proposition and if every proposition I believe is true. (p. 350; see also 1998, p. 140, Foley 1987, pp. 218–19, 1993, p. 17, Zagzebski 1996, p. 208, Goldman 1999, p. 73)

Two replies to this. First, there might be domains of truths so esoteric that (we know that) no useful beliefs can be inferred from them. Second, Horwich assumes that our beliefs "are the result of inferences that tend to preserve truth." The way this assumption is operating in the argument is to shore up the intuition that false beliefs are dangerous because of the tendency of falsehood to "spread." However, as I argued earlier (§2.9.7), false beliefs do not always "spread" and infect the rest of our beliefs. Although various species of bias are ubiquitous, massive error isn't. We should reject Horwich's assumption, which is effectively the assumption of human rationality. Some false beliefs, which are not at first glance instrumentally risky, might be seen on closer examination to be instrumentally risky because of the possibility that they will serve as premises in some future reasoning, infecting other beliefs with falsehood. But when false beliefs are insulated or compartmentalized, the threat of falsehood "spreading" is mitigated.

You might object that our interest in true belief is "general" or "unspecific" (cf. §6.2.2). It's not that every individual true belief has instrumental value, so the objection goes, but rather that true beliefs in general have instrumental value. This is likely what Hilary Kornblith (1993) has in mind when he considers the question of what sort of "cognitive system" we should prefer, for this requires us to consider beliefs in general as opposed to individual beliefs. Edward Craig's (1990) discussion of the value of true belief (pp. 130–3) proceeds at a similar level of generality. However, to maintain that true belief generally has instrumental value doesn't mean that true belief always has instrumental value. Our cases of true belief without instrumental value are still counterexamples to strong non-ideal instrumental value approaches. However, if to say that true belief "generally" has instrumental value is to say that there is no clearly identifiable pattern of cases in which true belief is useless (cf. §1.1.3), then it seems false that true belief "generally" has instrumental value, as we have identified patterns of cases where true belief is useless (trivial truths, inapplicable truths of science and mathematics, truths of aesthetic appreciation) and where false belief lacks instrumental disvalue (insulated or compartmentalized biased beliefs).

4.3 The constitutive value of true belief

It's often argued that true belief has not only instrumental value but final value as well (§1.5). Many philosophers have maintained that true belief has final eudaimonic value, in virtue of being a constituent of wellbeing—i.e. that true belief has constitutive value (§1.1.5). While you might worry that the instrumental value of true belief is hostage to a desire-fulfillment theory of wellbeing, constitutive value approaches to the eudaimonic value of true belief have no such commitment. This section considers such approaches, and argues that only a weak non-ideal constitutive value approach to the eudaimonic value of true belief is plausible.

4.3.1 Constitutive value approaches

Linda Zagzebski (2003a) sketches an Aristotelian constitutive value approach to the eudaimonic value of true belief:

[H]aving true beliefs is part of one's natural end, living a life of *eudaimonia*. Good cognitive activity contributes to the natural end of human life in the same way as good moral activity. (p. 140)

As Aristotle puts it in the *Nicomachean Ethics*, "[o]f the intellect that is contemplative…the good and bad state are truth and falsity respectively (for this is the work of everything intellectual)" (1139a 26–9). The constitutive value of true belief has been affirmed by a number of philosophers, inspired in this respect by Aristotle (Zagzebski, op. cit., 2003b, pp. 23–6, Rawls 1971, p. 425, Finnis 1980, Chapter 3, Sosa 2003, pp. 173–5, Greco 2010, pp. 97–101, Baehr 2011, p. 211, p. 222). Their view has been developed in more detail by Michael Lynch (2004) and Anne Baril (2010). Lynch argues that:

Knowing what you want helps you figure out how to get it. But knowledge of what you care about is more than useful. It is a constitutive part of some of the most important aspects of our psychic lives. In particular, it is essential for a certain network of attitudes we need to have towards ourselves. (2004, p. 123)

In particular, Lynch argues, self-knowledge is essential for having a "sense of self." "Having a sense of self is good in itself" (p. 124), but it is also essential for self-respect (ibid.) and for authenticity (pp. 124–6). True belief about what you care about, therefore, is "a constitutive good," and therefore "worth caring about for its own sake" (p. 128).

Baril likewise argues that true belief about certain topics is (sometimes) a constitutive good; her examples are not cases of self-knowledge but rather of scientific knowledge (e.g. a set of true beliefs about the correct physical theory) and aesthetic knowledge (e.g. a true belief about the expressive power of a painting). Beliefs of this kind "are such that having them is *partially constitutive* of the good human life," and thus they are "finally valuable … *as part of* a (non-derivatively) valuable whole" (p. 226).

In addition to the argument from self-knowledge (above), Lynch also argues that caring about the truth, per se and for its own sake, is a constitutive good, on the grounds that caring about the truth is required for intellectual integrity (2004, p. 36). Lynch suggests (pp. 128–9) that while considerations of self-respect and authenticity only explain the constitutive value of true beliefs about what I care about, considerations of integrity explain the constitutive value of true belief per se. That true belief per se has constitutive value is, at least, Lynch's view: he says that true belief is "good considered by itself" (p. 46 and passim) and "good as such" (p. 50 and passim; see also 2009a, p. 227). His is therefore a strong constitutive value approach.

4.3.2 Against ideal constitutive value approaches

I argued against ideal approaches to the eudaimonic value of true belief, above (Chapters 2 and 3), and these arguments apply against ideal constitutive value approaches. Although Lynch writes that "to say that something is partially constitutive of happiness or the good life is to say that your life would go better with it than without it" (2004, p. 136), which suggests the eudaimonic ideal of true belief, he makes clear elsewhere (pp. 46–51) that there are cases in which false belief is better than true belief, writing that true belief is "defeasibly good" (p. 46 and passim) and not good "all things considered" (p. 47 and passim).

4.3.3 Against strong non-ideal constitutive value approaches

Does true belief always have constitutive value? Or do some, but not all, instances of true belief have constitutive value? Two lines of reasoning support the latter view.

First, consider someone's true belief in some proposition that she finds (and has always found) **uninteresting**. S finds the proposition that p **interesting** iff she wants to know whether p, i.e. iff she is curious about the question of whether p, and finds the proposition that p uninteresting otherwise. I do not have, and have never had, any curiosity at all about whether the number of grains of sand on the beach at Coney Island is even. I just do not care about that question at all; I have no desire to know the answer. Suppose that I am now presented with conclusive evidence that the number of grains is even; I form a belief to that effect. Does this true belief have constitutive value? Recall that things that have constitutive value must partially explain the goodness of the whole of which they are a part (§1.1.5). Does my true belief, in this case, explain the goodness of my life in any way?

There seems to be nothing eudaimonically bad about not knowing the answers to questions that don't interest you; and there is likewise nothing eudaimonically good about knowing the answers to such questions (Goldman 1999, p. 88; see also Grimm 2009, Brady 2009). The contribution made to your wellbeing, in some cases, is vanishingly small, and in some cases appears nonexistent. This does not mean that, in coming to know the answer to some question, one might realize that one was, or had been, curious about its answer; as Alvin Goldman (2002) notes, "[s]ometimes the questions that interest a person are only implicit rather than explicit or fully conscious" (p. 88). And later on he proposes to include as valuable not only those propositions that are interesting to S, but also those that would be interesting to S if she thought about them, and those that would be interesting to S if she knew certain facts (pp. 94–6). But there can be true propositions that fall into none of these three categories, and when it comes to one of these, not believing it does not make my "credal corpus…impoverished" (ibid.), at least not from a eudaimonic point of view, and believing it would not add anything of eudaimonic value. True belief, therefore, does not always have constitutive value.

Second, true propositions seem to differ in their significance. By contrast with the interesting, the proposition that p is **significant** if it is *worth* knowing whether it is true, or if people *ought* to be curious about it, etc.[3] Compare the "trivial" questions Goldman mentions with such questions as: What is the fundamental physical structure of the universe? Did human life evolve through a process of natural selection? What is happiness? And so on. In light of this, many epistemologists have come out in defense of significant truth (Haack 1993, p. 203, Kitcher 1993, p. 94, 2001, p. 65, Goldman 2002, p. 60, Zagzebski 2003b, pp. 20–1, Alston 2005, p. 30, Treanor forthcoming a, forthcoming b).

The notion of significance is rather difficult to explicate—apart from saying that it is the "aim of inquiry" (Treanor forthcoming b) or that "cognitive progress" consists in discovering significant truths (Kitcher 1993, pp. 92–5). We might understand significance as an **epistemic** notion, although the notion of the "epistemic" is also difficult

---

[3] The distinction between what I am calling the interesting and what I am calling the significant could be drawn using alternative terminology; I don't intend a conceptual analysis of "interesting" and "significant." Both words have relativized versions ("interesting to," "of interest to," "significant to," "of significance to"). But (what I am calling) significance essentially differs from (what I am calling) interestingness in the fact that interestingness is *necessarily* relative to an individual. Significance need not be relative, either to individuals or to species, though one might defend a view on which it is.

to explicate (§1.3). Philip Kitcher (2001) defends a "context-dependent" conception of "epistemic" significance, on which:

Partially as the result of our having the capacities we do, partially because of the cultures in which we develop, some aspects of nature strike us as particularly salient or surprising. In consequence we pose broad questions, and epistemic significance flows into the sciences from these. (p. 81)

Ted Sider (2011) defends the "epistemic value" of beliefs which "carve the world at its joints," a value enjoyed by some true beliefs and not by others (pp. 61–5).[4] Nick Treanor (forthcoming b) argues that, of two propositions, it is "epistemically better" to know the one that is "more truth" than to know the one that is "less truth." Compare the proposition that Affan has a daughter (more truth) with the proposition that Affan has a child (less truth), or the proposition that the universe underwent massive exponential expansion shortly after the big bang (more truth) with the proposition that the number of grains of sand on the beach at Coney Island is even (less truth), or (less obviously) the proposition that x is green (more truth) with the proposition that x is grue (less truth). Knowing trivial truths "does not increase one's knowledge, or decrease one's ignorance, very much," (forthcoming a) because the "aim of inquiry" is to know as much truth as one can, not as many truths as one can.

But we can also understand significance in **eudaimonic** terms.[5] Zagzebski (2003b) argues that:

[T]rue belief…is thought to be desirable. That is to say, we think that true belief is good *for* us. But…surely not all true beliefs are desirable. [...] The unavoidable conclusion is that some knowledge is not good for us. (p. 21; see also 2004, p. 368)

And Baril (2010) proposes a "eudaimonist" conception of significance, "worthiness," where a true belief is "worthy" when it has constitutive value (§4.3.1); thus "certain beliefs," but not others, are "part of living well as a human being, even if nothing else is gained by them" (2010, p. 226). But this does not support the idea that true belief always has constitutive value: our beliefs in *significant* truths have constitutive value, but beliefs in insignificant truths seem eudaimonically worthless. As Baril (2010) argues, some true propositions seem unsuitable as contents for worthy beliefs, e.g. the familiar "utterly trivial…phonebook truths" (p. 227). Other beliefs may have instrumental value—e.g. a belief about the location of my keys—but not the constitutive value enjoyed by worthy beliefs. But even when a true proposition is suitable to serve as the content for a worthy belief, a true belief may fail to be worthy for either of two reasons. First, some truths may require context to contribute to the goodness of the believer's life, such that someone who believed such truths without the relevant

---

[4] I articulate and defend this view in "Limning Structure as an Epistemic Goal."

[5] The "epistemic" and eudaimonic understandings of significance need not be thought of as competitors; they might be understood as giving different senses of "significance," or as giving accounts of two different properties.

background knowledge would not thereby enjoy a worthy belief. For example, some true beliefs might be eudaimonically worthless unless combined with others to comprise a sufficiently comprehensive scientific understanding (p. 228). Second, some truths might require their believer to appreciate them in a certain way for her believing them to contribute to the goodness of her life (p. 227). Some people may be ill-suited to appreciate certain truths, perhaps because their form of the good human life does not involve curiosity about them (pp. 229–30). The upshot is that only beliefs in suitable truths, properly contextualized and appreciated, are "finally valuable as part of a good human life" (p. 227). If this is right, true belief does not always have constitutive value. The constitutive value of true belief is **conditional** rather than unconditional (Baril 2010, p. 227). We should therefore not adopt a strong non-ideal constitutive value approach to the eudaimonic value of true belief.

You might object that beliefs in uninteresting and insignificant truths have pro tanto eudaimonic value that is outweighed by other considerations. Lynch (2004) argues that:

> [T]here are all sorts of true beliefs (say, beliefs about how many threads there are in my carpet) that are not worth having, all things considered. But the fact that I should not bother with these sorts of beliefs doesn't mean that it isn't still [pro tanto][6] good to believe even the most trivial truth. (p. 55)

What other considerations outweigh the pro tanto value of believing these truths? Lynch doesn't say exactly. He compares believing trivial truths to helping an old lady cross the street: this is a pro tanto good, but often it would take too much time to find an old lady to make it worth pursuing said good. So perhaps the idea is that the time it would take to inquire about trivial truths is what outweighs their pro tanto value. Call this the **cost of inquiry**. Alternatively, you might think that believing itself is a waste of "mental energy" or "brain power"; call this the **cost of cognition**. The idea, then, is that true beliefs about uninteresting and insignificant propositions seem worthless, but only because we're focusing on the prohibitive costs of inquiry and cognition, and this mistaken focus obscures the trumped pro tanto value of those beliefs.

This explanation of the apparent worthlessness of true beliefs about uninteresting and insignificant propositions is essential. In paradigm cases in which a pro tanto good is trumped by other considerations, we still feel the pull of the pro tanto good in question: when I play hooky from a department meeting in favor of a brace of pints, I still appreciate the pro tanto goodness of attending the meeting, the value of attending still has some appeal, even as that appeal is o'erwhelmed by the appeal of the pints. But in the case of true beliefs about uninteresting and insignificant propositions, there is no appeal whatsoever (cf. Kraut 2007, pp. 164–5). We need an explanation of this intuition of worthlessness, if said beliefs really have pro tanto value.

---

[6] Lynch says "prima facie" here, but he means (what I mean by) "pro tanto" (cf. §1.1.3). Trivial truths don't seem eudaimonically valuable, "at first glance" or "on their face."

Lynch's undermining account of our intuition that true beliefs about uninteresting and insignificant propositions are worthless is available to the defender of a strong non-ideal version of the constitutive value approach. But note that it's also available to the defender of a strong non-ideal constitutive value approach to the eudaimonic value of owning gold (cf. §1.1.6), who maintains that owning gold always has pro tanto eudaimonic value. We might point to cases in which someone owns some intuitively worthless gold—imagine some tiny, ugly scrap of gold, despised by its owner (and also, for good measure, rendered useless by being embedded in an impenetrable block of steel)—but the defender of the pro tanto value of gold can always respond that our intuition is based on mistakenly focusing on the factors that trump the supposed pro tanto value of gold, e.g. the cost of extracting the gold from the steel, or whatever. This should make us skeptical of Lynch's argument.

Given the nature of constitution, we should not expect things that have constitutive value to be per se valuable. Constitutive value is a species of final value (§1.1.1), but not a species of intrinsic value (§1.5). When x has constitutive value, x is valuable in virtue of the fact that x partially constitutes wellbeing (§1.1.6). What this means is that tokens of x are valuable in virtue of being parts of tokens of wellbeing, i.e. good human lives. The value of a token of x depends on its bearing the right relationship to some good human life. If some tokens of x stand, but others do not stand, in the appropriate relationship to good human lives, it is not the case that x per se is eudaimonically valuable. To put this another way, we should expect the eudaimonic value of constituents of wellbeing to be conditional, rather than unconditional.

We might continue to pump our intuitions by considering cases in which uninteresting and insignificant truths are believed, but where the factors that Lynch says trump the value of such beliefs, in the ordinary case, are absent. Imagine a believer with infinite resources at her disposal, such that for her there is no cost of inquiry and no cost of cognition for believing any truth whatsoever. Do we have the intuition that *her* true belief about whether the number of grains of sand on the beach at Coney Island is even has eudaimonic value? Lynch does; he writes that "it is prima facie good to be omniscient" (2009a, p. 77), and suggests that "omniscience is the ultimate cognitive goal" (2004, p. 55). We have an intuition that it would be good, in some sense, to be omniscient, reflected in the idea that a perfect being would be omniscient; a strong non-ideal version of the constitutive value approach would explain this intuition. However, consider omnipotence, another standard property for a perfect being. We seem to have the intuition that it would be good, in some sense, to be omnipotent. But does this suggest that *power* always has pro tanto eudaimonic value? Power seems to be a paradigm example of something with conditional eudaimonic value: some cases of power are good (e.g. courage, healthy physical strength, the power to inspire those over whom one has legitimate authority) while others seem worthless or even bad (e.g. the ability to count blades of grass, the ability to torture people without remorse). Again, the defender of the eudaimonic value of power could appeal here to Lynch's strategy: power is always valuable, but its value is sometimes trumped. However, that power and true belief are sometimes valuable, and sometimes not valuable, seems at least as good an account of the phenomena.

We also should note that we may be imagining that a perfect being has unlimited curiosity, i.e. that she wants to know whether p, for any proposition that p. But it's then impossible for such a being to believe an uninteresting truth. You might think that beliefs about interesting truths always have pro tanto eudaimonic value, since there is always pro tanto eudaimonic value when someone gets what she wants. This might explain why we imagine a perfect being as omniscient, but since human beings do not have unlimited curiosity (§1.2.2), this would not support the idea that true belief always has pro tanto eudaimonic value.

We may be poorly served by appealing to our conception of God when we theorize about eudaimonic value. You might think that what is good for a human being is different from what is good for a non-human being (Baril 2010, p. 223). We can do justice to the idea that God's omniscience is eudaimonically valuable, by noting that what is good for God (knowing everything) is not the same as what is good for a human being (knowing what is worth knowing, for a human), just as what is good for a dog (kibble) is not the same as what is good for a human being (foie gras). This idea is natural in the context of constitutive value approaches to the eudaimonic value of true belief, since defenders of these approaches often appeal to essentialist theories of wellbeing (§1.1.6).

I conclude, therefore, that uninteresting and insignificant propositions provide counterexamples to strong non-ideal constitutive value approaches to the eudaimonic value of true belief. Only weak, non-ideal constitutive value approaches are plausible. Combining this with our conclusion above (§4.2), it seems that only weak approaches to the eudaimonic value of true belief are plausible.[7]

Note well, however, that even if you are unconvinced, and opt for a strong non-ideal constitutive value approach, we have found good reason to think that all beliefs are not created equal when it comes to their constitutive value. As Zagzebski (2003b) writes, "the value of true beliefs varies" (p. 21). True beliefs in interesting or significant propositions intuitively have greater constitutive value than do true beliefs in uninteresting or insignificant propositions, even if (though I have argued against this) they all have some constitutive value.[8] Thus we have found that some beliefs (namely, those about interesting or significant propositions) have more constitutive value than others (which either have less constitutive value, or none). And we found above (§5.2) that

---

[7] Ethical particularists should be attracted to this conclusion. Rather than thinking of eudaimonic value as attaching to types, as implied by the general principle that true belief always has pro tanto eudaimonic value, the particularist will prefer to think of eudaimonic value as attaching to tokens, such that "the eudaimonic value of true belief" will be present, or absent, in particular cases of belief.

[8] Cf. W.D. Ross (1930) on the variable intrinsic value of knowledge (cf. §1.5): "Knowledge of mere matters of fact…seems to be worth much less than the knowledge of general principles, or of facts depending on general principles—what we might call insight or understanding as opposed to mere knowledge" (p. 139).

some beliefs (e.g. a true belief about the way to Larissa) have more instrumental value than others (which either have less instrumental value, or none). Therefore, some true beliefs have more eudaimonic value than others.

4.4 The social value of true belief

We focused above (§4.2) on the instrumental eudaimonic value of true belief, i.e. the value of true belief *for the believer*. You might object that this ignores the *social* value of true belief, which has been emphasized by social epistemologists (Craig 1990, Goldman 1999, Williams 2002, Kusch 2009, Grimm 2009). So in this section I'll articulate the argument for the social value of true belief (§4.4.1) and then argue that true belief only sometimes has social value, and that some true beliefs have more social value than others (§4.4.2).

4.4.1 Clifford's argument

In his 1877 essay *The Ethics of Belief*, W.K. Clifford famously defends an evidentialist principle ("it is wrong, always, everywhere, and for anyone, to believe anything on insufficient evidence") on the grounds that false belief is dangerous (1999, p. 77). He describes two types of harm that can come from false belief: **direct harm** (pp. 70–3), as when a self-deceived shipbuilder falsely thinks that a certain ship is safe, and **testimonial harm** (pp. 73–6), as when a "village rustic" keeps "fatal superstitions" alive (p. 74). Our non-verbal actions can harm others if they are based on false beliefs (e.g. the ship sinks), and our verbal actions can harm others if they are based on false belief (e.g. false belief is passed on to the hearer).[9] And testimonial harm is insidious: false testimony threatens to spread from one person to those in her vicinity, and from those people to the people in their vicinity, and so on, ad infinitum. Our beliefs, therefore, are "common property," (p. 73) such that

> Whoso would deserve well of his fellows in this matter will guard the purity of his beliefs with a very fanaticism of jealous care, lest at any time it should rest on an unworthy object, and catch a stain which can never be wiped away. (p. 74)

Evidentially unsupported belief is like disease:

> That duty is to guard ourselves from such beliefs as from pestilence, which may shortly master our own body and then spread to the rest of the town. What would be thought of one who, for the sake of a sweet fruit, should deliberately run the risk of delivering a plague upon his family and his neighbours? (pp. 75–6)

Thus the life of the credulous man is essentially "one long sin against mankind" (p. 77). We have strong reason, therefore, to cleave to our evidence.

---

[9] The distinction between direct and testimonial harm isn't sharp. This is especially clear if false belief per se has eudaimonic disvalue: in that case, testimonial harm would constitute direct harm.

Many contemporary epistemologists have agreed, at least in rough outline, with Clifford's argument; these passages are representative:

Human beings need true beliefs about their environment, beliefs that can serve to guide their actions to a successful outcome. [...] It will be highly advantageous to them if they can also tap the [true beliefs] of their fellows...[s]o any community may be presumed to have an interest in evaluating sources of information[.] [T]he concept of knowledge is used to flag approved sources of information. (Craig 1990, p. 11)

Given the plausible assumption that human beings are naturally garrulous and that we often reveal our beliefs involuntarily, we cannot be accurate informants unless we have mostly true beliefs. Hence, we have a kind of responsibility to others to have accurate beliefs. (Zagzebski 2003a, p. 143)

Along the same lines, Stephen Grimm (2009) writes that:

[T]he best way to make sense of the value of true belief is to think of it along the lines of a *common good*. Consider, for example, the value we associate with other classic examples of common goods such as *clean water*. (p. 259–60; cf. Kusch 2009, p. 61)

Grimm asks us to imagine that we are passing some body of clean water, and to consider why it would be wrong to dump a barrelful of sludge into the water. There is at least one obvious reason: "that other people might well need this water to satisfy their needs" (p. 260).

Given the unpredictable nature of the needs of others, and given how contamination of this sort can spread in unpredictable ways, others very well might turn out to depend on this water. And since clean water plays such an indispensable role in human well-being, we plausibly have an obligation not to pollute in this way. (Ibid.)

Likewise, the thought goes (see also Zagzebski 1996, p. 208, 2004, p. 355, Papineau 1999, p. 27, Williams 2002, p. 57),[10] we ought not pollute our "web of beliefs" with falsehoods, given how such contamination can spread, via testimony, to others. Suppose that humans are naturally garrulous (i.e. disposed, under certain conditions, to testify that p when they believe that p) and trusting (i.e. disposed, under certain conditions, to believe that p when someone testifies that p), and suppose that false testimony is a harm, or tends to cause harm, to the hearer, and that true testimony is a benefit, or tends to cause benefit, to the hearer. From this, we can conclude that true belief is

---

[10] I am inclined to include Nietzsche here, but his views about the value of true belief are difficult to discern. He calls for a reevaluation of the value of true belief (e.g. *Beyond Good and Evil*, §34, *The Genealogy of Morals*, III, §24), and in some places seems to reject the "value of truth" (e.g. *Genealogy of Morals* III, §24, *The Will to Power*, §80, §§277–9, §§304, 465). The "will to truth" is a species of the "will to power" (*Will to Power*, §375, §423, §455, §480, §495, §515, §521, §552, §568, §579, §§583–5, §616; see also "On Truth and Lying in a Non-Moral Sense"), and the distinction between truth and falsity, and between reality and appearance, is a result of treating morality as the supreme value (*Will to Power*, §3, §7, §12, §583, §585). But at other times he praises truthfulness as a heroic virtue (*Beyond Good and Evil*, §39, *Untimely Meditations*, "On the Uses and Disadvantages of History for Life," §6, *Will to Power*, §445, §945, §1041)—and in these passages he sounds like a follower of Clifford. All this is complicated by his "perspectivalist" views about truth, which may be inconsistent with our realist Aristotelian assumption (§1.6.1).

valuable and false belief is disvaluable; the value in question is the **social value** of true belief.

4.4.2 True belief only sometimes socially valuable

The socio-epistemological argument (§4.4.1) is based on the premise that human beings are naturally garrulous. We might challenge this assumption. Although we often reveal our beliefs involuntarily, we often keep our beliefs to ourselves. This seems especially true of beliefs that result from self-enhancement bias: Jonathan Brown and Frances Gallagher (1992) found that subjects' self-evaluations varied depending on whether they were being watched by an experimenter (cf. §2.9.2). We may think highly of ourselves, but we often know well enough to keep this to ourselves, whether out of embarrassment, to appear modest, or to avoid social friction. In the *Treatise* (III. iii.2), Hume praises "self-satisfaction and vanity," but notes well that "good-breeding and decency require that we shou'd avoid all signs and expressions, which tend directly to show that passion" (1978, p. 597). "[W]e establish the *rules of good-breeding*," Hume writes, "in order to prevent the opposition of men's pride, and render conversation agreeable and inoffensive" (ibid.). And thus "some disguise in this particular is absolutely requisite" (p. 598). We ought to keep our biased beliefs concealed, Hume argues; if this is possible, then the moral risk that generally comes with false belief will be mitigated in this case. We might then conclude that self-enhancement bias is all-things-considered appealing, in as much as it sustains personal wellbeing, without harming anyone else.

But I won't pursue that line of criticism further. I'll argue that false belief is only sometimes dangerous, because there are socially useless true beliefs (and socially harmless false beliefs). Two kinds of cases show this.

First, consider cases of useless true beliefs (§4.2.3). Consider the prospect of having a true belief about whether the number of grains of sand on the beach at Coney Island is even. The social epistemologist might argue: although a true belief about this question would not benefit *me*, and although a false belief about this question would not harm *me*, a true belief about this question might potentially benefit *others*, and a false belief about this question might potentially harm *others*, so this seemingly trivial question about grains of sand is not so trivial after all: I owe it to other people to believe the truth about this, or at least not to believe falsely. What we must imagine is that *someone's* believing the truth about the number of grains of sand on the beach at Coney Island could, for all I know, be eudaimonically valuable. In this respect, as Clifford puts it, "no belief is insignificant" (1999, p. 74). But there are some truths such that I know that there will never be someone such that her believing them will have eudaimonic value. Suppose that there are presently 31 paperclips in the paperclip container on my desk, although neither I nor anyone else has counted them. Thus, a true proposition:

> *paperclip* At 11:53, 18 November, 2011, there were 31 paperclips in the paperclip container on Allan Hazlett's desk.

To be sure, it's hard to imagine how someone could benefit from believing this; the chance of someone's being affected by my belief in *paperclip* is vanishingly small. I now know that no one will ever benefit from believing this proposition. Could there be a TV quiz, with the question of whether *paperclip* is true as the $1,000,000 prize? No; by hypothesis no one has ever counted the clips; no one knows that *paperclip* is true. Could there be some form of human flourishing that involves inquiring after truths like *paperclip*? That is precisely the kind of form of life that desire-independent theories of wellbeing are designed to reject as counterflourishing. Truly believing *paperclip* would be socially useless. For the same reason, believing its negation would be socially harmless. True belief, in this case, has no social value—and false belief has no social disvalue.

Second, consider cases involving an isolated believer. The last person on earth knows that believing truly will never benefit anyone, and that believing falsely will never harm anyone. The chance of his belief affecting anyone—aliens?—is vanishingly small. True belief, in this case, has no social value, and false belief has no social disvalue.

Even if you are unconvinced that true belief sometimes has no social value, you should admit that all beliefs are not created equal when it comes to their social value. First, true beliefs differ in social value depending on the interestingness or significance of the proposition. For example, my belief in *paperclip* has less social value than my belief that the number 5 bus goes to Meadowbank, since the latter belief is much more likely to benefit somebody; for the same reason, false belief about the former proposition is less dangerous than false belief about the latter. Second, true beliefs differ in social value depending on the social circumstances of the believer. For example, consider Robinson Crusoe, stranded alone on an island, with a slim chance of ever seeing another person again. His true beliefs are less socially valuable than mine, since the risk of harm (potential for benefit) that comes from his being wrong (right) is greater than that which comes from my being wrong (right). Alternatively, compare me, a healthy loudmouth with many years of testimony ahead of me, with a shy old man, on the brink of permanent silence. I conclude that some true beliefs have more social value than others.

4.5 The necessity of true belief for wellbeing

The defender of the constitutive value of true belief might argue, at this point, that a "weak" constitutive value approach need not be all that weak. For one could reject strong constitutive value approaches as implausible, but nevertheless maintain that **having some true beliefs is necessary for wellbeing**. Never mind that some true beliefs are eudaimonically worthless, both instrumentally and constitutively. Living well *requires* having some true beliefs. Surely anything that is necessary for living well is of great eudaimonic value. And so true belief is of great eudaimonic value, even if it does not always have pro tanto eudaimonic value. We might motivate this either by appeal to the instrumental value of true belief or by appeal to the constitutive value of true belief.

Consider the instrumental value of true belief first. If we say that the instrumental value of true belief is such that living well requires having some true beliefs (cf. Kornblith 1993, Zagzebski 2004), we will not yet have shown that true belief has great eudaimonic value. Consider the instrumental value of clean air. Living well, for humans, requires clean air; no one lives well unless she has access to clean air. But clean air, you might think, is of no great eudaimonic value—it's merely a precondition of living well, a requirement for a human to even survive long enough to be in the business of living well. The fact that all those who live well have access to clean air doesn't tell us anything substantial about the good life: their access to clean air does not explain the goodness of their lives, since those who live badly have access to clean air, too. The defender of the eudaimonic value of true belief should not be satisfied by the idea—which seems plausible enough—that having *some* true beliefs is necessary for a human being to even survive long enough to attempt to live well, since such beliefs may not *explain* the goodness of the lives of those who succeed (cf. §1.1.5).

You might object that, as the contemporary self-help literature urges, there are "keys to happiness," the recognition of which is both necessary and sufficient for satisfaction with your life and personal mastery. "The most important things in life I learned in kindergarten"—and knowledge of these significant truths is not merely a precondition for survival (like clean air), but an essential tool for acquiring the goods that constitute a good human life. But the existence of such "keys to happiness" seems implausible. Take your pick of a truth, belief in which seems necessary for living well, and we will be able to imagine someone living well without believing said truth.

Consider then the constitutive value of true belief. Suppose we were to say that living well requires having some constitutively valuable true beliefs. We could say either that there are constitutive "keys to happiness," or (more plausibly) that everyone who lives well believes some significant truths, their believing of which (partially) explains their living well. This allows for the needed relativity (cf. Baril 2010, pp. 227–30): the true beliefs that partly constitute my good life may not have the same content as the true beliefs that partly constitute your good life. But every good life is partly constituted by some true beliefs.

But the point about necessary preconditions for living well applies here as well. As John Finnis (1980) argues, "[a] sound brain and intelligence are necessary conditions for the understanding, pursuit, and realization of truth, but neither brainpower nor intelligence should appear on a list of basic values" (p. 82). If all we can say about true belief is that it's necessary for the good life, we will not yet have justified its status as a "basic value," for true belief might resemble brainpower and intelligence: a prerequisite for wellbeing, rather than a constituent of it. For this reason, David Brink (1989) distinguishes between "components of human welfare that are intrinsically valuable" and "necessary conditions for human welfare" (p. 231). So perhaps although every good life *involves* some true beliefs, and in that sense true belief is necessary for wellbeing, these true beliefs do not *explain* the goodness of the lives of which they are parts.

So we must say that everyone who lives well necessarily has some true beliefs, which partially explain their living well. This inherits the vagueness of "living well." The appeal to pro tanto constitutive value (§4.3) is appealing in part because it jibes with the fact that wellbeing surely comes in degrees: your life might be going better than my life, and your possession of certain pro tanto wellbeing goods that I do not enjoy might explain this. The claim that having some true beliefs is necessary for living well is troubling in that it's not obvious how to articulate it without suggesting that there is a sharp boundary between "good lives" and "not good lives," as opposed to degrees of wellbeing.

But perhaps this can be gotten around; we might say, for example, that everyone who lives one of the *best* lives necessarily has some true beliefs, which partially explain their living well. But is it really plausible that someone couldn't live one of the best lives, without having some true beliefs with constitutive value? Consider the magnificent athlete or the benevolent saint, who has neither the time nor the inclination for reflection on questions of significance (cf. Kraut 2007, p. 191). The greatness of their lives does not derive from their "epistemic" goodness. Should we say that it would be better to be both a magnificent athlete *and* a believer of significant truths, and that the mere magnificent athlete and the mere benevolent saint are not living the *best* human lives? This is just to say, I think, that significant true belief has pro tanto constitutive value.

There is no plausible sense in which true belief is necessary for living well, apart from the sense provided by the claim that significant true belief has pro tanto constitutive value. Think of the things that can make a life good, even great: athletic excellence, devotion to others, bravery in combat, engaging with good music, commitment to a cause, raising a family, artistic excellence. Among these, I am sure, is knowledge of significant truths—if it can be had by creatures like us. But are any of these things plausibly such that everyone who lives well, or who lives one of the best lives, necessarily has it? The grounds for saying that truth belief is necessary for living well, in virtue of its constitutive value, seems no stronger than the grounds for saying that athletic excellence is necessary for living well, in virtue of its constitutive value, or that artistic excellence is necessary for living well, in virtue of its constitutive value. If we say that the naïve athlete is not living one of the best human lives, in virtue of not believing any significant truths, then we should also say that the clumsy sage is not living one of the best human lives, in virtue of her lack of athletic ability. What is more plausible is that there is nothing that is *necessary* for living well: the good life comes in a plurality of forms, each rich in constitutive goods. But there are no constitutive goods such that possession of *them* is required for the good life.

Recall Rosalind Husthouse's (1999) take on the eudaimonic value of virtue (§1.1.3). On her view, the virtues benefit the possessor, but this claim does not commit one to the view that the virtues are necessary for human flourishing. She asks us to consider a regimen prescribed by a doctor; the prudence of following the regimen is not undermined by the fact that it's not necessary for health. Likewise:

To claim that the virtues, for the most part, benefit their possessor, enabling her to flourish, is not to claim that virtue is necessary for happiness. It is to claim that no "regimen" will serve one better—no other candidate "regimen" is remotely plausible. (p. 173)

In other words, the virtues "are the only reliable bet" when it comes to human flourishing (p. 172). Might we understand the value of significant true belief along similar lines? We might say: the only reliable "regimen," vis-à-vis the goal of flourishing, is one that includes seeking significant true beliefs. (Recall that we have already considered, and set aside, the instrumental value of having some true beliefs; we can take this to be a precondition of human survival, whether to flourish or not.) Once we have adopted a pluralistic conception of human flourishing, as proposed above, it's hard to see how this might work. "Seek the truth about significant matters" isn't the only reliable bet when it comes to human flourishing; some are well served by following this advice, but others might not be; their "regimen" will consist in abiding by alternative maxims: "Play like a champion today" or "Love your neighbor." If we were right, above, that there are good lives without significant true beliefs, then the "regimen" of seeking truth is not, after all, the only reliable bet when it comes to human flourishing. We might say that all those who live well seek some of a plurality of goods, among which is that of having significant true beliefs. We should have no objection to this; but we have failed to find a plausible articulation of the idea that true belief is necessary for living well.

4.6 Conclusion

I've argued that only a weak approach to the eudaimonic value of true belief is plausible. I've suggested that the eudaimonic value of true belief is conditional in various ways: on whether the proposition believed is interesting, on whether it is significant, and on whether it partially constitutes the valuable whole that is the good life of the believer. My most important conclusion is that true beliefs are not all created equal, when it comes to their eudaimonic value (and their social value), but I have also argued that some true beliefs are eudaimonically (and socially) worthless, and (in previous chapters) that some false beliefs are eudaimonically valuable.

PART II

The Epistemic Value of True Belief

5

The Problem of the Source of Epistemic Normativity

Above (Part I) we examined the eudaimonic value of true belief. We now turn to the "epistemic" value of true belief. Consider the claim that true belief has "epistemic" value (§1.4). This leaves open questions about the comparative "epistemic" value of true belief as well as questions about whether true belief is the only thing that has fundamental "epistemic" value. However, our concern here is merely with understanding the "epistemic" value of true belief. Our approach will be to examine the status of "epistemic evaluation," which takes true belief to be good, and false belief to be bad, and to ask a metaethical question about it: what explains the appropriateness of epistemic evaluation? This is a basic question in what I'll call "the problem of the source of epistemic normativity." This chapter introduces that problem (§5.2), rejects a possible solution to it (§5.3), and sketches alternative solutions (§5.4), to be considered in what follows (Chapters 6–8). Along the way, some important assumptions are articulated and briefly defended (§5.2.3, §5.3.1, §5.5).

5.1 The "epistemic" value of true belief

In contemporary epistemology it's standard to maintain, or presuppose, that true belief has "epistemic" value. Epistemologists standardly say that the "epistemic" has something to do with treating truth as a good, or end, or goal (Alston 1985, BonJour 1985, pp. 7–8, Goldman 1986, p. 98, 1999, Chapter 3, 2002, Chapter 3, Foley 1987, pp. 8–11, 1993, p. 19, p. 94, Sosa 2007; cf. David 2001). Virtue epistemologists (Zagzebski 1996, pp. 168–76, Baehr 2011, pp. 100–2) standardly characterize intellectual virtue in terms of the love of truth, knowledge, and understanding, which are often described as "epistemic goods." As Jason Baehr (2011) argues, on this picture the value of the "epistemic goods" is needed to explain the value of the intellectual virtues: "it seems obvious that being motivated by or "loving" knowledge is good simply on account of the fact that knowledge itself is good" (p. 137), and if "knowledge were not good, or…we did not regard it as good," then it would not "still be plausible to think of a desire for knowledge as good" (p. 136). The plausibility of this picture of intellectual virtue, where intellectual virtue is understood as valuable, depends on the value of true belief (ibid. p. 101n).[1]

Recent epistemological discussions of "epistemic" value have centered on the "Meno problem" (Riggs 2002, Zagzebski 2003b, Kvanvig 2003, Sosa 2007, Pritchard 2010, Greco 2010). This is a problem that Socrates raises in Plato's *Meno* (97b): in terms of usefulness, knowledge is often no better than true belief that doesn't amount to knowledge. The person who knows the way to Larissa seems in no better a position, as far as her project of traveling to Larissa, than someone who has a true belief, not amounting to knowledge, about the way to Larissa. But we tend to think that knowledge is more valuable than mere true belief—as Meno puts it, "knowledge is prized far more highly than right opinion" (97d). Is knowledge really more valuable than mere true belief? How can this be so, given their apparent equality in usefulness? Socrates responds (so it seems to me) by rejecting the apparent equality in usefulness between knowledge and mere true belief. Knowledge has a kind of security or stability that is missing in mere true belief.[2] Imagine that you owned one of the statues of Daedalus—more like robots than statues, since they could move around and potentially quit your property:

> To possess one of his works which is let loose does not count for much in value; it will not stay with you any more than a runaway slave: but when fastened up it is worth a great deal, for his productions are very fine things. And to what am I referring in all this? To true opinion. For these, so long as they stay with us, are a fine possession, and effect all that is good; but they do not care to stay for long, and run away out of the human soul, and thus are of no great value until one makes them fast with causal reasoning. [O]nce they are fastened, in the first place they turn into knowledge, and in the second, are abiding. And this is why knowledge is more prized than right opinion: the one transcends the other by its trammels. (97e–98a)

Contemporary epistemologists, however, have not followed Socrates in arguing that knowledge has greater usefulness than mere true belief. They have conceded that knowledge may be no more valuable than mere true belief, when it comes to usefulness, but have sought to explain why knowledge is more "epistemically" valuable than mere true belief. This question presupposes that knowledge *is* "epistemically" more valuable than true belief. And to take the question to be at all interesting is to presuppose that true belief has some "epistemic" value (cf. Kvanvig 2003, p. 155). It's not like the question: why is knowledge "epistemically" more valuable than cottage cheese? This question is uninteresting because cottage cheese has no "epistemic" value. Consider, for example, the idea that the "epistemic" value of true belief threatens to "swamp" the would-be additional "epistemic" value of knowledge (Kvanvig 2003,

---

[1] Cf. Zagzebski 1996, p. 83, p. 203.

[2] This premise should be challenged. An intellectually virtuous knower will be more likely to abandon her true beliefs (which amount to knowledge), in the face of misleading evidence, than will a credulous nitwit (whose true beliefs do not amount to knowledge).

pp. 46–52, Pritchard 2010, pp. 8–16). This problem cannot arise unless true belief is taken to have some "epistemic" value.

5.2 The problem of the source of epistemic normativity

In this section I'll articulate two problems concerning the "source of epistemic normativity" (§§5.2.1–5.2.2), make a realist assumption about "epistemic normativity" (§5.2.3), and discuss the meaning of "epistemic" (§5.2.4).

5.2.1 Three questions about the source of epistemic value

A practice of evaluation will partition the elements of some domain into a hierarchy, in which some elements are said to be good, and others bad, or in which pairs of elements are said to stand in the relation of one being better than the other. In **epistemic evaluation**, beliefs are evaluated as true (good) or false (bad), as "epistemically" justified (good) or "epistemically" unjustified (bad), as "epistemically" rational (good) or "epistemically" irrational (bad), and as amounting to knowledge (good) or not (bad) (cf. Alston 1985, 2005, pp. 29–31, Sosa 2007, pp. 70–3). These evaluations are paradigm examples of "epistemic" evaluation, and of "epistemic" evaluation of beliefs, but the list is not meant to be exhaustive of "epistemic" evaluation, or of "epistemic" evaluation of belief.[3]

Consider the following epistemic principle:

Truth principle: For any subject S and proposition that p, S's belief that p is (in one respect) good iff it is true that p, and (in one respect) bad otherwise.

Someone who engages in epistemic evaluation will evaluate beliefs vis-à-vis this principle: she will count true beliefs as (in one respect) good, and false beliefs as (in one respect) bad. This rightly leaves open the possibility that there are other ways in which beliefs might be epistemically good. These might depend, in some sense, on the truth principle (e.g. a belief is good if formed in a reliable way), or not (if there are other fundamental epistemic goods). My discussion of epistemic value, in what follows, will be of the epistemic value of true belief, and for simplicity we shall often assume "truth value monism," on which truth is the only fundamental epistemic good (DePaul 2001, Sosa 2007, pp. 70–8, Pritchard 2010, pp. 13–16). This assumption will simplify our discussion, but our critical discussion of the epistemic value of true belief could be applied, mutatis mutandis, to other would-be fundamental epistemic goods.

---

[3] However, I'll treat this as enough to drop the scare quotes in what follows. We'll return to the characterization of the epistemic below (§9.3).

Evaluation seems to be in some sense "normative" (see also §5.2.2, §9.2.4): to say that something is good is to say that it is valuable, to recommend it, to praise it, to put it forward as something to be pursued, promoted, or admired, and to say that something is bad is to say that it is (in one respect) not valuable, to disapprove of it, to criticize it, to put it forward as something to be avoided or despised. In short, *evaluation* involves talking about *value*. Epistemic evaluation employs the truth principle, the truth principle says that true beliefs are good, therefore epistemic evaluation is (or at least seems) "normative." Some epistemologists have maintained that epistemic evaluation is "normative" (e.g. Alston 1988, Feldman 1988a, 2000). Epistemologists employ language that appears "normative": they speak of "epistemic justification," "epistemic warrant," what we "ought" to believe, or what we "should" believe, of "epistemic goodness" and "epistemic virtue," and so on. Epistemic evaluation seems sometimes to involve reactive attitudes (cf. §9.5.2). There seem to be cases in which we *blame* people for their epistemic failures: people should not have believed that there were weapons of mass destruction in Iraq; they were overly credulous. Such epistemic vice inspires our resentment and disapprobation. Similarly, there seem to be cases in which we *praise* people for their epistemic virtue: those who suspended judgment about the existence of such weapons in Iraq were appropriately careful in their thinking; they believed in the way that they should have. Such epistemic virtue inspires our admiration and respect. And epistemic evaluation of beliefs is, at least sometimes, the evaluation of persons. To say that David's *belief* that there are weapons in Iraq is unjustified is to say something about David—it's to say that *he* is unjustified in holding that belief. To evaluate a person's beliefs as irrational or unjustified is, at least sometimes, to say something about *her*: that she has fallen short of some standard, that she has done poorly, from an epistemic point of view. The same, mutatis mutandis, for evaluation of beliefs as rational or justified.

In any event, when it comes to epistemic evaluation, we can ask several explanatory questions. First, we can ask:

Basic question about epistemic evaluation: What (if anything) explains the fact that epistemic evaluation (e.g. evaluation of beliefs vis-à-vis the truth principle) is appropriate? What (if anything) justifies, or grounds, or warrants, or legitimates, this species of evaluation?

We will ask this question by asking about the appropriateness of evaluating beliefs vis-à-vis the truth principle and by seeking an account of the value of true belief (cf. §5.2.3). This is not to ignore other species of epistemic evaluation. But, even if "truth value monism" is false, an explanation of the epistemic value of true belief will surely be a first step in any explanation of epistemic value in general. Thus our focus in this book will be on the epistemic value of true belief.

We should not just say that the epistemic value of true belief explains the appropriateness of evaluation of beliefs vis-à-vis the truth principle (cf. §1.2.3, §9.1.1). We should seek an explanation of the appropriateness of epistemic evaluation that will *explain* the epistemic value of true belief. Otherwise we will have given no explanation at all: we will just have said that it's appropriate to call true beliefs good, because they are good. But to explain the value of true belief would be to explain the appropriateness of evaluating beliefs vis-à-vis the truth principle.

There is a question that is closely related to the basic question, concerning in particular the status of epistemic evaluation of beliefs. Consider:

Tuesday principle: For any subject S and proposition that p, S's belief that p is (in one respect) good iff S formed her belief that p on a Tuesday.

If we were to engage in evaluation of beliefs vis-à-vis the Tuesday principle, beliefs formed on Tuesdays would come out (in one respect) good, and beliefs formed on other days would come out (in one respect) bad. Many philosophers would say that evaluation of beliefs vis-à-vis the Tuesday principle is inappropriate in some sense, by contrast with epistemic evaluation.[4] Stephen Grimm (2009) writes:

It seems clear enough…that even though we can evaluate beliefs relative to countless different "fundamental values"…the end of realizing the truth enjoys a special sort of status when it comes to the evaluation of belief. (2009, p. 256)

Concerning this idea, we can ask:

Uniqueness question about epistemic evaluation: Does epistemic evaluation of beliefs (e.g. evalution vis-à-vis the truth principle) have a "special sort of status"? In what sense (if any)? Is epistemic evaluation of beliefs uniquely appropriate, in some sense? In what sense (if any)?

Finally, a satisfying account of epistemic value will also answer this question:

Scope question about epistemic evaluation: What principles, other than the truth principle, are *epistemic*? What defines or characterizes the standards of evaluation that are employed in *epistemic* evaluation? What *is* the domain of the epistemic?

The basic question about epistemic evaluation, the uniqueness question about epistemic evaluation, and the scope question about epistemic evaluation comprise the **problem of the source of epistemic value.**[5]

---

[4] The idea is that evaluation vis-à-vis the Tuesday principle would be inappropriate, given the way the world actually is. You can imagine situations in which evaluation vis-à-vis the Tuesday principle would be a kind of epistemic evaluation, e.g. if Tuesday were the only day of the week on which the newspaper is accurate.

[5] This problem is distinct from the Meno problem (§5.1), since the Meno problem presupposes the value of true belief. In this sense the problem of the source of epistemic value is more basic than the Meno problem. The problem of the source of epistemic value is also distinct from supposed problems for epistemic evaluation that arise from doxastic involuntarism (Alston 1988, Feldman 1988a, 2000, Ryan 2003, McHugh 2012b), although we shall return to doxastic involuntarism below (§§8.4–8.5).

The problem we have just articulated is based on Christine Korsgaard's (1996) "normative question" about "what *justifies* the claims that morality makes on us" (pp. 9–10). The question of justification arises because of the "normativity" of morality:

[E]thical standards are *normative*. They do not merely *describe* a way in which we in fact regulate our conduct. They make *claims* on us; they command, or oblige, recommend, or guide. Or at least, when we invoke them, we make claims on one another. When I say an action is right I am saying that you ought to *do* it; when I say that something is good I am recommending it as worthy of your choice. [...] Concepts like knowledge, beauty, and meaning, as well as virtue and justice, all have a normative dimension, for they tell us what to think, what to like, what to say, what to do, and what to be. (1996, pp. 8–9)

The same, mutatis mutandis, seems plausible when it comes to epistemic principles (like the truth principle): such principles seem to be "normative." Now despite this characterization, the notion of the "normative" is obscure. However, it is difficult to do without it in philosophy. As Korsgaard's characterization suggests, it is closely related to the notion of the prescriptive (which contrasts with the descriptive), with the notions of obligation and permission, and with the notions of value and reasons (which I'm concerned with here). We will proceed without giving a more explicit definition of the normative (and by dropping the scare quotes), but we will proceed with caution, and when some more articulated notion of the normative is in play, I'll say so.

So, along with the uniqueness question and the source question, our basic question is: what explains the appropriateness of epistemic evaluation? That's the problem of the source of epistemic value.

5.2.2 Epistemic value and epistemic reasons

Compare two principles:

Truth principle: For any subject S and proposition that p, S's belief that p is (in one respect) good if it is true that p, and (in one respect) bad otherwise.
Evidence norm: For any subject S and proposition that p, if S has evidence that p, then S has a pro tanto reason to believe that p.

We might distinguish between principles of the former kind, which speak of what is good or of what has value, and principles of the latter kind, which speak of reasons, by saying that principles of the former kind are **evaluative**, while principles of the latter kind are **narrowly normative**. The reasons posited by the evidence norm are **normative reasons**, rather than motivating or explanatory reasons. I understand "normative reasons" such that, necessarily, we ought to be responsive to the normative reasons that we have. When normative reasons exist, these reasons make demands on us, they require us to do (in a broad sense) certain things; as Korsgaard would put it (§5.2.1), normative reasons make claims on us. Evaluative principles tell us what is good or what has value; narrowly normative principles tell us what to do (in a broad sense), or what we ought to do (in a broad sense); they provide standards that ought to guide our conduct; they tell us about what normative reasons we have. The **broadly normative** covers both the evaluative and the narrowly normative. In what follows I'll use "normative" to mean "broadly normative," and explicitly note when we're considering narrow normativity.

Once this distinction is drawn, we can articulate a cousin of the problem of the source of epistemic value (§5.2.1): the **problem of the source of epistemic reasons**, which can be articulated by framing variants on our three questions:

Basic question about epistemic reasons attribution: What (if anything) explains the appropriateness of epistemic reasons attribution (e.g. utterances of <R is an epistemic reason for S to believe that p>).

Uniqueness question about epistemic reasons attribution: Does epistemic reasons attribution have a "special sort of status"? In what sense (if any)? Do, for example, epistemic reasons for belief have a special status as opposed to other sorts of reasons for belief?

Scope question about epistemic reasons attribution: What distinguishes *epistemic* reasons from non-epistemic reasons? What *is* the domain of the epistemic?

Together, the problem of the source of epistemic value and the problem of the source of epistemic reasons comprise the **problem of the source of epistemic normativity**.

Three positions on the relationship between epistemic value and epistemic reasons are available. The first is the view that epistemic value explains epistemic reasons. Suppose I have conclusive evidence that p, and thus have epistemic reason to believe that p. What explains the fact that I have epistemic reason to believe that p? On (one version of) the present view, the epistemic value of truth is what explains the fact that I have epistemic reason to believe that p. Believing on the basis of conclusive evidence will (if all goes well) lead to my acquisition of something of epistemic value: a true belief. In general, abiding by the evidence norm will conduce to my acquisition of things that are good, according to the truth principle. Asbjørn Steglich-Petersen (2011) calls this a **teleological conception of epistemic reasons**, on which "whether someone has a reason to believe some particular proposition p…depends on the value of the result of believing p" (p. 13). Thus the existence of epistemic value will explain the existence of epistemic reasons. This position is common among contemporary epistemologists; consider, for example, the appeal to truth as a good, or end, or goal (§5.1), and the idea that epistemic justification is a teleological notion (Goldman 1986, p. 98, 1999, Chapter 3, 2002, Chapter 3, Sosa 2007, Chapter 4, Greco 2003, 2010).

The second position is the view that epistemic reasons explain epistemic value (cf. Scanlon 1998, 78–107). On (one version of) this view, the fact that it is good for me to believe that p on conclusive evidence that p is explained by the fact that, in that situation, I have epistemic reason to believe that p.

The third position is the view that epistemic reasons and epistemic value are independent. On this view, the existence of epistemic reasons has nothing to do with the existence of epistemic value. Having epistemic reason to believe that p is not to be understood in terms of the (epistemic) value of believing that p, and vice versa. One might adopt this view on the basis of anti-realism about one, but not the other, of either epistemic reasons or epistemic value (cf. §5.2.3). So, for example, if you reject the existence of epistemic value, you might nevertheless want to defend the existence of epistemic reasons—in which case you would have to defend a conception of epistemic reasons on which they are independent of epistemic value.

We won't take a stand on the question of which of these three positions is correct. Rather, we will treat the problem of the source of epistemic value and the problem of the source of epistemic reasons as separate problems—in case the third position turns out to be correct. Because epistemic value has played such a prominent role in contemporary epistemology (§5.1), our primary concern is with epistemic evaluation, so our focus will continue to be on epistemic value, with a secondary concern being epistemic reasons. We'll consider both accounts of epistemic value, and in particular accounts of the epistemic value of true belief, as well as accounts of epistemic reasons. But we shall not, in general, assume any connection between them. However, since the teleological conception of epistemic reasons has been assumed by many contemporary epistemologists, I'll sometimes assume it for the sake of argument (§§5.3.1–5.3.2).

5.2.3 Realism about epistemic normativity

We will inquire after the appropriateness of evaluating beliefs vis-à-vis the truth principle, which says that true beliefs are good, by inquiring after the epistemic value of true belief. It seems clear, as we said above (§5.2.1), that an account of the value of true belief would be sufficient to explain the appropriateness of evaluation vis-à-vis the truth principle. We shall also tentatively assume the necessity of an account of the value of true belief, for explaining the appropriateness of evaluation vis-à-vis the truth principle. Let's make this realist assumption explicit:

Realism about epistemic value: The appropriateness of epistemic evaluation is explained by the existence of epistemic value.

Importantly, on this assumption, it is not the other way around (cf. Plato, *Euthyphro*, 10–11): it's not the case, for example, that true belief is good because it's appropriate to evaluate true beliefs as good. We'll make a similar assumption about epistemic reasons:

Realism about epistemic reasons: The appropriateness of epistemic reasons attribution is explained by the existence of epistemic reasons.

And not the other way around: it's not the case that S has epistemic reason to believe that p because it's appropriate to say that S has epistemic reason to believe that p. These two realisms together constitute **realism about epistemic normativity**.

Realism about epistemic normativity is prima facie plausible: evaluation of beliefs vis-à-vis the truth principle says that true beliefs are good, i.e. that they have value, so the most straightforward way to explain why evaluation of beliefs vis-à-vis the truth principle is appropriate is by appealing to the fact that true beliefs have value, otherwise evaluation of beliefs vis-à-vis the truth principle says something about them that isn't so. Similarly, the most natural way to explain the appropriateness of saying that someone has a reason to believe that p is by appealing to the fact that she does have reason to believe that p. Our strategy, therefore, will be to assume realism about epistemic normativity, and to see if we can find plausible realist accounts of epistemic value or epistemic reasons. Thus our inquiry will be an inquiry into the metaphysics of epistemic value and epistemic reasons, and in particular into the epistemic value of true belief. However, in the end (Chapter 9), I'll argue that we should reject realism about epistemic normativity.

5.2.4 *"Epistemic," "theoretical," "intellectual," "cognitive," "doxastic"*

It's common in contemporary philosophy to treat "epistemic" as synonymous with "theoretical," "intellectual," "cognitive," or "doxastic" (BonJour 1985, p. 7, Foley 1993, p. 41, Kelly 2003, p. 612, Lynch 2004, p. 47, 2009a, p. 228, Alston 2005, pp. 29–43, Sosa 2007, p. 160, Kvanvig 2010, p. 101, Baehr 2011, pp. 107–11). Above (§1.3) we resisted this move. Let's examine these matters more closely.

Below (§§5.3–5.4), we will consider some views which imply that "epistemic" is synonymous with "theoretical," "intellectual," "cognitive," and "doxastic." We'll call this a **doxastic conception of the epistemic**, since it defines the epistemic in terms of belief (theorizing, intellection, cognition). On this view, what fundamentally contrasts with the epistemic is the practical (cf. §1.3), and perhaps also the affective, the volitional, and other such domains of activity (broadly construed). This jibes with some uses of "epistemic" in contemporary philosophy. For example, "epistemic agency" is often used to refer to our active capacities as believers; for another, the question of whether an attitude is "epistemic" is often just the question of whether it is belief-entailing.

The alternative to this is to understand the epistemic in terms of the valuation of certain goods, like knowledge, truth, and understanding. This is an **axial conception of the epistemic**, since it defines the epistemic in terms of what is epistemically valuable. On this view, what fundamentally contrasts with the epistemic is the eudaimonic, the moral, the aesthetic, and other domains of value. I'll propose an axial account of the epistemic, below (§9.3).

From the perspective of an axial conception of the epistemic, the doxastic conception looks like it might involve a misuse of "epistemic," akin to the misuse of "moral" in "moral psychology." For what is called "moral psychology" does not concern morality per se, but rather a wide range of topics pertaining to affect and action. To call these topics "moral psychology" is to suggest, obliquely, that affect and action are essentially governed by morality. Similarly, to equate the epistemic with the doxastic likewise suggests, obliquely, that belief is essentially governed by epistemic principles.

That *is* a view that many philosophers hold, and it's the principal target of the rest of this book (Chapters 6–8). And I'll criticize another view that implies a doxastic conception of the epistemic (§5.3). We should not assume a doxastic conception of the epistemic, therefore, since this would stack the deck in favor of some controversial views.

5.3 Eudaimonic approaches to epistemic normativity

Linda Zagzebski argues that "[e]pistemic evaluation just *is* a form of moral evaluation" (1996, p. 256) and that "[t]here is no independent domain of epistemic value" (2004, p. 353; see also Baehr 2011, Appendix). The idea here is that epistemic evaluation is moral evaluation of people, in their capacity as believers; it is the moral evaluation of people's intellectual or cognitive conduct. On Zagzebski's (2004) view, this avoids the common "mistake of thinking that epistemic value is a special category of value in competition with, and perhaps incommensurable with, moral and pragmatic value" (p. 369). (Note that this implies a doxastic conception of the epistemic, §5.2.4.) Is this a plausible approach to epistemic normativity?

In this section I'll articulate and criticize a eudaimonic account of epistemic value (§5.3.1). Then I'll argue that the same criticism applies to an idea closer to what Zagzebski proposes: a "Cliffordian" account of epistemic value (§5.3.2). I'll then consider two ways that these accounts might respond to my objection (§§5.3.3–5.3.4).

5.3.1 The objection from universalism about epistemic normativity

Consider the following **eudaimonic account of epistemic value** (cf. Zagzebski 2003b, pp. 24–5): "epistemic" value is just eudaimonic value, when it comes to matters theoretical, intellectual, cognitive, or doxastic. (Note again that this implies a doxastic conception of the epistemic, §5.2.4.) To say that a belief is epistemically valuable is just to say that it is eudaimonically valuable. Indeed, to say that true belief has epistemic value is redundant: the eudaimonic value of true belief is "epistemic" just because true belief is a species of belief, so "epistemically valuable belief" is more perspicuously rendered "valuable belief" or "eudaimonically valuable belief."

This account faces three related objections. The first arises in connection with the existence of eudaimonically valuable false beliefs (Chapters 2 and 3). If epistemic value is just eudaimonic value, when it comes to matters doxastic, then biased beliefs are often epistemically valuable. Wishful thinking is often epistemically valuable. If anything is "intuitive" about the epistemic, it's that biased beliefs and wishful thinking are epistemically bad. I conclude that the eudaimonic account of epistemic normativity will not work.

The second objection arises if we assume a teleological conception of epistemic reasons (§5.2.2). Consider, for example, Hilary Kornblith's (1993) account of "epistemic normativity," on which everyone "has pragmatic reasons to favor a cognitive system which is effective in generating truths" (p. 371). Given this assumption, eudaimonically worthless true beliefs (§§4.2–4.3) will lie outside the scope of appropriate epistemic reasons attribution. As Zagzebski argues, "some true beliefs are undesirable" (2003b, p. 25) and "it is doubtful that every item of knowledge contributes to a flourishing life, so even if there is a demand…that we have conscientiously formed beliefs, the demand probably does not extend to every possible belief" (2004, p. 368). When it comes to eudaimonically worthless true beliefs, "I am violating no obligation if the belief is unjustified, that is, is not formed conscientiously" (p. 372).

But this seems wrong: it seems that we can have epistemic reasons in support of eudaimonically worthless true beliefs. As Tom Kelly (2003) argues, the possession of epistemic reasons to believe that p is not contingent on a person being curious:

[F]rom the fact that some subjects are matters of complete indifference to me, it does not follow that I will inevitably lack epistemic reasons for holding beliefs on those subjects. If, despite my utter lack of interest in the question of whether Bertrand Russell was left-handed, I stumble upon strong evidence that he was, then I have strong epistemic reasons to believe that Bertrand Russell was left-handed. (2003, p. 625)

As Richard Feldman (2000) puts it, "all people epistemically ought to follow their evidence, not just those who have adopted some specifically epistemic goals" (p. 682). But notice that the proposition in Kelly's example is also useless and insignificant. From the fact that some subjects are completely uninteresting *and* useless *and* insignificant, it does not follow that we lack epistemic reasons for holding beliefs on those subjects. If epistemic reasons derived from the eudaimonic value of true belief (or knowledge, or whatever), then I would have no epistemic reason to believe that Russell was left-handed. Making the same point, Stephen Grimm (2008) asks us to imagine a case of incurious belief formation: absent any desire to know the answer to the question of how many motes of dust there are on your doctor's waiting room coffee table, if you come to believe that there are 53 motes on the table, "we evidently *can* evaluate…the epistemic status of your belief. For example, if you were sloppy and careless in your counting, we would be inclined to judge your belief *unjustified*" (p. 742; see also 2009, pp. 253–7). Marian David (2001) points out that even someone without a desire to know the truth would have epistemically justified and epistemically unjustified beliefs (p. 156). And as Ernest Sosa (2001) argues, "[k]nowing the answer to a question does not require that one be motivated by a disinterested desire for the truth on that question, nor even by a desire for the truth as such, whether interested or disinterested" (p. 53). Someone lacking such a desire "can still know the answer to his question, so long as he accepts it on good enough evidence" (ibid. p. 52). Thus, Sosa (2003) concludes, the "aptness of a belief…is *not* proportional to how well that belief furthers" our goal of believing the truth and nothing but the truth (p. 159); belief in an uninteresting truth "may be epistemically rational to the highest degree" (ibid.). As Zagzebski (2003a) argues elsewhere, exempting beliefs about uninteresting propositions from epistemic evaluation "makes epistemic value too much a matter of personal preference," and "[e]pistemologists have rarely been so tolerant" (p. 139). But notice that the proposition in Grimm's example is also useless and insignificant. Given a teleological conception of epistemic reasons, we would have no epistemic reasons to believe this proposition. It seems that, in general, if epistemic value explains epistemic reasons, a eudaimonic account of epistemic value will have the implication that eudaimonically worthless true beliefs lie outside the scope of epistemic normativity. This, like the idea that biased beliefs and wishful thinking can be epistemically valuable, is counterintuitive.

We can make an assumption of this argument explicit:

Universalism about epistemic normativity: Epistemic evaluation is appropriate for all possible beliefs; epistemic reasons attribution is appropriate for all possible beliefs.

This assumption will play an important role in my criticism of "Cliffordian" (§5.3.2) and "Humean" (§6.3.1) approaches to epistemic normativity. Accounts that violate universalism about epistemic normativity seem to have failed, in an important way, to give an account of the appropriateness of epistemic evaluation or of epistemic reasons attribution. However, those skeptical of universalism may take comfort in the fact that I find no realist and universalist account of epistemic normativity plausible, and eventually turn to anti-realism about epistemic normativity (Chapter 9).

The third objection arises in connection with the fact that all beliefs are not created equal when it comes to their eudaimonic value (§§4.2–4.3). Again, assume a teleological conception of epistemic reasons. Suppose I have conclusive evidence both that the number of grains of sand on the beach at Coney Island is even *and* that the Higgs boson exists. Given our assumption, the eudaimonic account of epistemic normativity implies that I have *greater* epistemic reason to believe the latter than I have to believe the former, despite having conclusive evidence that both propositions are true. This is implausible.[6]

5.3.2 A Cliffordian account of epistemic value

Recall Zagzebski's idea that epistemic value is a species of moral value. We can develop this idea by articulating a **Cliffordian account of epistemic value**, on which "epistemic" value is social value (§4.4), when it comes to matters theoretical, intellectual, cognitive, or doxastic. (Note again that this implies a doxastic conception of the epistemic, §5.2.4.) Several contemporary epistemologists follow Zagzebski and write of

---

[6] Although it seems no less (and no more) plausible than the view, known as **pragmatic encroachment**, that epistemic justification, or knowledge, or epistemic virtue requires more reliability, evidence, or inquiry when the practical stakes are high than when they are low (Fantl and McGrath 2002, 2009, Zagzebski 2004, p. 374, Stanley 2005, Hawthorne 2006; cf. Baril forthcoming).

"epistemic" value in connection with the social value of knowledge (Kusch 2009, p. 60, Sosa 2010, p. 172; cf. Fricker 2009). My three objections to our eudaimonic account of epistemic value (§5.3.1) apply, mutatis mutandis, to this Cliffordian account.

First, there can be socially valuable false beliefs. Zagzebski (2004) writes that "[f]alse beliefs...can be beneficial to the agent or conducive to morality" (p. 369). But it's implausible that there can be *epistemically* valuable false beliefs. Second, assuming a teleological conception of epistemic reasons (§5.2.2), the Cliffordian account will imply that we cannot have epistemic reasons for or against **socially irrelevant** beliefs, i.e. true beliefs with no social value or false beliefs with no social disvalue (§4.4.2). Clifford argues that the risk of direct and testimonial harm that comes with false belief gives us a strong reason to cleave to our evidence. But such reason is absent, when the risk of direct and testimonial harm is absent. Someone who has conclusive evidence that *paperclip* is true will have no epistemic reason to believe that *paperclip* is true. And the last person on earth will have no epistemic reason to believe anything. Socially irrelevant beliefs will lie outside the scope of epistemic normativity. Third, again assuming a teleological conception of epistemic reasons, since some true beliefs are more socially valuable than others, our Cliffordian account will have the implausible implication that I have greater epistemic reason to believe that the number 5 bus goes to Meadowbank than I have to believe that *paperclip* is true, even when I have conclusive evidence that both propositions are true, and that I will have greater epistemic reason to believe that I am sitting in my office than Crusoe will have to believe that he is sitting in his hut, even though we both have conclusive evidence that both propositions are true. All this is counterintuitive.

It seems that we cannot give a purely socio-epistemological account of the value of true belief. While Edward Craig (1990) tells a social story about the origin of our concept of knowledge, his account of the value of true belief (pp. 130–3) is individualistic: an agent "needs true beliefs about what will happen if he undertakes such and such course of action" (p. 132), and this provides a crucial premise in his story: "Human beings need true beliefs about their environment, beliefs that can serve to guide their actions to a successful outcome" (p. 11). The original value of true belief isn't social value, on Craig's view: it's good old-fashioned instrumental eudaimonic value. Similarly, Bernard Williams' (2002, Chapter 3) genealogical account of the values of truth and truthfulness assumes that "the pooling of information" is "important to almost every human purpose" (p. 57), and that true belief is valuable because of "the value of getting what one wants, avoiding danger, mastering the environment, and so on" (p. 58). The value of true belief depends "on other, perhaps more primitive, values and needs, such as securing co-operative activity which is in everyone's interests" (p. 90). Consider, finally, Martin Kusch (2009) on the epistemic value of "protoknowledge," which is said to have had "a distinctive epistemic value: the value of having true beliefs coming from...a detectable good informant" (p. 67). The value of "protoknowledge" (and presumably the value of knowledge) here depends on the antecedent value of true belief. Thus these socio-epistemological accounts, in an important sense, pass the buck on the value of true belief. Why is it bad to believe falsely? Because of the risk of false testimony. Why is false testimony bad? Because it leads people to have false beliefs. And why are these bad? At this point we must appeal to some independent value of true belief that is not explained in terms of the risk of testimonial harm.

5.3.3 Epistemic value vs. the value of epistemic evaluation

You might object that this misses the point of the socio-epistemological argument (§4.4.1). It may have been true, at some early stage in our development, that we valued true belief only instrumentally—and thus its value might have been seen to vary with the interestingness or significance of the proposition believed (as with *paperclip*), or with the social circumstances of the believer (as with Crusoe). But we have come to value true belief *for its own sake*. As Williams (2002) argues, "no society can get by…with a purely instrumental conception of the values of truth" (p. 59). "The idea of this intrinsic value has to be shared," he says, "and it has to be understood as part of the culture that it is shared" (p. 90). Reflection on the social origins of the practice of epistemic evaluation explains why we presently engage in a **universalist practice** of epistemic evaluation (i.e. a practice consistent with universalism about epistemic evaluation)—why we treat every true belief as valuable (in epistemic evaluation) or why we treat every true belief as equally valuable (in epistemic reasons attribution). So we were wrong to maintain a tension between Cliffordian approaches and universalism.

I reply that this idea is orthogonal to the soundness of my argument. I have argued (for example) that the Cliffordian account (§5.3.2) implies that some true beliefs are epistemically worthless. It's consistent with this that we have social reason to engage in a *practice* of treating all true beliefs as valuable—i.e. the practice of epistemic evaluation (§5.2.1). My conclusion was about the value of true belief, not about the value of epistemic evaluation. It's one thing to vindicate the practice of treating x as valuable; it's another thing to explain the value of x.

My objection is that Williams has not explained the value of true belief, but only why "it is useful for people to treat it as though it had an intrinsic value" (p. 90). However, Williams writes that for true belief to have intrinsic value it is only required that "[t]hose who treat it as having an intrinsic value [are] able to make sense of it as having an intrinsic value" (p. 91). On this view:

[I]t is in fact a sufficient condition for something…to have an intrinsic value that, first, it is necessary (or nearly necessary) for basic human purposes and needs that human beings should treat it as an intrinsic good; and, second, they can coherently treat it as an intrinsic good. (p. 92)

The intrinsic value of true belief can thus be seen as "constructed" (p. 93; see also Kusch 2009, p. 76). This approach to the value of true belief rejects realism about epistemic value (§5.2.5): rather than explaining the appropriateness of epistemic evaluation by appeal to the value of true belief, Williams proposes to explain the value of true belief by appeal to the appropriateness of epistemic evaluation, which in turn is given a justification in terms of social utility. I am sympathetic to anti-realism about epistemic normativity, and I'll defend it below (Chapter 9). And I concede that an anti-realist Cliffordian approach to epistemic normativity might be plausible. I conclude here that, given our assumption of realism, a Cliffordian approach is not plausible.

5.3.4 Rule teleologism

You might object that our eudaimonic account of epistemic value (§5.3.1) or our Cliffordian account of epistemic value (§5.3.2) can avoid the objection from universalism by adopting a more subtle teleological account of epistemic reasons. Above, we assumed something like:

> **Simple teleologism:** S has epistemic reason to believe that p iff S's believing that p would be eudaimonically (or socially) valuable.

This led to unappealing implications, when combined with the premise that there are eudaimonically worthless true beliefs (or socially irrelevant beliefs). We could avoid these implications by adopting:

> **Rule teleologism:** S has epistemic reason to believe that p iff S's believing that p is licensed by norms whose adoption would be eudaimonically (or socially) valuable.

Consider, for example, the evidence norm (§5.2.2). We might argue that the individual adoption of this norm, as a guiding principle or rule, would be eudaimonically valuable (or that the group adoption of this norm, as an expectation or law, would be socially valuable). The problem with this move is that rule teleologism is not plausible unless we amend it to allow for exceptional cases. Consider rule utilitarianism: this is plausible as a form of utilitarianism only if we allow for permission to violate the rules in exceptional cases. This is why Mill writes, in *Utilitarianism*, that the rule prohibiting lying "admits of possible exceptions…when the withholding of some fact (as of information from a malefactor, or of bad news from a person dangerously ill) would save an individual…from great and unmerited evil" (2001, p. 23). If the value of happiness explains the rightness and wrongness of actions, then it may indeed generally be right to follow the rule "Do not lie," but it cannot always be right: there are exceptions, when the consequences of not lying would be bad enough. But for the same reason, if the eudaimonic (or social) value of true belief explains the existence of epistemic reasons, then there will be exceptions to the evidence norm. Consider a case in which I have conclusive evidence that p, but in which believing that p would be very bad for me (it will cause great pain and distress, and will have no benefit whatsoever). Any plausible defense of rule teleologism will need to allow this as an exception to the evidence norm. But this is implausible: even though believing that p would be very bad for me, I still have *epistemic* reason to believe that p, given the fact that I have conclusive evidence that p. (The same, mutatis mutandis, when it comes to a case in which I have conclusive evidence that p, but in which believing that p would be very bad for society.)

5.4 Epistemic essentialism about belief

From universalism about epistemic normativity (§5.3.1), we can deduce that, if some feature of belief explains the appropriateness of epistemic evaluation and epistemic reasons attribution, then it must be present in all possible beliefs, i.e. it must be a necessary feature of belief. Features that flow from the essential nature of belief are necessary features of beliefs. (The converse is not true: beliefs are necessarily such that $2 + 2 = 4$, but this doesn't flow from the essence of belief.) This thought (cf. McHugh 2011a, p. 371) motivates the view that we'll call "epistemic essentialism about belief," which is introduced in this section and critically examined below (Chapters 6–8).

5.4.1 Truth as the "aim of belief"

There is a rich philosophical tradition that maintains an essential connection between belief and truth. Such a connection, if it exists, would explain the appropriateness of evaluation of beliefs vis-à-vis the truth principle, and the inappropriateness of evaluation of beliefs vis-à-vis the Tuesday principle. Recall Aristotle's idea that "[o]f the intellect that is contemplative…the good and bad state are truth and falsity respectively (for this is the work of everything intellectual)" (1139a 26–9). In contemporary philosophy, we find the idea that truth is the "aim of belief" (Williams 1976, Humberstone 1992, Velleman 2000, Chapter 11, Sosa 2007, Chapter 4, 2009, Steglich-Petersen 2006, 2009, McHugh 2011a), that the biological function of belief is to be true (Millikan 1984, 1993, 2006, Papineau 1993, Neander 1991, 1995; cf. Alston 2005, pp. 29–30), and that truth is the constitutive standard of correctness for belief (Wedgwood 2002, Boghossian 2003, 2005, Shah 2003, Shah and Velleman 2005, Hieronymi 2006, Lynch 2009a, 2009b). All these views entail:

> **Epistemic essentialism about belief:** Epistemic evaluation of beliefs, in particular evaluation of beliefs vis-à-vis the truth principle, is the evaluation of beliefs, qua beliefs, i.e. the evaluation of beliefs as the kinds of things that they essentially are.

This suggests the following approach to epistemic value:

> **Epistemic essentialist approach to epistemic value:** Epistemic evaluation of beliefs (e.g. evaluation vis-à-vis the truth principle) is appropriate, because, and in the sense that, epistemic evaluation of beliefs is the evaluation of beliefs, qua beliefs.

What does it mean to say that epistemic evaluation of beliefs is the evaluation of beliefs, qua beliefs? Epistemic essentialism can take several forms (§5.4.2), and the details are different in each case. But the basic idea can be gotten at by considering the evaluation of an artifact, for example, this knife. Certain evaluations of this knife are appropriate in a way that other evaluations aren't. I have in mind evaluations of the knife in terms of how sharp it is, or how well it cuts, or stabs, or whatever—i.e. evaluations of the knife vis-à-vis standards that are set by its function or purpose, which standards flow from the essential nature of the knife. This is evaluation of the knife, qua knife. Compare evaluation of the knife in terms of how well it works as a paperweight, or as a doorstop, or evaluation of the knife that takes dullness to be good and sharpness to be bad, and so on. This would not be evaluation of the knife, qua knife.

Artifacts like knives are such that standards of evaluation flow from their essential nature. Although it's not plausible to analogize beliefs to artifacts (cf. §7.1), the epistemic essentialist's claim is that beliefs, too, are such that standards of evaluation flow from their essential nature. In particular, the truth principle is one that flows from the essential nature of belief. Call the evaluation of x vis-à-vis standards that flow from the essential nature of x **essential evaluation**. The epistemic essentialist's claim, then, is that epistemic evaluation of beliefs is essential evaluation. And this is how epistemic essentialism answers the basic question about epistemic evaluation (§5.2.1).

The epistemic essentialist might maintain not only that epistemic evaluation of beliefs is essential evaluation, but that *only* epistemic evaluation of beliefs is essential evaluation. For example, this would be natural on the view that truth is *the* "aim of belief." To say that epistemic evaluation of beliefs, and only epistemic evaluation of beliefs, is essential evaluation does not mean that there might not be situations in which it would be best, all things considered, to evaluate beliefs in some other way. In general, there are situations in which the best evaluation, all things considered, is not essential evaluation. Again, consider a knife. In desperate need of a paperweight, my best course of action might be to assess the suitability, qua paperweight, of all the objects on my desk; if I need a knife as a prop for a stage play, a dull knife might be best, and a sharp knife unacceptably dangerous. The epistemic essentialist's point is that epistemic evaluation will always be appropriate *in a sense that* non-epistemic evaluation isn't. Epistemic evaluation has a special status among ways of evaluating beliefs; it has pride of place among ways of evaluating beliefs. This is how epistemic essentialism could answer the uniqueness question about epistemic evaluation (§5.2.1).

If epistemic evaluation of beliefs is essential evaluation, then there is an obvious sense in which epistemic goods can be called "theoretical," "intellectual," "cognitive" or "doxastic" goods. Epistemic essentialist approaches to epistemic value, therefore, imply a doxastic conception of the epistemic (§5.2.4). This is how epistemic essentialists answer the scope question about epistemic evaluation (§5.2.1).

Related essentialist answers can be given to our three questions about epistemic reasons (§5.2.2). Three remarks about essential evaluation, in general, before turning to the various forms that epistemic essentialism can take.

Note first that not all things admit of essential evaluation. Consider this sample of barium. There is no such thing as "the evaluation of barium, qua barium." So even granting that the sample is essentially a sample of barium, there simply are no standards of evaluation that flow from its essential nature.

Second, the notion of "essential evaluation" is ambiguous, because "the evaluation of x, qua x" is ambiguous between a de re and a de dicto reading. On the de dicto reading, the evaluation of x, qua x, is evaluation vis-à-vis standards that flow from the essential nature of the kind denoted by $<x>$. On the de re reading, the evaluation of x, qua x, is evaluation vis-à-vis standards that flow from the essential nature of x itself. The difference is that essential evaluation, in the de dicto sense, may evaluate x vis-à-vis standards that flow from the nature of x-ness, even if x is not essentially an x. Essential evaluation, in the de re sense, is the evaluation of x vis-à-vis standards that flow from the de re essential nature of x. Consider this particular lawyer, Megan. We can evaluate this lawyer, qua lawyer, by evaluating her vis-à-vis standards that flow from the essential nature of the kind *lawyer*. But, so we may easily imagine, Megan is not essentially a lawyer. So this evaluation will not be essential evaluation, in the de re sense. Megan is many things other than a lawyer: a friend, a lover, an amateur golfer. We could just as well engage in essential evaluation, in the de dicto sense, by evaluating her vis-à-vis standards of evaluation that flow from the essential natures of the kinds *friend*, *lover*, and *golfer*. Epistemic essentialism is committed not only to the claim that epistemic evaluation of beliefs is essential evaluation, in the de dicto sense, but also that epistemic evaluation of beliefs is essential evaluation, in the de re sense. For only essential evaluation, in the de re sense, involves the evaluation of x as the kind of thing that x essentially is. According to epistemic essentialism, epistemic evaluation is the evaluation of beliefs vis-à-vis standards of evaluation that flow from the de re essential nature of individual beliefs. On the most natural version of this, epistemic evaluation is the evaluation of beliefs vis-à-vis standards of evaluation that flow from the essential nature of the kind *belief*, and beliefs are essentially beliefs.

Finally, essential evaluation is not eudaimonic evaluation (cf. §5.3). Epistemic essentialism alone has no eudaimonic implications. That truth is the "aim of belief" does not entail that true belief is always or ever good for us, because of either its instrumental or its constitutive eudaimonic value. If the epistemic value of true belief is explained by appeal to the thesis that truth is the "aim of belief," then this value is not eudaimonic value.

5.4.2 Three species of epistemic essentialism about belief

Epistemic essentialism, as formulated above, leaves open questions about the essential nature of belief. How is belief's essential nature to be understood? What explains the fact that standards of evaluation flow from belief's essential nature? Philosophers have offered radically different answers to these questions. Below (Chapters 6–8), we'll critically examine the three species of epistemic essentialism found in the contemporary literature. Here I'll briefly introduce them.

In general, when I attempt to do something and fail, my attempt warrants a negative evaluation, and when I attempt to do something and succeed, my attempt warrants a positive evaluation. There is a species of value that derives from attempting, or intending, or trying to do something, or from desiring some end, or from making something one's goal, or from aiming at something. When I aim at something and succeed in acquiring it, something good has happened, and when I aim at something and fail to acquire it, something bad has happened. Successes are good; failures are bad. Combine this with the view that beliefs are essentially attempts to believe the truth, or **Humean**

essentialism about belief, and you can give an account of epistemic normativity. On this view, belief is analogous to an archer's shot.[7] An archer's shot is successful if and only if it hits the target; a belief is successful if and only if it is true. We'll examine Humean essentialism, and other Humean approaches to epistemic normativity, below (Chapter 6).

You might think that this overintellectualizes belief, by understanding the "purpose of belief" too literally. Alternatively, we could understand the "purpose of belief" in terms of belief's natural history. Consider the human heart, whose biological function is to pump blood throughout the body. According to **Darwinian essentialism about belief**, just as the heart's biological function is to pump blood, belief's biological function is to represent the world accurately, in other words, to be true. This is the biological function of belief, given how it was "designed" by natural selection. We'll examine Darwinian approaches to epistemic normativity below (Chapter 7).

Another route of resistance to the Humean approach comes from philosophers of a Kantian persuasion. These philosophers maintain that it is an a priori conceptual truth that a belief that p is correct if and only if it is true that p, regardless of the desires of the believer. The concept of belief, on this view, is a normative concept. We'll examine this **Kantian essentialism about belief**, and its approach to epistemic normativity, below (Chapter 8).

All three versions of epistemic essentialism maintain that belief "aims at truth," although each would offer a different explanation of that slogan. To explain the sense in which non-epistemic evaluation is inappropriate, epistemic essentialists standardly maintain that truth is *the* "aim of belief."[8]

All three versions of epistemic essentialism maintain that truth is a constitutive standard of correctness for belief. There is a standard of correctness, namely, being true, for belief, and this standard is "constitutive" in the sense that it flows from the essential nature of belief—at least part of what it is to be a belief is to have this standard of correctness. What is distinctive of the different versions of epistemic essentialism is how they explain the fact that truth is the constitutive standard of correctness for belief. For Humeans this is a consequence of the fact that belief is an attempt to believe the truth. For Darwinians it's an a posteriori fact about belief's natural history. For Kantians it's a consequence of the normativity of the concept of belief.

Note well that Darwinian essentialism about belief, if true, is knowable only a posteriori (§7.6). Just as the question of the heart's biological function is an empirical matter, so is the question of belief's biological function. So this species of essentialism cannot be established a priori. On the other hand, Kantian essentialism, if true, is knowable a priori. Humean essentialism can be understood as a conceptual truth (Steglich-Petersen 2009, p. 396), although it need not be.

---

[7] On one understanding of archery; see §6.1.1.

[8] This isn't necessary; one could maintain that belief essentially aims at a plurality of positive epistemic statuses—truth, epistemic justification, knowledge—and still get to say that non-epistemic evaluation is not essential evaluation.

5.5 Naturalism and normativity

In what follows I shall assume that some form of philosophical naturalism is true, and that, if some form of philosophical naturalism is true, then we have pro tanto reason to avoid positing irreducible normative properties, in giving an account of epistemic normativity. In this section I'll give two arguments for why naturalists should try to avoid positing irreducible normativity.[9]

For our purposes here, a property is **irreducible** iff it cannot be reduced to natural properties. No friend of naturalism, Ralph Wedgwood (2007) writes that "[a] property counts as a 'natural property' if a constitutive account of the property need not refer to any normative or evaluative property or relation" (p. 145). Thus a normative property will be irreducible when it cannot be reduced to properties that we can account for in non-normative terms. And for our purposes we can adopt a relatively modest, if rough, conception of reduction: property P_1 is reducible to property P_2 when the instantiation of P_2 completely explains the instantiation of P_1. If my assumption is right, we naturalists have pro tanto reason to avoid positing irreducible value (i.e. the property of being good) and irreducible normative reasons (i.e. the property of being a normative reason). In other words:

> **First naturalistic constraint:** We have pro tanto reason to avoid positing irreducible normative properties.

Why think this? We might articulate philosophical naturalism either as a **metaphysical** thesis (a claim about the world) or as a **methodological** thesis (a claim about how we ought to proceed in philosophy). We might define naturalism as a metaphysical thesis, and build the nonexistence of irreducible value into our definition. Naturalism could be defined in *via negativa* fashion, as the thesis that there are no irreducible normative properties, no irreducible mental properties, no irreducible biological properties, and so on. Compare David Papineau and Barbara Montero's (2005) *via negativa* argument for physicalism, and Alvin Plantinga's (2002) definition of "philosophical naturalism," as "the belief that there aren't any supernatural beings—no such person as God, for example, but also no other supernatural entities, and nothing at all like God" (p. 1). Alternatively we might define naturalism as a methodological thesis, and build in the first naturalistic constraint. In either case, the first naturalistic constraint would follow straight away from the definition, and there would be a tight definitional connection between naturalism and avoiding irreducible normativity. Ruth Millikan (1984), for example, writes that we must articulate the notion of a proper function in "naturalist, nonnormative, and nonmysterious terms" (p. 17). In any event, many philosophers think that naturalism and irreducible normativity are in tension. Can we

---

[9] The naturalistic challenge to irreducible normativity articulated here is different from (though possibly related to) the idea that realists about reasons cannot explain the essential motivating force of normative reasons. I follow Parfit (2006, pp. 332–51) in rejecting any such motivational requirement on normative reasons.

delve deeper, and explain why some such naturalistic constraint follows from philosophical naturalism? Consider David Armstrong's (1978) definition of (metaphysical) naturalism as "the doctrine that reality consists of nothing but a single all-embracing spatio-temporal system" (p. 261). Armstrong takes this to imply that there are no "transcendent standards of value" (p. 263). But why think this?

One reason naturalists have, to avoid positing irreducible normative properties, is a reason that everyone has, based on the appeal of **parsimony**. For naturalists, the "spatio-temporal system" is all there is; but everyone agrees to the existence of the naturalist's "spatio-temporal system."[10] And normative properties are not straightforwardly part of that system. Consider a paradigm naturalistic worldview (in Armstrong's sense of "naturalistic"): **Humean supervenience**, on which "all there is to the world is a vast mosaic of local matters of particular fact, just one little thing and then another" (Lewis 1986, p. ix). What exists is "a system of external relations of spatiotemporal distance between points[, and] at those points we have local qualities…[a]nd that is all" (ibid.). Even if you reject the idea that Lewis' Humean world is "all there is to the world," you can agree that that world exists. But normative properties (being good, being valuable, being a reason) are neither spatiotemporal relations nor local properties of space–time points. And while properties reducible to natural properties are no ontological addition to the "spatio-temporal system," irreducible properties are an ontological addition. They are therefore unappealing from the perspective of parsimony. Thus everyone should endorse the first naturalistic constraint.

Why have we only pro tanto reason to avoid positing irreducible normativity, according to the first naturalistic constraint? Because parsimony isn't everything. An ontology without rhinos might be simpler and more austere, but we've come face-to-face with too many rhinos for this to be plausible. The idea behind the first naturalistic constraint is that there is an argumentative burden on the philosopher who wants to expand our ontology to include irreducible normative properties.

But for the naturalist, there is an additional reason to avoid positing irreducible normative properties (of a certain kind). This comes from a version of Jaegwon Kim's (1993a, 2000, 2007) **causal exclusion argument** against non-reductive physicalism. Kim's famous argument assumes physicalism and argues against mental properties that are not reducible to physical properties. My argument assumes naturalism and argues against normative properties that are not reducible to non-normative properties. Where Kim's argument assumes the causal closure of the physical (1993a, p. 280), mine assumes the **causal closure of the non-normative:** any non-normative event that has a cause has a sufficient non-normative cause. Naturalists, I maintain, must accept this. (Moreover, it seems implicated by the supervenience of everything on the natural.) Where Kim's argument assumes the causal efficacy of mental properties (p. 279), mine will assume (for the sake of argument) the **causal efficacy of normative properties**: the

---

[10] I exclude, perhaps, certain species of idealism.

fact that Mozart's music is good caused me to buy a ticket to the opera, the fact that suffering is bad caused me to donate to tsunami relief, the fact that it was my duty to vote caused me to vote, the fact that it would be wrong to vote for the other parties caused me to vote Green, the fact that I had normative epistemic reason to believe that p caused me to believe that p, and so on. But my buying a ticket, my donation, my voting Green, and my believing that p are all non-normative events, and thus (given the causal closure of the non-normative) they each have a (sufficient) non-normative cause. What then is the relationship between the normative causes of these events and their (sufficient) non-normative causes? We can say either:

(i)   that the non-normative cause completely explains the normative cause (i.e. the normative cause is reducible to the non-normative cause), or

(ii) that the non-normative cause does not completely explain the normative cause.

Option (ii) is unappealing. As Kim argues, "a cause, or causal explanation, of an event, when it is regarded as a full, sufficient cause of explanation, appears to *exclude* other *independent* causes or causal explanations of it" (ibid. p. 281). We should not maintain that my buying of an opera ticket, along with every other event caused by a normative event, has a sufficient non-normative cause *and* a normative cause. Our argument's crucial premise is that such systematic causal **overdetermination** is not credible. Better to accept that the normative can be explained in terms of the non-normative and accept option (i), i.e. that the normative properties in question are not irreducible.[11] Thus naturalists should accept the following:

Second naturalistic constraint: We have pro tanto reason to avoid positing (causally efficacious) irreducible normative properties.

Why have we only pro tanto reason to avoid positing (causally efficacious) irreducible normativity? Because, although systematic causal overdetermination is unappealing, it's not impossible. But there is a significant argumentative burden on the philosopher who wants to posit (causally efficacious) irreducible normative properties, since doing this commits us to unappealing systematic causal overdetermination.

The upshot of my Kim-style argument is that we naturalists are under pressure to explain normative properties in non-normative terms, to preserve their causal efficacy. Now Kim's argument against non-reductive physicalism is, of course, controversial (cf. Fodor 1989, Davidson 1993, Yablo 1992, Jackson 1996, Bennett 2003, Block 2003, Ney 2012). It's beyond the scope of the present inquiry here to provide a full defense of the causal exclusion argument for the naturalistic constraint; but in what follows, I'll assume that we have significant pro tanto reason to avoid positing (causally efficacious) irreducible normative properties.

---

[11] I understand this as a cousin of the argument defended in Harman 1977, Chapter 1.

Moreover, I'll assume that normative properties are causally efficacious. This is plausible; consider my examples above. So given this assumption, I'll be assuming that we have significant pro tanto reason to avoid positing irreducible normative properties.

I'll dismiss one objection. Wedgwood (2007) writes:

According to this argument against moral explanations, moral and normative facts are not causally efficacious because their causal role is excluded by the non-moral, non-normative facts in which those moral facts are realized. According to Kim's "exclusion" argument, mental facts are not causally efficacious because their causal role is excluded by non-mental...facts in which those mental facts are realized. (p. 193)

But Kim's argument is not, in fact, directed against the causal efficacy of the mental, but against non-reductive physicalism. The causal efficacy of the mental is a *premise* in Kim's argument; and the upshot of Kim's argument is that (if physicalism is true) the mental must be reduced to the physical to preserve the plausibility of its causal efficacy. My argument against irreducible normative properties, likewise, is not an argument against the causal efficacy of the normative, but rather an argument that assumes the causal efficacy of the normative and proceeds to argue that (if naturalism is true) the normative must be reduced to the non-normative to preserve the plausibility of its causal efficacy.

On Wedgwood's view, the normative is causally efficacious and yet irreducible. The naturalist's objection to this is that this commits Wedgwood to unappealing causal overdetermination. Can this objection be avoided? Wedgwood (2007) writes that:

[T]o defend the claim that moral and normative facts can be causally efficacious, we do not need to find cases in which these facts provide the *unique best* causal explanation. We need only find some cases in which they provide a *correct* causal explanation; it does not matter if there is another equally good causal explanation that appeals to the [non-natural] cause rather than the [normative] cause. [...] According to my proposal, correct normative explanations are ubiquitous: there is a correct normative explanation whenever anyone engages in rational reasoning of any kind. So there is nothing strange or exotic about such normative explanations. (p. 196)

But this doesn't yet give us any way to avoid Kim's worry about overdetermination—and it's the worry about overdetermination that motivates the idea that non-normative causes "exclude" normative causes, not the idea that normative causes are "strange or exotic."[12]

Note also that my Kim-style "exclusion" argument is not based on the premise that causal determination is incompatible with reasons-responsiveness. Derek Parfit (2011) writes that "even if...the mental processes in our brains are fully causally determined, that does not threaten the belief that we can reason in valid ways, and can respond to epistemic reasons" (v2, p. 500). My argument concedes the compatibility of causal

---

[12] You might think that the view Wedgwood defends is *obviously* not consistent with philosophical naturalism; he writes, after all, that "normative properties and normative facts are partially constitutive of reality" and that any "fundamental metaphysical account will have to mention them *as such*" (2007, p. 198).

determination and reasons-responsiveness; its crucial premise is that systematic causal overdetermination is not credible.

We could also get to a naturalistic constraint by starting with Terry Horgan and Mark Timmons' (1993) definition of naturalism as the view that "everything—including any particulars, events, facts, properties, etc.—is part of the natural physical world that science investigates" (p. 182). For the normative is not part of that world. This isn't because (as we saw for Lewis) the normative doesn't fit into a particular metaphysical conception, but because of the fact that science doesn't investigate the normative. Kim (1993b) explains this idea by saying that "the ontology of any acceptable discourse must be rendered naturalistically appropriate—that is, it must not posit entities and properties that cannot in principle be investigated by science" (p. 206). But the normative cannot be investigated in this way.

All these metaphysical considerations are related to motivations you might have for including the naturalistic constraints in your philosophical methodology. Anyone who thinks of philosophy as contiguous with natural science will hope to explain the normative in scientifically respectable terms. But since science doesn't investigate the normative per se, we should seek an explanation of the normative in non-normative terms.

5.6 Conclusion

We seek an account of epistemic evaluation and of epistemic reasons attribution—and of the thesis that belief "aims at truth." We proceed with the following defeasible assumptions:

- Realism about epistemic normativity (§5.2.3)
- Universalism about epistemic normativity (§5.3)
- The two naturalistic constraints (§5.5)

Finally (Chapter 9), I'll argue that we should reject realism about epistemic normativity. But we must first investigate realist approaches to epistemic normativity (Chapters 6–8).

6

Humean Approaches

Trying is the first step towards failure.

—Homer Simpson

We'll begin our investigation of epistemic normativity by considering Humean approaches to epistemic normativity, including those that appeal to Humean essentialism about belief (§5.4.2). I call these approaches "Humean" in virtue of their resemblance to approaches to practical reason, sometimes called "Humean" (see, e.g., Drier 2001), on which rational action is a matter of taking efficient means to your ends. On a natural way of spelling this out, it is a matter of doing what will (or what you believe will) bring about the satisfaction of your desires. Humean approaches to epistemic normativity propose something analogous when it comes to rational belief, which is understood as a matter of taking efficient means to the end of true belief.

It's unclear whether Hume himself endorsed anything like that approach to practical reason; arguably, he rejected the possibility of practical reason, rather than endorsing a particular species of it (Millgram 1995). In addition to this, it's important not to confuse the view that you ought to take the means to your ends, which is a normative principle, with any descriptive claim, like the view that no one is motivated to Φ unless she wants to Ψ and believes that Φing is a means to Ψing. This is sometimes called the "Humean theory of motivation," and Hume seems to have endorsed it. By the same token, the claim that you ought to take the means to your ends should not be conflated with the belief–desire model of action on which someone intentionally Φs only if her Φing was caused by her desire to Ψ and her belief that Φing was a means to Ψing.

I don't mean to suggest that Hume offered, or would offer, what I'm calling a "Humean" approach to epistemic normativity. On the one hand, his famous discussion of the passions (*Treatise*, II.iii.3) suggests that beliefs, not being "original existences," *are* subject to requirements of rationality in a way that desires are not. On the other hand, in his discussion of "curiosity, or the love of truth" (*Treatise*, II.iii.10) he offers a picture that is more "Humean," in the present sense: there he writes that "[t]he first and most considerable circumstance requisite to render truth agreeable, is the genius and capacity, which is employ'd in its invention and discovery" (1978, p. 449).

We'll begin by looking at a Humean essentialist account of epistemic value (§6.1.1) and a Humean essentialist account of epistemic reasons (§6.1.2). I'll then present an objection to both views (§6.2): not all beliefs involve the desire to believe nothing but the truth.

6.1   Humean essentialism and epistemic normativity

Humean essentialism about belief (§5.4.2) can be deployed in an account of epistemic value; it can also be deployed in an independent account of epistemic reasons. First (§6.2.1) we'll articulate a Humean essentialist account of epistemic value; then (§6.2.2) we'll articulate a Humean essentialist account of epistemic reasons.

6.1.1   A Humean essentialist account of epistemic value

Recall the problem of the source of epistemic value (§5.2.1). For the epistemic essentialist to explain the appropriateness of evaluating beliefs vis-à-vis the truth principle she needs to do two things. First, she needs to give an account of evaluation of beliefs vis-à-vis the truth principle as essential evaluation, i.e. she needs to say something about the essential nature of belief. Second, she needs to say something about epistemic value. The essentialist can then explain the appropriateness of evaluation vis-à-vis the truth principle. The Humean does this by defending the following two claims:

Attempt essentialism about belief: Necessarily, in virtue of the essential nature of belief, for any subject S and proposition that p, if S believes that p then S attempts to believe the truth about whether p.

Attempt principle: An attempt is (in one respect) good iff it is successful, and (in one respect) bad iff unsuccessful.

From these two claims it follows that true beliefs are (in one respect) good and false beliefs are (in one respect) bad. This conclusion, as Ernest Sosa (2007) argues, requires no verdict on the "intrinsic value of truth"; it "abstracts from such Platonic issues" (p. 72). It does not assume that successful doxastic attempts are always or ever eudaimonically or morally valuable. However, the attempt principle is compatible with the view that the value of successful attempts is eudaimonic; in this connection compare John Greco's (2010) account of the value of knowledge, on which "knowledge is a kind of success through ability, and in general success from ability is both intrinsically valuable and constitutive of human flourishing" (p. 99; cf. Sosa on "praxical value," 2003, pp. 171–5), and Duncan Pritchard's (2010) appeal to the idea that "[a] good life is, amongst other things, a life rich in achievement" (pp. 30–1). You might question a eudaimonic account of epistemic value for the reasons discussed above (§5.3). In any event, the attempt principle gives us the necessary premise connecting success and failure with goodness and badness, respectively, and we'll grant it for the sake of argument.

Attempt essentialism about belief is sometimes suggested by Sosa, who compares beliefs to shots made by an archer (2007, pp. 77–80, 2009, pp. 9–10; see also 2003, pp. 171–5), and epistemic evaluation to the evaluation of such shots. The analogy of the archer admits of two interpretations, however, only one of which is apt when it comes to Humean approaches to epistemic normativity. On this interpretation, we should consider archery as the activity of shooting arrows at a chosen target, where success is relative to the desires of the archer.[1] A shot is an attempt to hit something of the archer's choosing, and a successful shot is one that hits the archer's chosen target. The alternative interpretation considers archery as the activity of taking part in an archery competition, where the target is not chosen by the archer herself, but is determined by the conventional rules of the competition. A shot is successful, on this interpretation, if and only if it hits the conventional target, regardless of the desires of the archer. This alternative interpretation of the analogy of the archer is apt when it comes to Kantian approaches to epistemic normativity, and we'll return to it below (§8.1.3). Here, the relevant analogy is the archer who chooses her target.

The idea behind the Humean essentialist account of epistemic evaluation is that, just as we can evaluate the archer's shots as successes (if they hit her chosen target) or as failures (if they don't), we can evaluate beliefs as successes (if they are true) or as failures (if they are false).

This seems essential for what Sosa is really after: just as we can evaluate successful shots as "adroit" if they manifest the archer's skill, and as "apt" if they are successful because of the archer's skill, we can evaluate beliefs as epistemically adroit if they manifest the believer's epistemic virtue, and as epistemically apt if true because of the believer's epistemic virtue. Such adroit belief, Sosa argues, amounts to knowledge. To put this another way, knowledge is a cognitive or intellectual achievement, in other words, a cognitive or intellectual success manifesting cognitive or intellectual virtue. This view has been defended by several contemporary epistemologists (Zagzebski 1996, p. 295 and passim, 2003b, Riggs 2002, Greco 2003, 2010). These philosophers' aim has been to explain how knowledge is more epistemically valuable than mere true belief (§5.1), not to explain the epistemic value of true belief. So the solution to the problem of the source of epistemic value that I am attributing to them is not one they explicitly offer.

Now a digression. Are Sosa et al. committed to saying that true beliefs are attempts to believe the truth? Knowledge is a success-manifesting virtue only if true belief is a success. In virtue of what is true belief a success? One possibility—the possibility that I'm considering in this chapter—is that true beliefs are successes because beliefs are attempts to believe the truth, i.e. because attempt essentialism about belief is true. And one possible defense of this is by appeal to the premise that successes are a species of attempt, namely, attempts in which the attempter attains what she attempted.

---

[1] Here, and in what follows, I employ a broad sense of "desire," on which see §6.1.2.

You might object to this by pointing out that accidental successes are possible. Now one kind of accidental success can be set aside, as not a threat to our premise. You can attempt, in Φing, both to Ψ and to Π. Your Φing might be a success, with respect of your attempt to Ψ, but not with respect of your attempt to Π. This can happen when you attempt to Π by Ψing. Imagine that, craving an Egg McMuffin, you set out for the nearest McDonald's, which happens to sit on the opposite side of Ben Nevis. You walk towards the McDonald's, and end up climbing Ben Nevis on the way. Your climbing Ben Nevis seems intuitively to be some kind of achievement, and thus a success (granting the assumption that achievement is a species of success). But this kind of accidental success is no threat to our premise, since in this case you attempt to get to McDonald's by climbing Ben Nevis. Even if you do not make it to McDonald's, and so your attempt to get to McDonald's is unsuccessful, your attempt to climb Ben Nevis (as a means of getting to McDonald's) might be successful.[2]

Another kind of accidental success can be handled, but in a different way. Consider Alexander Fleming's discovery of penicillin, often described as an "accidental discovery." Fleming's carelessness in the laboratory led to a dish of *Staphylococcus* bacteria being contaminated with *Penicillium* mold; noticing that the mold had killed off the bacteria, he isolated and identified the antibacterial substance the mold was producing, and named it "penicillin." But this wasn't a case of success (or achievement) without attempt: Fleming had been trying, for years, to find an antibiotic substance.[3] So let us imagine a more difficult case, in which a scientist attempts to find one thing, and ends up finding another. Suppose Fleming had discovered not penicillin, but a new recipe for Beef Stroganoff (based, I suppose, on the addition of *Penicillium*). Would this be a success (or an achievement)?[4]

It depends on how we imagine the case. Imagine that at some point Fleming tastes a morsel of *Penicillium*, realizes that it's delicious, abandons his research on antibiotics, and embarks on a new series of experiments, designed to put the mold to culinary use. In this case, we have no counterexample to the premise that successes are a species of attempt. So imagine, alternatively, that Fleming never gives up his research on antibiotics, never starts up a culinary research project, and just cooks up a dish of Stroganoff one day, adding *Penicillium* for lack of button mushrooms, which he shares with his lab assistant, who remarks that it's a brilliant take on the classic Stroganoff. Although no doubt something good has happened, in this case, there is no inclination to call this a success (or an achievement).

---

[2] Note that you need not conceptualize your instrumental attempt as an attempt to climb Ben Nevis; you might just think: "To get to McDonald's I must get over *that*," and start climbing. This, I'm arguing, constitutes an attempt to climb Ben Nevis.

[3] If anything, Fleming's case might make trouble for the idea that achievement is incompatible with luck.

[4] There are *senses* of "success" and "achievement" where successes and achievements are not a species of attempt: winning the Nobel Prize is a great achievement, but only the most arrogant of us attempt to win the Nobel Prize. But these are not the senses of "success" and "achievement" that are relevant for Humean approaches, where the leading idea is that the believer is, in some sense, the "source" of epistemic normativity; see §6.2.1.

A final case: imagine an athlete who aims only to win her match, but ends up getting fit as an unintended side-effect of her efforts. You might argue that her getting fit is a success (or an achievement). Now one possibility here would be to say that this is analogous to the case of Fleming and the accidental Stroganoff: something good has happened, but there's no success (or achievement) here. However, suppose we say that the athlete's improved fitness is a success (or an achievement), despite there being no corresponding attempt. In virtue of what is her getting fit a success? Given that she did not attempt to get fit, we will have to appeal here to the value of fitness. But what makes fitness valuable? Why is fitness good? We can see now that the question of what makes true belief a success is intimately related to the question of the value of true belief, if these two questions are not in fact the same. So although Sosa et al. are not necessarily committed to the Humean explanation of true belief as a success, they owe us (it seems to me) some explanation. Attempt essentialism about belief is one attempt at such an explanation. End of digression.

Sosa (2009) endorses the attempt principle:

A performance is better than otherwise for not having *failed*, i.e., for not having fallen short of its objective. In line with that, it is *good* if it succeeds, if it reaches its objective. A performance is at least good *as such* for succeeding. (p. 9)

And he comes close to endorsing attempt essentialism about belief, when he writes that "belief is considered a kind of performance" (2009, p. 5) whose "internal aim" is truth (ibid p. 8). Note that an archer's shots are essentially attempts (to hit her chosen target); were they not attempts, they would not be shots. So if beliefs are analogous to shots, as Sosa argues, it would seem that beliefs are essentially attempts as well. Linda Zagzebski (2003b) defends a related view, on which "beliefs can be and perhaps typically are motivated," where "a motive is an affective state that initiates and directs action" (p. 17). Knowledge is understood as a kind of action (p. 16, see also 1996, pp. 264–73): true belief acquired with virtuous motivation. But she suggests that the value of true belief is another matter (2003b, p. 18).

Other philosophers have explicitly defended the claim that beliefs are attempts to believe the truth. Here are Lloyd Humberstone and Asbjørn Steglich-Petersen:

[U]nless one takes there to be a criterion of success in the case of an attitude towards the proposition that *p*, and, further, unless that criterion is truth, then whatever else it may be, the attitude in question is not that of belief. So unless the attitude-holder has what we might call a controlling background intention that his or her attitudinizing is successful only if its propositional content is true, then the attitude taken is not that of belief. (Humberstone 1992, p. 73)

Suppose … you judge that John believes that the London train leaves at 5 p.m. [Y]ou have [necessarily] judged that John has a certain aim or intention in so doing, namely, the aim of regarding that proposition as true only if it is in fact true. (Steglich-Petersen 2006, p. 499)

Believing, on this view, requires the "aim or intention [of] regarding [p] as true only if it is in fact true" (ibid.). Conor McHugh argues that "the attitude of belief has a characteristic and constitutive end, aim, goal or purpose" (2012a, p. 426), and in defense of the view that belief aims at knowledge, he suggests that "[f]alse beliefs are…defective," because they are "failures to do what the believer was aiming to do" (2011a, p. 370). To the extent that Humeans take these features of belief to be essential features of belief, they offer a **teleological conception of belief.** And as we'll see below (§6.2), there's good reason for Humeans to say that beliefs are essentially attempts to believe the truth, to avoid violating universalism about epistemic normativity (§5.3.1).

Let's look at how this version of Humean essentialism would solve the problem of the source of epistemic value. First, in answer to the basic question about epistemic evaluation, Humean essentialism explains the appropriateness of evaluation of beliefs vis-à-vis the truth principle by appeal to the attempt principle. A noteworthy feature of the value of attempts is that an attempt succeeds or fails if and only if the person who makes the attempt succeeds or fails. So Humean essentialism about belief would be well positioned to explain why epistemic evaluation of beliefs (sometimes) involves reactive attitudes (§5.2.1). More on this below (§6.2.1). Second, in answer to the uniqueness question about epistemic evaluation, Humean essentialism can explain the sense in which evaluation of beliefs vis-à-vis the truth principle is appropriate, by contrast with evaluation of beliefs vis-à-vis the Tuesday principle. In believing I necessarily attempt to believe something true, according to the Humean essentialist, but I do not necessarily attempt to form a belief on a Tuesday. So evaluation of my attempt vis-à-vis the truth principle is appropriate, in a way that evaluation vis-à-vis the Tuesday principle isn't (cf. Steglich-Petersen 2009, p. 396). On the scope question, the Humean essentialist can adopt a doxastic conception of the epistemic (§5.2.4).

6.1.2 A Humean essentialist account of epistemic reasons

Let's turn to a Humean essentialist account of epistemic reasons. Suppose I have conclusive evidence that p. Intuitively, I thereby have an epistemic reason to believe that p. What does this mean? What sort of a reason is this? And what is the source of its normative force, i.e. of the fact that I ought to believe that p? David Papineau (1999) argues that your reason is an instrumental reason, i.e. that believing that p is a means to some end of yours:

> [T]he adoption of a given end will standardly generate derivative norms about appropriate means to that end. Just as the adoption of car speed as an end generates the prescription "you ought to tune your car well", so will adoption of truth as an end generate prescriptions about the means of arriving at truth. (p. 29; cf. Kelly 2003, pp. 612–13)

On this view, epistemic principles can be understood as "hypothetical imperatives." A **hypothetical imperative**, then, is one that a person has reason to follow only in virtue of the fact that she has certain desires. Such an imperative will have the form: "If you want to Ψ, then Φ." As Philippa Foot (1972) notes, what I want or **desire** should be taken to include intentions, passing inclinations, long-term aims and projects, commitments to other people or to a cause (pp. 306–7), other elements of someone's "subjective motivational set" (Williams 1980, p. 105), her "ground projects" (Williams 1976, p. 12), and what she cares about or loves (cf. Frankfurt 1988, 1999).

Papineau's idea is that epistemology is a system of hypothetical imperatives, instances of <If you want to believe the truth and nothing but the truth, then Φ>. For Φ we can then substitute various **epistemic imperatives**: believe the logical consequences of your beliefs, trust the deliverances of sense perception and memory, and so on. The correct epistemic imperatives will just be those that in fact specify effective means of achieving the goal of believing the truth and nothing but the truth. This is a way of vindicating epistemological talk of truth as a good, end, or goal (§5.1). It would answer Sosa's (2003) pertinent question of why we should think about epistemic value in terms of a *goal* at all (p. 160).

Suppose I know that believing that p is a means to my end of believing that p only if p. A crucial assumption is needed to generate a hypothetical imperative commanding belief that p: that I have pro tanto reason to take the means to my ends. This, combined with the supposition that believing that p is a means to my end of believing that p only if p, entails that I have pro tanto reason to believe that p.

We'll formulate this crucial assumption as follows:

Means–ends rule: If S wants to Ψ and if by Φing, she will Ψ, then S has a pro tanto (normative) reason to Φ.[5]

If there are such things as (normative) instrumental reasons, some principle like this must be true. The means–ends rule is not trivial, when understood in the intended sense. The means–ends rule therefore allows us to go from a non-normative claim about someone's desires (broadly construed), along with other non-normative facts, to a normative claim about what reasons she has (cf. §5.2.2).

---

[5] Alternatively (cf. Drier 2001, p. 38, Williams 1980, p. 101), the principle could be formulated as "If S wants to Ψ and believes that by Φing, she will Ψ, then S has a pro tanto reason to Φ." The alternative formulation entails that I (who want to drink gin) have pro tanto reason to drink a glass of petrol which I believe to be gin; our formulation above doesn't. The alternative formulation says that you have pro tanto reason to do whatever you believe will promote your ends; our formulation says that you have pro tanto reason to do whatever will actually promote your ends. There are two reasons not to explain epistemic reasons by appeal to the alternative formulation of the means–ends rule (cf. Owens 2003, p. 286). First, this would make a person's possession of epistemic reasons (e.g. to believe that p) contingent on her having various second-order beliefs (e.g. about the means to believing the truth and nothing but the truth about whether p). Second, only epistemically well-grounded second-order beliefs should be allowed to generate epistemic reasons. But this begins an unacceptable regress, for the existence of an epistemic reason for S's second-order belief will require a third-order belief (to the effect that her second-order belief is a means to her "truth goal"), and the existence of an epistemic reason for this third-order belief will require in turn a fourth-order belief (to the effect that her third-order belief is a means to her "truth goal"), and so on *ad infinitum*. Such a regress is unacceptable for two reasons. First, it is psychologically crazy. No one has ever had such a chain of beliefs. And yet many have had epistemic reasons. Therefore, epistemic reasons do not require such a chain. Second, the regress seems explanatorily vicious: my original possession of an epistemic reason never gets explained. We keep explaining the notion of having an epistemic reason by using that same notion, over and over again. (Note that this problem doesn't arise for the alternative formulation of the means–ends rule, per se, but only when this principle is combined with the idea that epistemic reasons are instrumental reasons.)

With the means–ends rule in hand, we can appeal to a version of Humean essentialism about belief:

Truth goal essentialism about belief: Necessarily, in virtue of the essential nature of belief, S believes that p only if S wants to believe that p only if p.

Defenders of this include Steglich-Petersen (2006, 2009) and Humberstone (1992); I'll argue below (§6.2.1) that truth goal essentialism is a corollary of attempt essentialism about belief (§6.1.1). When truth goal essentialism and the means–ends rule are put together, we can offer an answer to the basic question about epistemic reasons attribution (§5.2.2): someone has epistemic reason to believe that p if believing that p will further her goal of believing that p only if p.[6] Thus, as Steglich-Petersen (2009) puts it, "[e]pistemic norms thus turn out to be instrumental norms, deriving their normative force from their ability to guide us to achieve our aims" (p. 396, cf. McHugh 2011a, p. 371). This also can provide an answer to the uniqueness question, by explaining "the peculiar authority that epistemic norms have over other kinds of considerations in forming beliefs" (Steglich-Petersen 2009, p. 396). Since the "truth goal" is built into the essence of belief, instrumental reasons we have that derive from this goal can be seen to have a special status when it comes to belief formation. And in answer to the scope question, again, the Humean can adopt a doxastic conception of the epistemic (§5.2.4).

6.1.3 Humean approaches and naturalism

A prima facie virtue of Humean approaches to epistemic normativity is that they do not seem to be in tension with philosophical naturalism (§5.5):

The naturalist avoids commitment to the idea that the metaphysical nature of belief involves normative properties, since it is notoriously difficult to explain these in a naturalistic framework. Aims, on the other hand, seem more palatable for a naturalist. It is usually assumed that trying to achieve something, having a goal of some sort, and being moved to act by having that goal, can all be explained in a naturalistic spirit. (Steglich-Petersen 2006, p. 500)

The source of epistemic normativity, on the Humean view, seems to be the desires of the believer. There seems to be nothing more to its being good when I believe the truth, and bad when I don't, than the fact that believing the truth was what I was trying to do, in believing. Someone who believes that p, where it is true that p, will be someone who has succeeded in getting something she wanted; someone who believes that p, where it is false that p, will have failed to get something that she wanted. A true belief will be a success, by the believer's own lights, and a false belief will be a failure, by her own lights.

However, this is not yet to consider the naturalistic credentials of the attempt principle and the means–ends rule. Recall the naturalistic constraints (§5.5), which

---

[6] The "only if" here must not be read as a material conditional; see §6.2.1.

enjoin us to avoid positing irreducible normativity. Whether or not Humean approaches are in some kind of tension with naturalism will depend on whether the normativity posited by the attempt principle and the means–ends rule is irreducible or not. We can bracket this question, however, and note that Humean approaches make significant headway for the philosophical naturalist. To the extent that we are antecedently committed to the attempt principle and the means–ends rule, we have made progress the naturalist can be proud of, in explaining the existence of epistemic value and epistemic reasons. For the Humean, epistemic imperatives turn out to be hypothetical imperatives, and as Papineau argues, "the problem of understanding the 'oughts' in hypothetical imperatives … presents a puzzle to all philosophers" (1999, p. 19). Reducing the puzzle of understanding epistemic "oughts" to the puzzle of understanding instrumental "oughts" is progress; we've exchanged two puzzles for one. If the Humean is right, the problem of the source of epistemic normativity poses no greater threat to naturalism than does the problem of the source of instrumental normativity.

Returning, however, to our question about the naturalistic credentials of the attempt principle and the means–ends rule, note that our issue can be usefully articulated as an issue about the "categorical normative force" of the means–ends rule. Tom Kelly (2003) writes:

It is widely thought, by both friends and foes of naturalism, that the existence of anything which possesses *categorical normative force*—that is, force which is binding on any rational agent, regardless of the goals or ends which he or she happens to hold—is not a possibility which the naturalist world view countenances. (p. 616)

Our crucial question for the Humean account of epistemic reasons, then, is whether the means–ends rule possesses this kind of "categorical normative force." Some philosophers argue that it does, since "[i]ts demands must be met by you, insofar as you are rational, no matter what desires you happen to have" (Drier 2001, p. 42, cf. Korsgaard 1997). Others (e.g. Kolodny 2005) would argue that the means–ends rule does not have this kind of "categorical normative force." We shall leave this question open, and note that the ultimate naturalistic credentials of Humean accounts of epistemic reasons are at stake.

The same point can be made when it comes to the attempt principle. The principle posits a certain species of value—the goodness of successful attempts and the badness of failed attempts. We've made no attempt here to explain away or reduce the value of attempts posited by the attempt principle. The naturalistic credentials of Humean accounts of epistemic value depend on whether the value posited by the attempt principle is irreducible.

None of this speaks against Papineau's point, that the reduction of epistemic normativity to instrumental normativity is progress the naturalist can be proud of. In any event, we shall assume in what follows that Humean approaches are naturalistically kosher. My critique will target Humean essentialism about belief, not the normative principles discussed here.

6.2 Against Humean approaches

A basic objection to Humean approaches (Kelly 2003, Grimm 2008, 2009) is that they are forced to reject universalism about epistemic normativity (§5.3.1). I'll argue that this objection cannot be overcome, and that Humean approaches should be rejected.

6.2.1 Against Humean essentialism

Attempts are necessarily intentional. Consider what Pritchard (2010) says about achievements:

> [I]t seems an essential part of achievements that they involve certain motivational states on the part of the subject with regard to the success in question—in particular, that the subject is actively seeking to bring this success about. (p. 29)

For Pritchard, cognitive or intellectual achievement is a species of successful attempt.[7] And what he says about achievements applies to successful attempts, and to attempts in general: for someone to attempt to Ψ, she must desire to Ψ. If this is right, attempt essentialism about belief (§6.1.1) entails truth goal essentialism about belief (§6.1.2): attempting to believe the truth about whether p requires wanting to believe that p only if p.

The requirement of a "truth goal" on the part of the believer in large part explains the plausibility and naturalistic appeal of Humean approaches. When I attempt to Ψ, and succeed, *I* am a success; when I attempt to Ψ, and fail, *I* am a failure. When I fail to respond to my instrumental reasons, I am failing *by my own lights*. The reason for this is that it is my desires that have been satisfied or frustrated in the successful or failed attempt. The source of normativity in such cases is, in part, my own desiring. Success and failure, in such cases, is success or failure *by my own lights*. When I attempt to Ψ, being an instance of Ψing becomes a standard of correctness for what I do, and this is in part because I *set that standard for myself*, by desiring to Ψ.[8] (If epistemic evaluation ever appropriately involves reactive attitudes, then something like this will be required; we will need to say that the epistemic badness of beliefs entails the epistemic badness of believers.) Consider, again, the archer. If she accidentally looses an arrow from her bow, without desiring to hit x, then her "shot" does not succeed or fail depending on whether it hits x or not.[9] Indeed, as indicated by the scare quotes, what has happened

---

[7] See my digression, above (§6.1.1).

[8] We can individuate intentional actions in terms of their literal aims. When I try to make a cornbread, part of what it is to be doing what I am doing is to be trying to make a cornbread. I would not be doing what I am doing were I not trying to make a cornbread. If this is right, then the standards of success involved in attempts are constitutive (or "internal," Sosa 2009, p. 8) standards of success.

[9] This is not the case on the alternative interpretation of the analogy of the archer that we considered above (§6.1.1) and will consider again below (§8.1.3).

is not a *shot* at all. Thus the value of attempts requires desire on the part of the person making the attempt. So we should understand attempt essentialism about belief in such a way that it entails truth goal essentialism about belief, for the sake of the plausibility of the idea that epistemic value flows from the value of attempts.

Might the Humean say that the fact that a belief is an attempt does not depend on some feature of the believer, such as her having a "truth goal," but on some feature of belief, e.g. its constitutive teleology (Steglich-Petersen 2006, McHugh 2011a, 2012a)? She should not say this, for the plausibility and naturalistic credentials of Humean approaches depend on the analogy between believing and intentional action. This is why defenders of a teleological conception of belief write that in believing falsely the believer fails "to do what *the believer* was aiming to do" (McHugh 2011a, p. 370, my emphasis) and that their view "attributes *to subjects* a specific aim each time they engage in forming a doxastic attitude" (McHugh 2012a, p. 427, my emphasis). Consider McHugh's (2012a) comparison of belief formation to "[t]he activity of doing a sudoku puzzle":

> The activity itself is not an agent that takes up aims. Rather, the activity has that aim in the sense that a token activity counts as an instance of doing a sudoku puzzle only if it is brought about and executed in a way that appropriately involves the aim of filling out the grid in the right way. (pp. 426–7)

In other words: doing a sudoku puzzle requires that *the person doing the puzzle* desire or intend to fill out the grid in the right way.[10] If the analogy with believing holds up, then, believing that p requires that *the believer* desire or intend that she believe that p only if p.

So we must inquire as to whether believing that p requires wanting to believe that p only if p. We encountered a related issue above (§1.2.2), in our discussion of Aristotle's principle of curiosity. Recall:

Unrestricted descriptive principle of curiosity: For any subject S and proposition that p, S wants to know whether p.

But as we saw, this principle isn't true, given the existence of apathetic and positive incuriosity. Sometimes people have no desire to know whether p, and indeed may form a belief about whether p absent such a desire. In your doctor's waiting room you absent-mindedly count the number of motes of dust on the coffee table, and come to believe that there are 53 motes. But you were, and remain, abjectly incurious about the number of motes (Grimm 2008, p. 742). This is a counterexample to the unrestricted descriptive principle of curiosity. You might object that there must be some sense in which you *are* curious about the number of motes, at least once you begin counting them, or at least once you get to the point where you are forming a belief about their number. Well, not in the ordinary sense: if asked whether you had ever been curious

---

[10] For an alternative understanding of the desires or intentions required for playing a game, see §8.1.3.

about the number of motes, you'd reply that you were never curious, but merely bored. You could, of course, be in bad faith about your curiosity, embarrassed at being curious about something so trivial. But the point here is that you could easily be absolutely authentic in your insistence that curiosity about the motes was never present. Which just means that, if there is a sense in which you were curious, it's not the ordinary sense.

What the Humean needs is a non-ordinary sense in which *every* belief involves curiosity. Our formulation of truth goal essentialism (§6.1.2) reflected this need: there we understood the "truth goal" as a desire to believe that p only if p (Sosa 2003, pp. 156–9; see also Sosa 2001, pp. 51–2).[11] The existence of incuriosity, our indifference to many truths, is no threat to the idea that belief that p requires a desire to believe that p only if p. The principle of curiosity proposed a universal desire for knowledge of every truth. Truth goal essentialism, by contrast, proposes a universal desire that one's beliefs have a certain feature, namely, that they be true. The principle of curiosity suggests that, by our lights, every truth is worth believing; truth goal essentialism suggests that, by our lights, only truths are worth believing. There's no reason to think that the latter suggests the former. Compare: Barron Points are the only oysters worth eating, by my lights, but this doesn't mean that I want to eat every Barron Point. It means that I want all the oysters that I eat to be Barron Points, i.e. that if I am hungry for oysters, I want to eat Barron Points and only Barron Points. The Humean's claim, that believing that p requires a desire to believe that p only if p, is not threatened by the fact that we are often incurious and that we merely have "fairly specific, particularized cognitive goals" (Kelly 2003, p. 624).

However, there are counterexamples to truth goal essentialism about belief. First, some individuals are capable of belief but not capable of higher-order desires about their beliefs: (some) non-human animals and (most) human children. Mittens believes that she is on the mat, but she does not want to believe that she is on the mat only if she is on the mat. She is just not capable of forming desires with that kind of complexity. As Papineau (1999) argues:

[T]he deliberate pursuit of true beliefs involves a sophisticated meta-representational concern *about* beliefs, and is therefore not something that we should expect to be present in all beings who have beliefs. (p. 32)

---

[11] There is something puzzling here. It seems that the Humean should not understand the "only if" here as the material conditional. Otherwise it would follow that the truth of p is sufficient for my possession of an epistemic reason to believe p, since the truth of p is sufficient for the truth of q ⊃ p. Rather, the goal of believing p only if p must be understood as the goal of safely believing p, where S's belief that p is safe iff S would not easily believe p falsely. Your desire to believe p only if p would therefore not be satisfied merely by your believing p truly. Should we really say, then, that beliefs are "performances aimed at truth"? It would be more accurate to say that they are performances aimed at truth and at safety. But Sosa may be on good ground here: the instrumental value of believing the truth (and avoiding error) may entail the instrumental value of believing safely. If so, a performance aimed at truth is a fortiori a performance aimed at safety, in the sense that anyone who wants to believe the truth (and avoid error) will have instrumental reason (via the means–ends rule) to believe safely.

Therefore it's false that S believes that p only if S wants to believe that p only if p. Call this (following Papineau) the **objection from unrefined thinkers**.[12]

Second, even when it comes to individuals who are capable of higher-order desires about their beliefs, such individuals often form beliefs without the accompanying higher-order desires. This will happen most commonly when beliefs are formed automatically and unconsciously. Obama walks from the Oval Office to the Rose Garden, surrounded by advisors and lackeys, with whom he is engaged in frantic discourse. Along the way he perceives his surroundings, and upon his arrival he is aware that he has arrived in the Rose Garden, i.e. he now believes that he is in the Rose Garden. But he never wanted to believe that he was in the Rose Garden only if he was in the Rose Garden. Therefore it's false that S believes that p only if S wants to believe that p only if p, and truth goal essentialism is false. Call this the **objection from unconscious belief formation**.[13]

I conclude that truth goal essentialism about belief is false, and since attempt essentialism entails truth goal essentialism, that attempt essentialism about belief is false as well. The proposed Humean accounts of epistemic value (§6.1.1) and epistemic reasons (§6.2.2) will not work.

6.2.2 On the general desire that one's beliefs be true

We have considered (§1.2) the idea that everyone wants knowledge, and above (§6.2.1) the idea that everyone wants to believe only truths. We took these claims to be instances of <For any subject S and proposition that p ...>. In other words, we took these claims to imply a multitude of desires on S's part. Perhaps we'd do better to take these claims to imply a single "general desire" on S's part, either a "general desire" for knowledge, or a "general desire" to believe only truths. Jonathan Kvanvig (2003) writes, in response to Sosa's (2003, p. 156) example of counting grains of sand:

> [W]e do have an interest in the truth...It is the nature of interests to lack specificity: We do not have an individuated interest in the truth of the claim that our mothers love us, that the president is not a crook, that Wyoming is north of Mexico, and so on. What we have is a general desire for the truth, and that interest attaches to particular truths in the manner of instantiation in predicate logic. The default position for any truth is that our general interest in the truth applies to it. (2003, p. 41)

---

[12] There is a connection between the idea that non-human animals and children have beliefs and the assumption that knowing entails believing. Bernard Williams (1973), for example, denies both. Similarly, the question of animal intelligence has always been at the heart of questions of normativity. Philosophers inspired by Kant posit (irreducibly normative) categorical imperatives that govern belief and action, while philosophers inspired by Hume reject categorical imperatives, countenancing only the hypothetical variety; philosophers inspired by Hume extend thought and action to non-human animals, taking these to be common natural phenomena, while philosophers inspired by Kant take belief and action to be rare phenomena, and rather hard to come by.

[13] Note that it's awkward to say that Obama believes that he's in the Rose Garden, because this implies that he isn't. We could have said that he knows he's in the Rose Garden; saying that he believes implies that he doesn't know (given the Gricean maxim of quantity), and since he clearly does know, it's awkward to *say* that he believes.

Suppose all believers have a "general desire" to believe only truths. Our Humean account of epistemic reasons (§6.1.2) could be amended to accommodate this:

Means–general–ends rule: If S has a general desire to Ψ and if by Φing, she will Ψ, then S has a pro tanto reason to Φ.

But what does it mean for someone to have a "general desire" to Ψ?

First conception: to have a general desire to Ψ is to desire to always Ψ. Thus, someone has a general desire to believe only truths iff she desires to, for any proposition that p, believe that p only if p. On this conception, it's false that all believers have a general desire to believe only truths. I do not desire to, for any proposition that p, believe that p only if p, because I have been convinced, by the arguments above (Part I), that false belief is sometimes better than true belief. The eudaimonic value of false belief undermines the reasonableness of a general desire (on this conception) to believe only truths, and for some this will lead to their not having a general desire (on this conception) to believe only truths.

In connection with the principle of curiosity (§1.2), Michael Lynch (2009a) notes that "truth is often the faintest of human passions, undesired or actively avoided" (p. 226), and Kelly (2003) argues that people simply "do not typically have this goal: believing the truth" (p. 624, cf. Grimm 2008, pp. 730–2). And Marian David (2001) writes:

> The claim that all of "us"…have such a standing desire for truth appears to be a somewhat daring empirical claim about human psychology—a claim not well supported by empirical evidence. (2001, p. 155)

This point applies equally against the claim that all believers have a general desire (on the present conception) to believe only truths. Most people have not given any thought to the question of what they want out of their beliefs. Our curiosity is aroused by certain questions or topics or subjects, and when this happens we desire to believe the truth, and nothing but the truth, about those questions or topics or subjects.

Second conception: to have a general desire to Ψ is to generally desire to Ψ. Thus, someone has a general desire to believe only truths iff she generally desires to believe that p only if p. Let's grant that this conception of a "general desire" can avoid our worries about the first conception. The problem here is that the means–general–ends rule is not plausible, on this conception. I generally want to eat oysters, and so I have a general desire (on the present conception) to eat oysters. But if I have just eaten three dozen Barron Points, in advance of a pair of lobsters and a formidable paella, it's absurd to say that I have a pro tanto reason to (try to make it the case that I) eat *more* oysters. It's not that my having some reason for eating oysters has been overridden by other considerations. I seem to have, in that situation, no reason to eat oysters at all.[14] My general desire for oysters, if anything, provides merely prima facie reasons to (try to make it the case that I) eat oysters (cf. Grimm 2008, pp. 730–2). But epistemic reasons are not prima facie reasons. When I have conclusive evidence that p, I do not have a

---

[14] Compare an acquaintance of Brillat-Savarin's who reported that he never stopped wanting oysters, and boasted that he could eat any finite number of them.

merely prima facie epistemic reason to believe that p, one that might be absent in some cases. That result is counterintuitive, and seems to violate universalism about epistemic normativity (§5.3.1), more on which below (§6.2.4).

Third conception: to have a general desire to Ψ is to desire to generally Ψ. Thus, someone has a general desire to believe only truths iff she desires to, in general, believe that p only if p. Again, let's grant that this conception of a "general desire" can avoid our worries about the first conception. The problem again is that the means–general–ends rule is not plausible, on this conception. Barron Points are the best oysters, and so I have a general desire (on the present conception) to eat only Barron Points: I desire to, in general, eat only Barron Points. This may provide me with prima facie reasons to eat only Barron Points, but it does not provide me with pro tanto reasons: when I have just eaten three dozen Barron Points, and I yearn for something new for my next dozen, the fact that I desire to generally eat only Barron Points gives me no reason at all to (try to make it the case that I) eat *more* Barron Points. In this case, I have no pro tanto reason to (try to make it the case that I) eat only Barron Points. This is a typical feature of general desires (on the present conception): if you desire to generally Ψ, but not to always Ψ, then you will not always have pro tanto reason to (try to make it the case that you) Ψ.

The same applies, mutatis mutandis, to the prospects for using the notion of a "general desire" to rescue the Humean account of epistemic value (§6.1.1). Attempting to Ψ requires a "particular desire" to Ψ; a general desire will not suffice. Someone who does not want to eat more oysters, but who has a general desire (on whatever conception) to eat oysters, does not enjoy a successful attempt if she (inexplicably) eats oysters in such a situation. There is nothing good about such an "attempt." In any event, even if all believers have a general desire to believe only truths, this does not imply that all beliefs are attempts to believe the truth. Universalism, again, will be violated (cf. §6.2.4).

A final point on the "general desire" that one's beliefs be true. The appeal to a general desire that one's beliefs be true does nothing to meet the objection from unrefined thinkers (§6.2.1). Even if all adult humans have a general desire (in some sense) to believe only truths, it's not plausible that children and non-human animals ever have such a desire. But most children and some non-human animals are capable of belief.

6.2.3 Unconscious, implicit, and tacit desires

Sosa (2007) is aware of the problem that many of our beliefs seem not to involve the kind of conscious intentionalty present in the case of an archer's shot. He writes:

Some acts are performances, of course, but so are some sustained states. Think of those live motionless statues that one sees at tourist sites. Such performances can linger, and need not be constantly sustained through renewed conscious intentions. The performer's mind could wander, with little effect on the continuation or quality of the performance. Beliefs too might thus count as performances, long-sustained ones, with no more conscious or intentional an aim than that of a heartbeat. (p. 23; see also 2009, p. 8)

Is belief such a performance? Sosa offers two analogies for belief in this passage. First, he compares believing to a mime's performance, in which the mime stands motionless over some interval of time, during which she does not consciously intend to perform. Second, he compares believing to the beating of a person's heart, which seems a kind of performance, although it involves no intentions, whether conscious or not, on the part of the person in question. Is believing analogous to either of these kinds of performance?

The mime's performance, although it remains a performance through the interval, during which the mime no longer consciously intends to perform, is unlike believing in two relevant respects. First, Sosa imagines that the mime initiates her performance with a conscious intention to perform; thus the idea that she need not "renew" her intention to perform. But an episode of believing (e.g. Obama's belief that he is now in the Rose Garden) seems to require neither a conscious intention (e.g. to believe that p only if p) that is present throughout the episode, *nor* a conscious initiating intention, present perhaps only at the beginning of the episode.[15] Second, while it sounds fine to say that a mime may perform, at *t*, while not, at *t*, consciously intending to perform, it sounds much less plausible to say that a mime may perform, at *t*, while not, at *t*, intending to perform. When the mime's mind wanders, during such a performance, she no longer consciously intends to perform. But does she no longer intend to perform? Intentions, like beliefs and desires, need not be conscious. My argument (§6.2.1) was that higher-order thoughts, conscious or unconscious, about our beliefs, are rare in adult humans and absent entirely in children and non-humans. The case of the mime gives us no reason to doubt that.

What about Sosa's example of the heartbeat? Here we have stretched the notion of a "performance" too far. It is *the heart*, and not the person, that beats; that's why we say that it beats within her. She does not beat her heart, as it were, for the beating of one's heart is not something that one does. This just shows that it's not a performance, in the relevant sense: for the basic Humean thought (§6.1.1) was that it's good when I attempt to do something, and succeed, and bad when I attempt to do something, and fail. But we would say that I digest my food, and this is also something that happens without my intending it to happen. But once we analogize belief to entirely unintentional activities, we have abandoned the Humean approach. Even if I digest my food, I never *attempt* to digest my food.[16] My heart beats, my food is digested, and so on—all without my desiring anything. (That was Sosa's whole point.) But if believing is like that, then we should appeal neither to the attempt principle nor to the means–ends rule to explain epistemic value or epistemic reasons. We'll look at the prospects for analogizing belief to biological organs such as the heart, below (Chapter 7).

---

[15] Obama's belief that he is in the Rose Garden is unconscious; it is also "dispositional," in the sense that his being in that state supervenes on his behavioral, cognitive, and conative dispositions. It is not "dispositional" in the sense of being merely a disposition to believe—Obama really does believe that he's in the Rose Garden.

[16] Maybe some people (competitive eaters, Shaolin monks) can control their digestion in such a way that they attempt to digest their food. Most of us are not like that.

So much for unconscious intentions, and with them unconscious desires, goals, and so on. You might want to argue that believing that p does require wanting to believe that p only if p, but that this desire is "implicit" or "tacit." Sometimes these words are just used to indicate an unconscious mental state, i.e. one that I am in, but am not consciously aware of. But we've discussed that idea already. So let's assume that "implicit" and "tacit" mean something else.

As David (2001) suggests, one way of understanding what this means would be to get an answer to the question: "What would be evidence for the claim that everyone has such an implicit desire?" (p. 156). An important grammatical point is that x can be "implicit" only if x is implicit in some y, as when someone's contempt is implicit in her choice of words. Indeed, one thing is implicit in another primarily in the context of language, with its implications and implicatures. An implication of an utterance is clearly, in some sense, implicit in that utterance. But it will not help the Humean if a desire to believe that p only if p is implicit in this linguistic way—for example if I imply that I desire to believe that p only if p by saying <I believe that p>. What the Humean needs is that my belief itself (not my belief report) is accompanied by a desire to believe only the truth. Could we say that such a desire is implicit in my belief itself? Is there a clear idea of what "implicit" would mean, outside of the context of language?

What about the idea that the desire to believe that p only if p is "tacit"? Here we speak of one's "tacit acceptance" of, or "tacit commitment" to, some rule or principle, or one's "tacit agreement" to some plan or compact. Such acceptance is proven in one's behavior: you never objected to the state's provision of security, so you tacitly agreed to follow its laws; you always fasten your seatbelt, so you tacitly accepted the principle that personal safety matters. Might believing that p, in similar fashion, tacitly commit you to desiring that you believe that p only if p? It seems more natural to speak of a tacit commitment to a rule or principle, rather than a desire. My behavior might, of course, reveal my desires: I fill my glass from a bottle clearly labeled "petrol," I prepare to drink, therefore, I must want to drink petrol. There may be a sense (although this sounds stupidly awkward) in which a desire to drink petrol was "tacit in my behavior," but in that case a "tacit desire" is just a desire, perhaps unconscious or perhaps conscious, and we have already discussed that, above. By pouring a glass of petrol did I "tacitly commit" myself to some rule or principle? Perhaps something like: "Petrol is to be drunk," or "It is good to drink petrol"? Kantian essentialism about belief (§5.4.2) could be formulated as the view that believing that p (and the doxastic practices that go with it) ("tacitly") commits the believer to the rule: believing that p is correct iff it is true that p. That seems, to me, the best interpretation of the idea that believers have a "tacit" desire to believe that p only if p, as well as of the idea that believers have a general desire to believe the truth (§6.2.2). We'll return to Kantian essentialism, below (Chapter 8).

6.2.4 A non-universalist Humean approach?

A natural move for the Humean would be to continue to appeal to the attempt principle or the means–ends rule, but to abandon truth goal essentialism, and admit that some beliefs are not accompanied by a desire to believe nothing but the truth. Call this a **non-essentialist Humean approach**. What speaks against this? Peter Railton (1997) notes that:

On the usual view of things, two agents in the same epistemic situation (same evidence, same background beliefs) would have the same reasons for believing any given propositions, regardless of possible differences in their personal goals. (p. 53)

Another way of putting this is that epistemic reasons—for example, conclusive evidence that p—are not merely prima facie reasons. A non-essentialist Humean approach would have to reject universalism about epistemic normativity (§5.3.1), because from such an approach it would follow that beliefs formed automatically or unconsciously are not appropriate objects of epistemic evaluation or epistemic reasons attribution, since they are not accompanied by a desire to believe nothing but the truth. It would also follow that the beliefs of children, non-humans, and other "unrefined thinkers" are not appropriate objects of epistemic evaluation or epistemic reasons attribution. An anti-essentialist Humean approach would have to say that two agents in the same epistemic situation, for example two agents who both have conclusive evidence that p, could differ in their epistemic reasons for believing that p. Someone with a desire to believe that p only if p would have epistemic reason to believe that p, in such a situation, but someone without such a desire would not. And someone with a desire to believe that p only if p, who believed p on the basis of such evidence, could be given a positive evaluation, as having succeeded in her attempt to believe the truth, while someone without such a desire, who believed p on the basis of such evidence, could not appropriately be so evaluated. This seems implausible (cf. Kelly 2003, Grimm 2008, 2009).

Consider, again, the archer. Unless she desires to hit her chosen target, her shot (or perhaps her "shot") cannot appropriately be evaluated as successful if and only if it hits her target. A shot that doesn't hit some "target" doesn't offend, qua attempt, if the archer was indifferent to hitting that "target." Believing seems different. Consider wishful thinking (cf. Chapter 2). A person's desire that p influences her belief formation without her being aware of it, resulting in a belief that p that she would not otherwise hold. But if wishful thinking is unconscious belief formation, then it cannot be vicious on Humean grounds. It cannot be bad because it's an instance of a failed attempt to believe nothing but the truth. Nor, for the same reason, can it be said to involve a failure to respond to one's epistemic reasons. If epistemic value were explained in Humean terms, therefore, wishful thinking would not be an epistemic vice.[17]

Papineau (1999) defends a non-universalist Humean account of epistemic reasons. He imagines someone who "arranges to avoid evidence that might undermine his

---

[17] My argument here seems to require the assumption that the appropriateness of epistemic evaluation, in general, can be explained by appeal to the appropriateness of evaluation vis-à-vis the truth principle (cf. §5.2.1). But even if this is not the case, we can get to the same conclusion, for the Humean will need to

sanguine belief that" he will not develop cancer, and someone who "deliberately seeks out evidence which will make him think overly well of himself," and asks:

> Are these people acting wrongly? Of course, they aren't doing what they need to, *if* they want their beliefs to be true. But by hypothesis they don't want their beliefs to be true. So is there any other sense in which they are proceeding improperly? It is not obvious to me that there is. (1999, p. 24)

There is a sense in which Papineau is right (cf. Chapter 9). But there is an obvious reply to what he says here: that of course there is *a sense* in which these people are proceeding improperly, namely, the *epistemic* sense. Papineau seems to assume that the only sense in which someone could ever be said to be "proceeding improperly" is the sense on which proceeding improperly is equivalent to violating the means–ends rule. But there are a number of other senses in which someone can be said to be "proceeding improperly." The traditional epistemologist maintains that there is at least one other sense: the epistemic sense.

6.2.5 Humean essentialism about judgment

My argument (§6.2.1) rested on the premise that belief is not necessarily intentional, and therefore does not "aim at truth" in the relevant sense. Conor McHugh (2011b) argues that **judgment**, unlike belief, is necessarily intentional:

> A judgment is an event in conscious thought with a propositional content; it is the conscious accepting, or endorsing, on the part of the thinker, of that propositional content as true, and thus the event of her committing herself to its being true. (p. 246)

In virtue of this, "in making a judgment about whether *p*, a thinker aims that the following state of affairs obtain: she judges *p* iff *p*" (p. 248). Call this **Humean essentialism about judgment.** My objections to Humean essentialism about belief do not apply to Humean essentialism about judgment: unrefined thinkers do not engage in judgment, and judgment is essentially conscious; there is no unconscious judgment-formation.

Although judgment that p results in believing that p, "judgments are conscious events, while beliefs are standing states that may or may not get manifested in consciousness" (p. 246). More importantly, believing that p does not require judgment that p, "as when you acquire the belief that there is a glass in front of you simply by seeing a glass there, without any conscious consideration" (pp. 246–7). Judgment is an episode or event, while belief is a state (p. 264).

Suppose Humean essentialism about judgment is true. We could combine this view with the attempt principle and explain the goodness of true judgments; or we could combine this view with the means–ends rule and explain the existence of epistemic

---

explain epistemic evaluation in terms of success and failure, achievement and lack of achievement, and so on. These are all intentional concepts, requiring motivation on the part of the person evaluated. If "unrefined thinkers" form beliefs without a desire to believe only the truth, surely they also form beliefs without a desire for any other positive epistemic status.

reasons for judgment. Given the diversity of judgment and belief, this would leave our questions about the value of true belief (§5.2.1) and the existence of epistemic reasons for belief (§5.2.2) unanswered. Contemporary epistemologists have taken the targets of certain paradigm species of epistemic evaluation and epistemic reasons attribution to be beliefs: epistemic justification is standardly taken to be a property of beliefs, knowledge is understood as a species of belief, epistemic reasons are reasons for belief. One response to the arguments of this chapter would be to abandon this idea, in favor of the idea that the targets of these species of epistemic evaluation and epistemic reasons attribution are judgments: judgments are epistemically justified or unjustified, knowledge is a species of judgment, and epistemic reasons are reasons for judgment. The principal drawback of this strategy would be that it is importantly revisionary vis-à-vis contemporary orthodoxy; consider the idea that wishful thinking is an epistemic vice (§6.2.4). On the other hand, again, such a revisionary strategy is appealing in that it avoids the objection to Humean essentialism about belief (§6.2.1).

An alternative strategy would be to understand the targets of epistemic evaluation and epistemic reasons attribution to be beliefs the formation of which are constituted by judgments (cf. McHugh 2011b, p. 247). But this has the same drawback as the previous strategy, in that it would exempt beliefs *not* formed in an act of judgment from epistemic evaluation and epistemic reasons attribution. Such a strategy would abandon universalism about epistemic normativity (§5.3.1). On this point, McHugh (2012b) writes that:

[O]ur ordinary practices do not presuppose that *every* doxastic state is properly subject to epistemic deontology. For example, certain pathological beliefs may not be. (p. 66)

But this is exactly what we have denied in assuming universalism about epistemic normativity: pathological beliefs are precisely the kinds of beliefs that we want to say are epistemically unjustified, epistemically irrational, and ones that we epistemically ought not hold.

A final possibility: Humean essentialism about judgment might ground epistemic evaluation and epistemic reasons attribution when belief is connected, in the right way, with judgment:

[B]elieving a proposition typically involves being disposed consciously to accept the proposition, should you consciously consider it[.] [T]he disposition to judge that *p* is a *central* or *canonical* disposition associated with belief in *p*. (McHugh 2011b, p. 247)

To say that this disposition is "canonical" means that cases of belief without said disposition "strike us as atypical or deviant," as "not the normal case of belief" (ibid.). From this premise, McHugh argues that:

Since you are responsible for your judgments, and believing *p* is constitutively connected to...being disposed to judge, that *p*, you are responsible for your belief [that *p*] in so far as you are disposed to judge that *p*. (Ibid. pp. 264–5)

We might take this idea up and say that your belief that p is subject to epistemic evaluation and epistemic reasons attribution in so far as you are disposed to judge that

p. Someone who judges that p ipso facto aims at judging that p iff p, and to judge that p is to form the belief that p. Therefore, if someone believes that p and is disposed to judge that p, she is disposed to aim at believing that p iff p. And this, so the argument goes, explains why her belief is subject to epistemic evaluation and epistemic reasons attribution.

This, again, has the benefit of avoiding the objection to Humean essentialism about belief and the drawback of violating universalism about epistemic normativity, as "subjects are not responsible in the normal way for...repressed beliefs and certain tacit beliefs" (p. 265). The plausibility of this idea, about responsibility, does not diminish the cost of rejecting universalism about epistemic normativity. That we are not responsible for some of our epistemically vicious believing does not diminish its epistemic viciousness (though it suggests that epistemic virtue and vice is not a matter of personal responsibility).

There is, however, a unique problem for this particular non-universalist strategy. The idea, again, is that my belief that p, not formed in judgment, is subject to epistemic evaluation and epistemic reasons attribution in virtue of the fact that I am disposed to aim at believing that p iff p. The present strategy amends the original Humean idea, on which belief is accompanied by a desire to believe nothing but the truth, in favor of the idea that belief (in the relevant cases) is accompanied by a disposition to desire to believe nothing but the truth. The problem is that it's not generally good (or bad) when I get (or don't get) what I merely dispositionally desire, and I do not generally have pro tanto reason to take the means to my merely dispositional ends. I stroll down Fifth Avenue, without a care in the world. The following might be true of me: were I to consider whether to check out the cufflinks at Zegna, I would want to check them out. This isn't because I've been meaning to check them out, because I had already formed the intention to check them out, at some earlier time; the thought has never crossed my mind and I presently have no desire to check them out. As it happens, the thought still doesn't cross my mind, even as I walk by the store, without entering. Now: Was this a failure? Did something bad happen? Was this a failed attempt to check out the cufflinks at Zegna? Does my behavior warrant a negative evaluation, qua attempt? Among the thousand natural shocks that flesh is heir to, we will not find the tragedy of our not getting what we merely would have wanted. Similarly, we may ask: Did I have pro tanto reason to check out the cufflinks at Zegna? Did I fail to respond to said reason by walking by the store? This is implausible. There are myriad things that I *would* desire, were I to consider them, but I do not *actually* have instrumental reasons to pursue those things.

Recall, again, one of the appealing features of Humean approaches to epistemic normativity (§6.1.1): when I attempt to Ψ, and succeed, *I* am a success; when I attempt to Ψ, and fail, *I* am a failure. If we appeal to dispositional desires we lose this appealing feature.

We may have the intuition that I've missed out on something by not checking out the cufflinks, and this intuition may have something to do with the fact that I would have wanted to check them out had I considered doing so. But this is explained by the fact that in this case we take my dispositional desire as a sign that I have actual, non-dispositional desires whose satisfaction would be furthered by checking out the cufflinks. Recall that we are allowing a broad conception of "desires," on which this includes various elements of my subjective motivational set, including my ground projects and what I care about or love. Someone who would want to check out the cufflinks at Zegna, were she to consider it, can be assumed to be someone who has an actual, non-dispositional interest in men's accessories. Dispositional desires sometimes reveal what a person's non-dispositional desires are, and when they do, they reveal her instrumental reasons. But instrumental reasons are absent in the absence of the relevant non-dispositional desires.[18] We might then think of our disposition to "aim at truth" as revealing a non-dispositional general desire for the truth; I criticized the appeal to such a desire above (§6.2.2).

6.2.6 Hypothetical goals

I have been defending the objection that Humean approaches to epistemic norma-tivity are forced to reject universalism about epistemic normativity (§5.3.1), given that not all beliefs are accompanied by a desire to believe nothing but the truth. Steglich-Petersen (2011) proposes a Humean account of epistemic reasons designed to vindicate universalism about epistemic normativity, which concedes the point that not all beliefs are accompanied by a desire to believe nothing but the truth. Steglich-Petersen's account is based on the existence of "purely hypothetical…instru-mental reasons that we have to pursue hypothetical aims, regardless of whether or not we do in fact have those aims" (pp. 27–8). For example, according to this idea, I pres-ently have hypothetical instrumental reason to go the airport in pursuit of the aim of going to Detroit. This reason exists in virtue of the fact that if I had the aim of going to Detroit, or if I had all-things-considered reason to pursue that aim, then I would have a (non-hypothetical) instrumental reason to go to the airport.

With this conception of purely hypothetical instrumental reasons in place, Steglich-Petersen offers an account of epistemic reasons:

[E]pistemic reasons are simply special cases of what we have called "hypothetical instrumental reasons". To be precise, they are instrumental reasons for believing particular propositions in pursuit of the hypothetical (i.e. present or non-present) aim of forming beliefs about those propositions. (p. 29)

Instrumental reasons are generated, via the means–ends rule, by the adoption of partic-ular aims, e.g. the aim of forming a (true) belief about whether p. Hypothetical instru-mental reasons exist regardless of whether a particular aim is adopted: I might have hypothetical instrumental reason to believe that p in pursuit of the aim of forming a (true) belief about whether p, even if I do not presently have (or have reason to pursue)

---

[18] I have spoken here of "dispositional desires" and "non-dispositional desires," but these are not two spe-cies of desire: "dispositional desire" is no more a species of desire than an egg is a kind of chicken.

that aim. This hypothetical instrumental reason is an epistemic reason to believe that p, which exists in the absence of any aim on my part to form a (true) belief about whether p. Likewise, given that he has evidence that he's in the Rose Garden, Obama has an epistemic reason to believe he's in the Rose Garden, absent any aim on his part to form a (true) belief about whether he's in the Rose Garden, and Mittens, given that she has evidence that she's on the mat, has epistemic reason to believe that she's on the mat, absent any aim on her part to form a (true) belief about whether she's on the mat.

Does Steglich-Petersen's proposal provide a plausible answer to the problem of the source of epistemic reasons (§5.2.2)? I'll argue that there are two ways of understanding Steglich-Petersen's proposal: on the first, it's an implausible account of epistemic reasons; on the second, it's a non-universalist Humean approach (§6.2.4).

The first interpretation: "purely hypothetical instrumental reasons" (e.g. epistemic reasons) are normative reasons. On this interpretation, I have a normative reason, right now, to go to the airport in pursuit of the aim of going to Detroit. But this is implausible. I don't have a normative reason, right now, to go to the airport in pursuit of the aim of going to Detroit. I don't have any normative reason, right now, to go to the airport. I *would* have a reason to go to the airport, if I had some reason to pursue the aim of going to Detroit (e.g. if I wanted to go to Detroit). But as things stand I have no such reason.

I assumed above (§5.2.2) that, necessarily, we ought to be responsive to the normative reasons that we have. This was my way of cashing out the idea that normative reasons make demands or claims on us. Given this assumption, it's not plausible that I have a normative reason to go to the airport in pursuit of the aim of going to Detroit. For although it would be the case that I ought to respond to such a reason, if I had reason to pursue the aim of going to Detroit, at present it's not the case that I ought to respond to any such reason. Even if I am presently totally unresponsive to my "purely hypothetical instrumental reasons," even if I totally ignore them, I am not failing to do what I ought. This suggests that "purely hypothetical instrumental reasons" are not normative reasons.

Steglich-Petersen replies to the worry that "purely hypothetical instrumental reasons" are ubiquitous: I presently have reason to go to the airport in pursuit of the aim of going to Detroit, to go to the train station in pursuit of the aim of going to Glasgow, to go down the hall in pursuit of the aim of cooking my own head in the microwave, to avoid the airport in pursuit of the aim of not going to Detroit, and so on. But this, Steglich-Petersen argues, is not a bad result:

If epistemic reasons are generated by evidence available to us, we have a large, perhaps infinite, number of epistemic reasons all the time, and far from all of them are about matters worth forming beliefs about. [...] [A]ny account of epistemic reasons must be able to explain why we are quite justified in not caring about the vast majority of them. The proposed account does just that. (2011, p. 31)

But the account achieves this by offering an account of epistemic reasons on which they are not plausibly taken to be normative reasons. I have normative (instrumental) reason to take the means to my ends, and when my end is believing nothing but the truth, I will have normative (instrumental) reason to, for example, cleave to my evidence. But when I have no such end, I will have no such normative (instrumental) reason.

Thus the second interpretation: "purely hypothetical instrumental reasons" (i.e. epistemic reasons) are not normative reasons; normative reasons to believe that p exist only when one has both a purely hypothetical instrumental reason to believe's that p in pursuit of the aim of forming a (true) belief about whether p *and* some reason to pursue the aim of forming a (true) belief about whether p. Steglich-Petersen suggests this interpretation, considering an objection on which his proposal "downplays the normative significance of epistemic reasons to an implausible extent" (p. 30). He replies, first, that since we do have reason to pursue the aim of forming a (true) belief about whether p for a "rather large number of propositions and subject matters," it turns out that epistemic reasons "very often" are "of normative significance" (p. 31). But this seems to abandon universalism about epistemic normativity (§5.3.1): genuine normative epistemic reasons are present only in certain cases. Even if those cases are common, we will get the counterintuitive result that when there is no reason to pursue the aim of forming a (true) belief about whether p, genuine normative epistemic reasons are not present. Consider, again, Grimm's (2008) example of the motes in the waiting room (p. 742), in which you have no reason to form a belief about the number of motes on the table: you would only have a "purely hypothetical instrumental reason," not a normative reason, to believe that there are 53 motes on the table. The present view suggests that someone who comes to believe that there are 3 motes on the table, on the basis of conclusive evidence that there are 53 motes on the table, is not failing to believe what she ought—for she lacks any normative reason to believe that there are 53 motes on the table. My argument here does not rely on the assumption that having conclusive evidence that p is sufficient for having a reason to form a belief about whether p. In Grimm's case, you have conclusive evidence that there are 53 motes on the table, but no reason to form a belief about the number of motes. The problem is that if, in spite of this, you do form a belief about the number of motes, Steglich-Petersen's account (on the second interpretation) implies that you have no normative reason to believe that there are 53 motes.[19]

6.3 Conclusion

In this chapter we considered Humean accounts of epistemic value (§6.1.1) and of epistemic reasons (§6.1.2), and presented a basic objection to them (§6.2): Humean approaches are forced to reject universalism about epistemic normativity (§5.3.1). We

[19] I'm sympathetic with the spirit of Steglich-Petersen's account; I favor rejecting the existence of normative epistemic reasons (Chapter 9). Steglich-Petersen's account resembles Richard Foley's (1987, 1993) account of epistemic rationality; I interpret Foley as an anti-realist, below (§9.2.3).

have thus seen a dilemma for Humean approaches to epistemic normativity. On the one hand, it's not plausible that believing that p requires desiring to believe that p only if p. On the other hand, it's not plausible to reject universalism about epistemic normativity. But the Humean must reject universalism if she admits the possibility of believing that p without wanting to believe that p only if p. This problem arises as a result of the Humean's crucial premise: that epistemic normativity is to be explained by appeal to the attempt principle or the means–ends rule.

7

Darwinian Approaches

Animals in evolutionary biology don't want to extend their family line, to produce progeny or improve, or even extend, their species; they just want to get laid.

—Adam Gopnik, *Angels and Ages*

Recall Darwinian essentialism about belief (§5.4.2), on which the biological function of belief is to represent the world accurately, i.e. to be true. Humean essentialism stumbled over the fact that beliefs need not be accompanied by the desires required for us to say that beliefs are essentially attempts (§6.2.1). Darwinian essentialism will not have this problem: the heart's biological function is to circulate blood, *sans* any desire on anyone's part for it to do so.

This chapter considers Darwinian approaches to epistemic normativity. These approaches are inheritors of the tradition in philosophical ethics that appeals to human nature (§1.2.3), and can be understood as a sophisticated, empirically informed instance of the sort of ethical "naturalism" that explains facts about what is good or right by appeal to claims about what is natural. However, I'll argue that Darwinian approaches depend on a problematic normative principle (§7.3), and that the plausibility of these approaches also depends on empirical knowledge about the natural history of human cognition that we presently do not possess (§7.4). First, we'll consider theistic accounts of epistemic value (§7.1), before sketching a Darwinian account (§7.2).

7.1 Theistic accounts of epistemic value

In his defense of the idea that "truth is the aim of belief," David Velleman (2000) writes that "to believe a proposition is to accept it with the aim of thereby accepting a truth," but that this "allows but does not require the aim of belief to be an aim on the part of the believer" (pp. 251–2). What's the alternative to this literal understanding of "aim" (cf. Chapter 6)? Velleman's answer is that:

A person can…aim cognitions at the truth without necessarily framing intentions about them. Suppose that one part of the person—call it a cognitive system—regulates some of his cognitions in ways designed to ensure that they are true, by forming, revising, and extinguishing them in response to evidence and argument. (Ibid. p. 253; see also Shah and Velleman 2005, p. 498)

An answer to the problem of the source of epistemic value beckons: true beliefs are good because true beliefs are as they were designed to be. Ernest Sosa (2009) appeals to the same idea in defense of his idea that "belief is a performance aimed at truth," comparing the idea that beliefs can perform well with the idea that "designed instruments…and…structures with a function" can perform well: "[a] bridge can perform well its function as a part of a traffic artery," and a "thermostat…may perform well in keeping the ambient temperature comfortable" (p. 8).

If analogizing beliefs, or cognitive systems, to designed artifacts is apt, then the answer just sketched seems credible: snow tires are designed to enable driving in the snow, and in virtue of this fact about their history, it's appropriate to evaluate a set of snow tires in terms of whether they enable one to drive in the snow, because that's what they were designed to do. And on the assumption that artifacts are to be individuated by their histories of design, so that a set of snow tires is essentially a set of snow tires, other species of evaluation of snow tires (e.g. in terms of whether they enable driving in sand), whatever they have going for them, will not be species of essential evaluation of snow tires.

It's easy to see how a theist could make sense of the artifact analogy. You might say that God designed our beliefs, or our cognitive systems, with truth in mind. This would explain the sense in which truth is the "aim of belief": in the same sense that truth is the "aim of belief" because God intends our beliefs to be true, regulating the temperature is the "aim of this thermostat" because its designer intended that it regulate the temperature, and safely supporting traffic over the river is the "aim of this bridge," because its designer intended that it safely support traffic over the river. Given our assumption about the essences of artifacts, we can say these "aims" are "internal" to beliefs, and to the thermostat, and to the bridge. But make no mistake: what literally aims at truth is God, not your beliefs, just like what literally aims at regulating the temperature is the thermostat's designer, not the thermostat.

The idea that God designed our beliefs with truth in mind has a rich pedigree in the history of philosophy. It is the cornerstone of Descartes' reasoning in the Fourth Meditation, and more recently Alvin Plantinga (1993) has based his epistemological theories on the premise that God created human beings with reliable faculties, and has challenged the foundations of naturalistic epistemology (2002) against this backdrop. But this theistic artifact analogy is not available to philosophical naturalists (§5.5).

Much of this chapter will be devoted in a roundabout way to explaining why that is so. The basic idea is simple enough: design requires a designer, artifact requires artificer, and function requires purpose. Jerry Fodor (1996) is right when he calls this point "obvious and dreary" (p. 252). Despite arguments to the contrary, arguments which have the ignoble distinction of vindicating popular misconceptions about evolutionary biology, namely, that what the theory of evolution by natural selection says is that our essential purposes come from Nature, not from God. As Fodor puts it, the "truly Darwinian idea" is that "*there isn't any Mother Nature*, so it can't be that we are her children or her artifacts" (ibid. p. 261).[1]

7.2 Darwinian essentialism about belief

Velleman's argument, however, isn't theistic. He goes on to write that beliefs "guiding the subject when true is what confers advantages on him, and so it appears to be what beliefs were selected for, in the course of evolution" (2000, p. 253n). His talk of our cognitive systems being "designed" is meant to imply that they are "designed by natural selection," not that they are literally designed by some designer (e.g. God). That's the idea behind Darwinian essentialism about belief. In this section we'll sketch this idea further (§7.2.1), before articulating a naturalistic account of biological functions (§7.2.2) and an account of truth as the biological function of belief (§7.2.3).

7.2.1 The very idea

We must tread carefully here. In speaking of things being "designed by natural selection" we run the risk of tacitly committing ourselves to a fundamentally mistaken interpretation of the theory of evolution by natural selection. There is a popular misconception of said theory that is little more than traditional theism, but with amoral and impersonal "nature" doing the work previously done by God. On this popular misconception, Nature has purposes, and these determine the proper functions of organisms and their parts, as well as of ecosystems and other supra-organismal entities. Nature designs things to be a certain way, sometimes things go according to design (this is good), and other times not (this is bad). But all this talk of "Nature's designs" and "Nature's purposes" is completely worthless to us, unless it can be reformulated in a way consistent with what evolutionary biology actually says.

The idea that beliefs are "designed by natural selection" to be true is popular in contemporary philosophy. W. V. O. Quine (1969) quipped that creatures with unreliable faculties "have a pathetic but praiseworthy tendency to die before reproducing their kind" (p. 126, and quoted sympathetically in Alston 2005, p. 30), and Daniel Dennett (1971) writes that "the capacity to believe would have no survival value unless it were a capacity to believe truths" (p. 101). This idea has led many philosophers to suggest the idea that being true is the biological function of belief, and to analogize beliefs to bodily organs, e.g. the human heart. Sosa (2009), for example, says that just as belief can

---

[1] Two naturalistic ways of conceiving of beliefs as artifacts should be rejected. First, you might conceive of the believer herself as the "designer" of her beliefs. We have in effect already discussed that idea above, in our consideration of Humean approaches to epistemic normativity (Chapter 6). Second, you might conceive of other people—e.g. the believer's parents—as the "designers" of her beliefs. But the considerations adduced above (§6.2) speak against this idea as well, mutatis mutandis.

perform well by being true, "[w]hen a heart beats...it may perform well in helping the blood circulate" (p. 8). And William Alston (2005) writes that:

The function of sense perception is to provide us with true beliefs about the immediate physical environment, in the same sense in which the function of the heart is to pump blood around the body. (p. 33)

The idea that cognition is "designed" for reliability is regularly cited by epistemologists (Sosa and Alston, op. cit., Goldman 1986, p. 98, Lycan 1988, p. 142). Formulating this idea more precisely will take some doing.

Darwinian essentialism about belief jibes with teleosemantic approaches to intentionality, content, and representation (Millikan 1984, 1993, Dretske 1968, Papineau 1993, pp. 55–101, 2001, Neander 1991, 1995, 2004, Macdonald and Papineau 2006). Three points about this. First, Darwinian essentialism about belief is a claim about belief in particular; some teleosemantic theorists have sought to cover more of the intentional landscape: not only belief but desire, or all mental representation, or representation in general (e.g. including linguistic representation), or all mental content (e.g. including non-conceptual content), or content in general (e.g. including linguistic content), or the mental in general (e.g. including apparently non-representational states like being in pain). Second, teleosemantic theorists typically aim to give a naturalistic account of content, e.g. of the fact that my belief that p has the content that it does. Darwinian essentialism about belief is not necessarily committed to this, although you might find it hard to imagine someone would be attracted to Darwinian essentialism about belief but not to a teleosemantic account of doxastic content. Third, one might adopt a teleosemantic account of belief, but reject Darwinian essentialism about belief, on the grounds that truth is not the (or a) biological function of belief.

We will not be concerned here with any problems for teleosemantics save those that arise for Darwinian essentialism about belief. So, for example, if teleosemantics cannot account for the content of non-conceptual, perceptual representation, that is not our concern here. We will also set aside the "swampman" objection (Davidson 1987; for replies see Millikan 1984, pp. 93–4, Papineau 2001), the "disjunction problem" (Fodor 1990; for replies see Dretske 1986, Millikan 1993, pp. 211–39, Papineau 1993, Neander 1995), and the epistemological objection raised by Frank Jackson (2006).

7.2.2 What is a biological function?

Darwinian essentialism about belief says that truth is the biological function of belief. What does it mean to say that to Φ is the biological function of x? I'll make a relatively uncontroversial assumption: biological function properties are historical (or etiological) properties.[2] Furthermore, I'll assume an etiological account of biological functions that

---

[2] There are non-etiological notions of "function" (Wright 1973, Cummins 1975; cf. Odenbaugh 2010). Given the relative ubiquity of false belief (Chapter 2), they would be of no use in articulating epistemic essentialism about belief. The assumption that biological function properties are etiological properties captures something important about biology's status, since Darwin, as an historical science. The theory of

is based on Ruth Millikan's (1984, 1993) influential account (see also Papineau 1993, Neander 1991, 1995, Kingsbury 2006), on which:

A proper function of…an organ or behavior is, roughly, a function that its ancestors have performed that has helped account for the proliferation of the genes responsible for it, hence helped account for its own existence. (1993, p. 14)

As Karen Neander (1995) puts it:

Some effect (Z) is the proper function of some trait (X) in organism (O) iff the genotype responsible for X was selected for doing Z because Z was adaptive for O's ancestors. (p. 111)

Let's look a bit closer at what is involved in a genuine case of something having a biological function, following Millikan's account (1984, pp. 17–50). Consider the barbels on this catfish, the function of which is to enable her to detect food. This is an historical claim about the natural history of the catfish, about her ancestors (other catfish and/or catfish-like organisms) and also about the "ancestors" of her barbels (parts of other catfish and/or catfish-like organisms). What the claim says is that the ancestors of this catfish had barbels (or "ancestors" of its barbels) that enabled them to detect food, and that this conferred evolutionary advantage on them (it enhanced their ability to survive and reproduce), and that as a result genes for having barbels proliferated, which explains why this catfish has those genes, and thus why she has barbels. That's what it means to say that the function of the barbels on this catfish is to enable her to detect food.

Notice that this claim is orthogonal to the question of whether having barbels *actually* confers evolutionary advantage on this catfish. This is an essential point, as Millikan urges (e.g. 1984, p. 29; see also Neander 1995, p. 111–12), because it allows us to make sense of cases of failure and malfunctioning, whether uncommon (e.g. a rare illness that causes heart failure) or ubiquitous (e.g. the failure of most sperm to fertilize an egg).

Notice that this claim is orthogonal to the question of whether having barbels *would have* conferred evolutionary advantage on the ancestors of this catfish. As Fodor (2002) notes:

What Darwinism requires as (roughly) sufficient for the evolution of a trait is *both* that the trait would be adaptive if the organisms were to have it; *and* that, in point of historical fact, there are some (rudimentary, approximate, proto-) instances of the trait actually on the ground for selection to operate upon. (p. 41; cf. Sober 1981, pp. 110–11, Feldman 1988b, p. 220)

What the biological function claim says is that having barbels *did* confer evolutionary advantage on the ancestors of this catfish.

Wearing cufflinks from Zegna confers evolutionary advantage on me, and (we can imagine) it would have conferred evolutionary advantage on my ancestors, but wearing such cufflinks is not among my biological functions. This is for two reasons. First,

evolution by natural selection is our best contemporary biological theory. If there is teleology (i.e. function, purpose) to be found in biology, it will be historically-based teleology.

my ancestors did not wear Zegna cufflinks. Second, there is no gene for wearing Zegna cufflinks. Thus, we cannot give the relevant sort of explanation for why I wear Zegna cufflinks that would be needed to establish that wearing them is among my biological functions.

When we say that to Φ is the biological function of x, where x is a part or feature of organism o, we are committed to (at least) these three claims:

i. (Natural historical claim) The ancestors of o had x (or some "ancestor" of x), and the fact that their x Φed conferred evolutionary advantage on them.
ii. (Genetic claim) There are genes for having x (and for having x that Φ).
iii. (Explanatory claim) The truth of the genetic claim and the natural historical claim explains why o has x.

Two comments on this understanding of biological functions. First, biological function claims will be true only relative to a species of organism. The function of catfish barbels, for example, could be different from the function of another animal's barbels. We shall here focus our attention on the biological function of *human* belief.[3] Second, for Millikan, biological functions are a species of "proper functions" (Millikan 1993, p. 14, Papineau 1993, p. 59), which is a broader category that includes, for example, the functions of artifacts. I have articulated the notion of a *biological* function in terms of genetic selection, but this is a simplification, and there's work that would need to be done to make good sense of the notion. For one thing, we have relied on the problematic notion of there being a "gene for" some trait (cf. Kendler 2005). For another, there are intuitive cases of biological function where the genetic claim is false. Songbirds, when all goes well, sing a song typical for their species, but the song an individual bird sings is not a matter of that bird's genotype, but rather a matter of the songs that that individual bird was exposed to as a juvenile. Singing a species-appropriate song thus seems, in some obvious sense, to be a biological function: present-day sparrow singing is explained by the evolutionary advantages conferred upon their ancestors who sang the sparrow-specific song. But whether a bird sings a species-appropriate song is a learned behavior, not a matter of genetics. However, this simplification will not make a difference when it comes to Darwinian essentialism about belief: it is not plausible that belief is a learned behavior. As Neander (1995) argues, "given that our interest ... is with innate information processing in natural cognitive systems, we can ignore other selection processes and focus on functions which derive from natural selection alone" (p. 111).

7.2.3 Darwinian essentialism about belief

Teleosemantic theorists argue that (roughly) to be true is the biological function of human belief (Millikan 1984, pp. 17–19, pp. 93–4, 1993, pp. 71–5, 2006, Papineau 1993,

---

[3] Which is not to say that we can ignore other animals. Facts about *Homo habilis* may be relevant to biological functions in *Homo sapiens*, but facts about lemurs are irrelevant.

pp. 55–101, 2001, Neander 1991, 1995). But this rough formulation requires some polish. Take my belief that Caticus is on the mat. Given our understanding of biological functions (§7.2.2), we should not say that the biological function of this belief is to be true. For my ancestors did not believe that Caticus is on the mat, nor are there genes for believing that Caticus is on the mat.

What did my ancestors have, for which there are genes, and which conferred evolutionary advantage on them? More plausibly, they had reliable cognitive faculties, i.e. faculties that produced mostly true beliefs.[4] Thus teleosemantic theorists speak of the evolution of "cognitive systems" (Millikan 1993, p. 11) and of "cognitive *mechanisms* and inference *strategies*" (Ramsey 2002, p. 22). The function of these, one might argue, is to produce true beliefs.[5] Let us assume, for the sake of argument, that the biological function of human cognition, and thus of my cognitive faculties, is to produce true beliefs.

We need two moves to recover Darwinian essentialism about belief. First, we need to introduce the notion of a "derived" biological function, where the notion we articulated above (§7.2.2) was the notion of an **original biological function**. Consider the "device" that enables this chameleon to change the color of its skin (Millikan 1984, pp. 439–5, Kingsbury 2006, pp. 46–8). Suppose that the original biological function of the color-change "device" is to make the chameleon invisible to predators. But now the chameleon sits on some brown-and-green surface. The biological function of the color-change "device," you might think, is to make the chameleon's skin match the particular color of the surface on which it's now sitting, i.e. to make the chameleon's skin brown and green. This is the **derived biological function** of the color-change "device."[6]

Second, we need to adapt this distinction to cases in which we want to speak of the biological function of some product—which I'll call the **productive derived biological function** of that product. Consider the token pattern that appears on the chameleon's skin on a particular occasion. The productive derived biological function of this token pattern is to match the color of the surface on which the chameleon is now sitting, i.e. to be brown and green. This is because the (derived) biological function of the color-change "device" is to make the chameleon's skin match the surface

---

[4] I speak here and in what follows of "faculties," but we could just as easily speak of systems, processes, mechanisms, or practices. Likewise, I speak here and in what follows of beliefs as "products" of cognition, but we could just as easily speak of them as outputs, or of what is yielded or caused.

[5] This ignores another wrinkle and another level of derivation (on "derivation," see below): teleosemantic theorists often argue that a function of belief is "to participate in inferences in such a manner as to help produce fulfillment of desires" (Millikan 1993, p. 71). A function of cognition, then, is to cause desire-satisfaction. In what sense, then, is the function of cognition to produce true beliefs? The answer requires appeal to Millikan's notion of a "Normal" explanation (1984, pp. 33–4): a Normal explanation of how cognition causes desire-satisfaction (how it fulfills its function) will appeal to the production of true beliefs (Kingsbury 2006, p. 29). In this sense, which is different from the sense articulated above (§7.2.2), the function of cognition is to produce true beliefs.

[6] A rigorous articulation of the notion of a derived proper function requires the notion of a "Normal" explanation (Millikan 1984, pp. 43–5, Kingsbury 2006, pp. 27–8).

on which the chameleon is sitting (the pattern on the chameleon's skin is, in this sense, a product of the color-change "device").[7]

We are now in a position to articulate Darwinian essentialism about belief. The original biological function of human cognition is to produce true beliefs.[8] The derived biological function of my cognitive faculties is to produce a true belief about whether Caticus is on the mat. And the productive derived biological function of my belief, about whether Caticus is on the mat, is to be true. Thus:

> **Darwinian essentialism about belief:** The productive derived proper function of human belief is to be true (in virtue of the fact that the original proper function of human cognition is to produce true beliefs).

Given the etiological account of (original) biological functions, Darwinian essentialism about belief is committed to three claims:

i. (Natural historical claim about human cognition) The ancestors of humans had cognitive faculties (or "ancestors" of cognitive faculties), and the fact that their cognitive faculties produced true beliefs conferred evolutionary advantage on them.

ii. (Genetic claim about human cognition) There are genes for having cognitive faculties (and for having cognitive faculties that produce true beliefs).

iii. (Explanatory claim about human cognition) The truth of the genetic claim and the natural historical claim explains why humans have cognitive faculties.

This view deserves the name "essentialism" on the assumption that the biological function of x reveals the essence of x (cf. Millikan 1984, p. 93). Given this assumption, the Darwinian offers a **biological conception of belief**.

7.3 Darwinian approaches to epistemic normativity

In this section we'll articulate a Darwinian essentialist account of epistemic value (§7.3.1), and I'll argue that the account is implausible (§§7.3.2–7.3.5). Then we'll briefly look at the prospects for a Darwinian account of epistemic reasons (§7.3.6).

7.3.1 A Darwinian essentialist account of epistemic value

Recall the basic question about epistemic evaluation (§5.2.1): what (if anything) makes epistemic evaluation (e.g. evaluation of beliefs vis-à-vis the truth principle)

---

[7] Again, because a Normal explanation of how this token pattern makes the chameleon invisible to predators (how it fulfills its function) will appeal to the fact that it matches the surface on which the chameleon is sitting. I assume that this avoids the worry that products do not always have a function (Fodor 1990, pp. 65–6). If not, so much the worse for Darwinian essentialism about belief.

[8] Modulo the wrinkle described above (this chapter, footnote 5).

appropriate? Let us grant Darwinian essentialism about belief. Does this answer the basic question? We need to combine this premise with a normative assumption:

Principle of (productive derived) biological value: Instances of (productive derived) biological functioning are (in one respect) good and instances of (productive derived) biological malfunctioning are (in one respect) bad.

We can now sketch a Darwinian essentialist account of epistemic value. The productive derived biological function of belief is to be true, and so true beliefs are instances of productive derived biological functioning (and false beliefs are instances of productive derived biological malfunctioning). Assuming the principle of (productive derived) biological value, we can conclude therefore that true beliefs are (in one respect) good and false beliefs are (in one respect) bad. This explains the appropriateness of evaluating beliefs vis-à-vis the truth principle. Given the assumption that the biological function of x reveals the essence of x (§7.2.3), this Darwinian account entails that evaluation of beliefs vis-à-vis the truth principle is essential evaluation of beliefs (§5.4.1).

Given the idea that truth is *the* (productive derived) biological function of belief, the Darwinian can answer the uniqueness question (§5.2.1) as follows: epistemic evaluation of beliefs (e.g. evaluation vis-à-vis the truth principle) is appropriate, in a way that other forms of evaluation of beliefs are not, because only epistemic evaluation is evaluation in terms of the (productive derived) biological function of belief. The idea that truth is *the* (productive derived) biological function of belief can be challenged, however; we'll return to this below (§7.4). Finally, in answer to the scope question, the Darwinian can adopt a doxastic conception of the epistemic (§5.2.4).

Is the principle of (productive derived) biological value true? I'm going to assume that it is plausible only if the following principle is plausible as well:

Principle of biological value: Instances of biological functioning are (in one respect) good and instances of biological malfunctioning are (in one respect) bad.

So, given the principle of biological value, it's good if and when the catfish's barbels enable her to detect food, and bad if and when said barbels fail to perform their function. This principle entails the principle of (productive derived) biological value, and it is hard to see how one could defend the latter without assuming the former. I think the most plausible picture of "biological value" would have to be one on which the value of *derived* biological functioning (including *productive* derived biological functioning) depends on the value of *original* biological functioning. Thus, for example, the reason it is good for the pattern of the chameleon's skin to match the surface on which she is sitting is *because* it is good for her to be invisible to predators.

7.3.2 Worthless proper biological functioning

In this section, I'll argue that the principle of biological value is implausible. This undermines the Darwinian essentialist account of epistemic value (§7.3.1).

Some teleosemantic theorists have rejected the principle of biological value. Neander (1995) writes that:

[T]he normativity of biological functions is [not] evaluative…Judging that something is functioning properly is not the same as judging that its functioning is good. (p. 111)

There are indeed reasons to be skeptical about the principle of biological value. Now it's not hard to come up with examples of biological functioning that seem not to be best, all things considered. But this would just illustrate the fact that the principle of biological value must be understood to concern pro tanto goodness, and only pro tanto goodness. However, you might well wonder whether some instances of proper biological functioning have any value at all—i.e. whether they enjoy even pro tanto goodness. Consider this catfish; it slowly swims through the muck, detecting food with its barbels, and eating what food it finds. Is this good? Grant, of course, that this is what "nature intended," that the catfish is "supposed" to be doing this, that the biological function of its barbels is to enable it to detect food. Is this a good thing? And, most importantly, is this necessarily a good thing because it's what "nature intended"? Cases can be multiplied, and it will be useful to consider organisms that we are not inclined to anthropomorphize. A single-celled protist divides; a fungus releases a puff of spores; a sea cucumber excretes a cloud of waste. Are all these events good, in virtue of being instances of biological functioning? You can of course imagine something that seems good about each of these, if you tell the story right: perhaps this fungus is food for some other species, so its spread will provide someone with a meal, and some (but not all) biological functions seem good for the organism that performs them. What we will not find, however, is some general sense, covering all instances of biological functioning, in which all such instances are good. For this reason, the principle of biological value is implausible.

7.3.3 Biological functioning and eudaimonic value

You might argue that biological functioning is good for the relevant organism. Mark Bedau (1993) proposes this conception of teleology, on which there is an "essential conceptual link between teleology and value" (p. 43). He argues that "it is difficult to find a value-free case of natural selection," as "examples of natural selection…typically involve traits that are *beneficial* to biological organisms" (ibid. p. 35). Bedau links the notion of teleology to the notion of value *for* something, and argues that "crystals, rocks, and other bits of inorganic matter are not the kinds of things for which the notion of better or worse off makes sense" (ibid. p. 43). Thus teleological-evaluative notions can be correctly applied only to organisms, on Bedau's view, and only in as much as they are capable of being better or worse off. Talk of the functions, purposes, and goals of an organism translates, on this proposal, into talk of what is good or bad for that organism.

It's possible to define "biological function" along these lines. But then we will need to substantially revise our treatment of many particular cases. Take the case of the fungus releasing its spores: this doesn't benefit the fungus, and therefore isn't an instance of biological functioning. Ditto for the division of the protist. In the standard sense of "biological function," biological functioning isn't always good for the relevant organism. Much of our medical practice involves putting a stop to biological functioning, for the good of the patient. Antihistamines interfere with the biological functioning of the human immune system. It's at least sometimes good for me when my immune system fails to function properly, as a result of my taking an antihistamine.

However, the real problem here, for our purposes, is that on Bedau's evaluative conception of biological teleology, talk of biological function translates into talk of eudaimonic value (§1.1.1). A Darwinian essentialist account of epistemic normativity, cashed out in Bedau's terms, would amount to a version of the eudaimonic account of epistemic normativity that I criticized above (5.3).

7.3.4 Is the principle of biological value trivially true?

You might argue that the principle of biological value is trivially true, or true by definition, or in some similar sense an obvious platitude or truism. After all, doesn't it just say that proper functioning is good? How could what is *proper* fail to be *good*? But if the principle of biological value is trivially true, then it can't do the work that the Darwinian essentialist needs it to do in answering the basic question about epistemic evaluation. What is needed is a principle to bridge the gap between the non-evaluative claim that truth is the biological function of belief, and the claim that evaluation of beliefs vis-à-vis the truth principle is appropriate. No triviality can bridge that gap; what is needed, given realism about epistemic normativity (§5.2.3), is a principle or principles affirming the goodness of biological functioning.

Could the Darwinian say that biological functioning is good, "qua biological functioning"? Compare the domain of epistemic value to the domain of "sodic value": the domain that takes ingesting salt, and only ingesting salt, to have value. The more salt someone ingests, the better she does when it comes to sodic evaluation. It would do nothing to *explain* the appropriateness of sodic evaluation by appealing to the trivial truth that ingesting salt is good, "qua ingestion of salt." There may be a trivial truth in the neighborhood: in some sense, ingesting salt *is* good, "qua ingestion of salt." But this triviality cannot explain the existence of "sodic value," which is needed for a realist account of sodic evaluation. What would be needed is the assumption that ingesting salt *really is good*, in some *non-trivial* sense. Thus we must understand the principle of biological value as making a non-trivial claim about the goodness of instances of biological functioning.

I said that biological function claims are non-evaluative. Teleosemantic theorists may balk at this (Millikan 1989, p. 296): isn't "proper" an essentially "normative term"?[9] If "proper function" is a term of art (Millikan 1993, pp. 14–15), then it will be an open question whether "proper" is normative. But biological function claims can't be

---

[9] Indeed, Millikan (1993) writes that "true" and "false" are "normative terms" (p. 72).

essentially normative, given the way we defined them above (§7.2.2): they're descriptive, historical claims. This leaves open the question of whether biological functioning is good, or bad, or neither, either all-things-considered or pro tanto.

Now there may be a sense in which biological function claims are normative. My only point here is that the biological function claims are not essentially normative in the sense required to answer the problem of the source of epistemic value. We have used a descriptive, historical definition to ground our talk of biological function, as a way of making naturalistic sense of the idea of "design by natural selection." As Fodor writes (in a related context), to adopt this language in connection with evolutionary biology "is not…a metaphysical breakthrough" (1996, p. 253). It may be (although Fodor denies this) a useful shorthand, a heuristic for thinking about organisms and their natural histories. But knowing that true beliefs are what "nature intended" will not alone tell me what I *ought* to believe (or whether it's appropriate to evaluate people's beliefs vis-à-vis the truth principle), just as knowing that ingesting salt is good from the sodic point of view will not alone tell me what I *ought* to ingest (or whether it's appropriate to evaluate other people's eating habits from the sodic point of view).

7.3.5 Sex and the open question argument

We have failed to find a sense in which instances of biological functioning are non-trivially good. Our discussion here recalls two well-known arguments: Hume's suggestion (*Treatise*, III.I.1) that one cannot derive an "ought" from an "is," and G.E. Moore's (*Principia Ethica*, I.B) "open question" argument. But you need not endorse either of those arguments to endorse the reasoning outlined here. My method has tended more towards particularism: I have reflected on the particular "is" claims made by evolutionary biology, and seen that they leave open the relevant questions of value. My argument was not that one cannot in general derive an "ought" from an "is," but that biological function claims do not support the relevant evaluative claims that we are looking for.

I have not employed the controversial "open question" strategy. That strategy imagines an analysis of "good" on which x is good iff F(x), and objects that it will always be an open question whether *being F* is valuable. The analogous strategy against the principle of biological value would object that it seems to be an open question whether *being an instance of biological functioning* is valuable. Rather, my objection was that some instances of biological functioning seem to have no value, or not to obviously have any value. One can object to the "open question argument" on the grounds that the correct analysis of goodness might not preserve our evaluative intuitions (DePaul 2010, pp. 133–5), but our argument above did not complain that we fail to find things valuable under the description "instance of biological functioning." On the contrary: perhaps it seems to many of us that instances of biological functioning are valuable, as such. The problem was that when we look at particular instances of biological functioning, there often does not seem to be any value to be found.

A final consideration may speak against a Darwinian approach to epistemic value. Suppose we grant the principle of biological value. This leaves open the *strength* or *importance* of the pro tanto goodness of instances of biological functioning. Consider the biological function of sexual intercourse. Among the biological functions of sexual intercourse—if this is not the unique biological function of sexual intercourse—is reproduction. What explains—what biologically explains—our having sexual intercourse is the fact that so doing proved advantageous to our ancestors when it led to reproduction. Tokens of sexual intercourse could thus be evaluated vis-à-vis standards implied by the biological function of sexual intercourse, namely, whether or not said tokens resulted in reproduction. Sexual intercourse is good, vis-à-vis this standard, when it results in reproduction, and bad otherwise. Call this **reproductive evaluation** of sex.

So far, so good. Given the principle of biological value, this gives us a sense in which reproductive evaluation of sex is appropriate. But you might well think that such evaluation is more often than not inappropriate, in myriad other senses—and, indeed, much more important senses. There are many ways of evaluating sex, other than reproductive evaluation; consider: evaluating tokens of sexual intercourse in terms of whether the intercourse was consensual (good) or not (bad); evaluating tokens of sexual intercourse in terms of whether the intercourse was pleasurable or satisfying to the parties involved (good) or not (bad); evaluating tokens of sexual intercourse in terms of whether one or more of the parties was cheating on someone (bad) or not (good); and so on.

The question we face is whether we are prepared to see epistemic evaluation of beliefs in the same way: as one of a plurality of species of evaluation of beliefs, perhaps a relatively unimportant species compared to others. I'm attracted to that idea (§9.4). My point here is that, even if we grant the principle of biological value, reflection on the strength or importance of biological value reveals that it may not count for much, all things considered.

But didn't we assume above (§7.3.1) that, for the Darwinian, epistemic evaluation of beliefs is essential evaluation of beliefs? Indeed; but given what we've just seen, we will need to take one of two routes. We might argue that, even though non-reproductive sex is bad, qua sex, we just don't care all that much about sex, qua sex, and it is of little importance to us. When hobos start a fire in an oil drum, they are unperturbed if their drum turns out to be bad, qua oil drum, because it lacks a crucial gasket. (This seems a fairly plausible response to reproductive evaluation of sex: the importance of consent is not a matter of the essential nature of sex, but it's far more important that sex be consensual than that it result in reproduction, or that it be good, qua sex, whatever you might take that to mean.) The value of true belief might then face a similar fate, as a relatively unimportant value, among others of much greater importance.

Alternatively, we might make the metaphysical argument that the biological function of sex doesn't determine the essential nature of sex (not for creatures like us, anyway), and thus that reproductive evaluation of sex is not essential evaluation. (This

seems at least partially right: someone who thinks that the purpose of sex is to reproduce has somehow missed the point; we want to say that such a person, in some sense,
doesn't really know what sex is.) In taking this route we would reject the idea that the
biological function of a thing determines its essential nature. Cognition might then
face a similar fate, to be understood as a non-biological category.

7.3.6 Darwinian essentialism and epistemic reasons

Recall the distinction between epistemic value and epistemic reasons (§5.2.2). Someone
attracted to a Darwinian approach to epistemic normativity might reject the principle
of biological value, and propose a Darwinian account of epistemic reasons, by rejecting the teleological conception of epistemic reasons. Our criticism of the principle of
biological value would not touch such an account. What we would need, to make such
an account plausible, is some general principle connecting facts about biological functions and the existence of a species of normative reasons, where the biological function facts explain the existence of that species of normative reasons. It's obscure how
this might go. Consider the fact that the biological function of the heart is to circulate
blood. Are there normative reasons whose existence is explained by this? Does this
fact about the heart, for example, give my heart a normative reason to circulate blood?
Does it, alternatively, give me a normative reason to promote my heart's circulation of
blood? Or to promote the circulation of blood by hearts, in general? This would be
easier had we not rejected the principle of biological value. For then we might explain
the existence of (normative) biological reasons by appeal to biological value. No philosopher, to my knowledge, has offered a Darwinian account of epistemic reasons of
the sort imagined here. So we won't spend any more time trying to articulate such an
account, apart from to say that such articulation seems difficult.

7.4 The many functions of belief?

Above (§7.2.3), we formulated Darwinian essentialism as the claim that *the* (productive
derived) biological function of belief is to be true. This claim was based, in turn, on the
idea that *the* original biological function of human cognition is to produce true beliefs.
This section considers whether that idea is plausible, or whether, alternatively, there are
a plurality of biological functions of human cognition.[10]

Some things have a plurality of biological functions. The ichthyologist will tell you
that the swim bladder of the channel catfish has two functions: to regulate the catfish's
buoyancy (so that it sinks to the bottom) and to enable the catfish to hear (vibrations
are passed from the bladder to the inner ear via parts of the skeleton). So perhaps we
ought to say merely that *a* function of human cognition is to produce true beliefs (cf.

---

[10] Compare the distinct question of whether human cognition is in fact reliable (Plantinga 2002, Ramsey
2002; cf. Fodor 2002, p. 42). The production of true beliefs might be the original function of human cognition, even if human cognition rarely performs that function.

Millikan 1984, p. 317), and leave open the question of whether reliability is *the* function of human cognition. If we said that some of these other biological functions were **non-epistemic functions**, in the sense that the performance of these functions had nothing to do with our cognitive faculties producing true beliefs, knowledge, understanding, etc., then the Darwinian would have to give a different answer to the uniqueness question (7.3.1), on which epistemic evaluation of beliefs would be merely one form of evaluation among many.[11]

First (§7.4.1), I'll consider some candidate reasons for thinking that human cognition has non-epistemic biological functions. Second (§7.4.2), I'll consider the idea that the evolutionary advantages of self-enhancement bias (Chapter 2) suggest that human cognition has the non-epistemic biological function of promoting motivation. I'll argue that we have just as much reason to think that a biological function of human cognition is to promote motivation as we have for thinking that a biological function of human cognition is to produce true beliefs. Third (§7.4.3), I'll respond to some objections to my argument.

7.4.1 Non-epistemic functions of human cognition?

You might appeal here to the possibility of **adaptive false positives**. The psychologist James Alcock (1995) imagines a rabbit whose survival depends on fleeing at even the slightest suggestion of danger, and concludes that "seeking truth does not always promote survival, and fleeing on the basis of erroneous belief is not always such a bad thing to do." If rats are irradiated while eating distinctively flavored food pellets, the resulting nausea gives rise to a strong disposition not to eat food pellets of that flavor (Garcia et al. 1972). However, the same rats did *not* manifest a disposition not to eat food pellets of the same size and shape as those that they ate prior to being made ill. Thus it seems that these rats associated food-related illness with the flavor of food, and not with its size or shape. They appeared to conclude that such-and-such flavor is an indicator of food contamination (or something to that effect).

What does this suggest when it comes to the question of whether there are non-epistemic functions of human cognition? Very little. For one thing, it's obscure whether the cases described involve false belief (Feldman 1988b, p. 222, McKay and Dennett 2009, p. 501; cf. Dretske 1986, pp. 304–8, Fodor 1990). For another, granting that the rats in Garcia's study falsely believed that such-and-such flavor is an indicator of food contamination, it's obscure whether this suggests that their cognitive faculties are unreliable, since we should surely answer the question of the reliability of rat cognition by looking at the reliability of rat cognition in the environments where rats are normally to be found—environments which resemble those in which rats evolved. If, in such environments, flavor is reliably correlated with food contamination, and post-dining sickness is also reliably correlated with food contamination, then the rats'

---

[11] A rigorous account of the notion of a non-epistemic function of cognition would require appeal to the notion of a "Normal" explanation (Millikan 1984, pp. 33–4).

inference would not easily go wrong in its natural environment, and unreliable cognition is not suggested by their behavior.

But even if unreliable cognition is suggested, for all we've said so far, all the cases suggest is that rat cognition is, and rabbit cognition might be, unreliable in some situations. Suppose we have reason to believe that human cognition is likewise unreliable in some situations. We did not need 20th-century empirical psychology to tell us that human cognition is fallible: "from time to time I have found that the senses deceive," Descartes meditated—and so have we all.

These cases bear on our question—about whether there are non-epistemic functions of human cognition—only if we start speculating about *why* an organism's cognitive faculties might be unreliable. Stephen Stich (1990) argues that:

Strategies of inference that do a good job at generating truths and avoiding falsehoods may be expensive in terms of time, effort, and cognitive hardware. [N]atural selection might well select a less reliable inferential system over a more reliable one because the less reliable one has a higher level of...fitness. (1990, p. 61; see also Stich 1985, pp. 124–5, 1990)

This is the premise behind **error management theory** (Haselton and Buss 2003, Haselton 2007), on which the fallibility of human cognition, at least in many cases, is the result of natural selection. This will happen when the costs of false positives are low and the costs of false negatives are high, as in the case of Alcock's rabbit. Error management theorists (Haselton and Buss 2000) argue that men's tendency to overestimate the sexual interest of women involves evolved fallibility of precisely this type.

But even if human cognition is fallible for these kinds of reasons, it does not suggest that there are non-epistemic functions of human cognition. For it is possible for an evolved "device" (to borrow Millikan's term) to malfunction most of the time—it's possible for malfunctioning to be ubiquitous, as in the case of sperm (§7.2.2). And it's possible that such ubiquitous malfunctioning is not a design flaw but a design feature, i.e. it's possible for ubiquitous malfunctioning to evolve. And this seems like exactly what we should say, if human cognition is fallible in the ways suggested by error management theorists. Less fallible faculties would have been costly (e.g. in terms of "time, effort, and cognitive hardware," Stich 1990, p. 61), with no particularly appealing payoff in terms of evolutionary advantage, and so fallible faculties evolved. But none of this suggests that the biological function of such faculties isn't to produce true beliefs. Error management theory could just be a footnote to Descartes: an account that may explain *why* we're sometimes deceived.

Some scientists argue that **sense perception** involves cognitive faculties that are evolutionarily advantageous but systematically unreliable (e.g. Marks et al. 2010). Color perception is often cited as a paradigm case (e.g. Wilson and Lynn 2009). We should concede that the appearance of the world in visual perception, in some important sense, does not match the intrinsic nature of the world that we perceive. But it is obscure whether this failure of match involves us in any false beliefs: my National Geographic Map of The World indicates political differences with color differences, but I do not believe that the land in Saudi Arabia is pink and the land in France is blue. A projectivist view of color perception, assumed by many scientists, is compatible with a charitable account of our beliefs about the colors of objects (Averill and Hazlett 2011).

There is a vast literature suggesting that we tend to use various **cognitive heuristics** (Kahneman et al. 1982, Nisbett and Ross 1980, Gilovich et al. 2002): e.g. the "representativeness heuristic," the "availability heuristic," and "adjustment and anchoring" heuristics. Furthermore, it is argued that our tendency to use such heuristics is a tendency to form false beliefs—and thus that human cognition is systematically unreliable. If this is right, it could serve as a first premise in an argument that such systematic unreliability is a product of natural selection (Stich 1985, pp. 116–20, 1990, pp. 4–10, pp. 60–3)—and perhaps then in an argument that there are non-epistemic functions of human cognition. However, it is controversial whether our tendency to use cognitive heuristics suggests systematic unreliability. Gerd Gigerenzer (2000, 2008; see also Gigerenzer et al. 1999; see Kahneman and Tversky 1996 for a reply) argues that our tendency to use heuristics does not suggest that human cognition is systematically unreliable. Gigerenzer's argument is motivated in large part by a worry about the ecological validity of the research suggestive of systematic unreliability. The cognitive faculties of the rats studied by Garcia and his colleagues led them astray in the lab, but in the right environment, the same faculties might be reliable. Similarly, human cognitive faculties may foul up in the lab, but in the right environment, the same faculties might be reliable. Gigerenzer (2008) argues that:

The rationality of heuristics is not logical, but ecological. Ecological rationality implies that a heuristic is not good or bad, rational or irrational per se, but only relative to an environment. (p. 23)

For example, consider "base-rate neglect" (Kahneman and Tversky 1982). Suppose you're told that 0.1% of people have disease X, that the test for disease X has a 5% rate of false positives, and that Sarah has just tested positive for disease X. What is the chance that Sarah has disease X? Most people will say that the answer is 95%, but the correct answer is 2%. However, the correctness of this answer depends on an assumption of random sampling—that Sarah was a randomly selected member of the population. But in the real world, people who take tests for a particular disease are usually people who have symptoms of that disease, or who are at risk of that disease, or who are otherwise more likely than a randomly selected member of the population to have that disease. The story was ambiguous on this point, but if one makes this assumption, then the correct answer isn't 2%. Thus, Gigerenzer argues (2000, pp. 251–4), it is obscure whether base-rate neglect involves a tendency to form false beliefs outside the psychologist's lab, where sampling is rarely random. In any event, it's controversial that our use of cognitive heuristics suggests that human cognition is systematically unreliable, and thus so is the idea that our use of cognitive heuristics provides evidence for the existence of non-epistemic functions of cognition.

Even if our tendency to use cognitive heuristics does suggest that human cognition is systematically unreliable, the explanation for this might be in terms of error management (see above), in which case we have not found evidence for the existence of non-epistemic functions of cognition.

We have found no promising candidate reason for thinking that human cognition has non-epistemic biological functions. But note well that the truth of this idea cannot be settled a priori. We cannot conclude a priori that there are no non-epistemic functions of human cognition. This is why our inquiry has turned to various empirical questions about human cognition.

7.4.2 Self-enhancement bias and motivation

Ryan McKay and Daniel Dennett (2009) argue that self-enhancement bias involves the formation of "adaptive misbeliefs." They offer two pieces of evidence for this. First, they argue that positive illusions about one's sexual partner(s) and children "can propel adaptive actions" (p. 506). Second, they argue that "positive illusions can directly sustain and enhance health" (ibid.; cf. §2.6.3). However, they concede that "we do not expect adaptive misbeliefs to be generated by mechanisms specialized for the production of beliefs that are false per se" (p. 508).

Does this suggest that there are non-epistemic functions of human cognition? It seems like the mechanisms of self-enhancement bias are functioning properly even when they output false beliefs, for these are the very beliefs that can "propel adaptive actions" and "sustain and enhance health." McKay and Dennett argue that "positive illusions" are adaptive, i.e. that such beliefs presently confer evolutionary advantage on the believer. They do not offer any reason to believe the relevant natural historical claim, genetic claim, and explanatory claim (§7.2.2). For this reason, even if they are right that "positive illusions" are adaptive misbeliefs, it would be premature to conclude that there are non-epistemic functions of human cognition, until we have natural historical and genetic evidence that the mechanisms of self-enhancement bias evolved for the purpose of producing "positive illusions."

I'll argue, though, for the following:

Parity claim: Our reasons for thinking that a biological function of human cognition is to produce true beliefs are just as good as our reasons for thinking that a biological function of human cognition is to promote motivation.

To evaluate the parity claim, we need to think about the reasons we have for thinking that a biological function of human cognition is to produce true beliefs. Our reasons turn out to be rather minimal, as they're based on a priori speculation about the natural history of human cognition. The argument is that reliable cognitive faculties would have been advantageous to our ancestors. Why think so? We should not appeal here to the argument that unreliable faculties, e.g. faculties that produced beliefs that were mostly false, would have been disadvantageous to our ancestors (Lynch 2004, p. 48, Alston 2005, p. 30), as this provides weak support for the claim that reliable faculties would have been advantageous to our ancestors. Rather, the argument needs to appeal to our intuitions about hypothetical cases of evolutionary advantage, for example:

Two groups of our ancestors leave their caves, on the hunt for mammoth. One group, as a matter of genetics, have more reliable perceptual faculties than the other. The group with more reliable faculties quickly spot a mammoth, and accurately throw their spears. The mammoth runs into the forest, but the hunters give chase; their keen ears track the mammoth's bellows. Finally they catch it, bring the meat back to the cave, etc. Compare the group with less reliable faculties: they mistake a mossy rock for a mammoth, their spears miss their target, they bring nothing back to the cave, they starve and die, etc.

And by finishing the story we can provide the natural history required to say that a biological function of human cognition is to be reliable:

Genes for more reliable faculties flourish; this explains (in part) why we are cognitive creatures.

However, given our conclusions about self-enhancement bias (Chapter 2), we have equally good reason to think that to promote motivation is among the biological functions of cognition. Consider:

Two groups of our ancestors (with equally reliable perceptual faculties) leave their caves, on the hunt for mammoth. One group, as a matter of genetics, enjoy a disposition towards self-enhancement bias. The self-enhancing group leave their cave with confidence, and pursue the mammoth relentlessly; an initial setback (the mammoth's flight into the forest) is met with renewed motivation in pursuit. They catch the mammoth, bring the meat back to the cave, etc. Compare the non-self-enhancing group, who leave their cave with a depressive pessimism at their chances; after an initial setback (the mammoth's flight into the forest) they decide to give up the hunt as hopeless, and return to the cave empty handed, they starve and die, etc.

Again, we can finish the story to provide the natural history required to say that a biological function of cognition is promoting motivation:

Genes for self-enhancement bias flourish; this explains (in part) why we are cognitive creatures.

This speculative natural-historical story is just as plausible as the one given above, in defense of the view that a biological function of cognition is to produce true beliefs. Both stories are essentially based on something we know about ourselves now: respectively, that reliable cognition is sometimes beneficial and that self-enhancing cognition is sometimes beneficial. On these bases, the stories speculate, respectively, that reliability would have been beneficial to our ancestors and that self-enhancement would have been beneficial to our ancestors. To get from that speculation to their respective conclusions (that a function of human cognition is to produce true beliefs, that a function of human cognition is to promote motivation), we made analogous assumptions. First, an assumption about **natural history**: that what would have been advantageous for our ancestors actually was advantageous for our ancestors. Second, an assumption about **genetics**: that there are genes for reliable cognition and self-enhancement bias, respectively. And finally, an **explanatory** assumption: that the relevant natural-historical idea (above) explains why we presently are cognitive creatures.

Suppose human cognition has non-epistemic functions. There are two important consequences of this. First, Darwinian approaches to epistemic normativity will need to give a different answer to the uniqueness question than the one we articulated above (§7.3.1). These approaches will have to say that epistemic evaluation of beliefs is one form of evaluation among many, with no special status. Epistemic evaluation of beliefs vis-à-vis the truth principle would be appropriate *in exactly the same way* that evaluation of beliefs in terms of how well they promote motivation is appropriate. Second, the Darwinian would not be able to offer a reduction of the epistemic value of true belief to the "biological value" of true belief, for we would have to admit non-epistemic "biological values" of belief—e.g. the goodness of beliefs that promote motivation. The scope question (§5.2.1) would remain unanswered.

7.4.3 Objections and replies

This section considers three objections to my argument for the parity claim. First, you might object that our reliable cognitive faculties (e.g. sense perception, inductive reasoning) are innate and our having them is a matter of genetics, while people's dispositions for self-enhancement bias are not innate and our having them is not a matter of genetics. Therefore, to promote motivation is not a biological function of cognition. Call this **the genetic objection**.

A priori speculation can tell us almost nothing about genetics.[12] Darwinian essentialism about belief, if it is true, is knowable only a posteriori.[13] So this objection is cogent only if there is empirical evidence that there are genes for reliable cognition but not for self-enhancement bias. You might appeal here to individual differences, to show that self-enhancement bias is not "a general law of human behavior applicable to all normal, psychologically healthy individuals" (John and Robins 1994, p. 208). But this fact doesn't suggest a disparity between self-enhancement bias and our reliable cognitive faculties, when it comes to their genetic basis, since there are individual differences in, for example, perceptual ability. More promising is the issue of cultural differences in self-enhancement bias. Self-enhancement bias is less pronounced for subjects in Japan and China than for American subjects (see Heine et al. 1999 for a review), and there is a debate among psychologists as to whether the self-enhancement "motive"

---

[12] There is a tempting thought here, in which there is a sense in which the heart is just by definition that organ whose function it is to pump blood. You might think: in as much as we are prepared to call something a "heart," its function is to pump blood, and likewise, in as much as we are prepared to call something a "belief," its function is to represent the world accurately. But this is to abandon the a posteriori method proper to Darwinian essentialism. We'll return to this a priori conceptual approach below (Chapter 8).

[13] This is neutral as to whether it is necessary or contingent. You might think that hearts are essentially (and thus necessarily) organs whose function is to pump blood, and if some organ's function was not to pump blood, it wouldn't be a heart. Or you might think it possible that there be hearts whose function was something other than pumping blood (Fodor 1996, p. 254). Either way the question is empirical (Feldman 1988b, p. 226).

is present in some cultures and not in others (Heine and Lehman 1997, Heine et al. 1999) or whether it is universal and "cultures vary in the degree to which they allow, encourage, or suppress the motive's expression" (Brown and Kobayashi 2003a, p. 492; see also Segall et al. 1998, Kurman 2001, 2003, Brown and Kobayashi 2002, 2003b, Kobayashi and Brown 2003, Sedikides et al. 2003). Given this controversy, the cogency of the genetic objection is an open empirical question. However, as suggested, cultural differences are compatible with underlying genetic similarities. Moreover, some cultural differences correlate with genetic differences (e.g. lactose tolerance). What is really needed to assess the cogency of the genetic objection is evidence correlating, or failing to correlate, individual differences in self-enhancement bias with individual genetic differences. Such evidence is not presently available.

Second, you might object that to produce true beliefs is the "primary" function of human cognition, while to promote motivation is merely a "secondary" function (Papineau 1993, pp. 61–5). On this basis, we can account for the special status of epistemic evaluation. Call this **the piggybacking objection** (for reasons to be explained).

What does it mean to say, of something that has two biological functions, that one of its functions is "primary" and the other "secondary"? Three bad answers. First, a statistical understanding of "primary": the primary biological function of x is that biological function that x performs more often than any other biological function. But frequency of performance is not generally a criterion for biological functions. Second, a nominal understanding of "primary," on which (e.g.) the primary function of the catfish's swim bladder is to regulate buoyancy, because it has the name "swim bladder." But this is a bad argument, which would imply that the "primary" biological function of the gall bladder is to regulate temper. Third, an originalist understanding of "primary": the primary biological function of x is the first biological function that "ancestors" of x ever had. But this involves unappealing vagueness (consier *Plesiadapis*, an early ancestor of primates; does the biological function of this creature's claws, which is currently a matter of controversy, make a difference when it comes to the biological function of my hands?) and seems inconsistent with the plausible idea that something's biological function can change over time (shall we say that the primary biological function of cetacean flippers is to enable whales to walk on land?).

More promising is an explanatory understanding of "primary." Recall that to say that Φing is the biological function of x is (among other things) to make an explanatory claim, to the effect that the fact that x's "ancestors" Φed explains why x presently exists. Now a state of affairs (T) could be explained by a plurality of states of affairs (e_1, e_2, e_3), and it might be the case, so the argument goes, that e_1 explains T to a greater degree than do either of e_2 or e_3. In that sense, e_1 can be said to be the primary explanation of p, with e_2 and e_3 providing secondary explanations. An example: Shaquille O'Neal and Justin Bieber are pushing a boulder up a hill; what explains the boulder's motion? Shaq's pushing is the primary explanation; Bieber's is only secondary.

Let's assume that this idea about explanation makes metaphysical sense. How can we tell that the reliability of our ancestors' faculties explains the fact that we are cognitive creatures to a greater degree than do the motivation-promoting features of our ancestors' faculties? Here's one kind of argument:

Let's grant that our ancestors faced two distinct problems: representing their environments accurately (the "representational problem") and keeping their spirits up (the "motivational problem"). And let's grant that cognition evolved as an effective strategy for solving both of those problems. There remain two important points: (1) cognition would have evolved even if our ancestors had faced only the representational problem, and (2) cognition wouldn't have evolved if our ancestors had faced only the motivational problem. Indeed, cognition *couldn't* have evolved only to solve the motivational problem. Notice the way in which our cognitive faculties solve the motivational problem: by "piggybacking" on their solution to the representational problem. Self-enhancement bias exploits an antecedently existing representational system whose function is to represent the environment accurately. Only if such a system were antecedently available could a cognitive solution to the motivational problem evolve. That's why the reliability of our ancestors' faculties explains the fact that we are cognitive creatures to a greater degree than do the motivation-promoting features of our ancestors' faculties, and that's why reliability is the primary function of cognition.

The disparity that the piggybacking objection draws our attention to seems real (cf. §2.10.1), and the explanation offered—that the primary reason we are cognitive creatures is that cognition is reliable—seems plausible. Further argument and empirical inquiry could shore up these ideas. But we should step back and ask what this means for the uniqueness question. Suppose we say that reliability is the primary biological function of human cognition in virtue of the fact that the reliability of our ancestors' cognitive faculties explains, more than anything else, the fact that we are cognitive creatures. Epistemic evaluation of beliefs is appropriate, in this sense, and non-epistemic evaluation of beliefs isn't. Recall the issues raised above in criticism of the principle of biological value (§7.3.5). Even if epistemic evaluation of beliefs is uniquely appropriate in virtue of the fact that reliability is the primary function of cognition, you might well wonder about the relative strength or importance of this species of value—the value instances of proper *primary* biological functioning—as compared to the strength or importance of other species of value. That the value of x derives from the value of primary biological functioning, while the value of y derives from the value of secondary biological functioning, tells us little about the relative all-things-considered values of x and y. We might quite reasonably care more for y than for x.

Third, you might object that, rather than saying that human cognition has a plurality of functions, we should say that different human cognitive faculties have different biological functions: the function of our perceptual faculties (say) is to produce true beliefs, but the function of the faculties involved in self-enhancement bias is to promote motivation. An attractive way of articulating this idea might distinguish between perception, in which an organism represents its environment via some sense modality (with characteristic sense organs), and social cognition, which involves representation of information about an individual organism, conspecifics of that organism, relations between that individual and its conspecifics, and relations between its conspecifics.

Perhaps social cognition has non-epistemic biological functions, while perception has none. (Recall that all our counterexamples to the eudaimonic ideal of true belief came from the domain of human social cognition.) Call this **the modularity objection**.

What we seek is an account of the value of true belief, i.e. some sense in which all true beliefs are good. But if there are a plurality of sources of beliefs, some of which have non-epistemic biological functions, what sense can we make of the idea that beliefs are good if and only if true, from a biological point of view? The idea that some human cognitive faculties have non-epistemic biological functions seems to have the same consequences as the idea that human cognition has non-epistemic biological functions (§7.4.2).

You might opt for a more radical idea: that those representational states we have been lumping together as "beliefs" are actually quite different sorts of things. If "perceptual beliefs" are the products of faculties that evolved for reliability alone, and "social-cognitive beliefs" are the products of faculties that evolved for a plurality of purposes, why think these states have anything essential in common, save the name "belief"? You might argue that epistemic evaluation of "perceptual beliefs" has special status, but that epistemic evaluation of "social-cognitive beliefs" has no special status. This would be a radical departure from traditional epistemology. Moreover, given the characteristic functional profile of belief (§1.6.2), there is good reason to think of "perceptual beliefs" and "social-cognitive beliefs" as having something essential in common. "Perceptual beliefs" and "social-cognitive beliefs" are united by their common functional profile. And these two would-be species of representational state can interact with one another in revealing ways: a "perceptual belief" that ~p can cause the abandonment of a "social-cognitive belief" that p, for example. The present proposal would require abandoning our functionalist criteria for belief attribution.

Suppose that we seek to understand the goodness of (human) social-cognitive beliefs by looking at the biological function of (human) social cognition. We will have to find out, then: Under what conditions did social cognition evolve? What selection pressures resulted in the emergence of social cognition? What feature or features did our ancestors' social cognitive faculties enjoy, which explain why we are social-cognitive creatures? One hypothesis that psychologists and biologists have generated is that social cognition evolves when there is a need to deal with an increasingly complex social environment. For an African wild dog to survive and reproduce as a member of a pack with a dominance hierarchy, she needs to keep track of the dominance relations between herself and the other members of the pack. This suggests accuracy as a function of social cognition in African wild dogs: with an accurate picture of one's status, within the pack's dominance hierarchy, an individual dog will have a better chance of surviving and reproducing. But what about social cognition in humans? Human societies have rarely had a rigid dominance structure of the sort found in African wild dogs, and even our more flexible social hierarchies are relatively recent, emerging in the Neolithic period. Early humans and our hominid ancestors lived somewhat egalitarian lives, relative to our unequal and stratified societies. So the story of the evolution of social cognition in humans will not be the same as for African wild dogs. And as I have urged, a priori speculation here is worthless. The emerging science of social cognition will be able to determine, perhaps, how and why social cognition evolved.

7.5 Individual differences

When it comes to the value of true belief, on a Darwinian approach to epistemic normativity, we should consider not the functions of cognition, but the functions of human cognition, and perhaps not even the functions of human cognition, but the functions of human social cognition. But further refinement may be needed, as it's possible for there to be individual differences, between members of a species, when it comes to biological function.

Consider *Physa* snails. Individuals of these species come in two distinct morphological types: some snails have "rotund" shells and some have "elongate" shells. Whether an individual snail will have a rotund or elongate shell is determined by what predator odors the snail is exposed to as it grows (DeWitt 1998): snails exposed to the smell of crayfish develop elongate shells, while snails exposed to the smell of sunfish develop rotund shells. This is explained (DeWitt et al. 2000) by the fact that rotund shells are more difficult to crush, while elongate shells have a smaller aperture, and by the fact that sunfish feed on these snails by crushing their shells (which is more difficult when the shells are rotund) while crayfish dine by extracting the *escargot* through the aperture (which is more difficult if the aperture is narrow). What is the biological function of *Physa* shells? What makes for a good *Physa* shell? It depends on the individual; in rotund individuals, the function of the shell is to prevent sunfish predation; in elongate individuals, the function of the shell is to reduce crayfish predation.

In this case, individual differences evolved as a result of selection pressures in tension: to combat sunfish predation the thing to do is to grow wide and strong; to combat crayfish predation the thing to do is to grow thin and narrow; but there are both sunfish and crayfish around every corner. *Physa* solved this problem by evolving individual differences in response to predator odor. Rotund snails are less susceptible to sunfish predation but vulnerable to crayfish predation, but if all goes well they're less likely to run into crayfish; elongate snails are less susceptible to crayfish predation but vulnerable to sunfish predation, but if all goes well they're less likely to run into sunfish.

Therefore: a possibility that needs to be considered is that cognition, or social cognition, or some more specific doxastic practice (e.g. self-evaluation), has different biological functions for different individuals. Individual differences, of the sort we are interested in here, evolve in response to selection pressures in tension. For an example from human psychology, consider extroversion (Nettle 2006). People with high extroversion scores have higher levels of social status, social attention, and increased physical activity (all good things when it comes to reproduction); but they also have higher levels of accidents, disease, and social conflict, and have a lower life-expectancy (all bad when it comes to survival). Score high on extroversion and you're likely to get laid, but only if you live long enough. Score low on extroversion and you'll live longer, and so have more chances to reproduce, but you'll likely be a chaste loser.

The idea that social cognition might have different biological functions for different (human) individuals is attractive, because of individual differences in self-enhancement bias (§2.4, §2.9.1). Perhaps just as *Physa* snails come in two types, humans come in two types:

Type 1	Type 2
Lower self-esteem	Higher self-esteem
Higher depression	Lower depression
Lower self-enhancement bias	Higher self-enhancement bias
Lower narcissism	Higher narcissism

Individual differences in human social cognition deserve the attention of epistemologists. The reason for this is that naturalistic philosophers must be open to the possibility—indeed they should expect—that we may be able to say nothing absolute when it comes to the eudaimonic and epistemic value of true belief, just as we can say nothing absolute when it comes to the proper shell shape for *Physa* snails. Recall, again, Hume's observation of "the vast variety of inclinations and pursuits among our species." Some philosophers consider themselves brave and perhaps profound when they ask: "But which of those inclinations and pursuits is *right*, or *good*, or *best*?" For those human differences that are analogous to the aforementioned differences among *Physa* snails, that question is confused.

7.6 Conclusion

Consider the role that we are asking evolutionary biology to play if we seek an account of epistemic value by appealing to Darwinian essentialism about cognition. We are asking evolutionary biology to play the epistemological role that natural theology plays for some philosophers. Thus Descartes, in his *Meditations*, sought to secure the reliability of his faculties by inquiring into God's nature as creator of those faculties. In our secular age, there is a temptation to speak of the reliability of our faculties as secured by "evolutionary design," in the same way that Descartes sought security in their divine design. But two deep differences between divine design and "evolutionary design" make this move problematic. The first is metaphysical, and we discussed it above (§7.1): God literally designs things; "Nature" doesn't. To analogize "Nature" to God is to invite a metaphysical mistake, since "natural design" grounds an entirely different notion of function or purpose than that notion of function or purpose grounded by divine design. The second deep difference, which we have just encountered (§7.5), is epistemological: God's designs, you might think, can be inquired after a priori; but "nature's designs" absolutely cannot be. Epistemology grounded in natural theology is plausibly a priori; epistemology grounded in natural selection absolutely is not (cf. Fumerton 1994, Fodor 1996, p. 251).[14] Reflection and meditation might very well yield a satisfying metanarrative in terms of divine design, but the narratives of evolutionary biology cannot be justified by reflection and meditation alone.

We have considered Darwinian approaches to epistemic normativity (§7.2), and I argued that we should reject the principle of biological value (§§7.3.2–7.3.5), which they assume. And I have argued that it is an open empirical question whether human cognition has non-epistemic biological functions. A Darwinian approach to epistemic normativity would require a posteriori empirical inquiry, focused on human cognition in particular (including social cognition), and drawing on the resources of anthropology, evolutionary psychology, genetics, social psychology, and cognitive science. Prior to such inquiry, the biological functions of human cognition are not yet known.

[14] This problematizes the casual comparison of naturalized and non-naturalized epistemology (Sosa 2004, p. 295, p. 299, p. 304).

8

Kantian Approaches

In this chapter we'll consider the third version of epistemic essentialism about belief (§5.4.2), on which a normative standard of correctness is part of the concept of belief. The existence of this standard depends not on the desires of the believer, as on Humean approaches (Chapter 6), nor on the natural history of cognition, as on Darwinian approaches (Chapter 7), but flows straight away from the concept of belief.

I call these approaches to epistemic normativity "Kantian" in virtue of their resemblance to the view, sometimes called "Kantian" or "constitutivist," that standards of right action are contained in the concept of action. On the constitutivist view of action, reflection on the nature of action will reveal standards of right action, just as, for the Kantian essentialist about belief (§5.4.2), reflection on the nature of belief will reveal standards of correct belief. A consequence of the constitutivist view of action is that standards of right action apply to you, regardless of whether you want to conform to those standards; Kantian essentialism about belief has an analogous consequence: that epistemic principles apply to you, regardless of whether you desire or intend to abide by those principles (cf. Shah 2011, pp. 102–7).

I don't mean to suggest that Kant did offer or would offer what I'm calling a "Kantian" approach to epistemic normativity. In his lectures on logic, he says that "a principal perfection of cognition, indeed, the essential and inseparable condition of all its perfection, is truth" (9:50; see also 24:56–8, 24:709, 24:806–10).[1] This is a "law of the understanding" (9:36), a necessary, objective, non-psychological "rule" of cognition (9:12–13, 24:25, 24:693–4, 24:791), and these Kant compares to natural laws like the law of gravity and the "hydraulic rules" that govern the movement of water (9:11, 24:21, 24:693), rules of grammar (24:693, 24:790–1), and the "rules of movement" that animals follow when they move around (9:11, 24:27). There are affinities between these remarks and what I'm calling "Kantian" approaches to epistemic normativity; of particular interest is the idea that there are normative rules essential to the understanding, grounding a special relationship between cognition and truth. But I'll say no more about Kant's own views.

---

[1] For English quotations from Kant I am using J. Michael Young's translations of the lectures on logic (Kant 1992) and Mary Gregor and Jens Timmerman's translation of the *Groundwork of the Metaphysics of Morals* (Kant 2012).

Kantian essentialism seems like a species of realism about epistemic normativity (§5.2.3), but this classification may offend its defenders; defenders of the Kantian or constitutivist view of action have traditionally understood their position as an alternative to both realism and anti-realism about standards of right action. I won't enter into this controversy, and will therefore not assume that Kantian essentialism about belief is a species of realism about epistemic normativity.

I'll offer two arguments against Kantian approaches. The first (§8.3) says that Kantian essentialism conflicts with the naturalistic constraints (§5.5). This puts pressure on the Kantian to offer reasons for accepting her view, despite this cost. The second argument (§§8.4–8.5) targets the best available argument for Kantian essentialism, which appeals to certain features of belief that are alleged to be necessary features of belief. I object that these features are contingent. Mine is thus a familiar Humean objection to Kantianism: the phenomena that Kantians treat as necessary features of agency and cognition are in fact contingent features of human agency and human cognition.

8.1 Formulating Kantian essentialism about belief

I'll formulate Kantian essentialism about belief by looking at the slogan "belief aims at truth." Attempting to articulate what this slogan amounts to will bring us to a formulation of Kantian essentialism.

8.1.1 Williams on "belief aims at truth"

Bernard Williams (1973, 2002) argues that belief "aims at truth," and it has seemed to many that this slogan captures something important about the essential nature of belief. Williams explains the slogan "belief aims at truth" as expressing three things:

1. "[T]hat truth and falsehood are a dimension of assessment of beliefs as opposed to many other psychological states or dispositions. Thus if somebody just has a habit of a certain kind…it is not appropriate to ask whether this habit of his is true or false." (1973, p. 137)
2. "[T]o believe that p is to believe that p is true. To believe that so and so is one and the same as to believe that that thing is true." (Ibid.)
3. Saying "I believe that p" "is a way…of asserting that p is true." (Ibid.)

I do not think claim (3) can be taken as an articulation of what the slogan "belief aims at truth" means. It's more plausible to take this claim as *evidence* that belief "aims at truth," which is what we'll do below (§8.6.1). So let's focus on claims (1) and (2) and see if they provide an adequate articulation of the idea that belief "aims at truth." I'll argue that they don't.

Claim (1), if understood in the way that Williams suggests, is obviously true. But this gives us very little by way of understanding what the slogan "belief aims at truth" means. What (1) affirms is that belief is a propositional attitude, and therefore something capable of having true or false content. Habits are not propositional attitudes; they have no propositional content, and therefore are incapable of having true or false content. But this at least does not exhaust the sense in which belief "aims at truth," for if it did, then we would have to say that anything with propositional content (desire, supposition, imagining) "aims at truth." That belief is a propositional attitude, and thus something capable of having true or false content, is a precondition for it being something that "aims at truth." But this fact about belief does little to explain what it is for belief to "aim at truth." However, you might note that truth is not a "dimension of *assessment*" (my emphasis) for desire; we'll return to this below (§8.1.2).

Claim (2) is inadequate for two reasons. First, it's false, because there are creatures capable of belief but without the concept of truth, and thus incapable of believing that it is true that p (Kvanvig 2003, p. 34; cf. Davidson 1982). Second, supposing it were true, then it would be an instance of a more general truth: that to adopt any propositional attitude towards the proposition that p is to adopt that propositional attitude towards the proposition that it is true that p. Thus to desire that p is to desire that it is true that p, to suppose that p is to suppose that it is true that p, to imagine that p is to imagine that it is true that p, and so on (Velleman 2000, pp. 247–8, Kvanvig 2003, p. 34, Shah 2003, p. 448). So if (2) articulates the sense in which belief "aims at truth," then again all propositional attitudes "aim at truth."

Suppose we revise claim (2) to:

2*. To believe that p is to regard the proposition that p as true; believing that p is one and the same thing as regarding the proposition that p as true.

But there are other propositional attitudes that are instances of regarding the proposition that p as true, namely, all the "cognitive" attitudes: supposing that p, imagining that p, and so on (Velleman 2000, p. 250). So, as with (1), this does not adequately articulate the idea that belief "aims at truth," for imagining that p does not "aim at truth." So to articulate the slogan that "belief aims at truth," we must find some "defensible connection" between belief and truth that doesn't hold between, e.g., imagining and truth (cf. Kvanvig 2003, p. 34, Owens 2003).[2]

8.1.2 The normative conception of the "aim of belief"

Defenders of the idea that belief "aims at truth" have articulated this idea in normative terms (Railton 1994, 1997, Wedgwood 2002, 2007, pp. 153–73, Boghossian 2003,

---

[2] Some defenders of the idea that belief "aims at truth" have wanted this idea to distinguish belief from all other propositional attitudes. It's beyond the scope of the present inquiry to give adequate attention to the question of the nature of belief. Briefly, we should be wary of drawing conclusions about the nature of belief based on a perceived need to distinguish it from other propositional attitudes, since the distinction between belief and other propositional attitudes is part of common sense. Compare Hume's discussion in his "Appendix" to the *Treatise* (1978, p. 629) and Thomas Reid's discussion in his *Essays on the Intellectual Powers of Man*, Essay 20, Chapter 20 (1983, pp. 198–9).

2005, Shah 2003, Shah and Velleman 2005, Heironymi 2006, Lynch 2009a, pp. 231–40, 2009b, pp. 76–83). The most promising version of this articulation takes truth to be the **standard of correctness** for belief. As Ralph Wedgwood (2002) puts it:

> [T]here is a fundamental epistemic norm of correct belief—to put it roughly, the principle that a belief is correct if and only if the proposition believed is true. (p. 272; see also 2007, p. 162, Shah 2003, p. 458)

So let's begin by considering:

> **The Standard of doxastic correctness:** Necessarily, for any subject S and proposition that p, S's belief that p is correct iff it is true that p, and incorrect otherwise.[3]

Correctness is normative, and the standard of doxastic correctness is not intended as an expression of any trivial truth, e.g. that it is true that p iff p. Wedgwood (2002) explains:

> To say that a mental state is "correct" is to say that in having that mental state, one has got things "right"; one's mental state is "appropriate". To say that a mental state is "incorrect" is to say that in having that mental state, one has got things "wrong" or made a "mistake"; one's mental state is in a sense "defective." (p. 267; see also 2007, p. 155, p. 157)

And Paul Boghossian (2003) argues that it is a "norm of belief" that "[o]ne ought to believe that p only if p" (p. 37, 2005, p. 210). Is the standard of doxastic correctness a necessary or a contingent truth, if it is true? You could see how it could be contingent if it depended on contingent facts about my natural history, as on a Darwinian approach. Having considered those approaches already, we will assume that the standard of doxastic correctness is necessarily true, if it is true.

Defenders of a normative conception of the "aim of belief" have taken the fact that belief "aims at truth" not only to be a necessary truth, but to be one that reveals the essential nature of belief (Wedgwood 2002, p. 270). In this sense, defenders of this approach take the standard of doxastic correctness to be a **constitutive standard**,[4] i.e. a member of a species of norms that "articulate…features that make belief the type of mental state that it is" (ibid. p. 271). As Boghossian (2003) puts it, that "belief aims at truth" is "constitutive of belief" because "the holding of this norm is one of the defining features of the notion of belief" (p. 38). Furthermore, that "belief aims at truth" is taken to be something knowable a priori—a necessary conceptual truth about belief. So Lloyd Humberstone (1992) writes that "the very concept of belief imports its own criterion of success [and] has its own 'internal axiology'" (p. 73), and Nishi Shah and David Velleman (2005) write that "part of the concept [of belief] is a standard of correctness" (p. 498; see also Shah 2003).

---

[3] Pamela Hieronymi writes that you believe that p iff you are "committed to *p* as true" (2006, p. 54), which amounts to being "answerable to certain questions and criticisms" (ibid. p. 69), e.g. criticism of believing that p in the form of arguments that it is false that p. Hieronymi's formulation is consistent with the spirit of the "standard of correctness" formulation that we'll employ here.

[4] Not to be confused with constitutive value (§1.1.5).

I follow Shah (2003) in taking Kantian essentialism to have the following corollary: that the concept of belief is a **normative concept** (pp. 465–74), in the sense that "exercising the concept of belief involves accepting that in some sense one *ought* to believe that p only if p is true" (p. 449). Wedgwood (2007) writes that "the very nature of these concepts and attitude types [e.g. belief] cannot be explained without mentioning normative properties and relations" (p. 171). The Kantian adopts a **normative conception of belief.**[5,6]

8.1.3 Kantian essentialism compared to Humean essentialism

We have not yet articulated a position that is obviously distinct from Humean essentialism about belief (§6.1). How is "doxastic correctness" in Wedgwood's sense different from "cognitive success" in the Humean's sense? The Humean has given us an articulation of the idea that belief "aims at truth," and she can take this to be a necessary truth about the essential nature of belief, and she can say that this is a conceptual truth about belief, knowable a priori (Steglich-Petersen 2009, p. 396).

Recall the analogy of the archer (§6.1.1), which admits of two interpretations. On both, beliefs are said to be analogous to the archer's shots. On the first, Humean, interpretation, archery is the activity of shooting arrows at a chosen target, where success is relative to the desires of the archer. The Kantian will resist this analogy. For the Kantian, your belief that p is correct iff p, regardless of your desires vis-à-vis believing the truth (either in general or about whether p). Thus Shah (2003) contrasts his account of the "aim of belief" with a teleological account on which belief must be "under the controlling influence of an intention to accept the truth" (p. 460; cf. Humberstone 1992, p. 73), and Humeans (Steglich-Petersen 2006, 2009, McHugh 2011b) explicitly offer their teleological accounts as alternatives to Shah et al.'s "normative account." The Kantian should interpret the analogy of the archer in a different way. On this second interpretation, archery is the activity of taking part in an archery competition, where the target is chosen not by the archer herself, but is determined by the rules of the competition. The archer's shot scores points iff it hits the target, regardless of her desires vis-à-vis hitting the target.

We can say, then, that to the extent that the Humean accepts the standard of doxastic correctness (§8.1.2), she takes it to be a kind of hypothetical imperative (§6.2.2). We are now in a position to formulate Kantian essentialism about belief:

---

[5] Cf. **Kantian essentialism about truth**, on which it is an a priori conceptual truth about the essential nature of *truth* that the truth is to be believed (cf. Rorty 1985, Wiggins 2002). On this view, the concept of truth is normative. This neither entails nor is entailed by Kantian essentialism about belief.

[6] Kantian essentialism about belief might be defended as part of various broader and more ambitious campaigns, for example: as an instance of the normativity of meaning in general (Boghossian 2003, 2005), or of intentionality in general (McDowell 1984, Wedgwood 2007, Chapter 7), or of mentality in general (Davidson 1970, Zangwill 1998, 2005).

Kantian essentialism about belief: It is an a priori conceptual truth, about the essential nature of belief, that, necessarily, for any subject S and proposition that p, regardless of the desires of S, S's belief that p is correct iff it is true that p, and incorrect otherwise.

Given this understanding of the doxastic standard of correctness, we must be cautious when analogizing the "aim of belief" to other constitutive norms. Consider, in addition to the analogy of the archery competition, Wedgwood's example of moves in a game of chess (2002, p. 268), or Shah's example (adopted from Gideon Rosen) of a performance of Jingle Bells (Shah 2003, p. 458). What these analogies suggest is the following way of understanding the idea that belief "aims at truth":

Thing x	Constitutive norm(s) for x
Shot in an archery competition	Rules of the competition
Move in a game of chess	Rules of chess
Performance of "Jingle Bells"	Score for "Jingle Bells"
Belief that p	Belief that p is correct iff it is true that p

These analogies are good for making the point that, for the Kantian, the standard of doxastic correctness is not grounded in desire. Suppose you move a pawn three spaces; your move is incorrect even if you are indifferent to following the rules of chess, even if you desire not to follow the rules of chess. Similarly, for the Kantian, if you believe something false, your belief is incorrect, even if you are indifferent to the standard of doxastic correctness, and even if you desire to flout the standard of doxastic correctness.

However, these analogies are misleading for two (related) reasons. The first is that it's not necessarily the case that believing is an intentional activity. But this is necessarily the case when it comes to taking place in an archery competition, playing chess, and performing "Jingle Bells." Necessarily, taking part in an archery competition requires a desire to take part, playing chess requires a desire to play, and performing "Jingle Bells" requires a desire to perform. Consider someone who wants to annoy her audience by singing "Jingle Bells" badly; such a person must still want to sing "Jingle Bells." None of this applies, mutatis mutandis, to believing: it's possible to believe that p without desiring to believe that p.

The second reason these analogies are misleading, at least when taken in conjunction, is that they encompass two very different kinds of constitutive norm (cf. Maitra 2011). With the rules of chess—e.g. the rule that bishops must move diagonally—following the rules is necessary for playing chess; if you are not following these rules then there is an important sense in which you are no longer playing chess. Therefore, someone who wants to play chess, which is, I just argued, necessary for playing chess at all, must follow the rules of chess, lest her desire be frustrated. Here the source of normativity is of the hypothetical Humean variety. With the rules of the archery competition, however, things are different. The archer who fails to hit her target, even repeatedly, is still taking part in the competition. Someone who wants to take part in the archery competition (which, again, is necessary for taking part), needn't always, or ever, hit the target with her shots, to take part. The rules of chess lay down what it is to play chess *at all*, but the rules of the archery competition—the ones that say that a shot scores points iff it hits the target—don't lay down what it is to take part in the competition, but rather what it is to take part in the competition *well*.

This matters when it comes to the source of normativity. Why ought I not move my pawn three spaces? The answer is that I would not even be playing chess were I to do that; to the extent that I want to play, I must not move my pawn three spaces. But why ought I to hit, or attempt to hit, the target in the archery competition, or to perform "Jingle Bells" in line with the score? Not because I would not even be taking part in the competition otherwise, or because I would not even be performing "Jingle Bells" otherwise. As Shah (2003) points out, "someone might want to play a silly or offbeat version of Jingle Bells as part of a comedic routine," and in such a case "playing Jingle Bells correctly is not what he should do" (p. 458). Someone can take part in an archery competition without wanting to score points, and someone can perform "Jingle Bells" without wanting to perform it correctly. Why then ought the archer to hit, or attempt to hit, the target, and why ought the musician to perform "Jingle Bells" correctly? The only plausible answer is Humean: it depends on the desires of the person involved. The archer should hit, or attempt to hit, the target, because she wants to win the competition; the musician should perform "Jingle Bells" correctly because she wants to please her audience with a correct performance. The proposed analogies, again, are cases in which the source of normativity is of the hypothetical Humean variety.

What this shows us is that the normativity posited by the Kantian is actually of a rather unfamiliar variety, and not something that we are familiar with from sports, or chess, or musical performance.

8.2 Kantian approaches to epistemic normativity

Recall our distinction (§5.2.2) between the evaluative and the narrowly normative. Given this distinction, Kantian essentialism about belief could be appealed to either in an account of epistemic value (§8.2.1) or in an account of epistemic reasons (§8.2.2).

8.2.1 A Kantian essentialist account of epistemic value

Some Kantians understand their view as providing an account of the epistemic value of true belief. Consider two principles defended by Michael Lynch (2009a; cf. 2009b, pp. 76–83):

> (TG) It is prima facie good that, relative to the propositions that one might consider, one believe all and only those that are true. (p. 226)
> (TN) It is correct to believe <p> if and only if <p> is true. (p. 228)

(TN), Lynch argues, supports (TG):

> It is a quick step between being committed to doing what is correct and being committed to the goodness of that which is correct. [...] Engagement in a goal-directed

practice commits me to the value of the goal I so pursue. [...] If I am committed to (TN), and I engage in inquiry, I am committed to (TG). (p. 230)

In this way, "(TN) ascribes value—what I'm here calling 'correctness'—to *believing* true propositions" (p. 228). Wedgwood (2002) suggests something similar when he writes, in connection with the idea that truth is the constitutive standard of correctness for belief, that:

[F]or every proposition p that one consciously considers, the best outcome is to believe p when p is true, the second best outcome is to suspend judgment about p, and the worst outcome is to believe p when p is false. (p. 273)

And elsewhere:

In explaining why someone forms a belief by pointing to the fact that it was rational for her to form that belief, it seems that we are explaining why a certain contingent event occurs…by appeal to a certain sort of goodness—specifically rationality—that is exemplified by the event. (2007, p. 197)

This language suggests that epistemic normativity is a matter of value. But in any event, if we sought to account for epistemic value by appeal to Kantian essentialism about belief, we would need an evaluative premise:

The Principle of constitutive doxastic value: For any subject S and proposition that p, S's belief that p is (in one respect) good iff S's belief that p is correct, and (in one respect) bad otherwise.

This provides an answer to the basic question about epistemic evaluation: epistemic evaluation is appropriate because it evaluates beliefs in terms of their constitutive standard of correctness. As Wedgwood (2002) puts it:

If there are some epistemic norms that apply to absolutely *all* beliefs…then these universal epistemic norms would apply to beliefs in virtue of the very essence or nature of *belief as such*. (p. 270)

For this reason, there will be no problem for the Kantian when it comes to vindicating universalism about epistemic normativity (§5.3.1).

When it comes to the uniqueness question about epistemic evaluation, there are a variety of options. One might maintain that truth is *the* "aim of belief" and articulate this by saying that truth is the unique constitutive standard of correctness for belief (Velleman 2000, Shah 2003, Shah and Velleman 2005). Alternatively, you might maintain merely that truth is *a* constitutive standard of correctness for belief, and posit a plurality of constitutive standards. Beliefs could then be said to be correct, in one sense, but incorrect, in another. Or one might defend a conjunctive standard of correctness, such as being true and rational, such that S's belief that p is correct iff it is true that p *and* it is rational for S to believe that p. Another option (Wedgwood 2002): belief has a plurality of essential "aims"; belief "aims at truth" in the sense that truth is the unique constitutive standard of *correctness* for belief, but there are other constitutive norms of belief, e.g. norms of rationality, such that belief also "aims at rationality." Here I will often speak of truth as *the* "aim of belief," but nothing will hinge on this. My critique of Kantian essentialism (§8.3–8.4) will target the idea that the standard of doxastic correctness is an a priori conceptual truth about the essential nature of belief. Whether or not there are other norms that flow a priori from the essential nature of belief will not be our concern.

Finally, the Kantian essentialist about belief can provide an answer to the scope question about epistemic evaluation, by equating the epistemic with the doxastic (§5.2.4).

8.2.2 A Kantian essentialist account of epistemic reasons

Some Kantian essentialists express doubt about the principle of constitutive doxastic value. Shah (2003) argues that "to claim that a playing of Jingle Bells is correct is [not] to endorse it as realizing any sort of value" (p. 458). For this reason, the philosopher attracted to Kantian essentialism about belief might choose to eschew accounting for epistemic value in Kantian terms, in favor of giving an account of epistemic reasons, where the evaluative and the narrowly normative (§5.2.2) are understood to be independent.[7] Recall:

Evidence norm: For any subject S and proposition that p, if S has evidence that p, then S has a pro tanto (normative) reason to believe that p.

In answer to the basic question about epistemic reasons, the fact that S has (pro tanto) reason to believe that p, when she has evidence that p, is explained by the fact that truth is the constitutive standard of correctness for belief: believing that p in response to evidence that p is what one ought to do, belief-wise, given that truth is the constitutive standard of correctness for belief.[8] There is, in some sense, for the Kantian, no gap between having evidence that p and having (pro tanto) reason to believe that p: that we are speaking here of *belief* ensures a priori that one ought to cleave, in belief, to one's evidence. If someone has evidence that p, then she has (pro tanto) reason to believe that p—and this regardless of her desires. The Kantian, as we noted above (§8.2.1), will therefore face no problems when it comes to vindicating universalism about epistemic normativity.

---

[7] However, Shah (2003) also says that "to claim that a playing of Jingle Bells is correct is [not] to say that it was played as it ought to be played" (ibid.). On the one hand, this may just mean that correctness claims do not ground all-things-considered "ought" claims. On the other hand, it may mean that correctness claims are neither evaluative nor narrowly normative (§5.2.2)—in which case, they cannot be of any use in solving the problem of the source of epistemic normativity.

[8] This seems to imply realism about epistemic normativity (§5.2.3): we have normative reason to believe that p, when confronted with conclusive evidence that p, because truth is the constitutive standard of correctness for belief, and not, for example, because it's appropriate to attribute reasons, as the anti-realist might have it.

As above, the Kantian has options when it comes to the uniqueness question about epistemic reasons. If truth is *the* standard of doxastic correctness, then epistemic reasons for belief will have a "special status," in that they will be the only sorts of reason for belief that flow from belief's constitutive standard. You might even think that this means that epistemic reasons for belief are the only possible kind of reason for belief (Shah 2006, Jones 2010, Hieronymi 2005; cf. Reisner 2008, 2009). Alternatively, so long as all of belief's constitutive norms are plausibly "epistemic" (cf. Wedgwood 2002), then all epistemic reasons will have the same "special status."

Finally, the Kantian can offer the same answer to the scope question about epistemic reasons offered above (§8.1.1): a doxastic conception of the epistemic (§5.2.4).

Because the principle of constitutive doxastic value is controversial among Kantian essentialists, I won't target it in what follows.

8.3 The objection from naturalism

Both critics and defenders of Kantian essentialism about belief have detected a tension between the view and philosophical naturalism. Asbjørn Steglich-Petersen (2006) notes that "[t]he naturalist avoids commitment to the idea that the metaphysical nature of belief involves evaluative properties, since it is notoriously difficult to explain these in a naturalistic framework" (p. 500). And defenders of Kantian essentialism have agreed that there is a prima facie tension between their view and naturalism (Shah 2003, p. 475, Kelly 2003, p. 616, Wedgwood 2007, Chapter 9). The basic worry is simple: Kantian essentialism adopts a normative conception of belief (§8.1.4), so on the Kantian view, the property of being a belief is a normative property.

If the normativity of belief is irreducible, then the naturalistic constraints (§5.5) explain why Kantian essentialism is in tension with naturalism. So we must ask: does Kantian essentialism posit irreducible normativity?

We can see that it does by noting that, for the Kantian, there is no analogue for epistemic normativity. Humeans could reduce epistemic reasons to instrumental reasons; Darwinians could explain epistemic normativity in terms of the normativity of biological functions. But the Kantian cannot do this; recall (§8.1.3) that the analogy to performances and game-playing was misleading. All this suggests that, for the Kantian, epistemic normativity is irreducible. For his part, Wedgwood accepts this consequence (2007, Chapter 9).

We can see this from another angle by asking an explanatory question. What explains, on the Kantian's view, the a priori conceptual truth that a belief that p is correct iff it is true that p? The answer has to be: nothing explains this. For the Kantian, the constitutive normativity of belief is where the explanatory buck stops. This, too, suggests that, for the Kantian, epistemic normativity is irreducible.

Given the naturalistic constraints, we therefore have pro tanto reasons to resist endorsing Kantian essentialism about belief. We cannot reject Kantian essentialism in advance, however. For perhaps these pro tanto reasons will be trumped by weightier considerations. Perhaps we cannot do without the irreducible epistemic normativity of belief.[9] We must therefore see whether there is a compelling argument for Kantian essentialism about belief. If there is, we should accept a Kantian essentialist approach to epistemic normativity.

8.4 The best explanation argument for Kantian essentialism

Arguments for Kantian essentialism have taken the form of inferences to the best explanation. In this section I'll present a master argument for Kantian essentialism by describing four phenomena involving belief (§8.4.1) and by showing how Kantian essentialism might explain those phenomena (§8.4.2). Then in the following section (§8.5) I'll criticize the master argument.

8.4.1 The phenomena

We'll canvass four closely related phenomena involving belief: (i) doxastic involuntarism, (ii) the exclusivity of epistemic considerations in conscious belief formation, (iii) the impossibility of recognized false belief, and (iv) the transparency of doxastic deliberation to truth. That we distinguish these "four" is not meant to suggest that they are not all aspects of some more general phenomenon; indeed as we shall see there are explanatory relations that are claimed to hold between these phenomena. For each of these phenomena, its reality is said to be a necessary truth. Indeed, as we'll see below (§8.4.2), on the Kantian's view, these are a priori necessary truths explained by the essential nature of belief.

Doxastic involuntarism A familiar idea in epistemology is that we do not have direct voluntary control over what we believe. I have **direct control** over whether I Φ when Φing is something that I can "just do," i.e. where my Φing is something that I can bring about "just like that," simply by intending to Φ, i.e. where I can Φ, and there is not some distinct Ψ such that I Φ by Ψing (cf. Alston 1988, p. 260, Bennett 1990, p. 89, Feldman 2000, p. 670, Hieronymi 2006, p. 48). The litmus test for whether I have direct control over whether I Φ has been taken to be to be whether I could Φ for no other reason than that I'll get a large cash prize if I do (Alston 1988, p. 263, Bennett 1990, p. 88, Ryan 2003, p. 50; cf. Kavka 1983). Even if I offered you a million dollars as a prize for believing that Australia won the 1979 Cricket World Cup (a proposition for which you have no evidence), you will not be able to do it. Thus many have concluded that,

---

[9] Just as you might argue (cf. Drier 2001) that we cannot do without the irreducible normativity of the means–ends rule (§6.1.2).

for any subject S and proposition that p, S does not have direct voluntary control over whether she believes that p.[10]

Some have maintained that this is a contingent truth about human beings (Alston 1988, Feldman 1988a, 2000, Foley 1993, p. 16, Ryan 2003, McHugh 2012b), including Hume, who wrote in the *Treatise* (I.iv.1) that "Nature, by an absolute and uncontroulable necessity has determin'd us to judge as well as to breathe and feel" (1978, p. 183; see also pp. 624–9). Those who think that doxastic involuntarism is evidence that belief "aims at truth" (Williams 1973, Hieronymi 2006; see also Williams 2002, p. 81), however, take the thesis to be a necessary truth about belief. They argue that it is a necessary truth about belief that, for any subject S and proposition that p, S does not have direct voluntary control over whether she believes that p.[11]

Why think doxastic involuntarism is a necessary truth? Williams (1973) writes that:

If in full consciousness I could acquire a "belief" irrespective of its truth, it is unclear that before the event I could seriously think of it as a belief, i.e. as something purporting to represent reality. (p. 148)

The argument must go like this: if doxastic involuntarism were contingent, then it would be possible to acquire a belief irrespective of its truth; since that's impossible, doxastic involuntarism is a necessary truth.

The exclusivity of epistemic considerations in conscious belief formation   Why is it impossible to acquire a belief irrespective of its truth? An answer, which awaits an explanation, is that epistemic considerations are exclusive in conscious belief formation. What does this mean?

As we said above, in defense of doxastic involuntarism, the fact that believing that p would earn me a cash prize does not seem capable of motivating me to believe that p. In general, non-epistemic considerations do not seem capable of motivating conscious belief formation; epistemic considerations alone can do so (Williams 1973, pp. 148–51, 2002, p. 83, Adler 2002, p. 52, Jones 2002, 2010, pp. 142–4, Owens 2003, Heironymi 2005, Shah 2006, p. 494, Lynch 2009a, pp. 228–30, McHugh 2011a, p. 371, 2011b, p. 249).

Imagine that Pascal reasons as follows: "I know it's false that God exists, but I conclude that I ought to believe that God exists, because so believing will be advantageous

---

[10] N.b. that the involuntariness of belief, whether necessary or contingent, does not imply that judgment (§6.3.5) is not an action.

[11] Heironymi (2006) worries that this focus on direct voluntary control is a mistake (2006, pp. 48–9). For if our lack of direct voluntary control over our beliefs is taken to mean that we cannot "believe at will," then we also must conclude that we cannot "prepare dinner at will," since a complex process is required to prepare dinner. But it is a contingent fact about human beings that we cannot prepare dinner at will: we can imagine a wizard who can prepare dinner "just like that." The Kantian's idea is that this is not possible when it comes to belief.

for me." Could Pascal come to believe that God exists on the basis of this reasoning? It seems that these deliberations cannot lead Pascal to believe that God exists, as they do not give him evidence that God exists. Pascal himself recognized something like this; in the *Pensées* (1660), he wrote that:

You want to find faith and do not know the way? You want to cure yourself of unbelief and ask for the remedies? Learn from those who have been bound like you[.] Follow the way by which they began: by behaving just as if they believed, taking holy water, having masses said, etc. That will make you believe quite naturally, and according to your animal reactions.[12]

Why is Pascal unmoved by his reasoning? Shah (2006) writes that it is "impossible [for someone] to come to believe that God exists directly on the basis of appreciating the practical argument expressed by the wager" (p. 494). Ward Jones (2010) argues that:

Some doxastic goods are such that my consciously realizing that coming to believe *p* will (or already does) allow me to attain them can, itself, determine my belief that *p*. Other doxastic goods, however, cannot. The latter can only work *surreptitiously* in bringing about belief; they cannot bring about belief in a way that is "open" to the believer. (p. 142; see also Jones 2002)

And Pamela Hieronymi (2005) writes that non-epistemic considerations that speak in favor of believing that p "are not the kind of reasons which, simply by finding convincing, one would believe *p*" (p. 448). Along the same lines, Lynch (2009a) says that "[i]n the typical conscious, deliberative case" belief is responsive to truth (p. 229, cf. 2009b, p. 80), and Williams (2002) maintains that, necessarily, "when beliefs are the products of wishful thinking, or in other ways become hostage to desires and wishes, they do so only as the result of hidden and indirect processes" (p. 83).[13]

We can remain neutral on the issue of whether non-epistemic considerations that speak in favor of believing that p are, or are not, reasons for believing that p, or reasons to believe that p, or the "right kind" of reasons for believing that p.[14] We will speak neutrally of "non-epistemic considerations"; Shah (2006) speaks similarly of "non-evidential considerations" (p. 483 and passim), and Jones (2002) argues that "seeing oneself as having a belief is inconsistent with offering a non-epistemic explanation of that belief" (p. 233). The considerations Pascal has adduced in favor of believing that God exists are "non-epistemic," in as much as they concern not the truth of that belief, but its utility. The "doxastic goods" that Jones argues are motivationally impotent—"the feeling of well-being or happiness that a belief can give us"; "the value of a

---

[12] From Honor Levi's translation in *Pensées and Other Writings* (Oxford University Press, 1995), pp. 155–6. The final sentence, "Naturellement même cela vous fera croire et vous abêtira," could be more literally translated: "Naturally, that will make you believe, and stupefy you."

[13] Cf. the "illusion of objectivity" (§2.10.1).

[14] One argument against non-epistemic reasons for belief relies on a premise that a reason to Φ must be capable of consciously motivating someone to Φ (cf. Williams 1980). Shah calls this the "deliberative constraint on reasons" (2006, p. 485; cf. Jones 2010, p. 149). For criticism of this premise, see Parfit 2009, pp. 336–45.

relationship which is made possible or better because of a belief"—are non-epistemic in the same sense (cf. §9.3).

We could also speak here of "object-given reasons" for belief (i.e. epistemic reasons for belief) and "state-given reasons" for belief (i.e. non-epistemic considerations in favor of believing). And our phenomenon is: that object-given reasons for belief can motivate conscious belief formation, but state-given reasons cannot.

Although non-epistemic considerations seem unable to *motivate* conscious belief formation, they surely can *influence* conscious belief formation. The distinction can be brought out by considering two cases:

(a) Amy has strong evidence that her beloved gerbil Horatio is dead. But she knows that she'll be happy if she believes that Horatio is still alive. And so she resolves to believe that Horatio is still alive, with the result that she believes that Horatio is still alive.

(b) Amy has ambiguous evidence suggesting that Horatio may have died. But she very much wants Horatio to be alive, and this desire causes her to interpret the evidence in a biased way ("those footprints leading to the edge of the cliff are from some other gerbil"), with the result that she believes that Horatio is still alive.

Case (a) is the case that seems impossible; case (b) is an ordinary case of wishful thinking and is clearly possible. So we should be clear: when we say that epistemic considerations are exclusive in conscious belief formation, we mean that non-epistemic considerations cannot consciously motivate belief formation, that they cannot be the basis on which a person consciously forms a belief, even though they may influence conscious belief formation. This is the phenomenon of exclusivity. The reality of this phenomenon, so the argument goes, is a necessary truth: necessarily, epistemic considerations are exclusive in conscious belief formation.

The impossibility of recognized false belief Williams (1973) writes that "[i]f a man recognizes that what he has been believing is false, he thereby abandons his belief" (p. 137; see also 2002, p. 67). In my view, this claim admits of several related sorts of counterexamples:

• Delusions. Some delusions involve belief, e.g. that your partner has been replaced by an impostor. But someone can recognize that her delusional belief is false, but be unable to rid herself of it.
• Phobias. Some phobias involve belief, e.g. that air travel is dangerous. But someone can recognize that her phobic belief is false, but be unable to rid herself of it.
• Indoctrination. Someone might be "brainwashed" into believing something, e.g. that the Dear Leader is the messiah. But someone can recognize that her indoctrinated belief is false, but be unable to rid herself of it.

- Prejudice. Some prejudices involve belief, e.g. that women are inferior to men. But someone can recognize that her prejudicial belief is false, but be unable to rid herself of it.

The kinds of cases I have in mind are cases in which, first, recognition is doxastic: the person believes (or knows) that her belief is false. (Compare cases in which someone insincerely admits that her belief is false.) Second, they are cases in which recognition is synchronic with the relevant belief: someone recognizes at t that she has a false belief at t. (Compare cases in which inconsistency is diachronic due to vacillation in belief.) Third, they are cases in which significant aspects of the characteristic functional profile of belief (§1.6.2) remain: the Capgras patient is made uncomfortable by her partner's presence and suspects her food has been poisoned; the aerophobic is upset and reluctant to board the airplane; the victim of indoctrination still finds herself admiring the Dear Leader and is disposed to rejoin the cult under certain circumstances; the sexist, a banker, systematically rejects loan applications from female entrepreneurs (Jones 2002, p. 239). In these cases, on my view, the attribution of one belief (that p) is justified on the basis of the person's affective and motivational profile, and the attribution of another belief (that the aforementioned belief is false) is justified on the basis of the person's sincere assertion that her belief (that p) is false. These will be cases of **intellectual akrasia** (cf. Mele 1987, Chapter 8, Zagzebski 1996, p. 154). And they will be cases in which someone believes that p, but also believes that ~p (but they will not be cases in which someone believes that p & ~p).

However, the possibility of intellectual akrasia is controversial. It's controversial that delusions ever involve belief; some defend this view (Bayne and Pacherie 2005, Bortolotti 2009) and others reject it (Currie 2000, Currie and Ravenscroft 2002, Chapter 8, Hamilton 2007). Some argue that what I have called phobic beliefs are not really beliefs but "aliefs" (Gendler 2008).[15] And some argue that unacknowledged racism does not involve racist beliefs (Jones 2002).[16] So I will assume, for the sake of argument, that my would-be counterexamples, to the claim that recognized false belief is impossible, are not counterexamples to that claim.

Again, we'll take the impossibility of recognized false belief to be a necessary truth about belief. So the idea is that, necessarily, someone cannot believe that p while at the same time recognizing that said belief is false.

---

[15] However, note well that we should not reject a would-be belief as not really a belief on the grounds that it is the result of habituation or of socialization (cf. Jones 2002, p. 239). The characteristic functional profile of belief (§1.6.2) is neutral on the origins of belief.

[16] However, note well that we should not require for belief (that p) that a person be willing to assert that p (cf. Jones 2002, p. 239). The characteristic functional profile of belief is more complex than that (§1.6.2). Someone who believes that p might have various kinds of reasons not to assert that p.

The transparency of doxastic deliberation Why are epistemic considerations exclusive in conscious belief formation? Shah (2006, p. 494) and Jonathan Adler (2002, p. 52) explain this phenomenon by appeal to what Shah calls the "transparency of doxastic deliberation" (2003, pp. 447–9, 2006, pp. 481–3; see also Shah and Velleman 2005, pp. 497–500). He articulates the idea (2003) in several ways:

[W]ithin the first-personal deliberative perspective…the question *whether to believe that p* seems to collapse into the question *whether p is true*. [T]hese two questions must be viewed as answered by, and answerable to, the same set of considerations. [W]e seamlessly move from the former question [whether to believe that p] to the latter question [whether p is true]. (p. 447)

[T]he question *whether to believe that p* immediately gives way to the question *whether p is true* within the first-personal deliberative context. In part this means that once one has discovered whether *p* is true, the question *whether to believe that p* is *closed*. (Ibid. p 463)

The phenomenology of deliberation…is that evidence is the only kind of consideration that can provide a reason for belief, because only evidence is relevant to answering the question "Is *p* true?" that one finds oneself directly faced with in deliberation about *whether to believe that p*. (Ibid. p. 464)

[D]eliberation that is framed by the particular question of *whether to believe p* is answered solely by considerations relevant to answering the question *whether p is true*. (Ibid. p. 467)

Are these claims true? That may depend on their precise meaning. First, the transparency thesis is to be understood as a necessary truth about belief (Shah 2006, pp. 482–3). Second, the transparency thesis is meant to be non-normative. The idea is not that the question of whether to believe that p ought to "collapse" into the question of whether p, nor that rational or epistemically justified doxastic deliberation is transparent to truth. When Shah says that we "must" answer the question of whether to believe that p by answering the question of whether it is true that p, the "must" here is meant to be descriptive, not prescriptive. Third, the transparency thesis concerns doxastic deliberation, not belief formation in general, nor believing in general. There is something "special about cases of deliberate belief" (Shah 2003, p. 473) that the thesis is meant to capture, which is not present in cases of non-deliberate belief.

People *do* sometimes attend to non-epistemic considerations in doxastic deliberation. Pascal deliberates as follows: "Setting aside the question of whether God exists, believing that God exists is advantageous, and therefore I ought to believe that God exists." Pascal deliberates about the question of whether to believe that p, and continues to deliberate about that question, but the content of his deliberation is not the question of whether it is true that p (which he explicitly sets aside), but the question of whether it is advantageous to believe that p. Or consider Hume on pride (§2.2): "It's good to have a sense of pride, because it makes you happy and gives you confidence." The question of whether to believe that p is being considered, and the question of whether it is true that p is (at least temporarily) being ignored. Indeed, I can consider the non-epistemic merits of believing that p even when I believe that p is false: even if I am convinced that God does not exist, or that having a sense of pride would involve having false beliefs, I can still consider the non-epistemic merits of believing in God or of having a sense of pride. You might argue that the only considerations that could *decide* doxastic deliberation, i.e. the only considerations that could put an end to deliberation about whether to believe that p by resulting directly in a belief that p, are considerations relevant to whether p. But here we have arrived at another way of articulating the exclusivity of epistemic considerations in conscious belief formation (see above). This is another way of describing that phenomenon, since doxastic deliberation is a conscious activity; when doxastic deliberation results directly in belief formation, said belief formation is necessarily conscious.[17]

Shah speaks of how things are "within the first-personal deliberative perspective" (or "context") and of "the phenomenology of deliberation," so we might seek an understanding of the transparency thesis on which it's a claim merely about the phenomenology of doxastic deliberation. (Think here also of Williams' appeal to what we could believe "in full consciousness.") Consider the idea that when doxastic deliberation results in wishful thinking, I do not take myself to be engaged in wishful thinking. Perhaps doxastic deliberation requires the appearance, to the deliberator, of being responsive to epistemic considerations only. But Pascal's doxastic deliberation is a counterexample to this claim. This may be what Shah and David Velleman (2005) have in mind when, in connection with "pragmatic reasons for believing," they write that there "are cases in which the deliberative question *whether to believe that p* is not transparent to *whether p*" (p. 517). But if this is the case, the reality of transparency is not a necessary truth.

However, suppose we said that doxastic deliberation requires that it seem to the deliberator that epistemic considerations are exclusive in conscious belief formation. Better: that deliberation about whether to believe that p requires that it seem to the deliberator that epistemic considerations will be exclusive in her conscious belief formation with respect to whether p. Pascal's doxastic deliberation doesn't speak against this: Pascal knows that the fact that believing that God exists would be beneficial will not decide deliberation about whether to believe that God exists. This is how I propose we understand the phenomenon of "transparency." Doxastic deliberation is transparent in the sense that doxastic deliberation requires awareness of the exclusivity phenomenon (see above). Or, more exactly: doxastic deliberation requires awareness of the relevant token instance of the exclusivity phenomenon; in deliberating about whether to believe that p I need not be aware that, in general, epistemic considerations are exclusive in

---

[17] You might object that Pascal doesn't deliberate about whether to believe that God exists, because he knows in advance that his reasoning will not decide his deliberation. But it is possible to deliberate about whether to Φ while knowing that your reasoning will not decide your deliberation, for you might hope that your deliberations will have surreptitious influence on whether you Φ. You might hope for rational akrasia (Audi 1990, Arpaly 2003), either practical or theoretical. Similarly, you might object that Pascal doesn't deliberate, because he knows he has no direct voluntary control over whether he believes that God exists. But you can deliberate about whether to Φ so long as you know you have some kind of voluntary control over whether you Φ; it need not be direct voluntary control.

conscious belief formation; I only need be aware that they will be exclusive vis-à-vis *my* belief formation *with respect to the proposition that p*. Likewise, I need not be aware of the necessity of exclusivity. The idea here, so the argument goes, is that, necessarily, if S deliberates about whether to believe that p, it seems to her that epistemic considerations will be exclusive in her conscious belief formation with respect to the proposition that p.

Compare the idea that belief is necessarily "regulated" by epistemic considerations, e.g. that belief is necessarily "regulated for truth" (Railton 1994, pp. 72–5, Velleman 2000, p. 252–5, Shah and Velleman 2005; cf. Wedgwood 2007, pp. 154–8). This is not prima facie plausible, as the beliefs of the victim of a deceptive demon do not seem to be "regulated for truth." Shah and Velleman (2005, p. 521) conclude from this that such a person wouldn't have genuine beliefs, but rather some virtual surrogate. The Kantian shouldn't bite that bullet, however. She should understand the requirement of regulation as a constraint on how things must seem, to the believer. On this view, necessarily, we must see our beliefs as responsive exclusively to epistemic considerations. What is required is not actual successful regulation, but a "self-representation" of actual successful regulation, as Peter Railton (1997) argues:

> In order for a propositional attitude to be an attitude of *belief*, it cannot represent itself as wholly unaccountable to truth or evidence. [...] A self-representation of certain of one's attitudes as 'aiming at' truth is *partially constitutive* of belief. (pp. 57–9)

You might worry that this talk of beliefs representing themselves as "aiming at" truth is to be avoided. But we can avoid it, by talking about the self-representations of believers, not beliefs: necessarily, doxastic deliberators must represent themselves as accountable, in conscious belief formation, to truth and evidence, or at least they must not represent themselves as unaccountable, in conscious belief formation, to truth and evidence. This, then, is the "transparency" of doxastic deliberation to truth.

8.4.2 The Kantian explanation

Consider the four phenomena described above (§8.4.1):

(i)   Necessarily, doxastic involuntarism is true.
(ii) Necessarily, epistemic considerations are exclusive in conscious belief formation.
(iii) Necessarily, recognized false belief is impossible.
(iv) Necessarily, doxastic deliberation is transparent to truth.

These phenomena call out for explanation. Given this, we can formulate an **inference to the best explanation** argument for Kantian essentialism about belief: the truth of Kantian essentialism explains these phenomena. In the absence of any better explanation of these phenomena, we should accept Kantian essentialism about belief.

On transparency, Shah (2003) writes:

> [A] competent user of the concept of belief must accept the prescription to believe that p [if and] only if p is true for any activity that he conceives of as belief-formation. Because one accepts this prescription insofar as one is deliberating about *whether to believe that p*, determining

whether p is true will be immediately imperative, to the exclusion of any other question, for anyone who entertains the deliberative question *whether to believe that p*. (p. 470)

In other words, if Kantian essentialism about belief is true, transparency is exactly what we should expect; the Kantian normative hypothesis explains the non-normative phenomenon of transparency. The reason that a representation of one's beliefs as accountable to truth and evidence is required is that the concept of belief contains a constitutive standard of correctness, viz. truth. Note that Shah's argument assumes that deliberation is a conscious activity, requiring awareness that one is deliberating. This is why someone who deliberates about the question of whether to believe that p can be assumed to employ the concept of belief in her deliberation.[18] So the argument goes, this reveals something about the concept of belief: that truth is its constitutive standard.

This, so the Kantian argument goes, explains the rest. If Kantian essentialism about belief is true, then we should expect the impossibility of recognized false belief, exclusivity, and doxastic involuntarism. To recognize a belief as false requires recognizing it as a belief, but employing the concept of belief requires awareness of belief's constitutive standard of correctness—thus ensuring that the state recognized as false cannot be recognized as a belief. Epistemic considerations are exclusive in conscious belief formation, because conscious belief formation requires the employment of the concept of belief, which requires, in turn, awareness of belief's constitutive standard of correctness, viz. truth (Shah 2006, p. 494, Adler 2002, p. 52). This, in turn, explains doxastic involuntarism, as Williams (1973) argues:

I cannot bring it about, just like that, that I believe something[.] Why is this? One reason is connected with the characteristic of beliefs that they aim at truth. If in full consciousness I could acquire a "belief" irrespective of its truth, it is unclear that before the event I could seriously think of it as a belief, i.e. as something purporting to represent reality. (p. 148; cf. 2002, p. 81, Jones 2002, pp. 233–7)

Recall the litmus test for direct voluntary control (§8.4.1): you have direct voluntary control over your beliefs only if you could believe for a cash prize.[19] Given exclusivity, you cannot pass the litmus test for direct voluntary control. Again, the normativity

---

[18] Note well that the argument does not assume that belief formation, in general, requires employing the concept of belief.

[19] Why accept this litmus test for basic voluntary control? Consider the immediate voluntary control I have over whether I shoot this gun in the direction of my best friend. I cannot bring myself to shoot, even if I am promised a cash reward. My relationship with whether I shoot doesn't pass the cash-prize litmus test, but this gives us no reason to think that I lack any kind of voluntary control over whether I shoot. In this case it is not that I haven't been given a reason to shoot, nor that I have the "wrong kind" of reason to shoot, but just that I have an incredibly strong reason not to shoot, such that no amount of cash can trump it (cf. Montmarquet 1986). The puzzle in the case of belief is not that cash prizes can't motivate belief (for cash prizes can't motivate certain obviously voluntary actions), but that cash prizes can't motivate belief even when there are relatively weak reasons against believing. Who won the 1979 Cricket World Cup? I know nothing of cricket so I suspend judgment on the question, and I care nothing for cricket so knowing who won matters nothing to me. If offered cash to believe that Australia won, I cannot bring myself to do it, simply on that basis. The puzzle is: why not?

of the concept of belief is doing the explanatory work here: to have basic voluntary control over my beliefs, I would need to be able to control them while recognizing them as beliefs, i.e. as states that are correct iff true.

To sum up: Kantian essentialism about belief provides a unified explanation of our four phenomena involving belief (§8.4.1). Since it's the best explanation of these phenomena on offer, we should accept Kantian essentialism about belief.

8.5 Against the best explanation argument for Kantian essentialism

Naturalists are under pressure to resist Kantian essentialism about belief (§8.3). Can the best explanation argument (§8.4) plausibly be resisted? Recall that the reality of each of our four phenomena is said to be a necessary truth. The necessity of these truths is crucial for the Kantian essentialist, who posits a necessary conceptual truth to explain them. Were these truths not necessary, they would not call for a necessary truth to explain them. More importantly, appealing to a necessary truth to explain them would explain too much, were the reality of these phenomena contingent, for the Kantian's explanation predicts that the reality of these phenomena is a necessary truth.[20] I'll argue here that the reality of these phenomena is not necessary, but merely contingent (§§8.5.1–8.5.2). Then I'll argue that, regardless of this, the Kantian's explanation of the phenomena isn't any good (§8.5.3), and sketch an alternative (§8.5.4).

8.5.1 Credamites

The Kantian essentialist must defend the view that doxastic involuntarism is necessarily true. I have no direct voluntary control over the weather in Scotland, and if the constitutive standard of correctness for Scottish weather is that it rain all the time, this would explain why I can't control the weather. But this is not a good reason to think that Scottish weather has a constitutive standard of correctness. My lack of control over the weather in Scotland is contingent. What this shows, again, is that only necessary involuntariness could suggest that a constitutive standard of correctness is at work; contingent involuntariness does no such thing. So is doxastic involuntarism necessarily true?

Jonathan Bennett (1990, pp. 92–4) asks us to imagine a community of "Credamites" who have the ability to at the same time induce in themselves the belief that p and to cause themselves to forget the origin of their belief that p. Credamites have direct voluntary control over their beliefs, and the idea that their beliefs are genuine is not threatened by Williams' argument (Williams 1973, p. 148), as Credamites do not "in

---

[20] You might object that, since the argument is an inference to the *best* explanation, the Kantian's explanation cannot be dismissed, even if the reality of these phenomena is contingent, without an alternative *better* explanation. I'll sketch such an explanation below (§8.5.4).

full consciousness" form beliefs at will—as soon as their direct voluntary control is exercised, it's forgotten, thus their beliefs still appear to "represent reality" in the relevant way. If what Bennett imagines is possible, then doxastic involuntarism is only contingently true. But what Bennett imagines surely is possible; we have no reason to think that our imagination has led us astray in this case.

Bennett builds into the story that Credamites only occasionally exercise their ability to believe at will, and that they cannot exercise their ability when the belief to be induced is "deeply and radically at odds with their belief systems" (p. 93). But this is inessential to the thought experiment. A community that very frequently employed their ability to believe at will might quickly run into trouble navigating and manipulating their environment; but one can imagine a Credamite community that is overseen by a benevolent community of non-Credamites, who ensure that the Credamites stay safe and well-fed, in spite of their frequently false beliefs. And one can imagine an ability to induce not only a single belief, but to change beliefs in a more systematic way. What is essential to the story is that the Credamites have the ability to cause "protective forgetfulness" (ibid.) whenever they alter their beliefs.[21] We can imagine a community of Credamites, which gives us prima facie reason to think that basic voluntary control over belief is possible.

Note well that we cannot appeal to phenomenology to defend the necessity of doxastic involuntarism—e.g., to the fact that when we try to alter our beliefs directly, we find ourselves unable. For the most that we could establish by appeal to phenomenology would be the contingent inability of humans to exercise basic voluntary control over their beliefs. This is why Hume took doxastic involuntarism to be contingent, by reflection on the phenomenology of belief (*Treatise*, I.iv.1). Through an introspective experiment we find that we have no direct voluntary control over our beliefs; but we also find that we have no direct voluntary control over the beating of our hearts, or over the weather in Scotland. But at least some of these are contingent facts about human (or individual) ability, not necessary truths about heartbeats or the weather in Scotland.[22]

---

[21] Bennett maintains that "immediately induced beliefs would have to be atypical or non-standard," as "a belief in this way would count as a belief in virtue of its relations—as exhibited in behavior—with the creature's desires and its other beliefs" (ibid. p. 95). He bases this conclusion on the idea that "[i]t is a conceptual truth that…sensory encounters with the world are the standard, typical source for beliefs about how the world is" (ibid. pp. 94–5). But this isn't a conceptual truth: we can imagine creatures that standardly and typically receive their information about the world in some other way (cf. Sosa 1991, pp. 186–9). Indeed, as I have suggested, we can imagine creatures that standardly and typically engage in wishful thinking (so long as we imagine some way for them to stay alive).

[22] Likewise, the fact that belief is a state, rather than an action or an event, does not support Kantian doxastic involuntarism. Being seated is a state, and while I seem to lack direct voluntary control over whether I am seated, since I can only go in or out of this state by doing something, namely, sitting down or standing up, we can imagine someone who has direct voluntary control over whether she is seated.

8.5.2 More Credamites

What about the other three phenomena (§8.4.1)? Is the reality of each of these phenomena also contingent? Given their selective forgetfulness, it's unclear whether the beliefs of Bennett's Credamites satisfy exclusivity and transparency and it's unclear whether they ever recognize any of their beliefs to be false (cf. Bennett 1990, p. 93). However, the selective forgetfulness of the Credamites isn't essential to the story. We can see this by thinking about why we included selective forgetfulness in the first place. The idea was to avoid Williams' (1973) objection that thinking of a belief as formed "irrespective of its truth" threatens our ability to think of it as a belief (p. 148). But is this *necessarily* true? I conceded above (§8.4.1) that delusions, phobias, indoctrination, and prejudice do not provide counterexamples to the claim that recognized false belief is impossible (although I am inclined to think that they do—and if you agree, then you should reject Williams' objection). But even if delusions, phobias, indoctrination, and prejudice don't provide counterexamples to the claim that recognized false belief is impossible, can't we *imagine* someone capable of believing that p while at the same time recognizing that said belief is false? Consider:

Lee's fear of flying is such that his non-verbal actions are entirely suggestive of belief that airplanes are dangerous: he will not ride on airplanes, he wishes his friends and family wouldn't ride on airplanes, and he gets upset and nervous when they do. But he judges that airplanes are not dangerous, and he sincerely asserts that airplanes are not dangerous. He tries to stop acting and feeling as though airplanes were dangerous, but he finds himself unable. Aware of his behavior and affective profile, he concludes that his beliefs about airplanes are inconsistent: he unconsciously believes, with unshakeable conviction, that they are dangerous, but judges, with equal force, that they are not dangerous. "I believe that airplanes are dangerous, but I recognize that my belief is false," he says.

You might object that you cannot make enough sense of Lee to attribute beliefs to him. It seems right that if we actually encountered someone like this, we might be at a loss as to what we should say about his beliefs. But that is consistent with it being possible that Lee's take on his situation is the correct one: he does believe that airplanes are dangerous, but he also recognizes that his belief is false. What the objector needs to argue is that, necessarily, Lee is wrong in his take on his situation. It seems to me that one might be independently committed to a philosophical theory on which, necessarily, Lee is wrong in his take on his situation, and it's beyond the scope of the present inquiry to discuss those philosophical theories.[23] But if we don't assume any such theory, it looks possible that Lee's take on his situation is correct.

But if that is right, we have the tool we need to modify the Credamite story. What we shall imagine are Credamites who can directly bring it about that they have an unshakeable conviction that p. They do not, as in Bennett's story, forget the origin of these beliefs, and they are aware before, during, and after the process of belief formation

---

[23] See, for example, Davidson 1973, 1974a, 1983.

that the induced belief is being formed on the basis of non-epistemic considerations. In some cases, they are aware that the induced belief is false. For these Credamites, as for Lee (above), recognized false belief is possible. As well, for them, it's not the case that doxastic deliberation is transparent to truth. They are fully aware that their induced beliefs are not accountable to truth and evidence. Finally, for them, it's not the case that non-epistemic considerations are exclusive in conscious belief formation.[24] If all this is right, the reality of each of our four phenomena (§8.4.1) is not a necessary truth, and a Kantian essentialist explanation of the phenomena is not supported.

8.5.3 Does Kantian essentialism explain the phenomena?

It is also doubtful that Kantian essentialism is sufficient to explain the phenomena in question. Consider Williams' (1973, p. 148) thought: belief at will is impossible, because belief "aims at truth." On its face, this can't be right: when Kobe Bryant aims to score, it's consistent with this that he shoots at will. So whether something has an aim, in the ordinary sense of "aim," doesn't have anything to do with whether or not it can be done at will. Why then should we think that constitutive standards of correctness have anything to do with whether or not something can be done at will?

Our question concerns how a thesis of this form:

(a) X is a constitutive standard of correctness for Φing

is explanatorily related to theses of these forms:

(i) Necessarily, one has no direct voluntary control over whether one Φs.
(ii) Necessarily, only X-related considerations can motivate conscious Φing.
(iii) Necessarily, it is impossible to Φ while recognizing that one's Φing is not X.
(iv) Necessarily, someone who deliberates over whether to Φ represents herself as responsive only to X-related considerations in consciously Φing.

But it's hard to see how a thesis of form (a) could explain theses of forms (i)–(iv). *Scoring* is a constitutive norm for taking a *shot* (in basketball), indeed it's plausibly *the* constitutive norm for taking a shot, but this does not imply a lack of direct voluntary control over whether one shoots. It certainly does not imply that *necessarily* one lacks direct voluntary control over whether one shoots. Nor does it imply that only scoring-related considerations can motivate conscious shooting: someone might consciously shoot while also trying to shoot in a particular way not related to scoring, as in a difficult reverse dunk. Alternatively, someone's motivation to shoot might be to attempt an unlikely shot from long-range, so as to possibly impress others.

---

[24] It might be objected that such beliefs are, in some important sense, atypical. But are they, in the relevant sense, *necessarily* atypical? We can imagine that such beliefs are statistically typical for our Credamites, since, as above (§8.5.1), we need only add a community to benevolent non-Credamites to run things. And we should grant that such beliefs are surely atypical relative to *our* beliefs, in as much as the Credamites' ability to indoctrinate themselves is atypical relative to the more modest human capacity for wishful thinking (Chapter 2).

Indeed, someone might shoot and try to miss, having taken a bribe. For all these reasons, someone might deliberate over whether to shoot without representing herself as responsive only to scoring-related considerations in coming to shoot: someone's deliberations about whether to shoot might be based solely on financial considerations (she was paid a bribe to shoot at such-and-such a point in the game), and she might be fully aware that these are the considerations that will decide the question of whether she shoots.[25]

This objection has been articulated by Asbjørn Steglich-Petersen (2006) and Conor McHugh (2011a). "[I]f transparency is produced by the norm of belief," Steglich-Petersen writes, then "this norm motivates one necessarily and inescapably to act in accordance with it" (p. 507), which makes it unlike norms in general: a norm of fulfillment flows from the nature of promising (if one promises to Φ, then one ought to Φ), but deliberation about whether to promise to Φ is not transparent to fulfillment (ibid. pp. 506–7). Considerations other than those related to whether one will Φ can enter into deliberation about whether to promise to Φ; someone can deliberately promise to Φ for reasons unrelated to the question of whether she will Φ. That fulfillment is a constitutive norm for promising implies none of the relevant theses of forms (i)–(iv): one could have direct control over whether one promises, non-fulfillment-related considerations can motivate conscious promising, and deliberating about whether to promise does not require representing oneself as responsive only to fulfillment-related considerations. As McHugh puts it, "[i]n general, we can deliberately violate constitutive norms, without thereby ceasing to be engaged in the activities constituted by those norms" (p. 372). It is standard to hold (cf. §8.6.2) that there is a constitutive norm for assertion—either truth, knowledge, or belief—but assertion can be deliberately false, ignorant, or insincere. None of the relevant theses of forms (i)–(iv) are even suggested by the existence of a constitutive norm of assertion. For the same reason, "that belief is subject to a constitutive norm…does not entail that we will have difficulty forming beliefs that are evidentially unsupported…nor that we will usually be inclined to believe strongly evidentially supported propositions" (McHugh 2011a, p. 372, cf. §2.3.1).

The thesis that truth is a constitutive standard of correctness for belief is one way of explaining the sense in which belief is representational (cf. §8.1.2). We should keep in mind that representation is not necessarily involuntary, and that conscious representation is not necessarily motivated by considerations having to do with representational accuracy. There are representational paintings, but painting is not involuntary, and painters can be motivated by considerations other than representational accuracy in consciously deciding what to represent in their paintings. Assertion is representational: when someone asserts that p she represents p as true,

---

[25] Similarly, consider the possibility of a constitutive norm (or norms) for action, e.g. the means–ends rule (§6.1.2) or Kant's categorical imperative. The existence of such a norm would not threaten our direct voluntary control over our actions, nor make deliberate and conscious violation of such a norm impossible.

or represents herself as believing that p, or as knowing that p. But assertion is voluntary, and one can consciously assert that p intending to mislead one's hearer, i.e. on the basis of considerations other than representational accuracy. It may be the case that, in some sense, someone who believes that p must represent herself, or her belief, as representing that p. But in the same sense, a representational painter must represent herself, or her painting, as representing its content, and an asserter must represent herself, or her assertion, as representing its content. But it's possible to consciously choose inaccurate representation, in the cases of representational painting and assertion, despite the fact that representational painting and assertion are representational.

Kantian essentialism does not provide a good explanation of the phenomena described (§8.4.1). What, then, explains these phenomena? One possibility is that a teleological conception of belief, rather than the Kantian's normative conception, can explain them (Steglich-Petersen 2006, 2009, McHugh 2011a, 2011b, 2012b). We have critically considered such accounts, in connection with the task of giving an account of epistemic normativity, above (Chapter 6). Another possibility is that the reality of each of these phenomena is not a necessary truth, but a contingent one, as I argued above (§§8.5.1–8.5.2).

8.5.4 The contingency of the connection between belief and truth

If the reality of our phenomena (§8.4.1) is contingent, what explains this? A fully satisfying answer to this question is beyond the scope of our inquiry. I'll sketch an answer, and if that answer is on the right track, a full account of our phenomena may require the resources of anthropology, sociology, and evolutionary psychology, and other scientific disciplines—as one would expect in giving an account of contingent phenomena having to do with human cognition.

A deep and universal love of truth might explain our exclusive responsiveness to epistemic considerations in conscious belief formation, and that might explain the rest. But we have found reasons to be skeptical of this idea (§1.2, §6.3); if our love of truth was not strong enough to ground Humean approaches to epistemic normativity, then it's not strong enough to explain our inability to believe at will and the other aspects of the seemingly deep, if contingent, connection between belief and truth.

In general, (contingent) involuntariness doesn't require an explanation in terms of a person's desires. That we can't control the weather in Scotland isn't to be explained by appeal to our deep and universal love of rain. But we should not ignore the fact that human cognition is, in some sense, directed at truth. So any account of the phenomena in question must vindicate this fact. Indeed, what I propose is that a successful account of our phenomena will put them center stage in its account of the sense in which human cognition is directed at the truth: it is "directed at the truth" in the sense that, for us, doxastic deliberation is transparent to truth, epistemic considerations are exclusive in conscious belief formation, recognized false belief is impossible (or difficult) for creatures like us, and we have no direct voluntary control over our beliefs.

A full explanation would explain why we are the way we are, in these respects. Such an explanation might appeal to a theory of our evolved biological nature, or to an historical story about our cultural inheritance. Here I'll briefly sketch the kind of explanation we should seek. Some aspects of our biological functioning are automatic and involuntary, e.g. we have no direct voluntary control over the beating of our hearts. Other aspects are deliberate and voluntary, e.g. we have direct voluntary control over the movement of our bodies. Other aspects are somewhere in between, e.g. the blinking of our eyelids. Nature, as it were, has left some tasks up to us—to feed ourselves, we must act, we must choose when and where to eat, we must acquire food through action, and so on—but has kept other tasks out of our hands. We can imagine a creature that had direct voluntary control over the beating of its heart, a creature that was forced to perform that task itself, in the same way that we are left with the task of feeding ourselves. But just as easily we can see why a creature with an automatic heartbeat would be better off. This is the form of explanation we should seek in the case of doxastic involuntarism: we can imagine a creature with direct voluntary control over its beliefs, but we can see why a creature with automatic and involuntary cognition would, or at least might, be better off. And we should seek it not by a priori speculation, but by empirically informed inquiry into the natural history of cognition.

The curiosity of doxastic involuntarism is further lessened when we consider doxastic deliberation as an evolutionary descendant of simpler cognitive systems. Such simple systems allowed our ancestors to detect basic changes in their environments—light and darkness, temperature—and over millennia developed into systems capable of more complex representation. If it seems obvious that the primitive perceptual system of the tuatara (a kind of lizard) would be more beneficial if its operation were automatic and involuntary, then it should not be entirely surprising that our relatively sophisticated cognitive system is automatic and involuntary—for even if direct voluntary control over our beliefs might seem as though it would benefit us *now*, an automatic and involuntary cognitive system may simply be our inheritance, from creatures who would have had no use for the capacity for belief at will.

As I've said, this is just a sketch. And even if doxastic involuntarism is explained, more will need to be said concerning the other phenomena. But I shall suggest that we should be looking for the same *kind* of explanation: we should ask what benefit might accrue to a creature motivated only be epistemic considerations in conscious belief formation, to one that cannot recognize her beliefs as false, and to one that represents herself as responsive to truth and evidence. The answer, as I have suggested, might delve into our evolutionary origins, or into our more recent history, by, for example, explaining transparency as a contingent cultural phenomenon (cf. Williams 2002). The account might appeal to the eudaimonic value of true belief, whether instrumental or final (Chapter 4).This sketch awaits a fuller account of the nature, scope, and origin of our "tendency" towards the truth.

In that respect, I've offered a promissory note. This sketch of an account of the contingent connection between belief and truth is incomplete. I have suggested the route towards its completion: evolutionary psychology and historical genealogy will explain our *explananda*. In light of the incompleteness of this account, however, we should step back and consider Kantian essentialism about belief by contrast with the present proposal. Each view, we can now see, owes us an explanation. The Kantian owes us an explanation of the existence of normative properties in a non-normative world (§8.3). The view proposed here owes us an explanation of our (contingent) "tendency" towards the truth. In this light, the view proposed here is in better shape than Kantian essentialism: our *explananda* are the kinds of thing that science and naturalistic philosophy have resources to explain, whereas irreducible normativity is a paradigm example of the kind of thing that science and naturalistic philosophy cannot make sense of (§5.5).

It's important to keep in mind that in explaining the contingent connection between belief and truth we may appeal to any of the following platitudes about belief:

- Necessarily, if S believes that p, then S takes it to be the case that p.
- Necessarily, if S believes that p, then S represents that p.
- Necessarily, if S believes that p, then S thinks it is true that p.

In this, I assume something controversial: that the notions of thought and representation are not normative (cf. Papineau 1999, p. 21). If they are, then surely philosophical naturalism is false (cf. Fodor 1996, p. 260).

I argued above that someone might recognize that the proposition that p is false, but find herself unable to give up her belief that p. It does not seem possible, however, to recognize that it is *true* that p without forming a *belief* that p. Recall Shah's (2003) idea that "once one has discovered whether *p* is true, the question *whether to believe that p* is *closed*" (p. 463). Pamela Hieronymi writes that "for certain attitudes, settling a question amounts to forming the attitude" (2005, p. 447), and she argues that belief is an attitude of this kind:

If you find the reasons that (you take to) bear positively on whether *p* to be convincing, and so settle for yourself the question of whether *p*, you have thus, *ipso facto*, formed a belief that *p*. (Ibid.; see also Hieronymi 2006, pp. 50–4)

Answering the question of whether p positively *just is* to believe that p, and answering the question of whether p negatively *just is* to disbelieve that p. It seems, therefore, to be a necessary truth about belief that, for any subject S and proposition that p, answering the question of whether p settles the question of whether S believes that p, in the sense that if S answers the question of whether p positively, S ipso facto believes that p, and if S answers the question of whether p negatively, S ipso facto disbelieves that p. It's not that answering the question of whether p puts an end to my deliberation about whether to believe that p (I might go on deliberating, Pascal-style), but rather that answering the question of whether p puts an end to my suspension of judgment about whether p. To borrow the language Richard Moran (1988) employs in this context, once I have answered the question of whether p, I have made up my mind about whether p.

Does this suggest Kantian essentialism about belief? No. Heironymi's phenomenon does not require explanation. It is true, and necessarily true, but its truth is trivial, and not something we need to posit the normativity of belief to explain.[26] We should add it to our list of platitudes—and it may serve us well in explaining our *explananda*. Once someone asks the question of whether p, all it means to "answer that question" is for her to believe that p or disbelieve that p. But this trivial truth does not require an explanation; in particular it does not require an explanation in terms of a constitutive standard of correctness for belief.

8.6 The argument(s) from assertion

There are some arguments for Kantian essentialism that are based on claims about assertion. This section considers those arguments. I'll argue that the question of the norm(s) of assertion is orthogonal to the question of the norm(s) of belief.

8.6.1 "I believe" as an assertion

In articulating the slogan "belief aims at truth," Williams (1973) writes:

[T]o say "I believe that *p*" itself carries, in general, a claim that *p* is true. To say "I believe that *p*" conveys the message that *p* is the case. It is a way, though perhaps a somewhat qualified way, of asserting that *p* is true. (p. 137)

As above (§8.5), if this suggests Kantian essentialism about belief, it must be a necessary truth. It must be that, necessarily, for any subject S and proposition that p, if S says that she believes that p, then S thereby asserts that p. Let's first ask whether Williams' principle is true, and then ask whether, if it's true, its truth suggests Kantian essentialism about belief, e.g. because Kantian essentialism is the best explanation of its truth.

First, there are counterexamples to Williams' principle. Consider a discussion of some controversial political issue, for example, whether British airstrikes in Libya should continue. After much discussion, you and I still disagree about the issue. When someone asks us what we think about the Libya question, I might say: "Well, I believe that airstrikes should end, but my friend here believes that they should continue." I have said that I believe that airstrikes should end, but I have not asserted that they should end. I have not even asserted this "in a somewhat qualified way" (Williams 1973, p. 137). Compare the kind of case Williams is thinking about: you ask me whether the National Portrait Gallery has reopened, and I say: "I believe it'll reopen in November."

---

[26] As above (§8.4.1), I remain neutral here on the issue of whether non-epistemic reasons are "the wrong kind" of reason for belief, which is Heironymi's (2005) topic.

This, indeed, amounts to a "somewhat qualified" assertion that the National Portrait Gallery will reopen in November. The difference between this case (in which saying that I believe that p amounts to asserting that p), and the previous case (in which saying that I believe that p doesn't amount to asserting that p), is that in this case the topic of the conversation is, and remains throughout the conversation, the question of whether p (i.e. the question of when the National Portrait Gallery reopens), whereas in the previous case the topic of conversation becomes the question of what you and I believe about whether p (i.e. the question of what we believe about the Libya question). The humility of my response shifts the topic of conversation away from the question of whether p to the question of what we believe about the question of whether p, and the result is that I may report on my belief that p without thereby asserting that p.[27]

Second, let's consider why sometimes saying that you believe that p amounts to asserting that p. Compare saying that you desire that p. It does not seem to be the case that saying that you desire that p *ever* amounts to an assertion that p, whereas saying that you believe that p at least sometimes amounts to an assertion that p. What explains this?

A relatively simple Gricean explanation will do the trick here.[28] Given the idea that people are assumed to be trying to follow a cooperative principle, on which you should "[m]ake your conversational contribution such as is required, at the stage at which it occurs, for the accepted purpose or direction of the talk exchange in which you are engaged" (Grice 1989, p. 26), you can ask what my purpose was in saying that I believe that the National Portrait Gallery will reopen in November. Someone who sincerely asserts that she believes that p can be assumed to be someone who believes that p (since people as a matter of fact are not that often wrong about what they believe), so if you take me to be sincere, you can assume that I believe that the National Portrait Gallery will reopen in November. But, again, why would I express this belief in response to your question? On the assumption that I am abiding by the cooperative principle, two answers to this question seem obvious: first, that I was trying to provide the information you sought (about when the Gallery will reopen), and, second, that I was trying to indicate how certain I am of the information provided (by adding the hedge "I believe"). In other words, given the assumption that I am abiding by the cooperative principle, and the fact that someone who sincerely says that she believes that p can be assumed to believe that p, you can conclude, in this context, from my saying that I believe that p, that I am, in a "somewhat qualified way," asserting that p. We need not think of belief as a normative concept to understand the case in this way: all that is needed is a platitudinous assumption about the functional role of belief vis-à-vis action (e.g. assertion), and the assumption of the cooperative principle. Given these assumptions, a good explanation of someone's expressing what she believes is that she intends to communicate what she believes to her interlocutor.

---

[27] The difference between these kinds of cases is sometimes a matter of stress: "I *believe* that p" suggests a qualified assertion that p; "*I* believe that p" suggests a belief report, and not an assertion that p.

[28] The Gricean "maxim of quality" (Grice 1989, p. 27) says that you should assert only what you believe. But this alone doesn't explain why saying that you believe that p sometimes amounts to asserting that p.

This is as it should be. Consider some other ways of asserting that p. Most of the time we assert that p just by uttering a sentence that expresses the proposition that p; you ask when the Gallery will reopen, and I say: "It'll reopen in November." You can assert that p by answering affirmatively when someone asks you whether p. Saying that you know that p is sometimes a way of asserting that p; you ask me what restaurants are open on Sunday and I say: "I know that Café Royal is." What explains the fact that saying that you know that p can be a way of asserting that p? Not the fact (if it is a fact) that truth is a constitutive standard of correctness for knowledge, nor the fact that truth is a constitutive standard of correctness for belief. For neither would explain why an assertion of <I know that p> is an unqualified assertion, as opposed to an assertion of <I believe that p>, which is a qualified assertion. It's a mistake to explain the fact that saying that you know that p can be a way of asserting that p by appeal to any constitutive standard of correctness for knowledge. But this should make us skeptical of the idea of explaining the fact that saying that you believe that p can be a way of asserting that p by appeal to any constitutive standard of correctness for belief.

8.6.2 The norm(s) of assertion

There seem to be distinctive norms that apply to assertion and other speech acts (cf. Grice 1989), and many philosophers maintain that there is a constitutive norm of assertion: a norm that flows from the essential nature of assertion, such that, necessarily, something is an assertion iff it is governed by said norm—and this is at least part of what it is to be an assertion. There is controversy about the content of such a norm or norms, however, with (at least) three contenders emerging:

Belief norm (cf. Williams 2002, pp. 71–5): It is proper to assert that p only if you believe that p.

Truth norm (Weiner 2005): It is proper to assert that p only if p.

Knowledge norm (Williamson 1996, 2000, Chapter 11, DeRose 2002; cf. Unger 1975): It is proper to assert that p only if you know that p.

None of these, alone, suggests a normative connection between belief and truth. However, it's possible that assertion is governed by a plurality of norms, and so it's possible that both the belief norm and the truth norm are true. The former asserts a normative connection between assertion and belief, and the latter asserts a normative connection between assertion and truth. Might we appeal to these *two* norms in defense of some normative connection between belief and truth?

As stated, the belief norm and the truth norm suggest no normative connection between belief and truth. We might strengthen the belief norm, however:

Stronger belief norm: It is proper to assert that p iff you believe that p.

And from this we might try to argue in favor of a normative connection between belief and truth: belief is sufficient for assertion (stronger belief norm), but truth is necessary for assertion (truth norm), therefore truth is a norm of belief. But the stronger belief norm is false: there are myriad things that I believe that it would be improper to assert—and not because such assertions would be false or not knowledgeable, but because they would be irrelevant, rude, pointless, and so on.[29] What we can conclude, to be sure, is that an assertion that violates neither the belief norm nor the truth norm will express a true belief. If both the belief norm and the truth norm govern assertion, then true belief is a norm of assertion. But the question of whether truth is a norm of belief is orthogonal to the issue of the norm(s) of assertion.[30]

8.6.3 Moore's paradox

Williams (1973, p. 137) and Railton (1994, p. 72) associate the idea that belief "aims at truth" with "Moore's paradox." Williams says that it "constitutes a paradox" to assert something of the form:

(i) ~p and I believe that p.

But as I argued above (§8.5.2), Lee might assert that airplanes are not dangerous, while admitting that he believes that airplanes are dangerous. Compare the utterance that Moore found paradoxical: "Though I don't believe it's raining, yet as a matter of fact it really is raining" (Moore 1993, p. 207), i.e. something of the form (switching the order):

(ii) p and I don't believe that p.

It really is "paradoxical" or incoherent to assert something of this form. Why? Philosophers have developed two strategies for answering this question. The first strategy is to understand "Moore's paradox" as revealing something about assertion, and to explain the incoherence of asserting something of form (ii) by appealing to norms of assertion. Thus defenders of the knowledge norm of assertion (Williamson 1996, pp. 506–7, DeRose 2002, pp. 180–1; cf. Sosa 2009) argue that the incoherence of asserting something of form (ii) along with the (supposed) incoherence of asserting something of the form:

(iii) p and I don't know that p

is explained by the fact that knowledge is necessary for proper assertion. And defenders of the truth norm of assertion (Weiner 2005, pp. 232–8) argue that their norm, plus familiar Gricean machinery, can explain the same. But as we saw above, the existence and nature of norms of assertion is orthogonal to the question of whether truth is a norm of belief. So if these accounts of "Moore's paradox" are right, then the "paradox" can be explained without positing an "aim" of belief.

---

[29] John Hawthorne (2004, p. 23n) moots the idea that knowledge is sufficient for "epistemically correct" assertion. Even if this notion can be made sense of (and Hawthorne is hesitant about this), it won't help with the current problem: we seek an explanation of epistemic normativity, and thus we cannot appeal to the "epistemic correctness" of knowledgeable assertions in our explanation.

[30] Note that (cf. §8.1.3, §9.1.6) assertion, unlike belief, is intentional: someone asserts only if she desires to assert. Even the liar, who intends to deceive her hearer by asserting something false, intends to assert.

The second strategy for explaining the incoherence of asserting something of form (ii) understands the "paradox" as revealing something about belief, rather than about assertion. We can see the appeal of this strategy by noting that while it seems incoherent to assert something of form (ii), it also seems incoherent to even *think* something of form (ii). If this is right, then our explanation can and should go deeper than the appeal to norms of assertion. We could argue that believing something of form (ii) is impossible (Shoemaker 1995) or that rationally believing something of form (ii) is impossible (de Almedia 2001, Williams 2004, Fernández 2005), to explain the apparent incoherence of believing something of form (ii). We could then appeal to the belief norm of assertion (Shoemaker 1995, p. 213) to explain why it would be improper to assert something of form (ii). I favor a version of this approach, which appeals to the fact that propositions of form (ii) cannot be truly believed. You cannot believe something of form (ii) and end up believing something true.[31] Belief in the proposition expressed by <p, but I don't believe that p> is guaranteed to be false. A "Moore paradoxical" thought is, in this respect, the opposite of Descartes' cogito thought. If you think the thought expressed by "I exist," then your belief is guaranteed to be true, even though its content is contingent (and therefore possibly false). If you think the thought expressed by "It's raining, but I don't believe it's raining," your belief is guaranteed to be false, even though its content is contingent (and therefore possibly true). That's why thinking something of form (ii) is incoherent. And we can now appeal to the true belief norm of assertion, suggested above, to explain why it would be improper to assert something of form (ii).[32,33] But although this strategy understands "Moore's paradox" as revealing something about belief, it reveals nothing about belief in general, nor does it reveal a norm of belief. No appeal needed to be made, in our account, to an "aim" of belief. So, again, "Moore's paradox" is orthogonal to the question of whether there is an "aim" of belief.

We have considered several strategies for solving "Moore's paradox." All make appeal, at some point, to a norm or norms of assertion, although the second kind of strategy goes further, explaining the impossibility or epistemic irrationality of believing propositions of form (ii). But we have found no reason to posit a norm of belief, in connection with "Moore's paradox."

---

[31] The argument assumes that believing that p & q suffices for believing that p, at least in the relevant cases. To the extent that this assumption is an assumption of the believer's rationality, the present version of the second strategy is not significantly different from the other versions mentioned.

[32] Note that this will not explain the incoherence of asserting or believing something of form (i). But this is as it should be: the incoherence involved in asserting or believing something of form (ii) is different from that involved in asserting or believing something of form (i). Propositions of form (i) can be truly believed, although someone who believes a proposition of form (i) is not fully rational—she has inconsistent beliefs. In believing or asserting a propostion of form (i), someone admits her own irrationality. By contrast, propositions of form (ii), I have just argued, cannot be truly believed. To believe a proposition of this form is not to admit one's irrationality, but to manifest it.

[33] This leaves open the (supposed) incoherence of asserting or believing something of form (iii). I do not think that asserting or believing something of form (iii) is incoherent (cf. Weiner 2005, McGlynn 2013), so that this is left open seems to me a virtue of the present version of the second strategy.

8.7 Postulating the standard of doxastic correctness

I maintain that truth is not a constitutive standard of correctness for belief. You might object as follows:

To argue about whether truth is a constitutive standard of correctness for belief is misguided, because the question turns out to be terminological. We can just define **belief*** as a propositional attitude such that, for any subject S and proposition that p, S's belief* that p is correct iff p. To think of a propositional attitude as a belief* is to see it as governed by the standard of doxastic correctness (§8.1.2). And the concept of belief* is the concept we apply when we engage in epistemic evaluation of beliefs, so the normativity of the concept of belief* explains the appropriateness of epistemic evaluation of beliefs. (Knowledge, for example, should be thought of as a species of belief*.)

Shah and Velleman (2005, pp. 508–11) propose a similar strategy. They propose that "[a]pplying the standard of truth to an attitude as a standard of correctness … can … be imagined as a way of conceiving of the attitude—conceiving of it … as being correct if and only if its content is true" (p. 509). To think of a belief as a belief* is to conceive of it as correct iff true; when we engage in epistemic evaluation we conceive of beliefs as beliefs*, and therefore—so the argument might go—epistemic evaluation is appropriate.

However, compare the concept of **tulief**, defined as a propositional attitude such that, for any subject S and proposition that p, S's tulief that p is correct iff it was formed on a Tuesday. Shall we then say that it's appropriate to evaluate beliefs vis-à-vis the Tuesday principle, in as much as they are conceived of as tuliefs? And in the same way that it's appropriate to evaluate beliefs vis-à-vis the truth principle, in as much as they are conceived of as beliefs*? On the present proposal, I see no way of avoiding the conclusion that evaluation of beliefs vis-à-vis the truth principle is appropriate in the same way that evaluation of beliefs vis-à-vis the Tuesday principle is appropriate. Thus, on the present proposal, we must answer the uniqueness question about epistemic evaluation (§5.2.1) by saying that there is no sense in which epistemic evaluation of beliefs is uniquely appropriate. But you might wonder, as well, whether this gives us any kind of answer to the basic question about epistemic evaluation. What, after all, justifies our conceiving of beliefs as beliefs* (and not conceiving of them as tuliefs)? Is it the case that all beliefs are beliefs* (and not tuliefs)? If so, then the issue isn't merely terminological, and we are back to our original formulation of Kantian essentialism. Perhaps some beliefs are beliefs*, but not others. But what makes this the case? Perhaps the desires of the believer (Chapter 6), or the natural history of those beliefs (Chapter 7); but in those cases we have abandoned Kantian essentialism about belief.[34]

---

[34] Note also that the present proposal has given up the de re reading of "essential evaluation" in favor of a de dicto reading (§5.4.1), given that beliefs are not essentially beliefs*. Epistemic evaluation of beliefs, then, is not evaluation vis-à-vis standards that flow from the de re essential nature of beliefs. This violates universalism about epistemic normativity (§5.3.1).

Shah and Velleman, cognizant of this problem, develop their idea that applying the standard of doxastic correctness is a matter of conceiving of an attitude as a belief, within the framework of **norm-expressivism**. On their view, it's a factual question whether I accept or do not accept some proposition, but not a factual question whether I believe or do not believe that proposition. "[A]pplying the belief-constituting standard of correctness to one's own acceptance that p consists in accepting the norm of truth for that acceptance," they argue, and "[w]hether to apply the truth-norm to an acceptance…is not a factual question" (2005, p. 510). Thus "there is no fact of the matter as to whether an acceptance that p must be true in order to be correct" (ibid.). We will return to expressivism about epistemic normativity below (§9.2.2). For now, note that Shah and Velleman's account of epistemic normativity would have to abandon realism about epistemic normativity (§5.2.3). For on their view, there is no fact of the matter as to whether an acceptance that p must be true in order to be correct, and thus no fact of the matter about the existence of epistemic value and epistemic reasons.

Our discussion so far has assumed **realism about belief**—that sometimes people have beliefs. For the anti-realist about belief, there is no fact of the matter as to whether true belief is good, because there are no facts of the matter about belief. To reject realism about belief is to reject realism about epistemic normativity. And there are two ways to do this. A modest strategy is to argue that there are no facts of the matter about the normative aspect of belief, while conceding that there are facts of the matter about the non-normative aspect. This is Shah and Velleman's strategy, who admit facts about acceptances, but reject facts about beliefs.

A more radical anti-realism about belief is suggested by Daniel Dennett's (1971, 1987, 1991) theory of the **intentional stance**. Belief, on Dennett's view, is normative in the sense that "[f]or the concept of belief to find application…[i]n general, normally, more often than not, if x believes p, p is true," and thus "the norm for belief is evidential well-foundedness" (1971, p. 102). But there is more to belief than this. We attribute beliefs and desires to "intentional systems" by way of explaining and predicting their behavior, but "a particular thing is an Intentional system only in relation to the strategies of someone who is trying to explain and predict its behavior" (ibid. p. 87). This is where the anti-realist suggestion arises:

[O]n occasion a purely physical system can be so complex, and yet so organized, that we find it convenient, explanatory, pragmatically necessary for prediction, to treat it as if it had beliefs and desires and was rational. (Ibid. p. 92)

The question of whether such a system "really" has beliefs and desires is "misguided" (ibid. p. 91). Dennett (1991) describes himself as a "semirealist" (p. 27); on his view beliefs (and other propositional attitudes) are real because "they serve in perspicuous representations of real forces, 'natural' properties, and the like" (p. 29). Beliefs are compared to "abstract objects" like centers of gravity (pp. 27–9). Dennett is right to reject debate about whether he is "really" a realist about propositional attitudes or "really" an anti-realist about propositional attitudes.[35] However, the anti-realist aspect of his view is clear enough when he articulates his understanding of the indeterminacy of translation:

I see that there could be two different systems of belief attribution to an individual which differed substantially in what they attributed...and yet where no deeper fact of the matter could establish that one was a description of the individual's *real* beliefs and the other not. [...] The choice...would indeed be up to the observer, a matter to be decided on idiosyncratic pragmatic grounds. (Ibid. p. 49)

Dennett, following Quine, admits that to adopt the intentional stance is to adopt a "dramatic idiom" (ibid. p. 48). But if, in general, there is no fact of the matter as to whether S believes that p, and saying that S believes that p is to adopt a pragmatically useful idiom, then, in general, there is no fact of the matter as to whether S's belief that p is good, and saying that S's belief that p is good is to adopt a pragmatically useful idiom.

Kantian essentialism about belief could be combined with Dennett's theory of the intentional stance to yield an anti-realist answer to the problem of the source of epistemic normativity. Employing the normative concept of belief (i.e. the concept of a propositional attitude that is correct iff true) is useful in predicting and explaining human behavior—and perhaps is worthwhile for other reasons (§9.1.4). The basic question about epistemic evaluation (§§5.2.1), for example, is then easy to answer: evaluation of people's beliefs vis-à-vis the truth principle is appropriate, because truth is the constitutive standard of correctness for belief (Kantian essentialism), and the concept of belief is useful in predicting and explaining human behavior (theory of the intentional stance). This view will not face the naturalistic problem of irreducible normativity (§5.5), because it does not posit epistemic values or epistemic reasons. That it's *useful* to employ irreducibly normative concepts is in no kind of tension with philosophical naturalism. We'll return to anti-realism about epistemic normativity, below (Chapter 9).

8.8 Conclusion

This chapter has considered approaches to epistemic normativity based on Kantian essentialism about belief: the thesis that truth is a constitutive standard of correctness for belief. This was seen to be in tension with philosophical naturalism (§8.3), giving us reason to resist it. I then criticized the master argument for Kantian essentialism (§§8.4–8.5), and considered an alternative motivation for it, from phenomena

---

[35] Cf. the issue of what separates Davidson and Dennett. In Dennett's view (1991, pp. 45–9), not much, but enough for Davidson to be a "regular strength realist," and Dennett a "mild realist" (ibid. p. 30).

involving assertion (§8.6). Finally, I conceded that those who reject realism about belief are free to adopt Kantian essentialism about belief (§8.7).

We have now considered (Chapters 6–8) three articulations of the idea that belief "aims at truth," and three accounts of epistemic normativity that could be offered by appeal to those three articulations. I have argued that none of these articulations of the idea that truth is the "aim of belief" can provide a plausible realist account of epistemic normativity.

9

Anti-Realism about Epistemic Normativity

A knowledge of etiquette is of course essential to one's decent behavior, just as clothing is essential to one's decent appearance; and precisely as one wears the latter without being self-conscious of having on shoes and perhaps gloves, one who has good manners is equally unselfconscious in the observance of etiquette, the precepts of which must be so thoroughly absorbed as to make their observance a matter of instinct rather than of conscious obedience.

—Emily Post, *Etiquette*

Several times, in our inquiry into the source of epistemic normativity, we have encountered the suggestion that we should reject realism about epistemic normativity (§5.2.3). In this chapter I'll give a sketch, and a provisional defense, of anti-realism about epistemic normativity.

Before we begin, let's take stock of the argument so far. First (Part I), I argued that true belief is at most sometimes eudaimonically valuable. False belief is sometimes better for a person than true belief (Chapters 2–3), and some true beliefs are eudaimonically (and socially) worthless (Chapter 4). Second (Chapters 5–8), I argued against various realist approaches to epistemic normativity. I rejected eudaimonic approaches to epistemic normativity, by appeal to my conclusions about the eudaimonic value of true belief (§5.3). When it came to Humean approaches (Chapter 6), I argued that these approaches run afoul of universalism about epistemic normativity (§5.3). When it came to Darwinian and Kantian approaches (Chapters 7 and 8), I argued that these approaches fail for other reasons.

Here I'll give a sketch of anti-realism about epistemic value (§9.1) and present promising accounts of epistemic evaluation (§9.1.4, §9.2). I'll answer the scope question by defining "epistemic" (§9.3), and articulate an appealing pluralism about doxastic evaluation (§9.4). My aim is to show that the anti-realist alternatives are appealing enough to stick with the provisional rejection of realism suggested by the failure of realist approaches to epistemic normativity (Chapters 5–8).

9.1 Rejecting realism

In this section I'll articulate anti-realism about epistemic normativity (§9.1.1), and in particular anti-realism about epistemic value (§9.1.2), before discussing the distinction between accounts of epistemic value and accounts of the appropriateness of epistemic evaluation (§9.1.3). I'll then sketch an anti-realist account of the social function of epistemic evaluation (§9.1.4), before responding to two objections to anti-realism about epistemic normativity (§§9.1.5–9.1.6).

9.1.1 Anti-realism about epistemic normativity

We have found no plausible account of epistemic normativity consistent with realism about epistemic normativity (§5.2.3). Note also that the difficulties with teleological (§6.1.1), biological (§7.2.3), and normative (§8.1.4) conceptions of belief suggest that the idea that truth is the "aim of belief" cannot be given a rigorous articulation (or, in the case of the biological conception, an a priori defense). I have not argued that there aren't alternative approaches available to the realist. But it's time to consider the anti-realist alternative.

Anti-realism about epistemic normativity is the conjunction of anti-realism about epistemic value and anti-realism about epistemic reasons:

> **Anti-realism about epistemic value:** The appropriateness of epistemic evaluation is not explained by the existence of epistemic value.
>
> **Anti-realism about epistemic reasons:** The appropriateness of epistemic reasons attribution is not explained by the existence of epistemic reasons.

In their simplest forms, anti-realism about epistemic value and anti-realism about epistemic reasons reject the existence of epistemic value and epistemic reasons, respectively. Alternatively, anti-realism about epistemic value could take the form of the claim that there is nothing more to "the existence of epistemic value" than the fact that people value true belief, knowledge, understanding, and the like—e.g. that epistemic value and epistemic reasons are not "real," but "subjective" or "constructed" (cf. §5.3.3). In any event, anti-realists of all stripes are at pains to offer an explanation of the appropriateness of epistemic evaluation and of epistemic reasons attribution that does not appeal to the existence of epistemic value and epistemic reasons.

Such explanations are needed for several reasons. First, they satisfy our theoretical curiosity, making anti-realism about epistemic normativity more appealing. Second, I criticized realist explanations above; without the offer of competing explanations, the case for anti-realism will be weak. Third, the realist about epistemic normativity might retreat to the position that the existence of epistemic value and the existence of epistemic reasons, which explain, respectively, the appropriateness of epistemic evaluation and epistemic reasons attribution, are themselves brute and inexplicable. We might call this **primitivism about epistemic normativity**. You might object that such irreducible normativity is incompatible with philosophical naturalism. But the naturalistic constraints (§5.5) describe pro tanto reasons to avoid positing irreducible normative properties; these pro tanto reasons might be overridden by the implausibility of anti-realism about epistemic normativity. At the very least, if the anti-realist offers no explanation of the appropriateness of epistemic evaluation and epistemic reasons attribution, she will face a dialectical standoff with the primitivist. But if she offers a satisfying explanation, she will win the day.

The anti-realist accounts of epistemic evaluation that we'll examine (§9.1.4, §9.2) are compatible with a kind of **skepticism about epistemic normativity**. The sort of skeptic I have in mind is someone who suspends judgment about the existence of epistemic value and epistemic reasons.

Derek Parfit (2011) notes that certain naturalistic objections to normative reasons for action would apply, mutatis mutandis, to normative reasons for belief:

[O]n such views…there aren't really any normative reasons. [If this] were true, we could not have reasons to have any particular beliefs. Such epistemic reasons are also irreducibly normative, and therefore are open to the same Naturalist objections. (VI, p. 110)

One might then argue that since there are surely normative reasons for belief, the naturalistic objections to normative reasons for action must be unsound. This, as Tom Kelly (2003) puts it, is "[t]he strategy of defending moral reasons by tying their fate to that of epistemic reasons" (p. 617n). This strategy has been elaborated by Russ Shafer-Landau (2006, p. 225) and Terence Cuneo (2007, Chapter 3).[1] The tenability of anti-realism about epistemic normativity is obviously of great importance, when it comes to assessing this strategy.

Even if the fate of normative reasons for action is thus tied to that of epistemic reasons, anti-realism about epistemic normativity does not commit us to anti-realism about normative reasons for action. Suppose that, although we have pro tanto reasons to avoid positing irreducible normative properties (§5.5), anti-realism about normative reasons for action proves indefensible. The naturalist might then find her pro tanto reasons overridden, and be forced to admit (irreducible) normative reasons for action. But this would not force her to admit normative reasons for belief, so long as anti-realism about epistemic normativity is defensible. So while Parfit et al. are right that some ways of rejecting normative reasons for action commit you to anti-realism about epistemic normativity, anti-realism about epistemic normativity per se does not commit you to rejecting normative reasons for action.

9.1.2 Anti-realism about epistemic value

From here we shall confine our attention primarily to anti-realism about epistemic value. We will tentatively assume that what we say about epistemic value will apply,

---

[1] Taking the same premise in the opposite direction, Matthew Chrisman (2011) motivates an anti-realist-friendly account of epistemic evaluation by appeal to naturalistic worries about ethical facts that apply equally to epistemic facts (p. 117; see also p. 125).

mutatis mutandis, to epistemic reasons. This assumption can be made less tentative if we assume that epistemic value explains epistemic reasons (§5.2.2). But in any event, we shall confine our attention to epistemic value.

We can distinguish anti-realism about epistemic value from three other positions with which it might have been confused. First, anti-realism about epistemic value isn't the view that true belief (along with knowledge, understanding, and the like) isn't valued—by many, or by most, or even by all (although we have found reason to be suspicious of the principle of curiosity, §1.2.2). Michael Lynch (2004) argues that "truth does matter to most of us" (p. 119); anti-realism about epistemic value doesn't deny this. We might speak of something's "really" mattering, as opposed to its mattering to or for someone. Anti-realism denies that true belief (etc.) "really" matters; it doesn't deny that they matter to many, or most, or even all people.

Second, anti-realism about epistemic value isn't the view that we ought not value true belief (along with knowledge, understanding, and the like). Stephen Stich (1990) argues that:

[O]nce we have a clear view of the matter, most of us will not find any value, either intrinsic or instrumental, in having true beliefs. (p. 101)

On Stich's view, we may value having true beliefs, but we ought not value having true beliefs; his argument is "against according intrinsic [or final] value to having true beliefs" (p. 120). But anti-realism about epistemic value is a distinct position. For one, anti-realism about epistemic value is consistent with true belief having eudaimonic value (Part I). We found no reason (Chapter 4) to reject weak instrumental and constitutive value approaches to the eudaimonic value of true belief. But anti-realism about epistemic value is consistent with any position you might want to take on the eudaimonic value of true belief. For another, anti-realism is consistent with there being good reason for some or many or all people to value true belief. We might appeal to the social benefits of valuing true belief (§5.3.3). We'll return to this point (§9.1.4).

Third, anti-realism about epistemic value isn't the view that true belief (or knowledge, or understanding, or whatever) is epistemically disvaluable or epistemically bad. That view sounds close to incoherence, and the fact that it does may tell us something important about the notion of the "epistemic" (§9.3). The anti-realist rejects the "real" existence of epistemic value whole hog; she does not denigrate true belief in favor of some other epistemic good (cf. Stich 1990, pp. 117–19).

This leads us to a final point. Anti-realism about epistemic value is a thesis that concerns epistemic value in particular. The letter of anti-realism about epistemic value, at least, is consistent with realism about other species of value—and in particular it's consistent with realism about instrumental value and instrumental reasons, to which I'll appeal below (§9.1.4). My leading motivation has been philosophical naturalism (§5.5), which enjoins us to avoid positing irreducible normativity. But positing irreducible normativity may be unavoidable, so our naturalistic motivation does not rule out realism about any species of value. On the other hand, anti-realism about epistemic value is consistent with anti-realism about all species of value.

Recall the problem of the source of epistemic value (§5.2.1). We'll now turn to sketching an anti-realist approach to this problem. First, we'll consider how the nihilist can answer the basic question about epistemic evaluation (§9.1.4, §9.2). Then we'll turn to the scope question (§9.3), and the uniqueness question (§9.4). My goal will be to show that anti-realism is viable; this will show that rejecting irreducible epistemic normativity is viable, which is good news for the naturalist.

9.1.3 Accounts of epistemic value vs. accounts of the appropriateness of epistemic evaluation

Recall the basic question about epistemic evaluation (§5.2.1): why is epistemic evaluation appropriate? Realists about epistemic value answer this question by appeal to the existence of epistemic value. How shall the anti-realist proceed?

We must distinguish here between giving an account of epistemic value and giving an account of the appropriateness of epistemic evaluation; the anti-realist seeks to give an account of the appropriateness of epistemic evaluation without (e.g.) giving an account of the value of true belief—or, at least, without appealing to the value of true belief in her explanation of the appropriateness of epistemic evaluation. John Greco (2010) articulates the distinction well, in connection with the "Meno problem" (§5.1):

> [W]e should distinguish ... Plato's question in the *Meno* ... from a different question that we have already answered: Why is the *concept* of knowledge valuable? Our answer to that question was that the concept plays valuable roles in the lives of information-using, information-sharing beings such as ourselves. The human form of life demands good information and the reliable flow of that information. The concept of knowledge, along with related concepts, serves those needs. That is not yet to say, however, why knowledge is valuable. We may put things this way: The concept of knowledge is valuable because it allows us to identify and share reliable information. But why is *knowledge* valuable? That question remains to be answered. (p. 91)

One upshot of this is that giving an account of epistemic evaluation is not the same as giving an account of epistemic value. The anti-realist can give an account of epistemic evaluation without giving an account of epistemic value. Compare Christine Korsgaard's (1996) distinction between three questions about ethical concepts:

> It is obvious that human beings apply ethical concepts ... The philosopher is ... concerned with three important features of these concepts. First, what exactly do they mean, or what do they contain: that is, how are they to be analyzed or defined? Second, of course, to what do they apply? Which things are good, and which actions are right or obligatory? And third, the philosopher wants to know where ethical concepts come from. How did we come into possession of them, and how does it come about that we use them? (p. 10)

We can ask the same three questions about "epistemic concepts," like the concept of epistemic value. There is a semantic question about the meaning of the concept, there is a normative question about its application, and there is a genealogical question about its origins. Our present point can be put like this: one might answer the semantic and genealogical questions, even while giving an anti-realist answer to the normative question.

As we saw above (§5.3.3), the distinction I'm drawing here can also be seen by considering social-genealogical approaches to epistemic normativity, which offer explanations of the *practice* of epistemic evaluation. This distinction applies whether such explanations are meant merely to describe the evolution of epistemic evaluation or whether they are meant to justify our practice of epistemic evaluation. The value of engaging in the practice of epistemic evaluation and the value of true belief are conceptually distinct: it might be valuable to engage in the practice of epistemic evaluation even if true belief is not valuable.[2]

To answer the basic question about epistemic evaluation, then, the anti-realist will need to give an account of epistemic evaluation that explains its appropriateness. This account will seek to justify or vindicate or legitimate the practice of epistemic evaluation. So, for example, the anti-realist will seek to explain the appropriateness of evaluating beliefs vis-à-vis the truth principle. But in doing so she will not appeal to the value of true belief.

It's worth pausing to consider the Meno problem again. How, or why, or in what way, is knowledge epistemically more valuable than mere true belief? In our inquiry we have considered the value of mere true belief, by asking: how, or why, or in what way, is true belief valuable? But recall that Meno's question is not actually articulated as a question about the greater value of knowledge, but rather about the greater value *we place* on knowledge: "it makes me wonder," he says, "why knowledge is prized far more highly than right opinion" (97d). When Socrates gives his answer to this question, it's an explanation of "why knowledge is prized higher than correct opinion" (98a). A successful anti-realist account of epistemic evaluation, in similar fashion, will explain why true belief is prized. We turn now to that question; we'll approach this by asking the basic question about epistemic evaluation (§5.2.1): why is epistemic evaluation appropriate?

9.1.4 A socio-epistemological account of the appropriateness of epistemic evaluation

Social epistemologists (§4.4.1) can be understood as offering an account that both explains the evolution of our practice of epistemic evaluation and vindicates it as a continuing practice.[3] Sinan Dogramaci (2012) makes this explicit. His question concerns "the function of words like 'irrational' as used in ordinary epistemic evaluation,"

---

[2] Klemens Kappel (2010) argues that "treating a belief as known is beneficial in the right sort of circumstances," and concludes from this that "knowledge is valuable, or more valuable than, say, mere true belief" (pp. 183–4). But this conclusion does not follow from the adduced premise: what the premise affirms is the "pragmatic" value of *attributing* knowledge; it does not provide a "pragmatic account of the value of *knowledge*" (p. 183, my emphasis). Compare Matthew Chrisman's (2012) apt discussion of the fact that "we value knowledge more than mere true belief," in connection with expressivism about epistemic evaluation (p. 122; cf. §9.2.2).

[3] A more modest account might merely explain the existence of our practice, without vindicating it. The more ambitious account sketched here seems committed to realism about normative reasons for action (cf. §9.1.1).

and asks after "the utility of our epistemically evaluative practice" (p. 514), seeking "a clear and plausible function that all our epistemically evaluative practice services" (p. 516). Dogramaci assumes that "the utility of our epistemically evaluative practice is just an instrumental utility it has by helping us get true beliefs" (p. 514), and that "we each want true beliefs, and no false beliefs, about the topics that are important to us" (p. 523). He argues, on the basis of some claimed correlations between evaluation and human behavior, that the function of epistemic evaluation is the promotion of coordination in our following of belief-forming rules; this "allows us to put together every individual's evidence into a vastly larger communal pool," thus extending "our common epistemic reach by enabling each person to serve as an 'epistemic surrogate' for any other person" (p. 524). Because of this:

> If "rational" (and "justified" and all the others) were suddenly expunged from our vocabulary, and nothing new were introduced to take their place, our communal support system would be weakened, and the credibility of testimony would suffer. (Ibid.)

And in turn we would suffer in our pursuit of true beliefs about important topics. Thus we have good (instrumental) reason to engage in the practice of epistemic evaluation.[4]

The emergence of such a practice would naturally involve a suite of evaluative practices, including but not limited to the use of such words as "(epistemically) rational" and "(epistemically) justified." For example, as Sanford Goldberg (2011, p. 178) argues, we take ourselves to be entitled to blame someone for asserting that p, if she lacked adequate epistemic support for believing that p. Given society's interest in reliable testimony, epistemic norms have to be enforced: this might require personal sanctions (Goldberg's point), or institutional pressure (e.g. ensuring conformity with high academic standards through the selective distribution of grant money), or regulation through the internalization of epistemic norms (e.g. the inculcation of honesty, curiosity, and intellectual integrity). These are all aspects of "the institution of testimony," (Kusch 2009, p. 76; cf. Williams 2002, esp. Chapters 4–6) which on the present proposal is designed to ensure conformity to epistemic norms, with society as the chief beneficiary.

Note well: this account is consistent with anti-realism about epistemic value. The appropriateness of epistemic evaluation, on Dogramaci's view, is explained by the social value of that practice; the collective practice of epistemic evaluation is a means to the collective good of acquiring instrumentally valuable true beliefs, and avoiding false beliefs, about important topics. The anti-realist about epistemic value can accept all this. And she could incorporate the idea that true belief, in some sense, "acquires intrinsic value" at some point in the genealogy of epistemic evaluation (§5.3.3). But she needn't make this "constructivist" move. The question of the appropriateness of epistemic evaluation is distinct from the question of the existence of epistemic value.

---

[4] As Dogramaci points out (p. 514n), this does not mean that the present account is a Humean account (Chapter 6).

Is this account compatible with rejecting the eudaimonic value of true belief per se (Chapter 4)? It is: the sometime eudaimonic value of true belief gives us social reason to engage in a universalist practice of epistemic evaluation (§5.3.3). The sometime eudaimonic value of true belief gives us good social reason to *treat* true belief as though it always has value—a value which we come to call "epistemic." (It might in the same way give us good reason to conceive of such value as final, intrinsic, and non-eudaimonic, cf. §9.3.)

9.1.5 The political objection

Michael Lynch begins his book *True to Life* (2004), a defense of the value of true belief, as follows:

In early 2003 George Bush claimed that Iraq was attempting to purchase the materials necessary to build nuclear weapons. [Although this turned out to be false,] various members of the administration [argued that] the important thing was that the subsequent invasion of Iraq achieved stability in the region and the liberation of the country. [...] To paraphrase Nietzsche, the truth may be good, but why not sometimes take untruth if it gets you to where you want to go? (p. 1)

Lynch then asks: "is it always better to believe and speak the truth?" (ibid.) and goes on, in the remainder of the book, to critically examine "cynicism" about the value of truth. The suggestion seems to be that a failure to appreciate the value of truth is politically problematic: cynicism about the value of truth motivates and justifies a relaxed attitude towards political dishonesty, in general, and towards the politically motivated lies that George Bush told to the American public, and that Colin Powell told at the United Nations, in the build-up to the Iraq war. Along the same lines, Bernard Williams (2002) writes that "an individual's commitment to the virtues of truth may stand opposed to a political culture which destroys and pollutes the truth" (p. 127), and that a "dedication to science and to standards of scientific truthfulness," and a desire "to discover and hold on to reality...can stand against such forces as political corruption and terror" (p. 141). And Ernie Sosa (1987) has written that "serious philosophy," which rejects subjectivist and relativist views about truth and objectivity, is the only philosophy capable of coherently resisting "the soft sell of the hidden persuaders, or the hard boot of political tyranny" (p. 724, see also p. 714, p. 726). All this suggests the idea that embracing or rejecting the value of truth has political implications.

Let us consider, with Lynch, the American scene. The left casts their right-wing opponents as enemies of truth, as Orwellian obfuscators, as Nixonian schemers, as hawks who will tell any lie to justify their wars, as Fox News bullshit-spewers, as fanatics devoted to faith rather than reason, as defenders of secret black-ops sites, classified and redacted documents, as against transparent government, and so on. For the left, to speak up for Truth is to take a stand in defense of liberal democracy, justice, and progress. Might anti-realism about epistemic value, along with my critical conclusions about the eudaimonic value of true belief (Part I), involve me in complicity with right-wing politics? No. For the right sees things exactly the other way. For them, "liberals [*sic*]" are the real enemies of truth: post-modern cultural relativists, subjectivists, left-wing academics who don't even believe there is such a thing as the truth. To speak up for Truth, then, is to take a stand in defense of traditional values, absolutism, and moral seriousness. The defense of the value of true belief is neither a left-wing nor a right-wing enterprise. And thus neither is the critique of the value of true belief that I've presented here.

Does anti-realism about epistemic value leave one unable to resist "a political culture which destroys and pollutes the truth"? Does it leave one powerless against "Big Brother and the police state" (Sosa 1987, p. 726)? First, my argument against the value of true belief is not an argument against valuing true belief—there may be all kinds of benefits to valuing true belief, including, perhaps, an increased ability to resist political oppression (cf. §9.1.4). Second, my critique of the value of true belief does not threaten the idea that we care about the truth, especially on certain topics, very much, and that we may be owed the truth, especially on certain topics, by our governments. Even if x is worthless, you may come to owe me x, and I may have a morally powerful claim on you to give me x, such that your failure to give me x is a great violation of my rights. Much political obligation seems to have this feature. So we can conclude that anti-realism about epistemic value, and a cynical attitude towards the value of truth in general, does not have the political implications that were suggested.

9.1.6 The objection from self-defeat

Another objection to anti-realism about epistemic normativity is the objection that anti-realism about epistemic normativity is self-defeating (Finnis 1980, p. 75, Cuneo 2007, pp. 117–18, Lynch 2009a, pp. 232–3, Shah 2011, Parfit 2011, v2, p. 522). This objection is based on the idea that it's in some way incoherent to assert or defend anti-realism about epistemic normativity.[5] Note well, to begin, that this objection does not suggest that anti-realism about epistemic normativity is *false*, only that it cannot coherently be asserted or defended. It is therefore, from the beginning, a curious kind of objection—since it does not suggest that the view, against which it is an objection, is false.

This objection from self-defeat can be articulated in several ways. Terence Cuneo (2007) writes that:

If epistemic nihilists hold that we do have reasons to believe their position, then their position is self-defeating in the sense that it presupposes the existence of the very sorts of entity that it claims not to exist. [But if they] hold that we do not have epistemic reason to believe their position, then their position is polemically toothless. (p. 117; see also Finnis 1980, p. 75)

---

[5] Here I focus on this objection as it applies to any version of anti-realism about epistemic normativity, leaving aside certain worries about expressivism about epistemic evaluation (more on which below, §9.2.2) in particular (on which see Cuneo 2007, Chapters 5 and 6, Lynch 2009a, pp. 233–4, 2009b, pp. 85–6).

Let us grant that the anti-realist is committed to the view that there are no epistemic reasons, and therefore that there are no epistemic reasons in favor of anti-realism. Following Jonas Olson's discussion (2011, p. 83), my reply is that the view the anti-realist defends is that anti-realism is *true*, not the view that there are reasons to believe that it is true. The anti-realist takes a stand in "debates on where the truth lies in meta-ethics and metaepistemology" (ibid.). Cuneo's objection, in other words, trades on a confusion between the ability to argue that a view is true and the ability to argue that there are reasons to believe that view.[6]

Recall the standard of doxastic correctness (§8.1.2), which Michael Lynch (2009a) formulates as:

(TN) It is correct to believe <p> if and only if <p> is true. (p. 228)

Lynch argues against the view that (TN) is neither true nor false on the grounds that this view is "self-undermining" (pp. 232–3). His argument is that asserting the view commits one to believing the view, and that, given Kantian essentialism about belief (§8.1), this commits one to the following:

(A) It is correct to believe <(TN) is neither true nor false> if and only if <(TN) is neither true nor false> is true.

And this, Lynch argues, commits one to believing that (TN) is true. However, this conclusion does not follow from the adduced premise. Being committed to (A) does not commit one to (TN), since (TN) is a universally quantified claim about all propositions, whereas (A) is merely an instance of (TN). Moreover, Lynch's argument relies on the truth of Kantian essentialism about belief. But this is inconsistent with the view that (TN) is neither true nor false. So the argument could have been much quicker, but it would not show that the view in question is "self-undermining." Objections that appeal to Kantian essentialism about belief as a premise (Lynch 2009a, p. 236, 2009b, p. 87) face my criticism of Kantian essentialism, above (Chapter 8).

Finally, Nishi Shah (2011) argues that anti-realism about reasons for belief is incoherent, on the grounds that the anti-realist "must attribute judgments about reasons for belief and demonstrate that these beliefs are systematically false" (p. 99). But "to ascribe belief one must judge, implicitly at least, that the mental state so classified is *correct* if its content is true and incorrect if its content is false" (p. 100), which in turn commits one to the existence of reasons for belief, since "[a] reason for belief is just a consideration that indicates that believing *p* would be correct" (p. 101). This argument, like Lynch's, appeals to Kantian essentialism about belief as a premise. One possibility here is that anti-realism about reasons for belief, properly understood, is compatible

---

[6] Cuneo (2007) associates anti-realism about epistemic normativity with "a sweeping form of epistemological skepticism," on which "no entity can display an epistemic merit or demerit" (p. 119). Many forms of philosophical skepticism are incompatible with this idea; consider the skeptical view that our beliefs about the external world are unjustified. The invocation of the specter of skepticism, in this connection, is not illuminating.

with Kantian essentialism about belief, properly understood (Olson, pp. 91–3). For my purposes, I'll note only that anti-realism is a metaphysical position about the existence of epistemic value and epistemic reasons (and about the explanatory relations between the appropriateness of epistemic evaluation and epistemic reasons attribution, on the one hand, and the existence of epistemic value and epistemic reasons, on the other). As such, the assertion of anti-realism does not involve the attribution of belief, nor does it commit one to the view that anyone believes anything false, e.g. that anyone falsely believes realism about epistemic value or epistemic reasons. Anti-realism commits one to the *falsity* of realism, not to the view that anyone *believes* realism falsely.

The assertion or defense of anti-realism about epistemic normativity commits one to the truth of anti-realism about epistemic normativity. Does it commit one to anything else, anything incompatible with anti-realism about epistemic normativity? Does it commit one, say, to a norm of assertion? Perhaps, but this is compatible with anti-realism about epistemic normativity (§8.6.2). As Fred Drestske (2000) argues:

Saying (asserting, claiming) that P (unlike believing that P) is, generally speaking, a purposeful, goal-directed action and, thus, the language of entitlements, commitments, rules, and norms more easily finds a home here. (p. 251)

And as Olson (2011) argues:

[Anti-realists] can recognize reasons for belief that apply to some agents in virtue of their roles, or in virtue of being engaged in some rule-governed or goal-oriented activities. (p. 84)

For the same reason, anti-realism about epistemic normativity is consistent with the view that inquiry (as opposed to belief) aims at truth (*pace* Lynch 2009a, p. 238, 2009b, p. 86). Asserting that p and inquiring about whether p are intentional actions or activities; my rejection of the idea that truth is the "aim of belief" (Chapters 6–8) therefore does not suggest that truth is not the "aim of assertion" or the "aim of inquiry." You might think that truth is an aim of inquiry in a quite literal sense: as Susan Haack (1995) puts it, "[i]f you aren't trying to find out how things are, to get truth, you aren't really inquiring" (p. 199). Even in the case of assertion, as Dretske (2000) suggests, it's plausible that "the norms emerge from the associated intentions" (p. 251; cf. Williams 2002, pp. 70–3),[7] but this is immaterial to the present point. The assertion of anti-realism, like any assertion, may commit you to truth as the norm of assertion. And inquiry about whether anti-realism is true, like any inquiry, may commit you to truth as a norm of inquiry. But neither of these things commits you to truth as a norm of belief, nor in general to the falsity of anti-realism about epistemic normativity.

---

[7] Note a crucial difference between belief and assertion: S asserts that p only if S intends to assert that p, but it is not the case that S believes that p only if S intends to believe that p. For this reason, assertion, unlike belief, is a plausible candidate for being analogous to a move in a game (cf. §8.1.3, §8.6.2).

9.2 Anti-realist accounts of the semantics of epistemic evaluation

An account of the social function of epistemic evaluation (§9.1.4) is not the same as an account of the semantics of epistemic evaluation. An account of the latter kind will tell us the *meaning* of the words, expressions, sentences, and utterances involved in epistemic evaluation—e.g. an account of the meaning of utterances of <*x* is epistemically good> or <S epistemically ought to believe that p> or <S knows that p>. And it will tell us the *content* of the thoughts involved in epistemic evaluation—e.g. an account of what it is to think that something is epistemically good, or that someone epistemically ought to believe something, or that someone knows something. One might give diverging accounts of the meaning of these different expressions—one kind of account might be appropriate for epistemic goodness attribution, but a very different kind of account might be appropriate for knowledge attribution. But I'll assume, for the sake of simplicity, that the anti-realist's account will be unified.

This section considers three anti-realist accounts of epistemic evaluation: error theory (§9.2.1), expressivism (§9.2.2), and what I'll call "convention-relativism" (§9.2.3). All three, I'll argue, are promising, but convention-relativism is the account I prefer; I'll conclude by sketching an argument for it (§9.2.4), and further clarifying and defending my proposed approach to epistemic normativity (§§9.2.5–9.2.6).

9.2.1 Error theory

Recall the idea (§5.2.3) that the most straightforward way to explain why evaluation of beliefs vis-à-vis the truth principle is appropriate is by appeal to the fact that true beliefs have value, otherwise evaluation of beliefs vis-à-vis the truth principle says something about them that isn't so. You might argue that since epistemic evaluation in general says things that aren't so, epistemic evaluation in general is false. This is an **error theory** about epistemic evaluation.

Error theory about epistemic evaluation has attracted a few detractors (Cuneo 2007, Chapter 4, Lynch 2009a, p. 232) but, to my knowledge, no defenders (although Olson 2011 offers a critique of the detractors). One might resist error theory on the grounds that it is uncharitable. But this would be too quick, for the error theorist can offer an account of the appropriateness of epistemic evaluation, thereby charitably vindicating the practice; such an account might appeal to a socio-epistemological account of the appropriateness of epistemic evaluation (§9.1.4). In any event, like error theorists about other parts of ordinary talk and thought, the error theorist about epistemic evaluation will need to offer a vindicating account of the ordinary practice of epistemic evaluation.[8]

---

[8] Compare Trenton Merricks' (2003, Chapter 7) vindicating account of ordinary talk about inanimate composite objects, which is systematically false on his view, and David Braun and Ted Sider's (2007, pp. 135–7) vindicating account of ordinary vague utterances, which is false on their view.

9.2.2 Expressivism

A number of philosophers have proposed **expressivism about epistemic evaluation** (Gibbard 1990, 2003, pp. 227–9, Shah and Velleman 2005, p. 510, Chrisman 2007, Field 2009, Kappel 2010). The leading idea behind these accounts is that the talk (and thought) involved in epistemic evaluation is essentially (though not necessarily exclusively) expressive of (or constituted by) certain non-cognitive attitudes. What is meant by "non-cognitive"? This is controversial, but we can say relatively uncontroversially that our beliefs about the world are paradigm cognitive attitudes. Non-normative talk (and thought) is essentially expressive of (constituted by) such beliefs; normative talk (and thought) is essentially different.

For example, Allan Gibbard (1990) defends and elaborates the view that "to call something rational is not…to attribute a property to it," but rather "to express a state of mind" (p. 9). In particular, "to think something rational is to accept norms that permit it" (p. 46). Gibbard's account applies equally to actions, feelings, and beliefs, so to think a belief is rational is (among other things) to accept norms that permit it, and to say that a belief is rational is (among other things) to express such acceptance. More recently, Gibbard (2003, pp. 227–9) has argued that to think that S knows that p is to plan to rely on S's judgment about whether p, and thus to say that S knows that p is to express such planning. "Coherence and agreement on the plain facts doesn't guarantee agreement on whether" someone knows, for whether we attribute knowledge to someone will depend on our plans; the concept of knowledge is thus "plan-laden" (p. 228).[9] And Matthew Chrisman (2007, p. 241) articulates a "norm-expressivist" account of (linguistic) knowledge attributions, on which the attribution of knowledge to S expresses a complex state of mind consisting of both (i) the belief that S is entitled by norms e to her true belief that p *and* (ii) the non-cognitive acceptance of those norms.

An expressivist account of epistemic evaluation will maintain that the talk (and thought) involved in epistemic evaluation is essentially (though not necessarily exclusively) expressive of, or constituted by, certain non-cognitive attitudes. This is compatible with adopting an error theory about epistemic evaluation (§9.2.1). It's also compatible with the view, defended by early expressivists, that the utterances involved in epistemic evaluation are not "truth apt." But contemporary expressivists typically reject this view, in favor of the view that the relevant utterances are "truth apt" (Chrisman 2007, p. 237, Field 2009, p. 267, Gibbard 2003, pp. 18–20, pp. 180–4).[10]

---

[9] Gibbard thus defends expressivist accounts of "rational" (as applied to beliefs) and of "knows." Elsewhere (2005), he seems to adopt a somewhat different approach to the normativity involved in the "correctness" of true belief, where he argues that the correctness of true beliefs is a kind of hypothetical imperative (pp. 342–3). Compare Shah and Velleman's (2005) expressivist account (pp. 509–11).

[10] An expressivist account of epistemic evaluation could be articulated by appeal to John MacFarlane's (2005a, 2005b) notion of "assessment sensitivity," with differences in assessor's accepted epistemic norms making for differences in relative truth (cf. Field 2009, pp. 262–4, pp. 272–8).

Expressivism is an account of the semantics of epistemic evaluation, not a metaphysical view, but it coheres nicely with anti-realism about epistemic value (§9.1.2). Gibbard (1990) writes that his "analysis is not directly of what it is for something to *be* rational, but of what it is for someone to *judge* that something is rational" (p. 8, cf. p. 46), and that on his view "apparent normative facts" are "no real facts at all; instead there [are] facts of what we are doing when we make normative judgments" (p. 23).[11] This is why the expressivist can be said to "change the question" from that of the nature of goodness and of the definition of "good," to the question of "what *states of mind* ethical statements express" (2003, p. 6). This is why Gibbard can "weasel" (2003, p. 182) about the existence of normative properties, facts, and truths: because his account of normative thought and talk is free of commitment to the existence of normative properties, facts, and truths. As Chrisman (2012) explains, expressivism about epistemic evaluation is a "metaepistemological" view about "what it means to claim that a belief is justified, rational, known, etc.," rather than a "normative epistemological" view about what it is for a belief to be justified, rational, known, etc. (p. 119). The anti-realist about epistemic value can embrace expressivism.

How might the expressivist answer the basic question about epistemic evaluation (§5.2.1)? Gibbard (1990) suggests an evolutionary answer: "Humanity evolved in groups" (p. 24), he writes; "we are, in effect, designed for social life," and "[o]ur normative capacities are part of the design" (p. 26). The crucial idea here is that of "the need for complex coordination" (ibid.) among human beings. Of course, natural history might only take us so far: it might explain why we are epistemic evaluators without explaining why epistemic evaluation is appropriate. A certain kind of anti-realist about epistemic value might want to stop there. But we can, if we are comfortable, go further, by adopting a socio-epistemological account of the appropriateness of epistemic evaluation (§9.1.4). "Knowledge attributions," Chrisman writes, "could be seen as playing a crucial role in keeping track of who can be trusted about which kinds of information" (2007, p. 242–3). For these (and other) reasons, "treating a belief as a known belief is beneficial in the right sort of circumstances" (Kappel 2010, p. 184); in connection with this we might "debate norms by debating whether they are likely to lead to desirable results—in particular, truth-oriented results of various sorts" (Field 2009, p. 278). But we should be careful here: the anti-realist about epistemic value can say that epistemic evaluation is good because engaging in this practice is beneficial or useful or socially desirable; but she must be careful not to appeal to the epistemic value of true belief in her explanation of the appropriateness of epistemic evaluation. The anti-realist can say that not adopting these policies would lead to "things that we...dislike" (Field 2009, p. 256); she can't say that not adopting these policies would be epistemically disvaluable in virtue of the epistemic value of truth (cf. p. 260).[12] That would be to give up her anti-realism.

---

[11] Although compare his "quasi-realism" (2003, pp. 18–20, pp. 180–4).
[12] The anti-realist may also consider adopting an inferentialist account of epistemic evaluation (Chrisman 2011).

9.2.3 Convention-relativism

We now turn to what I'll call "convention-relativism" about epistemic evaluation. I'll focus mostly on epistemic goodness attribution (with a few remarks on the epistemic "ought"); the account I'll sketch could be extended to other types of epistemic evaluation (and to epistemic reasons attribution).

My view is based on Sosa's (2007) idea of a "critical domain," which is "a set of interrelated entities evaluable through correspondingly interrelated values" (p. 73). Sosa asks us to:

> Consider the world of coffee—of its production, elaboration, and consumption. One central value organizes the critical assessment distinctive of that domain. I mean the value of liquid coffee that is delicious and aromatic. Think of the assessment of coffee beans, fields, coffee machines, baristas, ways of making liquid coffee, plantations, harvests, etc. What organizes all such evaluation, the value at the center of it all, from which the other relevant values are derivative, is the value of good coffee, of liquid coffee that is delicious and aromatic. (Ibid.)

Various things—cups of coffee, fields of coffee beans, methods of making coffee—can be evaluated relative to the fundamental standard of delicious and aromatic liquid coffee. And, as Sosa argues, we might understand epistemology as a critical domain of this kind, organized around the fundamental standard of true belief.[13] Although we'll speak of "standards" here, we could just as easily conceive of critical domains as organized around fundamental rules, or norms, or principles, or values (although speaking of "values" is ambiguous in this context, see below).

So far this is consistent with expressivism (§9.2.2)—drinking delicious and aromatic liquid coffee is what we approve of or endorse, and individual cups, fields of coffee beans, and methods of making coffee are all evaluated as means to our approved or endorsed end of drinking delicious and aromatic liquid coffee. But this is not the only way of developing this strategy. Sosa writes that evaluation within a critical domain presupposes "no domain-transcendent value":

> Thus, someone knowledgeable about guns and their use for hunting, for military ends, and so on, may undergo a conversion that makes the use of guns abhorrent. The good shot is thus drained of any real value that he can discern. Nevertheless, his critical judgment within that domain may outstrip anyone else's, whether gun lover or not. Critical domains can be viewed as thus *insulated*. (pp. 73–4)

Here, our evaluator does not evaluate guns (etc.) as means to some approved or endorsed end of hers; she does not want, or care about, or value, the good shot— but she can evaluate guns (etc.) relative to the standard of a good shot nonetheless.

---

[13] Cf. Richard Feldman (2000) on "role oughts" (p. 676) and Richard Foley (1987) on the evaluation of a person's beliefs relative to a "point of view" that "can be identified by identifying a goal, and by identifying a perspective from which the evaluation concerning how effectively the person is satisfying the goal is made" (1987, p. 140; see also 1993, p. 34). Crucially, for Foley, the "goal" need not be a psychologically real goal of the believer (1987, p. 2, pp. 10–12, p. 124, p. 143, 1993, pp. 3–4, pp. 32–3).

"Convention-relativism" thus rejects the expressivist's leading idea. On this view, the fundamental standards, relative to which evaluation within a critical domain operates, are "values," in some sense, but they are not necessarily things that the evaluator values.

Nor must the fundamental standards of a critical domain "really" have value:

> Our present worry abstracts from such Platonic issues of epistemic normativity. Truth may or may not be intrinsically valuable absolutely, who knows? Our worry requires only that we consider truth the *epistemically fundamental* value. (p. 72)

But if it's not the value of true belief that explains its status, as the fundamental standard of the critical domain of epistemology, what explains its status? The view I propose says: convention. The fundamental standards of a critical domain are conventional standards. The fundamental standards of the critical domain of the epistemic will be fundamental **epistemic standards**, and what makes it the case that one thing, rather than another, is a fundamental epistemic standard is mere convention (cf. Foley 1987, pp. 136–7). Evaluation within a critical domain is relative to the conventional standards of that domain, and presupposes nothing about the value of said conventional standards—that's the point about "insulation." We might say: that this, rather than that, is a fundamental epistemic standard comes down to nothing more than what we mean by "epistemic." And in the case of "epistemic," this is a term of art employed by epistemologists—so the conventional epistemic standards will be a matter of **epistemological convention**. We'll return to the task of articulating our conventional epistemic standards below (§9.3).

We can articulate a semantic claim to complete this picture:

Convention-relativist semantics for epistemic goodness attribution: There exist conventional fundamental epistemic standards, such that an utterance of <x is epistemically good> is true iff x does well relative to those fundamental epistemic standards. (The same, mutatis mutandis, for the thought that x is epistemically good.)

And similar semantic claims could be articulated when it comes to epistemic reasons attribution, for talk and thought involving the epistemic "ought," and so on. This semantic account, on its own, is consistent with expressivism. On Chrisman's (2007) view, to say that S knows that p is to express the belief that S is entitled by norms e to her true belief that p (p. 241), and on Field's view, to evaluate something positively in epistemic evaluation is to think or say that it does well vis-à-vis some set of norms (2009, pp. 258–61). But expressivists will insist that we have not yet captured the essence of epistemic evaluation: we must add that epistemic evaluation expresses (or is constituted by) non-cognitive attitudes as well. For Chrisman, to say that S knows that p is essentially to express acceptance of the relevant norms (op. cit.), and for Field, it's essential to epistemic evaluation that the set of norms in question be preferences that the speaker has or policies that she endorses (op. cit., p. 274). **Convention-relativism about epistemic evaluation** is the conjunction of (i) the present semantic account and (ii) the negation of these expressivist claims. What distinguishes convention-relativism from expressivism is that the convention-relativist rejects the view that the expression of a non-cognitive attitude is essential in epistemic evaluation (more on which in a moment).

Convention-relativism is distinct from **speaker-relativism**, on which an utterance of <*x* is epistemically good> is true iff *x* does well relative to standards that the speaker accepts (Boghossian 2006, pp. 84–5; see also Kalderon 2009).[14] On convention-relativism, epistemic evaluation in general does not require any such acceptance.[15] Convention relativism is also distinct from the view that an utterance of <*x* is epistemically good> is true iff the speaker believes that *x* does well relative to conventional fundamental epistemic standards.

It's useful to compare epistemic evaluation, on convention-relativism, with another case of evaluation relative to a set of conventions: evaluation relative to the rules of a club. Suppose that Plantation Club rules strictly forbid eating peas with a spoon. The avoidance of eating peas with a spoon, we could then say, is among the fundamental standards of a critical domain, the domain of evaluating things relative to the fundamental standards determined by the rules of the Plantation Club. "Club-rule evaluation" evaluates things relative to these fundamental "club-rule standards." To think or say that something is "club-rule good" is just to think or say that it does well relative to club-rule standards. It is true, then, that eating peas with a spoon is *not* club-rule good, and eating peas with anything else *is* (other things being equal) club-rule good. These truths are determined by the conventional rules of the Plantation Club. Convention-relativism about epistemic evaluation understands truths about epistemic value—for example, that true belief is epistemically good—in the same way. That eating peas with a spoon is not club-rule good is a trivial truth, determined entirely by the conventional rules of the Plantation Club. On the present proposal, that true belief is epistemically good is, likewise, a trivial truth, determined entirely by the conventional meaning of "epistemic" (cf. §9.3). Setting aside epistemic evaluation proper, consider uses of the epistemic "ought." The convention relativist should treat these as analogous to uses of the club-rule "ought." "You ought not eat your peas with a spoon," one member of the Plantation Club says to another; this can be understood as expressing the belief that eating peas with a spoon is forbidden by the rules of the Plantation Club. Likewise, "You ought not believe in ghosts" can be understood as expressing the belief that believing in ghosts is forbidden by the epistemic rules.

Convention-relativism about epistemic evaluation jibes with anti-realism about epistemic value—critical domains are "insulated" and free from commitment to the

---

[14] Speaker-relativism has trouble making sense of disagreement in epistemic evaluation (cf. Chrisman 2007, p. 234).

[15] Convention-relativism about epistemic evaluation is a "metaepistemological" view (§9.2.2) about epistemic evaluation. Issues of "metaepistemology" are orthogonal to issues in "normative epistemology." Consider, for example, "epistemic subjectivism," on which "what I (epistemically) ought to believe depends on which epistemic rules *I* happen to adopt" (White 2007, p. 117). Convention-relativism about epistemic evaluation is orthogonal to this.

existence of values.[16] For the convention-relativist, the use of "good" in "epistemically good" is an "attributive" use of "good" (cf. Geach 1956, Ridge 2011): <x is epistemically good> does not entail that x is good, just as <S is a good assassin> does not entail that S is good, and just as "Not eating peas with a spoon is club-rule good" does not entail that not eating peas with a spoon is good. Moreover, to say that x does well relative to some standard is to say nothing about the value of that standard, just as to say that eating peas with a spoon is not club-rule good is to say nothing about the value of the Plantation Club's rule against eating peas with a spoon.

However, it might be unclear what the rules of the Plantation Club are; we might disagree about that, and make inquiries to find out. Likewise, it might be unclear what the epistemic standards are, and inquiry might be required to find out—a project to which we'll return below (§9.3). We might also debate whether the rules of the Plantation Club ought to be changed, or whether we ought to adopt a new set of rules. Likewise for epistemic standards. But once we have established what the rules of the Plantation Club are, there is no further question of whether those are "really" the "correct" rules of the Plantation Club. Likewise, once we have established what the epistemic standards are, there is no further question of whether those are "really" the "correct" epistemic standards. Consider, again, the epistemic value of true belief— once we establish that true belief is a fundamental standard of the critical domain of the epistemic, there is no further question of whether true belief is "really" valuable.

The comparison to club rules may suggest the idea that epistemic evaluation is capricious or arbitrary, and thus might suggest that epistemic evaluation is somehow groundless and unjustified. But the comparison shouldn't put us off: the Plantation Club might have good reasons for adopting the rules that it does, including rules that may, in some important sense, be arbitrary. The conventionalist, in other words, is in no worse a position than any other anti-realist about epistemic value, when it comes to answering the basic question about epistemic evaluation. She might, for example, appeal to a social-functional account of the appropriateness of epistemic evaluation (§9.1.4).

Alternatively, she might offer something more modest. Consider, again, the rules of the Plantation Club. Why follow these rules? One might appeal to the benefits of membership and to the fact that following these rules is necessary to remain a member. But one might also simply say that these are the rules that we members of the Plantation Club choose to follow. Why not eat peas with a spoon? Because it disgusts us, or offends us, or pains us, to see peas eaten with a spoon—or because we simply don't like it. The same might explain the appropriateness of epistemic evaluation, as Fred Dretske (2000) argues:

The only *fault* with fallacious reasoning, the only thing *wrong* or *bad* about mistaken judgments, is that, generally speaking, we don't like them. [...] This...leaves the normativity of false belief

---

[16] Modulo the issue of how to combine a charitable semantics with an austere metaphysics; see van Inwagen 1990, Chapter 10, Cameron 2010a, 2010b.

and fallacious reasoning in the same place as the normativity of foul weather and bad table manners—in the attitudes, purposes, and beliefs of the people who make judgments about the weather and table behavior. (p. 248)

A final clarification. As the case of the club-rule "ought" shows, someone can engage in (linguistic) evaluation relative to conventional standards, without explicitly mentioning those standards: in the right context, one way of saying that Plantation Club rules forbid eating peas with a spoon is by uttering the sentence "You ought not eat peas with a spoon." Moreover, one need not explicitly conceive of epistemic standards as conventional to engage in epistemic evaluation. Epistemic standards, like standards of etiquette, can be internalized: just as the life-long Plantation Club member instinctively disapproves of the eating of peas with a spoon, the life-long epistemologist instinctively disapproves of falsehood and epistemic irrationality.

9.2.4 The reverse open question argument

Consider an objection to convention-relativism about epistemic evaluation (§9.2.3), which if correct would count in favor of an expressivist account:

> In an evaluative claim…one doesn't intend to be making a claim about a specific norm…[A] claim about what is *justified according to a specific norm* would be straightforwardly factual, with no evaluative force. (It would encourage the Moore-like response "Sure that's justified *according to that norm*; but is it justified?") (Field 2009, pp. 251–2)

Convention-relativism, unlike expressivism, treats epistemic evaluation as involving "straightforwardly factual" claims—at least, it treats it as involving claims that are "straightforwardly factual" according to the correct account of them, the truth of which account may not be straightforward. Expressivism, by contrast, can be motivated by appeal to the idea that attributions of knowledge and epistemic justification are "normative" (Chrisman 2012) and do not merely "express purely factual beliefs" (p. 121). The present objection, then, is that epistemic evaluation is normative, in some sense incompatible with the convention-relativist account of it.

As I said above (§5.2.2), the notion of the normative is obscure, so we'll proceed with caution here. Suppose that the convention-relativist has it that epistemic evaluation is not normative (in the relevant sense). Is this a mark against convention-relativism? Richard Fumerton (2001) argues that epistemic evaluation isn't normative (in what seems like the relevant sense):

> [I]ndividual beliefs are justified or not in virtue of exemplifying certain general properties, where we think of the "rules" of epistemology as generalizations describing the kinds of conditions under which beliefs are justified. (p. 54)

But these "rules" "will take the form of propositions that assert that one is justified in believing certain propositions" (ibid.), but given the fact that these "rules" are just true generalizations about the conditions for justification, it's unclear that epistemic evaluation is normative. "Epistemic judgments," Fumerton argues, "are no more normative than judgments about lawful necessity and possibility are normative" (ibid.). If Fumerton is right, that convention-relativism says epistemic evaluation isn't normative is a mark in its favor, rather than a mark against it.

But we still have not explicitly articulated the relevant sense of "normative." Field has given us a clue to the sense of "normative" that we seek: the claim that x is justified according to a specific norm is non-normative, in the sense that this invites—i.e. allows the coherent articulation of—the question of whether x really is justified. A genuinely normative claim, in the relevant sense of "normative," would not invite this question. This conception of the normative derives from G.E. Moore's "open question argument." Moore (on one reading of the argument) argues that various theories of goodness are inadequate, because they fail to respect the fact that goodness attribution is normative, where F attribution is **normative** iff, if you grant that x is F, then it's incoherent to ask whether x really is good, or justified, or rational, or whatever.

But if this is the criterion of normativity, then epistemic evaluation is not normative. For even granting that x is *epistemically* good, it *is* coherent to ask whether x really is good. I do not just mean that epistemic value is always pro tanto value—that even granting that x is pro tanto good, it is coherent to ask whether x is all-things-considered good. I mean that, even granting that x is (pro tanto) epistemically good, it is coherent to ask whether x really is (pro tanto) good, i.e. to ask whether x is good *in any way*. This question is coherent in particular cases—you might grant that some particular true belief is epistemically good, but coherently ask whether it is really good in any way—but also in the case of a more general consideration of epistemic value: you might grant that true belief, epistemic justification, knowledge, etc. have *epistemic* value, but still wonder whether true belief, epistemic justification, knowledge, etc. are really valuable in any way.

This point applies, mutatis mutandis, in other cases: even granting that S *epistemically* ought to Φ, it is coherent to ask whether S really ought to Φ. Again, I do not just mean that the epistemic "ought" is not the all-things-considered "ought." I mean that, even granting that S epistemically (but not all-things-considered) ought to Φ, it is coherent to ask whether x really ought to Φ, i.e. whether S is really under any kind of obligation to Φ. The case of epistemic evaluation is analogous to the case of club-rule evaluation: even granting that Φing is required by the rules of the Plantation Club, I can coherently ask whether I am under any kind of obligation to Φ. Compare Gibbard's (1990) critique of the "irrationalist," who thinks that in many cases the rational thing is not what is to be done. But "[t]he irrationalist cannot be what he thinks himself to be, for whatever he endorses he thereby thinks rational" (pp. 48–9). Given this, "what is rational to believe settles what to believe" (p. 49). But this is not true of *epistemic* rationality: the question of what to believe is left open by a conclusion about the requirements of *epistemic* rationality.

Call this the **reverse open question argument** against the normativity of epistemic evaluation. This argument appeals to the Moorean conception of normativity, and is based on the premise that epistemic goodness attribution is not normative. While Moore concludes that an adequate theory of goodness would have to respect the fact that goodness attribution is normative; I conclude that an adequate theory of epistemic goodness attribution must respect the fact that epistemic goodness attribution is not normative.

The only way to resist this argument, I think, is to say that epistemic rationality is essentially rationality in belief, and, more broadly, that epistemic evaluation is essentially evaluation of beliefs. Then the question of whether some belief is epistemically good (or epistemically justified, or epistemically rational, or whatever) is just the question of whether that belief is good (or justified, or rational, or whatever). We've encountered this doxastic conception of the epistemic (§5.2.4) before. However, recall our characterization of epistemic evaluation (§5.2.1) by appeal to paradigm epistemic evaluation, on which true beliefs are said to be epistemically good and false beliefs are said to be epistemically bad. If epistemic evaluation is essentially evaluation of beliefs, this is no longer an obvious paradigm of epistemic evaluation—why not evaluation vis-à-vis the Tuesday rule, for example, or evaluation of beliefs in terms of their eudaimonic value? Eudaimonic evaluation of beliefs—e.g. in terms of their benefits to the believer—would count as epistemic evaluation (cf. §5.3.1). And it would be an open question whether true belief is of any epistemic value. But that question is surely closed: it is not coherent to ask whether true belief has epistemic value. You might resist this reply by appeal to epistemic essentialism about belief (§5.4). True belief is epistemically good, you might argue, because belief "aims at truth," because truth is belief's constitutive standard of correctness. Epistemic evaluation is essentially evaluation of beliefs, and since beliefs essentially "aim at truth," true belief is epistemically good. But we have found epistemic essentialism about belief to be implausible (Chapters 6–8).

However, we should not conclude that epistemic evaluation is never normative— although we must articulate a different sense of "normative" to make this point. Recall expressivism about epistemic evaluation, on which epistemic evaluation essentially expresses a non-cognitive attitude. For example, the (linguistic) attribution of knowledge could be said to be the expression of one's acceptance of a norm entitling the knower to her true belief. Such expression, on the expressivist view, flows from the meaning of the utterances involved in (linguistic) knowledge attribution. The conventionalist rejects this, but should maintain that the attribution of knowledge *sometimes* involves the expression of one's acceptance of a norm entitling the knower to her true belief. And she should say the same, mutatis mutandis, for (linguistic) epistemic evaluation in general. In this sense—on which some utterance is **normative** iff it expresses a non-cognitive attitude—epistemic evaluation is normative, even for the convention-relativist. But for the convention-relativist, the normativity associated with epistemic evaluation is not part of the meaning of the utterances involved in epistemic evaluation, but is rather a pragmatic feature of their use in some contexts. Let me explain.

An utterance of a non-normative sentence can have normative implications.[17] Suppose the president of the Plantation Club looms over an offending diner and says, gravely, "Club rules forbid eating peas with a spoon." This would amount to censure of the offending diner—the president would express her disapproval of the diner's eating peas with a spoon, and expresses her own commitment to the rules of the Club. But this is not down to the meaning of the sentence she has uttered. Compare the announcement of a rebellious diner: "Club rules forbid eating peas with a spoon, but damn the rules, let's do it anyway!" She utters the same sentence as the president, but expresses no disapproval of eating peas with a spoon, and expresses no commitment to the rules of the Club. Likewise with epistemic evaluation. To say that a belief is epistemically bad, for example, amounts to censure in many contexts—but not in all. "Pascal's belief is epistemically bad," we might note, "but that just shows how worthless epistemic justification is." Convention-relativism explains why epistemic evaluation is sometimes normative and sometimes isn't—such normativity is not built in to the meaning of the utterances involved—and this is a mark in favor of convention-relativism, and against expressivism.[18]

9.2.5 Categorical, hypothetical, inescapable

Epistemic norms are sometimes said to be "categorical" (Kelly 2003, p. 616, Railton 1997, pp. 54–9). As Philippa Foot (1972) notes, there are two senses in which a principle, rule, imperative, or norm could be said to be "categorical." The first corresponds to what is "inescapable," in this sense:

> Both [morality and etiquette] are inescapable in that behavior does not cease to offend against either morality or etiquette because the agent is indifferent to their purposes and to the disapproval he will incur by flouting them. (p. 311)

Consider a rule of etiquette that forbids eating peas with a spoon (cf. §9.2.3). Even if you are indifferent to the rules of etiquette, or to this rule in particular, you violate the rule when you eat peas with a spoon. Such rules must be distinguished from hypothetical imperatives (cf. §6.1.2), which prescribe means to some end, such that someone who happens not to have said end is not thereby under any obligation to perform the means to it. By contrast, a non-hypothetical imperative "would necessarily apply to any agent as such, regardless of her contingent personal ends" (Railton 1997, p. 58).

However, the rules of morality are thought to be "categorical" in a sense which distinguishes them from non-hypothetical rules of etiquette:

> [O]ne may reasonably ask why anyone should bother about what...should from the point of view of etiquette...be done, and [conclude] that such considerations deserve no notice unless reason is shown. So although people give as their reason for doing something the fact that it

---

[17] In connection with this paragraph, compare Rawls 1971, pp. 404–7.

[18] Compare Fumerton (2001) on the criticism of artifacts (p. 57).

is required by etiquette, we do not take this consideration as in itself giving us reason to act. Considerations of etiquette do not have any automatic reason-giving force. (Foot 1972, p. 309)

As Jamie Drier (2001) puts it, "a categorical imperative is one that each person has reason to follow, no matter what his desires" (p. 30). So let us call some species of normativity **inescapable** iff whether someone conforms to or violates its principles (rules, imperatives, norms) does not depend on her desire to conform to those principles, and a reason **strongly categorical** iff it is a normative reason that someone has no matter what her desires.

On the version of anti-realism about epistemic normativity (§9.1.1) that I favor, there are no strongly categorical epistemic reasons. By contrast, the Kantian account of epistemic reasons (§8.2.2) posits strongly categorical epistemic reasons. However, according to the convention-relativist account of epistemic evaluation (§9.2.3) that I favor, epistemic normativity is inescapable. This combination of views allows one to vindicate universalism about epistemic normativity (§5.3.1) and to respect the intuition that epistemic norms are in some sense "categorical," without the costs (Chapters 6–8) of realism about epistemic normativity (§5.2.3). Consider the person who believes that p as a result of wishful thinking, in the face of strong evidence that it is false that p. Such a person may be indifferent to the value of true belief, but her wishful thinking nonetheless offends against epistemic principles, just like the boor who eats peas with a spoon, indifferent to the rules of the Plantation Club.

Recall (§5.2.1) Stephen Grimm's (2009) idea that epistemic evaluation has a "special sort of status when it comes to the evaluation of belief" (p. 256). He motivates this by appeal to the idea that epistemic evaluation involves "some apparently binding sense of 'should'" (p. 254). Grimm asks us to imagine someone who recognizes that atheism would lead to "tremendous psychological distress" (p. 255) and who concludes that she has reason to believe, and that she should believe, that God exists.

But it seems clear that neither the "reason" nor the "should" at issue here is binding in the way considered above—in neither case does it seem that we can justly be blamed or criticized for failing to orient towards the goal of psychological comfort, for example. (Ibid.)

Epistemic reasons, on the other hand, are "binding," and when I epistemically should or should not believe something, this is a "non-optional sense of 'should'" (pp. 255–6). Does this make trouble for anti-realism about epistemic normativity?

Two replies to Grimm's objection. First, Grimm suggests that epistemic evaluation always involves reactive attitudes, as compared to other "non-binding" or "optional" species of evaluation. I argued against this above—epistemic evaluation is not always normative (§9.2.4). More importantly, Grimm suggests that non-epistemic evaluation of beliefs never involves reactive attitudes. This is not obvious. Suppose that James is suffering from tremendous psychological distress on account of his belief that he is a bad tennis player. His evidence for this is far from conclusive, although his belief is, in fact, true. James spends all day in bed, weeping, imagining losing at tennis, and watching video of himself playing tennis badly. In a non-epistemic, eudaimonic sense of "should," James should not believe that he is a bad tennis player. He should forget about the evidence that he is, and turn his mind to other things. He should stop dwelling on it and stop inquiring about it. He should never have thought about it so much in the first place. Moreover, James deserves censure for all this: his belief is causing him tremendous psychological distress, and believing the truth about this will have no great eudaimonic value for him (this, I think, is the difference between this case and Grimm's case—the truth about the existence of God is significant). We might say that James' entire cognitive approach, his style of thinking, his intellectual way of proceeding, when it comes to his tennis skills, is eudaimonically improper—he should not adopt this approach, he should not engage in this style of thinking, he should not proceed in this way. And these "shoulds" involve as much censure as "shoulds" ever do.[19]

Second, Foot (1972) writes that "[p]eople talk...about the "binding force" of morality, but it is not clear what this means if not that we *feel* ourselves unable to escape" (p. 310). Similarly, we might experience the "binding force" of epistemic normativity. But the feeling of being bound by epistemic principles is not strong evidence for the existence of strongly categorical epistemic reasons. Our sense of being bound may simply indicate that epistemic normativity is inescapable—we feel, in this sense, bound by the rules of the Plantation Club, but this doesn't suggest the existence of strongly categorical reasons to abide by those rules. Alternatively, our sense of being bound may indicate that we have internalized the epistemic norms of our society (§9.1.4). Finally, we may feel bound by epistemic principles because of our commitment to epistemic goods, e.g. because of our love of truth. As Harry Frankfurt (1988, 1999) has urged, the sense of being constrained by some principle can—or may always—arise from the fact that one cares about satisfying that principle, in virtue of loving the things that the principle treats as having value. Love does not feel optional, and the demands of love do not feel like hypothetical imperatives. For someone who loves true belief, epistemic demands will feel as binding as demands ever feel.

9.2.6 The objection from reactive attitudes

You might wonder how reactive attitudes can ever be involved in epistemic evaluation, if epistemic evaluation is mere evaluation relative to conventional standards, akin to evaluation relative to the rules of the Plantation Club. I've already gestured at a partial reply to this objection: we have instrumental reasons to engage in the practice of epistemic evaluation, reactive attitudes and all (§9.1.4). But more can be said in defense of these reactive attitudes.

As Williams (1995) notes, an internalist about practical reasons faces a similar problem. To blame S for Φing seems to require thinking that S had reason to Φ (p. 41). But consider now a man who is a "very hard case": he treats his wife badly, and

---

[19] Alternatively, consider the morally charged "should" that Clifford employs in his articulation of his evidentialist principle (§4.4.1).

in response to our criticism ("you ought to be nicer to your wife," "you have a reason to be nicer to her, namely, that she's your wife") he responds with indifference ("Don't you understand? I really do not care"). He has no internal reason to be nicer to his wife, and if all reasons are internal reasons (as the internalist claims), then he has no reason to be nicer to his wife. Blaming him for his cruelty, therefore, seems impossible, given our assumption connecting blame and reasons for action. Williams articulates two possible lines of response for the internalist. The first appeals to the idea that blame is a "proleptic mechanism" (p. 44), such that hard cases may have "a motivation to avoid the disapproval of other people," as part of "a general desire to be ethically well related to people they respect." In virtue of this:

[T]he expression of blame serves to indicate the fact that in virtue of this, they have a reason to avoid those things they did not have enough reason to avoid up to now. (p. 41)

In blaming the hard case:

Our thought may…be this: if he were to deliberate again and take into consideration all the reasons that might now come more vividly before him, we hope he would come to a different conclusion. (p. 42)

And among his reasons for coming to this different conclusion might be "this very blame and the concerns expressed in it" (ibid.). The convention-relativist about epistemic evaluation can say something similar about those cases in which epistemic evaluation involves reactive attitudes. When I blame David for believing that there were weapons of mass destruction in Iraq, I express my hope that he will proceed with more intellectual caution in the future, and aim ideally to bring this about, in part, through David's recognition of my disapprobation. Epistemic blame, I propose, can be understood as a "proleptic mechanism": the expression of disapprobation aimed at epistemically improving the offender, through her recognition of said disapprobation. Even someone who is entirely indifferent to epistemic goods—the "anti-epistemologist" imagined by Peter Railton (1997, pp. 54–9), who rejects the value of truth and criticizes cleaving to the evidence—might not be indifferent to recognition and approval, and might be brought into the epistemic fold, so to speak, as a response to our disapproval.

But what if the "anti-epistemologist" is indifferent not only to epistemic goods, but to recognition and approval as well? What if she lacks "any general disposition to respect the reactions of others?" (Williams 1995, p. 43). In this case, and this is Williams' second line of response, blame is once again problematic for the internalist. But this is as it should be: such people we "regard as hopeless or dangerous characters rather than thinking that blame is appropriate to them" (p. 43). And this applies for epistemic blame as well. The sociopathic "anti-epistemologist" is not a suitable object for the reactive attitudes; she deserves pity, perhaps, but not blame (or perhaps she is so dangerous that she deserves to be ostracized—think here of the worst cases of mental illness, which are perhaps simply cases of extreme epistemic vice). Nonetheless, her false beliefs are epistemically bad. The reactive attitudes are not required for epistemic evaluation (cf. Fumerton 2001, p. 57)—this is predicted by convention-relativism, and that convention-relativism predicts this speaks in its favor.

If she rejects the existence of strongly categorical epistemic reasons, the anti-realist has to concede something to the "anti-epistemologist." For once the "anti-epistemologist" has made clear that she is completely indifferent to epistemic goods, the anti-realist cannot insist that she, for example, has strongly categorical epistemic reason not to believe some proposition. We are confined to saying that she is epistemically unjustified in her belief, that her belief manifests her dogmatism, her lack of intellectual integrity, her bias, that it would be epistemically better were she not to believe as she does. We can still plead our case, just as we can plead our case against the "hard case" (§9.2.4):

There are many things I can say about or to this man: that he is ungrateful, inconsiderate, hard, sexist, nasty, selfish, brutal...that it would be better if he were nicer to her. (Williams 2005, p. 39)

What Williams thinks we cannot say is that "the man has a reason to be nicer" (ibid.). And what I have conceded the anti-realist may not be able to say to the "anti-epistemologist" is that she has strongly categorical reasons to not believe as she does.

9.3 Defining "epistemic"

I conclude that the anti-realist has promising options—a socio-epistemological account of the appropriateness of epistemic evaluation (§9.1.4), combined with an account of the semantics of epistemic evaluation (§9.2)—when it comes to answering the basic question about epistemic evaluation (§5.2.1). We turn now to the scope question: what is the domain of the *epistemic*? In answering this question, I'll provide a missing element of the convention-relativist semantics sketched above (§9.2.3): an articulation of our conventional fundamental epistemic standards.

The term "epistemic" is ubiquitous in contemporary epistemology, but its meaning is rarely defined or explained. One ambiguity needs to be handled immediately: "epistemic" is ambiguous as between a doxastic and an axial conception (§5.2.4). To define "epistemic," for the purposes of articulating convention-relativism, we must set aside the doxastic conception of the epistemic (cf. §9.2.4).

We seek to articulate the conventional standards distinctive of epistemic evaluation, and so, I maintain, we seek a definition of "epistemic" that jibes with epistemologist's use of the term—since "epistemic" is an epistemological term of art. I propose that the critical domain of epistemology can be understood as a domain of evaluation relative to a fundamental standard of accurate representation, or of "cognitive contact with reality" (Zagzebski 1996, p. 167). True belief, knowledge, understanding—these should all be understood as species of cognitive contact with reality. This means we should adopt a broad notion of "reality" here: mathematical knowledge and moral understanding involve contact with reality, but perhaps not with spatio-temporal reality, and self-knowledge and self-understanding may involve no contact with mind-independent reality. "Cognitive contact with reality" is intended to cover a broad range of relations that a thinking creature may bear to the objects of her thoughts: these relations need not be propositional (so, for example, non-propositional understanding is not ruled out) nor doxastic (so, for example, non-doxastic perceptual acquaintance is not ruled out).

This conception of the epistemic jibes with the idea that "epistemic evaluation...is most naturally understood along broadly teleological lines, as evaluating beliefs relative to the standard...of believing truth and avoiding error" (David 2001, p. 154), and that the "epistemic point of view...is defined by the aim of maximizing truth and minimizing falsity" (Alston 1985, p. 59, see also 2005, p. 33). But the present conception is broader than the view that true belief (and avoiding error) is the only fundamental epistemic standard.

In characterizing a critical domain, in addition to specifying a fundamental standard (or standards), we must also specify the *way* in which said standard is valued, from the perspective of that critical domain (Hazlett 2012). A critical domain that treated gold as having instrumental value would differ importantly from a critical domain that treated gold as having final value: the former might endorse speculation in gold futures; the latter might reject this as offensive to the dignity of gold. On my conception of the epistemic, cognitive contact with reality is *finally* and *intrinsically* valued from the epistemic perspective. This preserves the intuition that epistemic evaluation is distinct from "practical or prudential" evaluation (§1.3): epistemic value is final value, as opposed to instrumental eudaimonic value, but it's also final intrinsic value, as opposed to constitutive eudaimonic value. Thus:

Definition of "epistemic": The fundamental standard of the critical domain of the epistemic is cognitive contact with reality, where this is finally and intrinsically valued.

This definition has an appealing consequence: we can explain Richard Feldman's (1988) idea that epistemic obligations are "obligations that arise from a purely impartial and disinterested perspective" (p. 236). For the epistemic perspective has been defined such that, from this perspective, the instrumental and constitutive eudaimonic value of cognitive contact with reality is ignored. Such a perspective will therefore be impartial and disinterested, in the relevant sense. That this consequence is appealing will be controversial for those who favor a eudaimonic account of epistemic normativity (§5.3).

Given this conception of the epistemic, we can now see the sense in which the epistemic value of true belief is a trivial consequence of the meaning of "epistemic" (§9.2.3). This is important for appreciating the difference between convention-relativism about epistemic evaluation and epistemic essentialism about belief (§5.4). For the epistemic essentialist, the epistemic value of true belief is a consequence of the nature of belief; for the convention-relativist, the epistemic value of true belief is a consequence of the nature of the epistemic. Recall, finally, Aristotle's principle of curiosity, which we might understand as affirming that everyone epistemically ought to want knowledge (§1.2.3). On the present conception of the epistemic, this is a trivial truth, if it is true. This contrasts sharply with the non-triviality of the Socratic maxim (§1.1.1), the eudaimonic ideal of knowledge (§1.1.3), the eudaimonic ideal of true belief (§1.4), and constitutive value approaches to the values of true belief and knowledge (§1.1.5, §4.3).[20]

9.4 Pluralism about doxastic evaluation

Recall, finally, the uniqueness question about epistemic evaluation (§5.2.1). Anti-realists about epistemic value must answer this question by saying that epistemic evaluation of beliefs has no "special sort of status," and that there is no sense in which epistemic evaluation of beliefs is uniquely appropriate. We might say that epistemic evaluation of beliefs is uniquely *epistemically* appropriate, but in whatever sense this might be true, it is trivially true, just as is the fact that evaluation of beliefs vis-à-vis the Tuesday principle is uniquely Tuesday-principle-wise appropriate. Compare the epistemic essentialist's answer to the uniqueness question (§5.4), on which epistemic evaluation of beliefs is uniquely appropriate, given the essential nature of belief.

This negative answer to the uniqueness question leads the anti-realist to **pluralism about doxastic evaluation**, on which there are a plurality of equally appropriate species of evaluation of beliefs. Several epistemologists have embraced pluralism:

It is easy enough as well as altogether appropriate to depart from [the] epistemic point of view in order to evaluate S's beliefs from other points of view. Indeed, theoretically there is no limit to the number of viewpoints other than the...epistemic one from which S's beliefs can be evaluated. (Foley 1987, p. 125; see also p. 11, 1993, p. 32)

[R]eliability for truth is simply one potentially valuable feature of belief-forming processes, alongside importance, economy, and possibly others. [...] For naturalists, truth-conducive norms of judgment constitute just one dimension among a number of possible ways of evaluating belief-forming methods. (Papineau 1999, p. 30)

Consider, for example, the following norm:

Eudaimonic principle: For any subject S and proposition that p, S's belief that p is good if believing that p contributes to S's wellbeing.

The pluralist about doxastic evaluation will say (roughly) that it's equally appropriate to employ the eudaimonic principle in evaluating beliefs as it is to employ the truth principle (§5.2.1), and that there is no non-trivial sense in which epistemic evaluation of beliefs is appropriate and eudaimonic evaluation inappropriate. However, the pluralist need not deny that a particular species of doxastic evaluation might be (non-trivially) appropriate to a particular situation: some situations might call, as a matter

---

[20] Note that, if the anti-realist adopts this conception of the epistemic, she can vindicate the idea (§1.3) that epistemic value is distinct from, and irreducible to, eudaimonic (and other species of) value. This idea is incompatible with eudaimonic and Cliffordian accounts of epistemic value (§5.3) and it is unclear whether it can be vindicated on Humean approaches (cf. §6.1.1). This idea is, however, consistent with Kantian approaches (cf. §8.1.3).

of practical reason, for epistemic evaluation, while others might call for eudaimonic evaluation. What the pluralist will say (less roughly), and what the epistemic essentialist will deny, is that there is no non-trivial, situation-independent sense in which epistemic evaluation of beliefs is appropriate and eudaimonic evaluation of beliefs inappropriate.[21]

Should we say the same about evaluation vis-à-vis the Tuesday principle? We can imagine two forms of pluralism, both incompatible with epistemic essentialism about belief. According to **restricted** pluralism about doxastic evaluation, there are a plurality of species of appropriate doxastic evaluation, not limited to epistemic evaluation, but there are species of doxastic evaluation that are (non-trivially, situation-independently) inappropriate. One might accept epistemic and eudaimonic evaluation as appropriate species of doxastic evaluation, but reject evaluation vis-à-vis the Tuesday principle as inappropriate. Alternatively, **unrestricted** pluralism maintains that there is no (non-trivial, situation-independent) sense in which any species of doxastic evaluation is appropriate and another inappropriate.

To maintain that epistemic essentialism is compatible with pluralism about doxastic evaluation, one would need to argue that the fact that some species of evaluation is essential evaluation does not provide a sense in which that species of evaluation is "appropriate." The best way to see why this is implausible is to think about the way that contemporary epistemologists tend to think about cases of eudaimonically valuable biased beliefs. "Sure, those beliefs are eudaimonically valuable," we say, "*but not epistemically justified.*" Now on the one hand, we might just be articulating the distinction between the eudaimonic and the epistemic. But why is the eudaimonic value of biased beliefs a concession ("sure"), to be contrasted ("but") with their lack of epistemic justification? We can't escape the sense that contemporary epistemologists take eudaimonic evaluation of beliefs to somehow fail to get to the heart of the matter—and that the heart of the matter is gotten to once we arrive at epistemic evaluation of beliefs. And this seems to be exactly what epistemic essentialism predicts: it says that you have gotten to the heart of the matter when you engage in epistemic evaluation of beliefs, because you've gotten to evaluation of them in terms of their essential nature. The sense in which epistemic evaluation has pride of place among species of doxastic evaluation is difficult to articulate. The defender of epistemic essentialism seems perfectly poised to articulate it, in terms of the appropriateness of essential evaluation.

---

[21] I have said that epistemic essentialism about belief is incompatible with pluralism about doxastic evaluation. But even if this were not so, my argument against epistemic essentialism (Chapters 6–8) was not based on pluralism about doxastic evaluation. So that argument stands, regardless of whether epistemic essentialism is compatible with pluralism about doxastic evaluation.

9.5 Conclusion

In this chapter I have sketched the anti-realist alternative to realism about epistemic normativity. I presented some anti-realist accounts of epistemic evaluation (§9.1–9.2), defined "epistemic" (§9.3), and proposed pluralism about doxastic evaluation (§9.4). I conclude that the prospects for anti-realism are bright, given the difficulties faced by realist approaches (Chapters 5–8).

It's worth pausing to consider the most substantial assumptions that I made in arriving at this conclusion. The most substantial, it seems to me, was philosophical *naturalism* (§5.5): an aversion to irreducible normativity has driven me in the direction of anti-realism. An assumption about the *criteria for belief attribution* (§1.6.2) has proven to be central to the question of the value of true belief: treating belief as essentially functional vis-à-vis action, thought, and emotion has been crucial in arriving at my anti-realist conclusion. Finally, some readers may complain of a kind of un-philosophical *empiricism*, legitimating the mustering of empirical evidence in pursuit of conclusions about wellbeing, and the rejection of a priori speculation about the functions of cognition. I think these are the three things that have made the anti-realist conclusion, for me, inevitable.

Epilogue

Imagine again that you have just fallen in love, and are now faced with good evidence that your relationship is likely to end. We can say that, from the epistemic point of view, you should believe that your relationship is likely to end. But the question remains: what should you believe?

There is a reply to this that we didn't consider above: that there is no absolute answer to this question, that the correct answer will depend, in some way, on to whom the question is addressed. Here's a sketch of a reply of this sort. Let's assume that, in your case, believing that your relationship is likely to end is risky: there is a significant chance that this belief will be unpleasant, or that it will have a negative effect on your relationship, or that it will make your beloved unhappy, or whatever. What should you believe? This depends on what you care about, and on the relative strength or weight of your cares. Imagine that believing the truth, in your case, will make your beloved unhappy. What should you believe? The answer depends, in part, on what you care about more: true belief or your beloved's happiness. If you care little for true belief and a great deal about your beloved's happiness, then you should not believe this true proposition. But if you care a great deal for true belief and little for your beloved's happiness, then you should believe this true proposition.

You might object that I've set up the case so that it's skewed in favor of one answer, rather than the other. Who could be so callous as to care more for true belief than for her beloved's happiness? But I think the dilemma is pressing. Imagine that someone you love is pained by some evidentially well-supported belief of yours, a belief about some matter of importance, and not some triviality. Would you give up the belief, for the sake of your beloved's peace of mind? Imagine you are offered a way to do it: an amnesiac serum, for example. Would you drink it? The case is outré, but its structure resembles more ordinary dilemmas. Will you tolerate a romantic partner's bad reasoning in defense of deeply held political convictions? Will you agree to some erroneous opinion, for the sake of amity? In all these cases, epistemic virtue—where "epistemic" is understood in terms of the final and intrinsic value of cognitive contact with reality—and our romantic interests come into conflict. On the approach I'm sketching, we should not say that there is a universally correct answer to the question of whether epistemic virtue should triumph over romance, or whether romance should triumph over epistemic virtue. For some people, the choice is obvious; for others, it's difficult. There are extremes on both sides: compare Diogenes of Sinope (made socially intolerable by his relentless pursuit of truth) and Don Juan (whose only interest is seduction). In any event, in answer to the question of what you should believe, when you're in love, my suggestion is that some people ought to sacrifice epistemic virtue for romance, and others ought to sacrifice romance for epistemic virtue.

A theme of my arguments in this book has been individual differences (which have always been emphasized by philosophical skeptics): some people love true belief, but others don't. There is no universal curiosity, no universal "aim of belief," and thus no universal value of true belief. In my view, a defense of which is beyond the scope of the present inquiry, and which is at least in this sense skeptical, there is nothing more to the value of true belief than the fact that some people, contingently, care about, or love, or value, true belief.

Philosophers are lovers of truth. Do my conclusions here suggest a critique of philosophy? Consider Socrates' characterization of "the nature of philosophers" in the *Republic* (485a–487a). Philosophers must seek wisdom, i.e. knowledge of what is unchanging and most real (485b), and for this reason "they must be without falsehood—they must refuse to accept what is false, hate it, and have a love of the truth" (485c). This is because of a kinship between wisdom and truth, which ensures that it is impossible "for the same nature to be a philosopher—a lover of wisdom—and a lover of falsehood" (485d). And thus "someone who loves learning must strive for every kind of truth" (ibid.). I've argued that true belief is at most sometimes eudaimonically valuable, and in favor of anti-realism about the epistemic value of true belief. What does this mean for the truth-loving philosopher?

Not very much. First, I have not criticized the view that believing significant truths can have constitutive value, and recall the Socratic maxim, which affirmed the importance of seeking wisdom, which we defined as knowledge about the answers to philosophical questions in ethics and metaphysics—and which Socrates, in the passage just described, takes to involve knowledge of what is unchanging and most real. If this is right, then we should not follow Socrates in concluding that a philosopher must seek "every kind of truth." Rather, we should conclude that a philosopher must seek *significant* truth—the sort of truths knowledge of which constitutes wisdom. Compare the athlete, who must (by definition) seek strength, but not (necessarily) strength of every kind: she must seek only the strength appropriate to athletics, or to her particular sport. Likewise the philosopher must (by definition) seek true beliefs, but not (necessarily) true beliefs of every kind, but only true beliefs appropriate to philosophy. For the same reason, the philosopher (by definition) must only refuse to tolerate falsehood about matters philosophical.

Second, suppose that we concede that a philosopher must (by definition) seek true belief of every kind and refuse to tolerate falsehood in any form. True belief per se does not have eudaimonic value, and its "epistemic value" is a trivial consequence of the meaning of "epistemic." But why should the philosopher be troubled by this?

Assume the kind of desire-fulfillment theory of wellbeing that I favor. The lover of true belief, in as much as she acquires an ample quantity, will in that respect live well. Compare the lover of strength, who trains and becomes stronger, or the lover of fine wine, who acquires an impressive collection of good vintages, or the lover of justice, who makes a positive contribution to her cause. Some people love strength, some wine, some justice, and *some* love truth—some love truth more than anything, some love it so much they would be willing to die rather than give up seeking it, some love it and nothing else, some love it at the expense of other things that they love. The premise that true belief has no universal value has no bearing on the eudaimonic status of philosophers, given the desire-fulfillment theorist's relativistic approach.

(Some love truth even at the expense of their own wellbeing. But this isn't to say that such people are irrational or in any way defective: there are things worth doing that are personally harmful, as when a soldier sacrifices her life to protect others. We might put this point by saying that such self-sacrifice was a good thing to do, but that it was not good for her. We mean just that it was good for her to do it, even though it did not benefit her, it did not make her life go well.)

Lovers of truth (those who care about true belief, those who value true belief) should not feel threatened by a critique of the value of true belief. There is no shame in loving something that is revealed to lack universal or "objective" value. Love is not always, or often, justified by such value. We love our friends, our parents and children, our sisters and brothers, our romantic partners, to a degree and in a manner unlike that involved in our love of strangers, and our love for our friends is not threatened by the "discovery" that they lack universal or "objective" value that would justify our love. To think otherwise assumes that love stands in need of some universal or "objective" justification. Some loves may be like that, but many aren't.

When we are in the grip of love, of course, we may imagine that our beloved has some universal or "objective" value. As Hume points out in "The Sceptic," we find our pursuits the most engaging, the objects of our passion the most valuable, and the road we pursue the only one that leads to happiness. In the case of the love of truth, this can lead to a kind of philosophical self-righteousness: the inchoate sense that the pursuit of truth, or the practice of philosophy, is the only pursuit that is really worthwhile. This can involve tacit commitment to the view that non-philosophers cannot be "truly happy"; it can be mingled with the sentiment that the pursuit of truth is brave, or manly, or noble, such that the practice of philosophy requires eschewing a kind of plebian cowardice. It's revealing, although not surprising, that philosophy has so far never articulated an ethics that didn't praise the philosophical life. In this respect, philosophical ethics has been a rarefied and elaborate exercise in manifesting the bias Hume describes. But the world deserves better philosophizing than this, and we can deliver. What we need to do, to deliver the real ethical goods, is to resist the temptation of philosophical self-righteousness.

A critique of the value of true belief does not speak against a love of truth (and certainly not against a love of significant truth). One might conclude, however, based on my critique of the eudaimonic ideal of true belief, that for most people true belief is best consumed in moderation. Compare, obviously, drink, the consumption of which is part of many of the best human lives. Excessive consumption can threaten one's wellbeing; one can have too much of a good thing. The same, mutatis mutandis, when it comes to truth. If you love true belief, you are surely a philosopher. (The relevant analogue is the hard drinker.) If you love true belief so much that you hold it above all else, seek it anywhere and everywhere, and would trade anything for it, you are an extreme version of the philosophical type. (Compare the alcoholic.) But should you find someone else whose passion for truth is less than yours, or even more importantly, someone for whom such quantities of truth lead to nothing but pain and suffering, you would be a fool (and no philosopher) to think that this other person is somehow worse off than you, because she doesn't want, or can't handle, what you prize so dearly. If philosophers were to admit the possibility of individual differences in valuing true belief—and to really *admit* those differences, as grounding potentially equally good and equally human ways of living—then they would exhibit, to a much greater degree than they typically do, the virtues of humility and toleration, and their love of truth might appear something admirable and heroic, rather than pretentious and self-righteous.

In the *Groundwork of the Metaphysics of Morals*, Kant wrote:

We do find that the more cultivated reason engages with the purpose of enjoying life and with happiness, so much the further does a human being stray from true contentment; and from this there arises in many, and indeed in those who are most experienced in its use, if only they are sincere enough to admit it, a certain degree of *misology*, i.e. hatred of reason, since after calculating all the advantages they derive—I do not say from the invention of all the arts of common luxury, but even from the sciences (which in the end also appear to them to be a luxury of the understanding)—they still find that they have in fact just brought more hardship upon their shoulders than they have gained in happiness, and that because of this they eventually envy, rather than disdain, the more common run of people, who are closer to the guidance of their natural instinct, and do not allow their reason to much influence their behavior. (4:395)

What Kant describes here in the case of practical reason is also possible in the case of theoretical reason. This critique of the value of true belief can be understood as a defense of a modest form of theoretical misology. (It would be a defense of misology not in the sense of providing reasons for misology, but of removing the objection that the misologist fails to respect the value of true belief.) I envy, and do not despise, the "common run of people," who do not allow their reason to much influence their beliefs. And I sometimes find myself wishing that I loved true belief less, and happiness more.

Kant's objection to practical misology is that:

[E]xistence has another and much more worthy purpose, for which, and not for happiness, reason is quite properly intended, and which must, therefore, be regarded as the supreme condition to which the private purpose of men must, for the most part, defer. (Ibid.)

We have considered in this book the idea that the intellect also has a "more worthy purpose," by considering the epistemic value of true belief, and the thesis that belief "aims at truth." You might think, following Kant, that the intellect has a more worthy purpose than promoting our happiness, that it was intended for something grander. But I found no plausible way of articulating this idea. For my part, the claim that the intellect has a more worthy purpose seems false. Each of us has our own purposes—the things we desire, love, and care about—and some of us love true belief very much. But to the extent that our love of true belief interferes with our happiness, we cannot in good faith take refuge in the kind of consolation that Kant imagines. We cannot say that the intellect was not meant to make us happy. The intellect was not meant for anything. True belief is valued by philosophers—not because human beings naturally want knowledge, not because the unexamined life isn't worth living, not because belief essentially aims at truth, and not because God or Mother Nature intended that our beliefs be true—but simply because the love of truth is our ruling passion.

Bibliography

Abramson, L.Y., and Alloy, L.B. (1981), "Depression, Nondepression, and Cognitive Illusions: Reply to Schwartz," *Journal of Experimental Psychology: General* 110, pp. 436–47.

Ackrill, J.L. (1973), *Aristotle's Ethics* (Faber).

Adler, J. (2002), *Belief's Own Ethics* (MIT Press).

Alcock, J. (1995), "The Belief Engine," *Skeptical Inquirer* 19:3.

Alicke, M.D. (1985), "Global Self-Evaluation as Determined by the Desirability and Controllability of Trait Adjectives," *Journal of Personality and Social Psychology* 49:6, pp. 1621–30.

Alloy, L.B., and Abramson, L.Y. (1979), "Judgment of Contingency in Depressed and Nondepressed Students: Sadder but Wiser?," *Journal of Experimental Psychology: General* 108:4, pp. 441–85.

—— (1982), "Learned Helplessness, Depression, and the Illusion of Control," *Journal of Personality and Social Psychology* 42:6, pp. 1114–26.

—— (1988), "Depressive Realism: Four Theoretical Perspectives," in L.B. Alloy (ed.), *Cognitive Processes in Depression* (Guilford Press), pp. 223–65.

Alloy, L.B., Abramson, L.Y., and Viscusi, D.V. (1981), "Induced Mood and the Illusion of Control," *Journal of Personality and Social Psychology* 41:6, pp. 1129–40.

Alloy, L.B., and Ahrens, A.H. (1987), "Depression and Pessimism for the Future: Biased Use of Statistically Relevant Information in Predictions for Self versus Others," *Journal of Personality and Social Psychology* 52, pp. 366–78.

Alston, W.P. (1985), "Concepts of Epistemic Justification," *The Monist* 68, pp. 57–89.

—— (1988), "The Deontological Conception of Epistemic Justification," *Philosophical Perspectives* 2, pp. 257–99.

—— (2005), *Beyond "Justification": Dimensions of Epistemic Evaluation* (Cornell University Press).

Aristotle (1984), *Complete Works*, revised edition, edited by J. Barnes (Princeton University Press).

Armor, D.A., and Taylor, S. (2002), "When Predictions Fail: The Dilemma of Unrealistic Optimism," in T. Gilovich, D.W. Griffin, and D. Kahneman (eds.), *Heuristics and Biases: The Psychology of Intuitive Judgment* (Cambridge University Press), pp. 334–47.

—— (2003), "The Effects of Mindset on Behavior: Self-Regulation in Deliberative and Implemental Frames of Mind," *Personality and Social Psychology Bulletin* 29, pp. 86–95.

Armstrong, D. (1978), "Naturalism, Materialism, and First Philosophy," *Philosophia* 8, pp. 261–76.

Aronson, E. (1969), "The Theory of Cognitive Dissonance: A Current Perspective," in L. Berkowitz (ed.), *Advances in Experimental Social Psychology* 4 (Academic Press), pp. 1–34.

Arpaly, N. (2003), *Unprincipled Virtue: An Inquiry into Moral Agency* (Oxford University Press).

Audi, R. (1990), "Weakness of Will and Rational Action," *Australasian Journal of Philosophy* 68, pp. 270–81.

Averill, E., and Hazlett, A. (2011), "Color Objectivism and Color Projectivism," *Philosophical Psychology* 24:6, pp. 751–65.

Badhwar, N.K. (2008), "Is Realism Really Bad for You? A Realistic Response," *Journal of Philosophy* 1005, pp. 85–107.

Baehr, J. (2011), *The Inquiring Mind: On Intellectual Virtues and Virtue Epistemology* (Oxford University Press).

Baker, J. (1987), "Trust and Rationality," *Pacific Philosophical Quarterly* 68, pp. 1–13.

Bandura, A. (1977), *Social Learning Theory* (Prentice Hall).

Baril, A. (2010), "A Eudaimonist Approach to the Problem of Significance," *Acta Analytica* 25:2, pp. 215–41.

—— (forthcoming), "Pragmatic Encroachment in Accounts of Epistemic Excellence," *Synthese*.

Baron, M. (1988), "What is Wrong with Self-Deception?," in B.P. McLaughlin and A.O. Rorty (eds.), *Perspectives on Self-Deception* (University of California Press), pp. 431–49.

—— (1991), "Impartiality and Friendship," *Ethics* 101:4, pp. 835–57.

Baumeister, R. (1989), "The Optimal Margin of Illusion," *Journal of Social and Clinical Psychology* 8, pp. 176–89.

Baumeister, R., Heatherton, T.F., and Tice, D.M. (1993), "When Ego Threats Lead to Self-Regulation Failure: Negative Consequences of High Self-Esteem," *Journal of Personality and Social Psychology* 64, pp. 141–56.

Bayne, T., and Pacherie, E. (2005), "In Defense of the Doxastic Conception of Delusions," *Mind and Language* 20:2, pp. 163–88.

Beck, A.T., and Alford, B.A. (2009), *Depression: Causes and Treatment*, second edition (University of Pennsylvania Press).

Bedau, M. (1993), "Naturalism and Teleology," in S.J. Wagner and R. Warner (eds.), *Naturalism: A Critical Appraisal* (University of Notre Dame Press), pp. 23–51.

Bennett, K. (2003), "Why the Exclusion Problem Seems Intractable and How, Just Maybe, to Tract It," *Noûs* 37:3, pp. 471–97.

Bergmann, M. (2009), "Rational Disagreement After Full Disclosure," *Episteme* 6:3, pp. 336–53.

Blaney, P.H. (1986), "Affect and Memory: A Review," *Psychological Bulletin* 99, pp. 229–46.

Block, N. (2003), "Do Causal Powers Drain Away?," *Philosophy and Phenomenological Research* 67:1, pp. 133–50.

Boghossian, P. (2003), "The Normativity of Content," *Philosophical Issues* 13, pp. 31–45.

—— (2005), "Is Meaning Normative?," in Nimtz and Beckermann (eds.), *Philosophy—Science—Scientific Philosophy* (Mentis), pp. 205–18.

—— (2006), *Fear of Knowledge: Against Relativism and Constructivism* (Oxford University Press).

BonJour, L. (1985), *The Structure of Empirical Knowledge* (Harvard University Press).

Borkenau, P., and Liebler, A. (1993), "Convergence of Stranger Ratings of Personality and Intelligence With Self-Ratings, Partner Ratings, and Measured Intelligence," *Journal of Personality and Social Psychology* 65:3, pp. 546–53.

Bortolotti, L. (2009), *Delusions and Other Irrational Beliefs* (Oxford University Press).

Boyd-Wilson, B.M., McClure, J., and Walkey, F.H. (2004), "Are Wellbeing and Positive Illusions Linked? The Answer May Be Yes, but...," *Australian Journal of Psychology* 56:1, pp. 1–9.

Bradley, G.W. (1978), "Self-Serving Biases in the Attribution Process: A Reexamination of the Fact or Fiction Question," *Journal of Personality and Social Psychology* 36, pp. 56–71.

Brady, M.S. (2010), "Curiosity and the Value of Truth," in A. Haddock, A. Millar, and D. Pritchard (eds.), *Epistemic Value* (Oxford University Press), pp. 265–83.

Braun, D., and Sider, T. (2007), "Vague, So Untrue," *Noûs* 41:2, pp. 133–56.

Brickman, P., Coates, D., and Janoff-Bulman, R. (1978), "Lottery Winners and Accident Victims: Is Happiness Relative?," *Journal of Personality and Social Psychology* 35, pp. 917–27.

Brink, D.O. (1989), *Moral Realism and the Foundations of Ethics* (Cambridge University Press).

Brinthaupt, T.M., Moreland, R.L., and Levine J.M. (1991), "Sources of Optimism among Prospective Group Members," *Personality and Social Psychology Bulletin* 17, pp. 36–43.

Brown, J.D. (1986), "Evaluations of Self and Others: Self-enhancement Biases in Social Judgments," *Social Cognition* 4:4, pp. 353–76.

—— (1990), "Evaluating One's Abilities: Shortcuts and Stumbling Blocks on the Road to Self-Knowledge," *Journal of Experimental Social Psychology* 26, pp. 149–67.

—— (1993), "Self-Esteem and Self-Evaluation: Feeling is Believing," in J.M. Suls (ed.), *Psychological Perspectives on the Self* (Erlbaum), 27–58.

—— (1998), *The Self* (McGraw-Hill).

—— (2009), "Positive Illusions and Positive Collusions: How Social Life Abets Self-Enhancing Beliefs," *Behavioral and Brain Sciences* 32:6, pp. 514–15.

Brown, J.D., and Dutton, K.A. (1995), "Truth and Consequences: The Costs and Benefits of Accurate Self-Knowledge," *Personality and Social Psychology Bulletin* 21, 1288–96.

Brown, J.D., and Gallagher, F.M. (1992), "Coming to Terms with Failure: Private Self-Enhancement and Public Self-Effacement," *Journal of Experimental Social Psychology* 28, pp. 3–22.

Brown, J.D., and Kobayashi, C. (2002), "Self-Enhancement in Japan and America," *Asian Journal of Social Psychology* 5, pp. 145–67.

—— (2003a), "Introduction: Culture and Self-Enhancement Bias," *Journal of Cross-Cultural Psychology* 34:5, pp. 492–5.

—— (2003b), "Motivation and Manifestation: The Cross-Cultural Expression of the Self-Enhancement Motive," *Asian Journal of Social Psychology* 6, pp. 85–8.

Brown, J.D., and Rogers, R.J. (1991), "Self-Serving Attributions: The Role of Physiological Arousal," *Personality and Social Psychology Bulletin* 17, pp. 501–6.

Buunk, B.P., Collins, R.L., Taylor, S.E., Van Yperen, N.W., and Dakof, G.A. (1990), "The Affective Consequences of Social Comparison: Either Direction Has Its Ups and Downs," *Journal of Personality and Social Psychology* 59:6, pp. 1238–49.

Cameron, R. (2010a), "Quantification, Naturalness, and Ontology," in A. Hazlett (ed.), *New Waves in Metaphysics* (Palgrave-Macmillan), pp. 8–26.

—— (2010b), "How to Have a Radically Minimal Ontology," *Philosophical Studies* 151, pp. 249–64.

Campbell, J.D. (1986), "Similarity and uniqueness: The Effects of Attribute Type, Relevance, and Individual Differences in Self-Esteem and Depression," *Journal of Personality and Social Psychology* 50, pp. 281–94.

Carver, C.S., and Gaines, J.G. (1987), "Optimism, Pessimism, and Postpartum Depression," *Cognitive Therapy and Research* 11, pp. 449–62.

Chrisman, M. (2007), "From Epistemic Contextualism to Epistemic Expressivism," *Philosophical Studies* 135, pp. 225–54.

—— (2010), "From Epistemic Expressivism to Epistemic Inferentialism," in A. Haddock, A. Millar, and D. Pritchard (eds.), *Social Epistemology* (Oxford University Press), pp. 112–28.

—— (2012), "Epistemic Expressivism," *Philosophy Compass* 7:2, pp. 118–26.

Clifford, W.K. (1999), *The Ethics of Belief and Other Essays* (Prometheus Books).

Cokely, E.T., and Feitz, A. (2009), "Adaptive Diversity and Misbelief," *Behavioral and Brain Sciences* 32, p. 516.

Collins, R.L., Taylor, S.E., and Skokan, L.A. (1990), "A Better World or a Shattered Vision? Changes in Life Perspectives Following Victimization," *Social Cognition* 8:3, pp. 263–85.

Colvin, C.R., and Block, J. (1994), "Do Positive Illusions Foster Mental Health? An Examination of the Taylor and Brown Formulation," *Psychological Bulletin* 116, pp. 3–20.

Colvin, C.R., Block, J., and Funder, D.C. (1995), "Overly Positive Self-Evaluations and Personality: Negative Implications for Mental Health," *Journal of Personality and Social Psychology* 68:6, pp. 1152–62.

Conway, M., and Ross, M. (1984), "Getting what you want by revising what you had," *Journal of Personality and Social Psychology* 47, pp. 738–48.

Coyne, J.C., and Gotlib, I.H. (1983), "The Role of Cognition in Depression: A Critical Appraisal," *Psychological Bulletin* 94:3, pp. 472–505.

Craig, E. (1990), *Knowledge and the State of Nature* (Oxford University Press).

Crandall, V.J., Solomon, D., and Kellaway, R. (1955), "Expectancy Statements and Decisions Times as Functions of Objective Probabilities and Reinforcement Values," *Journal of Personality* 24:2, pp. 192–203.

Crocker, J., and Park, L.E. (2004), "The Costly Pursuit of Self-Esteem," *Psychological Bulletin* 130:3, pp. 392–414.

Crocker, J., Thompson, L., McGraw, K., Ingerman, C. (1987), "Downward Comparison, Prejudice, and Evaluation of Others: Effects of Self-Esteem and Threat," *Journal of Personality and Social Psychology* 52, pp. 907–16.

Cross, K.P. (1977), "Not Can, but Will College Teaching be Improved?," *New Directions for Higher Education* 17, pp. 1–15.

Cummins, R. (1975), "Functional Analysis," *Journal of Philosophy* 71, pp. 741–65.

Cuneo, T. (2007), *The Normative Web* (Oxford University Press).

Currie, G. (2000), "Illusion, Delusions, and Hallucinations," *Mind & Language* 15(1), pp. 168–83.

Currie, G., and Ravenscroft, I. (2002), *Recreative Minds: Imagination in Philosophy and Psychology* (Oxford University Press).

Cutrofello, A. (1999), "The Transcendental Pretensions of the Principle of Charity," in L.E. Hahn (ed.), *The Philosophy of Donald Davidson* (Open Court), pp. 333–41.

David, M. (2001), "Truth as the Epistemic Goal," in M. Steup (ed.), *Knowledge, Truth, and Duty: Essays on Epistemic Justification, Responsibility, and Virtue* (Oxford University Press), pp. 151–69.

Davidson, D. (1970), "Mental Events," in L. Foster and J.W. Swanson (eds.), *Experience and Theory* (Duckworth), and reprinted in D. Davidson, *Essays on Actions and Events* (Oxford University Press, 1980), pp. 207–24.

—— (1973), "Radical Intepretation," *Dialectica* 27, pp. 313–28, and reprinted in D. Davidson, *Essays on Truth and Interpretation* (Oxford University Press, 1984), pp. 125–40.

—— (1974a), "Belief and the Basis of Meaning," *Synthese* 27, pp. 309–23, and reprinted in D. Davidson, *Essays on Truth and Interpretation* (Oxford University Press, 1984), pp. 141–54.

—— (1974b), "On the Very Idea of a Conceptual Scheme," in D. Davidson, *Essays on Truth and Interpretation* (Oxford University Press, 1984), pp. 183–98.

—— (1982), "Rational Animals," *Dialectica* 36, pp. 317–27, and reprinted in D. Davidson, *Subjective, Intersubjective, Objective* (Oxford University Press, 2001), pp. 95–106.

—— (1983), "A Coherence Theory of Truth and Knowledge," in D. Henrich (ed.), *Kant oder Hegel?* (Klett-Cotta), and reprinted in D. Davidson, *Subjective, Intersubjective, Objective* (Oxford University Press, 2001), pp. 137–53.

—— (1987), "Knowing One's Own Mind," *Proceedings and Addresses of the American Philosophical Association* 60, pp. 441–58.

—— (1993), "Thinking Causes," in J. Heil and A. Mele (eds.), *Mental Causation* (Oxford University Press), pp. 3–17.

Almeida, C. (2001), "What Moore's Paradox is About," *Philosophy and Phenomenological Research* 62:1, pp. 33–58.

Dennett, D. (1971), "Intentional Systems," *Journal of Philosophy* 68: 4, pp. 87–106.

—— (1982), "Making Sense of Ourselves," in J. Biro and R. Shahan (eds.), *Mind, Brain, and Function* (University of Oklahoma Press), pp. 63–81.

—— (1987), *The Intentional Stance* (MIT Press).

—— (1991), "Real Patterns," *Journal of Philosophy* 88:1 (1991), pp. 27–51.

DePaul, M. (2001), "Value Monism in Epistemology," in M. Steup (ed.), *Knowledge, Truth, and Duty: Essays on Epistemic Justification, Responsibility, and Virtue* (Oxford University Press), pp. 170–83.

—— (2010), "Ugly Analyses and Value," in A. Haddock, A. Millar, and D. Pritchard (eds.), *Epistemic Value* (Oxford University Press), pp. 112–38.

DeRose, K. (2002), "Assertion, Knowledge, and Context," *Philosophical Review* 111:2, pp. 167–203.

DeWitt, T.J. (1998), "Costs and Limits of Phenotypic Plasticity: Tests With Predator-Induced Morphology and Life History in a Freshwater Snail," *Journal of Evolutionary Biology* 11, pp. 465–80.

DeWitt, T.J., Robinson, B.W., and Wilson, D.S. (2000), "Functional Diversity among Predators of a Freshwater Snail Imposes an Adaptive Trade-off for Shell Morphology," *Evolutionary Ecology Research* 2, pp. 129–48.

Dogramaci, S. (2012), "Reverse Engineering Epistemic Evaluations," *Philosophy and Phenomenological Research* 84:3, pp. 513–30.

Dretske, F. (1986), "Misrepresentation," in R.J. Bogdan (ed.), *Belief, Form, and Content* (Oxford University Press), reprinted in A. Goldman (ed.), *Readings in Philosophy of Mind and Cognitive Science* (MIT Press), pp. 297–314.

—— (2000), "Norms, History, and the Constitution of the Mental," in his *Perception, Knowledge, and Belief* (Cambridge University Press), pp. 242–58.

Drier, J. (2001), "Humean Doubts about Categorical Imperatives," in E. Millgram (ed.), *Varieties of Practical Reasoning* (MIT Press), pp. 27–47.

Driver, J. (1989), "The Virtues of Ignorance," *Journal of Philosophy* 86:7, pp. 373–84.

—— (1999), "Modesty and Ignorance," *Ethics* 109:4, pp. 827–34.

—— (2001), *Uneasy Virtue* (Cambridge University Press).

Dunning, D., Meyerowitz, J.A., and Holzberg, A.D. (1989), "Ambiguity and Self-Evaluation: The Role of Idiosyncratic Trait Definitions in Self-Serving Assessments of Ability," *Journal of Personality and Social Psychology* 57:6, pp. 1082–90.

Dunning, D. (1995), "Trait Importance and Modifiability as Factors Influencing Self-Assessment and Self-Enhancement Motives," *Personality and Social Psychology Bulletin* 21:12, pp. 1297–306.

—— (2005), *Self-Insight: Roadblock and Detours on the Path to Knowing Thyself* (Psychology Press).

—— (2009), "Misbelief and the Neglect of Environmental Context," *Behavioral and Brain Sciences* 32, pp. 517–18.

Elga, A. (2005), "On Overrating Oneself ...And Knowing It," *Philosophical Studies* 123(1/2), pp. 115–24.

Elgin, C. (2009), "Is Understanding Factive?," in A. Haddock, A. Millar, and D. Pritchard (eds.), *Epistemic Value* (Oxford University Press), pp. 322–30.

Epley. N., and Dunning, D. (2006), "The Mixed-Blessings of Self-Knowledge in Behavioral Prediction: Enhanced Discrimination but Exacerbated Bias," *Personality and Social Psychology Bulletin* 32:5, pp. 641–55.

Epstein, S., and Meier, P. (1989), "Constructive Thinking: A Broad Coping Variable with Specific Components," *Journal of Personality and Social Psychology* 57:2, pp. 332–50.

Fantl, J., and McGrath, M. (2002), "Evidence, Pragmatics, and Justification," *The Philosophical Review* 111, pp. 67–94.

—— (2009), *Knowledge in an Uncertain World* (Oxford University Press).

Feldman, F. (2004), *Pleasure and the Good Life: Concerning the Nature, Varieties, and Plausibility of Hedonism* (Oxford University Press).

Feldman, R. (1988a), "Epistemic Obligations," *Philosophical Perspectives* 2, 235–56.

—— (1988b), "Rationality, Reliability, and Evolution," *Philosophy of Science* 55:2, pp. 218–27.

—— (2000), "The Ethics of Belief," *Philosophy and Phenomenological Research* 60:3, pp. 667–95.

—— (2006), "Epistemological Puzzles about Disagreement," in S. Hetherington (ed.), *Epistemology Futures* (Oxford University Press), pp. 216–36.

Feldman, S., and Hazlett, A. (2012), "What's Bad About Bad Faith?," *European Journal of Philosophy* 21(1), pp. 50–73.

—— (forthcoming), "Authenticity and Self-Knowledge," *Dialectica*.

Feldman, S. (forthcoming), *Against Authenticity: Why You Shouldn't Be Yourself* (Lexington Books).

Felson, R.B. (1984), "The Effect of Self-Appraisals of Ability on Academic Performance," *Journal of Personality and Social Psychology* 47, pp. 944–52.

Fernández, J. (2005), "Self-Knowledge, Rationality, and Moore's Paradox," *Philosophy and Phenomenological Research* 71:3, pp. 533–56.

Festinger, L. (1954), "A Theory of Social Comparison Processes," *Human Relations* 7, pp. 117–40.

Field, H. (2009), "Epistemology without Metaphysics," *Philosophical Studies* 143, pp. 249–90.

Finnis, J. (1980), *Natural Law and Natural Rights* (Oxford University Press).

Fiske, S.T., and Taylor, S.E. (2008), *Social Cognition: From Brains to Culture* (McGraw-Hill).

Flanagan, O. (2009), "'Can Do' Attitudes: Some Positive Illusions are not Misbeliefs," *Behavioral and Brain Sciences* 32, pp. 519–20.

Fodor, J. (1989), "Making Mind Matter More," *Philosophical Topics* 17: 59–79.

—— (1990), *A Theory of Content and Other Essays* (MIT Press).

—— (1996), "Deconstructing Dennett's Darwin," *Mind and Language* 11:3, pp. 246–62.

—— (2002), "Is Science Biologically Possible?," in J. Beilby (ed.), *Naturalism Defeated? Essays on Plantinga's Evolutionary Argument Against Naturalism* (Cornell University Press), pp. 30–42.

Foley, R. (1987), *The Theory of Epistemic Rationality* (Harvard University Press).

—— (1993), *Working Without a Net: A Study of Egocentric Epistemology* (Oxford University Press).

Foot, P. (1972), "Morality as a System of Hypothetical Imperatives," *Philosophical Review* 81:3, pp. 305–16.

—— (2001), *Natural Goodness* (Oxford University Press).

Frankfurt, H. (1988), *The Importance of What We Care About* (Cambridge University Press).

—— (1999), *Necessity, Volition, and Love* (Cambridge University Press).

Frey, D., and Stahlberg, D. (1986), "Selection of Information After Receiving More or Less Reliable Self-Threatening Information," *Personality and Social Psychology Bulletin* 12:4, pp. 434–41.

Fricker, M. (2009), *Epistemic Injustice: Power and the Ethics of Knowing* (Oxford University Press).

Fumerton, R. (1994), "Skepticism and Naturalistic Epistemology," *Midwest Studies in Philosophy* 19, pp. 321–40.

—— (2001), "Epistemic Justification and Normativity," in M. Steup (ed.), *Knowledge, Truth, and Duty: Essays on Epistemic Justification, Responsibility, and Virtue* (Oxford University Press), pp. 49–60.

Garcia, J., McGowan, B.K., and Green, K.F. (1972), "Biological Constraints on Conditioning," in A.H. Black and W.F. Prokasy (eds.), *Classical Conditioning II: Current Research and Theory* (Appleton-Century-Crofts), pp. 2–27.

Geach, P.T. (1956), "Good and Evil," *Analysis* 17, pp. 33–4.

Gibbard, A. (1990), *Wise Choices, Apt Feelings: A Theory of Normative Judgment* (Oxford University Press).

—— (2003), *Thinking How to Live* (Harvard University Press).

—— (2005), "Truth and Correct Belief," *Philosophical Issues* 15, pp. 338–50.

Gibbons, F.X. (1983), "Self-Attention and Self-Report: The "Veridicality" Hypothesis," *Journal of Personality* 51(3), pp. 517–42.

Gibbons, F.X. (1986), "Social Comparison and Depression: Company's Effect on Misery," *Journal of Personality and Social Psychology* 51, pp. 140–8.

Gigerenzer, G. (2000), *Adaptive Thinking: Rationality in the Real World* (Oxford University Press).

—— (2008), *Rationality for Mortals* (Oxford University Press).

Gigerenzer, G., Todd, P.M., and the ABC Research Group (1999), *Simple Heuristics that Make Us Smart* (Oxford University Press).

Gilovich, T., Griffin, D.W., and Kahneman, D. (eds.) (2002), *Heuristics and Biases: The Psychology of Intuitive Judgment* (Cambridge University Press).

Goldberg, S. (2011), "Putting the Norm of Assertion to Work: The Case of Testimony," in J. Brown and H. Cappelen (eds.), *Assertion: New Philosophical Essays* (Oxford University Press), pp. 175–95.

Goldman, A. (1986), *Epistemology and Cognition* (Harvard University Press).

—— (1999), *Knowledge in a Social World* (Oxford University Press).

—— (2002), *Pathways to Knowledge: Private and Public* (Oxford University Press).

Golin, S., Terrell, F., and Johnson, B. (1977), "Depression and the Illusion of Control," *Journal of Abnormal Psychology* 86:4, pp. 440–2.

Golin, S., Terrell, F., Weitz, J., and Drost, P.L. (1979), "The Illusion of Control Among Depressed Patients," *Journal of Abnormal Psychology* 88:4, pp. 454–7.

Gollwitzer, P.M., and Kinney, R.F. (1989), "Effects of Deliberative and Implemental Mind-Sets on Illusion of Control," *Journal of Personality and Social Psychology* 56, pp. 531–42.

Gosling, S.D., John, O.P., Craik, K.H., and Robins, R.W. (1998), "Do People Know How They Behave? Self-Reported Act Frequencies Compared with On-Line Codings by Observers," *Journal of Personality and Social Psychology* 74:5, pp. 1337–49.

Greco, J. (2003), "Knowledge as Credit for True Belief," in M. DePaul and L. Zagzebski (eds.), *Intellectual Virtue: Perspectives from Ethics and Epistemology* (Oxford University Press), pp. 111–34.

—— (2010), *Achieving Knowledge: A Virtue-Theoretic Account of Epistemic Normativity* (Cambridge University Press).

Greenberg, M.S., and Alloy, L.B. (1989), "Depression versus Anxiety: Processing of Self- and Other-Referent Information," *Cognition and Emotion* 3:3, pp. 207–23.

Greenwald, A.G. (1980), "The Totalitarian Ego: Fabrication and Revision of Personal History," *American Psychologist* 35:7, pp. 603–18.

Grice, H.P. (1989), *Studies in the Way of Words* (Harvard University Press).

Grimm, S.R. (2006), "Is Understanding a Species of Knowledge?," *British Journal of the Philosophy of Science* 57:3, pp. 515–35.

—— (2008), "Epistemic Goals and Epistemic Values," *Philosophy and Phenomenological Research* 77:3, pp. 725–44.

—— (2009), "Epistemic Normativity," in A. Haddock, A. Millar, and D. Pritchard (eds.), *Epistemic Value* (Oxford University Press), pp. 243–64.

—— (forthcoming), "Understanding as Knowledge of Causes."

Haack, S. (1993), *Evidence and Inquiry: Towards Reconstruction in Epistemology* (Blackwell).

—— (2001), "'The Ethics of Belief' Reconsidered," in M. Steup (ed.), *Knowledge, Truth, and Duty: Essays on Epistemic Justification, Responsibility, and Virtue* (Oxford University Press), pp. 21–33.

Hackmiller, K.L. (1966), "Threat as a determinant of downward comparison," *Journal of Experimental Social Psychology* (Supplement 1), pp. 32–9.

Hahn, L.E. (ed.) (1999), *The Philosophy of Donald Davidson* (Open Court).

Hamilton, A. (2007), "Against the Belief Model of Delusion," in M.C. Chung, K.W.M. Fulford, and G. Graham (eds.), *Reconceiving Schizophrenia* (Oxford University Press), pp. 217–34.

Haselton, M.G. (2007), "Error Management Theory," in R.F. Baumeister and K.D. Vohs (eds.), *Encyclopedia of Social Psychology, Volume 1* (Sage Press), pp. 311–12.

Haselton, M.G., and Buss, D.M. (2000), "Error Management Theory: A New Perspective on Biases in Cross-Sex Mindreading," *Journal of Personality and Social Psychology* 78(1), pp. 81–91.

Haselton, M.G., and Nettle, D. (2006), "The Paranoid Optimist: An Integrative Evolutionary Model of Cognitive Biases," *Personality and Social Psychology Review* 10:1, pp. 47–66.

Hawthorne, J. (2004), *Knowledge and Lotteries* (Oxford University Press).

Hazlett, A. (2010), "The Myth of Factive Verbs," *Philosophy and Phenomenological Research* 80:3, pp. 497–522.

—— (2012), "Non-Moral Evil," *Midwest Studies in Philosophy* 36, pp. 18–34.

Heathwood, C. (2010), "Welfare," in J. Skorupski (ed.), *The Routledge Companion to Ethics* (Routledge), pp. 645–55.

Heckhausen, J., and Krueger, J. (1993), "Developmental Expectations for the Self and Most Other People: Age Grading in Three Functions of Social Comparisons," *Developmental Psychology* 29:3, pp. 539–48.

Heine, S.J., Lehman, D.R., Markus, H.R., and Kitayama, S. (1999), "Is there a Universal Need for Positive Self-Regard?," *Psychological Review* 106, pp. 766–94.

Heine, S.J., and Lehman, D.R. (1997), "The Cultural Construction of Self-Enhancement: An Examination of Group-Serving Biases," *Journal of Personality and Social Psychology* 72, pp. 1268–83.

Helgeson, V.S., and Taylor, S.E. (1993), "Social Comparisons and Adjustment Among Cardiac Patients," *Journal of Applied Social Psychology* 23:15, pp. 1171–95.

Helweg-Larsen, M., and Shepperd, J.A. (2001), "Do Moderators of the Optimistic Bias Affect Personal or Target Risk Estimates? A Review of the Literature," *Personality and Social Psychology Review* 5:1, pp. 74–95.

Hieronymi, P. (2005), "The Wrong Kind of Reason," *Journal of Philosophy* 102:9, pp. 437–57.

—— (2006), "Controlling Attitudes," *Pacific Philosophical Quarterly* 87, pp. 45–74.

Horgan, T., and Timmons, M., (1993), "Metaphysical Naturalism, Semantic Normativity, and Meta-Semantic Irrealism," *Philosophical Issues* 4, pp. 180–204.

Horwich, P. (1998), *Truth*, second edition (Oxford University Press).

—— (2006), "The Value of Truth," *Noûs* 40:2, pp. 347–60.

Humberstone, I.L. (1992), "Direction of Fit," *Mind* 101, pp. 59–83.

Hume, D. (1978), *A Treatise of Human Nature*, second edition, edited by P.H. Nidditch (Clarendon Press).

—— (1985), "The Sceptic," in D. Hume, *Essays Moral, Political, and Literary* (Liberty Fund), pp. 159–80.

Hurka, T. (1993), *Perfectionism* (Oxford University Press).

—— (2001), *Virtue, Vice, and Value* (Oxford University Press).

Hursthouse, R. (1991), "Arational Actions," *Journal of Philosophy* 88:2, pp. 57–68.

—— (1999), *On Virtue Ethics* (Oxford University Press).

Ingram, R.E. (1989), "Unique and Shared Cognitive Factors in Social Anxiety and Depression: Automatic Thinking and Self-Appraisal," *Journal of Social and Clinical Psychology* 8:2, pp. 198–208.

Ingram, R.E., and Smith, T.W. (1984), "Depression and Internal versus External Focus of Attention," *Cognitive Therapy and Research* 8:2, pp. 139–52.

Irwin, F.W. (1953), "Stated Expectations as Functions of Probability and Desirability of Outcomes," *Journal of Personality* 21:3, pp. 329–35.

Jackson, F. (1996), "Mental Causation," *Mind* 105: 377–413.

—— (2006), "The Epistemological Objection to Opaque Teleological Theories of Content," in G. Macdonald and D. Papineau (eds.), *Teleosemantics* (Oxford University Press), pp. 85–99.

James, W. (1950), *Principles of Psychology*, volume I (Dover).

Janoff-Bulman, R. (1989), "The Benefits of Illusion, the Threat of Disillusionment, and the Limitations of Inaccuracy," *Journal of Social and Clinical Psychology* 8:2, pp. 158–75.

John, O.P., and Robins, R.W. (1994), "Accuracy and Bias in Self-Perception: Individual Differences in Self-Enhancement and the Role of Narcissism," *Journal of Personality and Social Psychology* 66:1, pp. 206–19.

Joiner, T.E., Vohs, K.D., Katz, J., Kwon, P., and Kline, J.P. (2003), "Excessive Self-Enhancement and Interpersonal Functioning in Roommate Relationships: Her Virtue is His Vice?," *Self and Identity* 2, pp. 21–30.

Jones, W. (2002), "Explaining Our Own Beliefs: Non-Epistemic Believing and Doxastic Instability," *Philosophical Studies* 111, pp. 217–49.

—— (2009), "The Goods and the Motivation of Believing," in A. Haddock, A. Millar, and D. Pritchard (eds.), *Epistemic Value* (Oxford University Press), pp. 139–62.

Kahneman, D., Slovic, P., and Tversky, A. (eds.) (1982), *Judgment Under Uncertainty: Heuristics and Biases* (Cambridge University Press).

Kahneman, D., and Tversky, A. (1996), "On the Reality of Cognitive Illusions," *Psychological Review* 103(3), pp. 582–91.

Kalderon, M.E. (2009), "Epistemic Relativism," *Philosophical Review* 118:2, pp. 225–40.

Kant, I. (1992), *Lectures on Logic*, edited by J. Michael Young (Cambridge University Press).

—— (2012), *Groundwork of the Metaphysics of Morals*, edited by Mary Gregor and Jens Timmerman (Cambridge University Press).

Kappel, K. (2010), "Expressivism about Knowledge and the Value of Knowledge," *Acta Analytica* 25, pp. 175–94.

Kavka, G. (1983), "The Toxin Puzzle," *Analysis* 43:1, pp. 33–6.

Keller, S. (2004), "Friendship and Belief," *Philosophical Papers* 33:3, pp. 329–51.

Kelly, T. (2003), "Epistemic Rationality as Instrumental Rationality: A Critique," *Philosophy and Phenomenological Research* 66:3, pp. 612–40.

Kendler, K.S. (2005), "'A Gene for…': The Nature of Gene Action in Psychiatric Disorders," *American Journal of Psychiatry* 162, pp. 1243–52.

Kim, J. (1993a), "The Myth of Nonreductive Materialism," in J. Kim, *Supervenience and Mind* (Cambridge University Press), pp. 265–84.

—— (1993b), "Naturalism and Semantic Normativity," *Philosophical Issues* 4, pp. 205–10.

—— (2000), *Mind in a Physical World* (MIT Press).

—— (2007), *Physicalism, or Something Near Enough* (Princeton University Press).

Kingsbury, J. (2006), "A Proper Understanding of Millikan," *Acta Analytica* 21(3), pp. 23–40.

Kitcher, P. (1993), *The Advancement of Science: Science without Legend, Objectivity without Illusions* (Oxford University Press).

—— (2001), *Science, Truth, and Democracy* (Oxford University Press).

—— (2004), "The Ends of the Sciences," in B. Leiter (ed.), *The Future for Philosophy* (Oxford University Press), pp. 208–29.

Klein, C.T.F., and Helweg-Larsen, M. (2002), "Perceived Control and the Optimistic Bias: A Meta-Analytic Review," *Psychology and Health* 17:4, pp. 437–46.

Kobayashi, C., and Brown, J.D. (2003), "Self-Esteem and Self-Enhancement in Japan and America," *Journal of Cross-Cultural Psychology* 34:5, pp. 567–80.

Kolodny, N. (2005), "Why Be Rational?," *Mind* 114, pp. 509–63.

Kornblith, H. (1993), "Epistemic Normativity," *Synthese* 94, pp. 357–76.

Korsgaard, C. (1983), "Two Distinctions in Goodness," *Philosophical Review* 92:2, pp. 169–95.

—— (1996), *The Sources of Normativity* (Cambridge University Press).

—— (1997), "The Normativity of Instrumental Reason," in G. Cullity and B. Gaut (eds.), *Ethics and Practical Reason* (Oxford University Press), pp. 215–54.

Kraut, R. (1979), "Two Conceptions of Happiness," *Philosophical Review* 88:2, pp. 167–97.

—— (2007), *What is Good and Why* (Harvard University Press).

Kriegel, U. (2010) "Interpretation: Its Scope and Limits," in A. Hazlett (ed.), *New Waves in Metaphysics* (Palgrave-Macmillan), pp. 111–35.

Krueger, J. (1998), "Enhancement Bias in Descriptions of Self and Others," *Personality and Social Psychology Bulletin* 24, pp. 505–16.

Krueger, J., and Dunning, D. (1999), "Unskilled and Unaware of It: How Difficulties in Recognizing One's Own Incompetence Lead to Inflated Self-Assessments," *Journal of Personality and Social Psychology* 77:6, pp. 1121–34.

Kuiper, N.A., MacDonald, M.R., and Derry, P.A., (1983), "Parameters of a Depressive Self-Schema," in J. Suls and A.G. Greenwald (eds.), *Psychological Perspectives on the Self*, pp. 119–217.

Kuiper, N.A. (1978), "Depression and Causal Attributions for Success and Failure," *Journal of Personality and Social Psychology* 36, pp. 236–46.

Kunda, Z. (1987), "Motivation and Inference: Self-Serving Generation and Evaluation of Evidence," *Journal of Personality and Social Psychology* 53, pp. 636–47.

Kunda, Z. (1990), "The Case for Motivated Reasoning," *Psychological Bulletin* 108:3, pp. 480–98.

Kurman, J. (2003), "Why is Self-Enhancement Low in Certain Collectivist Cultures?: An Investigation of Two Competing Explanations," *Journal of Cross-Cultural Psychology* 34:5, pp. 496–510.

—— (2006), "Self-Enhancement, Self-Regulation, and Self-Improvement Following Failures," *British Journal of Social Psychology*, 45, pp. 339–56.

Kusch, M. (2009), "Testimony and the Value of Knowledge," in A. Haddock, A. Millar, and D. Pritchard (eds.), *Epistemic Value* (Oxford University Press), pp. 60–94.

Kvanvig, J.L. (2003), *The Value of Knowledge and the Pursuit of Understanding* (Cambridge University Press).

—— (2010), "The Swamping Problem Redux: Pith and Gist," in A. Haddock, A. Millar, and D. Pritchard (eds.), *Social Epistemology* (Oxford University Press), pp. 89–111.

Kwan, Y.S.Y., John, O.P., Kenny, D.A., Bond, M.H., and Robins, R.W. (2004), "Reconceptualizing Individual Differences in Self-Enhancement Bias: An Interpersonal Approach," *Psychological Review* 111:1, pp. 94–110.

Langer, E.J. (1975), "The Illusion of Control," *Journal of Personality and Social Psychology* 32:2, pp. 311–28.

Langer, E.J., and Roth, J. (1975), "Heads I Win, Tails It's Chance: The Illusion of Control as a Function of the Sequence of Outcomes in a Purely Chance Task," *Journal of Personality and Social Psychology* 32:6, pp. 951–5.

Langton, R. (2007), "Objective and Unconditioned Value," *Philosophical Review* 116:2, pp. 15785.

Larwood, L. (1978), "Swine-Flu: A Field Study of Self-Serving Biases," *Journal of Applied Social Psychology* 8:3, pp. 283–9.

Larwood, L., and Whittaker, W. (1977), "Managerial Myopia: Self-Serving Biases in Organizational Planning," *Journal of Applied Psychology* 62:2, pp. 194–8.

Lawrence, G. (1993), "Aristotle and the Ideal Life," *Philosophical Review* 102:1, pp. 1–34.

—— (2009), "Is Aristotle's Function Argument Fallacious?," *Philosophical Inquiry* 31:1/2, pp. 191–224.

Lazar, A. (1999), "Deceiving Oneself or Self-Deceived? On the Formation of Beliefs 'Under the Influence,'" *Mind* 108, pp. 265–90.

Leary, M.R. (2007), "Motivational and Emotional Aspects of the Self," *Annual Review of Psychology* 58, pp. 317–44.

LePore, E. (ed.) (1986) *Truth and Interpretation: Perspectives on the Philosophy of Donald Davidson* (Blackwell).

Lewinsohn, P.M., Mischel, W., Chaplin, W., and Baron, R. (1980), "Social Competence and Depression: The Role of Illusory Self-Perceptions," *Journal of Abnormal Psychology* 89:2, pp. 203–12.

Lewis, D. (1974), "Radical Interpretation," *Synthese* 23, pp. 331–44, reprinted in D. Lewis, *Philosophical Papers I* (Oxford University Press), pp. 108–18.

Lycan, W. (1988), "Epistemic Value," in his *Judgment and Justification* (Cambridge University Press), pp. 128–56.

Lynch, M.P. (2004), *True to Life: Why Truth Matters* (MIT Press).

—— (2009a), "The Values of Truth and the Truth of Values," in A. Haddock, A. Millar, and D. Pritchard (eds.), *Epistemic Value* (Oxford University Press), pp. 225–42.

—— (2009b), "Truth, Value, and Epistemic Expressivism," *Philosophy and Phenomenological Research* 79:1, pp. 76–97.

Macdonald, G., and Papineau, D. (2006), "Introduction: Problems and Prospects for Teleosemantics," in G. Macdonald and D. Papineau (eds.), *Teleosemantics* (Oxford University Press), pp. 1–22.

MacFarlane, J. (2005a), "Making Sense of Relative Truth," *Proceedings of the Aristotelian Society* 105:1, pp. 205–23.

—— (2005b), "The Assessment Sensitivity of Knowledge Attributions," *Oxford Studies in Epistemology* 1, pp. 197–233.

MacIntyre, A. (2007), *After Virtue*, third edition (Duckworth).

Marks, J.T., Marion, B.B., and Hoffman, D.D. (2010), "Natural Selection and Veridical Perceptions," *Journal of Theoretical Biology* 266, pp. 504–15.

Marks, R. (1951), "The effect of probability, desirability, and 'privilege' on the stated expectations of children," *Journal of Personality* 19:3, pp. 332–51.

Martin, D.J., Abramson, L.Y., and Alloy, L.B. (1984), "The Illusion of Control for Self and Others in Depressed and Non-Depressed College Students," *Journal of Personality and Social Psychology* 46, pp. 125–36.

Maslow, A.H. (1950), "Self-Actualizing People: A Study of Psychological Health," *Personality* 1, pp. 11–34.

McFarland, C., and Ross, M. (1982), "Impact of Causal Attributions on Affective Reactions to Success and Failure," *Journal of Personality and Social Psychology* 45, pp. 937–46.

McGlynn, A. (2013), "Believing Things Unknown," *Noûs* 47:2, pp. 385–407.

McGraw, A.P., Mellers, B.A., and Ritov, I. (2004), "The Affective Costs of Overconfidence," *Journal of Behavioral Decision Making* 17, pp. 281–95.

McHugh, C. (2011a), "What Do We Aim At When We Believe?," *Dialectica* 65:3, pp. 369–92.

—— (2011b), "Judging as a Non-Voluntary Action," *Philosophical Studies* 152, pp. 245–69.

—— (2012a), "Belief and Aims," *Philosophical Studies* 160:3, pp. 425–39.

—— (2012b), "Epistemic Deontology and Voluntariness," *Erkenntnis* 77:1, pp. 65–94.

McKay, R., and Dennett, D. (2009), "The Evolution of Misbelief," *Behavioral and Brain Sciences* 32, pp. 493–561.

McLaughlin, B. (1988), "Exporing the Possibility of Self-Deception in Belief," in B. McLaughlin and A.O. Rorty (eds.), *Perspectives on Self-Deception* (University of California), pp. 29–62.

Mead, G.H. (1934), *Self, and Society* (University of Chicago Press) 20.

Mele, A. (1987), *Irrationality: An Essay on Akrasia, Self-Deception, and Self-Control* (Oxford University Press).

—— (1997), "Real Self-Deception," *Behavioral and Brain Sciences* 20, pp. 91–102.

—— (2001), *Self-Deception Unmasked* (Princeton University Press).

Merricks, T. (2003), *Objects and Persons* (Oxford University Press).

Millgram, E. (1995), "Was Hume a Humean?," *Hume Studies* 21:1, pp. 75–94.

Millikan, R. (1984), *Language, Thought, and Other Biological Categories* (MIT Press).

—— (1993), *White Queen Psychology and Other Essays for Alice* (MIT Press).

—— (2006), "Useless Content," in G. Macdonald and D. Papineau (eds.), *Teleosemantics* (Oxford University Press), pp. 100–14.

Montmarquet, J. (1986), "The Voluntariness of Belief," *Analysis* 46, pp. 49–53.

Moore, G.E. (1993), *Selected Writings* (Routledge).

Morton, A. (1988), "Partisanship," in B.P. McLaughlin and A.O. Rorty (eds.), *Perspectives on Self-Deception* (University of California Press), pp. 170–82.

Murray, S.L., and Holmes, J.G. (1993), "Seeing Virtues in Faults: Negativity and the Transformation of Interpersonal Narratives," *Journal of Personality and Social Psychology* 65, pp. 707–22.

—— (1997), "A Leap of Faith? Positive Illusions in Romantic Relationships," *Personality and Social Psychology Bulletin* 23, pp. 586–604.

Nagel, T. (1999), "Davidson's New *Cogito*," in L.E. Hahn (ed.), *The Philosophy of Donald Davidson* (Open Court), pp. 195–206.

Neander, K. (1991), "The Teleological Notion of a Function," *Australasian Journal of Philosophy* 69, pp. 454–68.

—— (1995), "Misrepresenting & Malfunctioning," *Philosophical Studies* 79, pp. 109–41.

—— (2004), "Teleological Theories of Mental Content," *Stanford Encyclopedia of Philosophy*.

Nettle, D. (2006), "The Evolution of Personality Variation in Humans and Other Animals," *American Psychologist* 61:6, pp. 622–31.

Ney, A. (2012), "The Causal Contribution of Mental Events," in S. Gozzano and C.S. Hill (eds.), *New Perspectives on Type Identity: The Mental and the Physical* (Cambridge University Press), pp. 230–50.

Nisbett, R., and Ross, L. (1980), *Human Inference: Strategies and Shortcomings of Social Judgment* (Prentice-Hall).

Nussbaum, M. (1993), "Non-Relative Virtues: An Aristotelian Approach," in M. Nussbaum and A. Sen (eds.), *The Quality of Life* (Oxford University Press), pp. 242–69.

—— (1995), "Aristotle on Human Nature and the Foundations of Ethics," in J.E.J. Altham and R. Harrison (eds.), *World, Mind, and Ethics: Essays on the Ethical Philosophy of Bernard Williams* (Cambridge University Press), pp. 86–131.

—— (2000), *Women and Human Development: The Capabilities Approach* (Cambridge University Press).

Odenbaugh, J. (2010), "On the Very Idea of an Ecosystem," in A. Hazlett (ed.), *New Waves in Metaphysics* (Palgrave-Macmillan), pp. 240–58.

Owens, D. (2003), "Does Belief Have an Aim?," *Philosophical Studies* 115, pp. 283–305.

Pace, G.M. (2011), "The Epistemic Value of Moral Considerations: Justification, Moral Encroachment, and James' 'The Will To Believe'," *Noûs* 45:2, pp. 239–68.

Papineau, D. (1993), *Philosophical Naturalism* (Blackwell).

—— (1999), "Normativity and Judgment," *Proceedings of the Aristotelian Society* 73, pp. 16–43.

—— (2001), "The Status of Teleosemantics, or How to Stop Worrying about Swampman," *Australasian Journal of Philosophy* 79, pp. 279–89.

Papineau, D., and Montero, B. (2005), "A Defense of the Via Negativa Argument for Physicalism," *Analysis* 65:287, pp. 233–7.

Parfit, D. (1984), *Reasons and Persons* (Oxford University Press).

—— (2006), "Normativity," in R. Shafer-Landau (ed.), *Oxford Studies in Metaethics*, volume 1, pp. 325–80.

—— (2011), *On What Matters*, two volumes (Oxford University Press).

Paulhus, D.L. (1998), "Interpersonal and Intrapsychic Adaptiveness of Trait Self-Enhancement: A Mixed Blessing?," *Journal of Personality and Social Psychology* 74:5, pp. 1197–1208.

Pietromonaco, P.R., and Markus, H. (1985), "The Nature of Negative Thoughts in Depression," *Journal of Personality and Social Psychology* 48:3, pp. 799–807.

Plantinga, A. (2002), "Introduction: The Evolutionary Argument Against Naturalism," in J. Beilby (ed.), *Naturalism Defeated? Essays on Plantinga's Evolutionary Argument Against Naturalism* (Cornell University Press), pp. 1–12.

Plato (1997), *Complete Works*, edited by J.M. Cooper (Hackett Publishing).

Price, H.H. (1954), "Belief and Will," *Proceedings of the Aristotelian Society, Supplementary Volume* 28, pp. 1–26.

Pritchard, D. (2010), "Knowledge and Understanding," in D. Pritchard, A. Millar, and A. Haddock (eds.), *The Nature and Value of Knowledge: Three Investigations* (Oxford University Press), pp. 3–88.

Pronin, E., Lin, D.Y., and Ross, L. (2002), "The Bias Blind Spot: Perceptions of Bias in Self Versus Others," *Personality and Social Psychology Bulletin* 28: pp. 369–81.

Pronin, E., Gilovich, T., and Ross, L. (2004), "Objectivity in the Eye of the Beholder: Divergent Perceptions of Bias in Self Versus Others," *Psychological Review* 111:3, pp. 781–99.

Pryor, J.B., Gibbons, F.X., Wicklund, R.A., Fazio, R.H., and Hood, R. (1977), "Self-focused attention and self-report validity," *Journal of Personality* 45, pp. 513–52.

Pyszczynski, T., and Greenberg, J. (1987a), "Toward an integration of cognitive and motivational perspectives on social inference: A bias hypothesis-testing model," in L. Berkowitz (ed.), *Advances in Experimental Social Psychology*, volume 20 (Academic Press), pp. 297–340.

—— (1987b), "Depression, Self-Focused Attention, and Self-Regulatory Perseveration," in C. R. Snyder and C. E. Ford (eds.), *Coping with Negative Life Events: Clinical and Social Psychological Perspectives* (Plenum Press), pp. 105–29.

Pyszczynski, T., Hamilton, J.C., Herring, F.H., and Greenberg, J. (1989), "Depression, Self-Focused Attention, and the Negative Memory Bias," *Journal of Personality and Social Psychology* 57:2, pp. 351–7.

Pyszczynski, T., Holt, K., and Greenberg, J. (1989), "Depression, Self-Focused Attention, and Expectancies for Future Positive and Negative Events for Self and Others," *Journal of Personality and Social Psychology* 52, pp. 994–1001.

Railton, P. (1994), "Truth, Reason, and the Regulation of Belief," *Philosophical Issues* 5, pp. 71–93.

—— (1997), "On the Hypothetical and Non-Hypothetical in Reasoning about Belief and Action," in G. Cullity and B. Gaut (eds.), *Ethics and Practical Reason* (Oxford University Press), pp. 53–79.

Ramsey, W. (2002), "Naturalism Defended," in J. Beilby (ed.), *Naturalism Defeated? Essays on Plantinga's Evolutionary Argument Against Naturalism* (Cornell University Press), pp. 15–29.

Rawls, J. (1971), *A Theory of Justice* (Harvard University Press).

Reed, G.M., Taylor, S.E., and Kemeny, M.E. (1993), "Perceived Control and Psychological Adjustment in Gay Men with AIDS," *Journal of Applied Social Psychology* 23:10, pp. 791–824.

Regan, P.C., Snyder, M., and Kassin, S.M. (1995), "Unrealistic Optimism: Self-Enhancement or Person Positivity?," *Personality and Social Psychology Bulletin* 21:10, pp. 1073–82.

Reisner, A. (2008), "Weighing Pragmatic and Evidential Reasons for Belief," *Philosophical Studies* 138:1, pp. 17–27.

—— (2009), "The Possibility of Pragmatic Reasons for Belief and the Wrong Kind of Reason Problem," *Philosophical Studies* 145:2, pp. 257–72.

Ridge, M. (2011), "Getting Lost on the Road to Larissa," *Noûs* 47(1), pp. 181–201

Riggs, W. (2002), "Reliability and the Value of Knowledge," *Philosophy and Phenomenological Research* 64:1, pp. 79–96.

—— (2009), "Two Problems of Easy Credit," *Synthese* 169, pp. 201–16.

Robertson, L.S., (1977), "Car Crashes: Perceived Vulnerability and Willingness to Pay for Crash Protection," *Journal of Community Health* 3(2), pp. 336–41.

Robins, R.W., and Beer, J.S. (2001), "Positive Illusions About the Self: Short-Term Benefits and Long-Term Costs," *Journal of Personality and Social Psychology* 80:2, pp. 340–52.

Ross, W.D. (1930), *The Right and the Good* (Oxford University Press).

Ryan, S. (1999), "What is Wisdom?," *Philosophical Studies* 93:2, pp. 119–39.

—— (2003), "Doxastic Compatibilism and the Ethics of Belief," *Philosophical Studies* 114:1/2, pp. 47–79.

Sacco, W.P., and Hokanson, J.E. (1982), "Expectations of Success and Anagram Performance of Depressives in a Public and Private Setting," *Journal of Personality and Social Psychology* 42, pp. 377–85.

Sackheim, H.A., and Wegner, A.Z. (1986), "Attributional Patterns in Depression and Euthymia," *Archives of General Psychiatry* 43, pp. 553–60.

Sanbonmatsu, D.M., Harpster, L.L., Akimoto, S.A., and Moulin, J.B. (1994), "Selectivity in Generalizations about Self and Others from Performance," *Personality and Social Psychology Bulletin* 20, 358–66.

Sartre, J.P. (1956), *Being and Nothingness* (Washington Square Press).

Sartwell, C. (1992), "Why Knowledge is Merely True Belief," *Journal of Philosophy* 89, pp. 167–80.

Scanlon, T. (1993), "Value, Desire, and Quality of Life," in M.C. Nussbaum and A. Sen (eds.), *The Quality of Life* (Oxford University Press), pp. 185–205.

—— (1998), *What We Owe to Each Other* (Harvard University Press).

Scheier, M.F., and Carver, C.S. (1992), "Effects of Optimism on Psychological and Physical Well-being: Theoretical Overview and Empirical Update," *Cognitive Therapy and Research* 16, pp. 201–28.

Sedikides, C. (1993), "Assessment, Enhancement, and Verification Determinants of the Self-Evaluation Process," *Journal of Personality and Social Psychology* 65:2, pp. 317–38.

Sedikides, C., Gaertner, L., and Toguchi, Y. (2003), "Pancultural Self-Enhancement," *Journal of Personality and Social Psychology* 84, pp. 60–70.

Sedikides, C., and Green., J.D. (2000), "On the Self-Protective Nature of Inconsistency-Negativity Management: Using the Person Memory Paradigm to Examine Self-Referent Memory," *Journal of Personality and Social Psychology* 79:6, pp. 906–922.

Sedikides, C., and Gregg, A.P. (2003), "Portraits of the Self," in M.A. Hogg and J. Cooper (eds.), *The SAGE Handbook of Social Psychology* (SAGE Publications), pp. 110–38.

—— (2008), "Self-Enhancement: Food for Thought," *Perspectives on Psychological Science* 3:2, pp. 102–16.

Sedikides, C., Herbst, K.C., Hardin, D.P., and Dardis, G.J. (2002), "Accountability as a Deterrent to Self-Enhancement: The Search for Mechanisms," *Journal of Personality and Social Psychology* 83:3, pp. 592–605.

Sedikides, C., Rudich, E.A., Gregg, A.P., Kumashiro, M., and Rusbult, C. (2004), "Are Normal Narcissists Psychologically Healthy?: Self-Esteem Matters," *Journal of Personality and Social Psychology* 87:3, pp. 400–16.

Sedikides, C., and Strube, M.J. (1995), "The Multiply Motivated Self," *Personality and Social Psychology Bulletin* 21:12, pp. 1330–5.

Segall, M.G., Lonner, W.J., and Berry, J.W. (1998), "Cross-Cultural Psychology as a Scholarly Discipline: On the Flowing of Culture in Behavioral Research," *American Psychologist* 53, pp. 1101–10.

Seligman, M., Abramson, L., Semmel, A., and Von Baeyer, C., "Depressive Attribution Style," *Journal of Abnormal Psychology* 12, pp. 133–40.

Shafer-Landau, R. (2006), "Ethics as Philosophy," in T. Horgan and M. Timmons (eds.), *Metaethics after Moore* (Oxford University Press), pp. 209–32.

Shah, N. (2003), "How Truth Governs Belief," *Philosophical Review* 112, pp. 447–82.

—— (2011), "Can Reasons for Belief be Debunked?," in A. Reisner and A. Steglich-Petersen (eds.), *Reasons for Belief* (Cambridge University Press), pp. 94–108.

Shah, N., and Velleman, J.D. (2005), "Doxastic Deliberation," *Philosophical Review* 114, pp. 497–534.

Shoemaker, S. (1995), "Moore's Paradox and Self-Knowledge," *Philosophical Studies* 77, pp. 211–28.

Sider, T. (2011), *Writing the Book of the World* (Oxford University Press).

Smith, T.W., and Greenberg, J. (1981), "Depression and Self-Focused Attention," *Motivation and Emotion* 5:4, pp. 323–31.

Smith T.W., Ingram, R.E., and Roth, D.L. (1985), "Self-Focused Attention and Depression: Self-Evaluation, Affect, and Life Stress," *Motivation and Emotion* 9:4, pp. 381–9.

Snyder, M.L., Stephan, W.G., and Rosenfield, D. (1976), "Egotism and Attribution" *Journal of Personality and Social Psychology*, 33, 435–41.

Sosa, D. (2009), "Dubious Assertions," *Philosophical Studies* 146, pp. 269–72.

Sosa, E. (1987), "Serious Philosophy and Freedom of Spirit," *Journal of Philosophy* 84:12, pp. 707–26.

—— (1991), *Knowledge in Perspective: Selected Essays in Epistemology* (Cambridge University Press).

—— (2001), "For the Love of Truth?," in A. Fairweather and L. Zagzebski (eds.), *Virtue Epistemology: Essays on Epistemic Virtue and Responsibility* (Oxford University Press), pp. 49–61.

—— (2003), "The Place of Truth in Epistemology," in M. DePaul and L. Zagzebski (eds.), *Intellectual Virtue: Perspectives from Ethics and Epistemology* (Oxford University Press), pp. 155–79.

—— (2007), *A Virtue Epistemology: Apt Belief and Reflective Knowledge, Volume 1* (Oxford University Press).

—— (2009), "Knowing Full Well: The Normativity of Beliefs as Performances," *Philosophical Studies* 142, pp. 5–15.

—— (2010), "Value Matters in Epistemology," *Journal of Philosophy* 107:4, pp. 167–90.

Sperber, D. (1997), "Intuitive and Reflective Beliefs," *Mind and Language* 12:1, pp. 67–83.

Stanley, J. (2005), *Knowledge and Practical Interests* (Oxford University Press).

Steglich-Petersen, A. (2006), "No Norm Needed: On the Aim of Belief," *Philosophical Quarterly* 56, pp. 499–516.

—— (2009), "Weighing the Aim of Belief," *Philosophical Studies* 145:3, pp. 395–405.

—— (2011), "How to be a Teleologist about Epistemic Reasons," in A. Reisner and A. Steglich-Petersen (eds.), *Reasons for Belief* (Cambridge University Press), pp. 13–33.

Stevenson, L. (2002), "Six Levels of Mentality," *Philosophical Explorations* 5:2, pp. 105–24.

Stich, S. (1985), "Could Man be an Irrational Animal?," *Synthese* 64, pp. 115–35.

—— (1990), *The Fragmentation of Reason: Preface to a Pragmatic Theory of Cognitive Evaluation* (MIT Press).

Stocker, M. (1976), "The Schizophrenia of Modern Ethical Theories," *Journal of Philosophy* 73, pp. 453–66.

Stroud, B. (1999), "Radical Interpretation and Philosophical Scepticism," in L.E. Hahn (ed.), *The Philosophy of Donald Davidson* (Open Court), pp. 139–61.

Stroud, S. (2006), "Epistemic Partiality in Friendship," *Ethics* 116, pp. 289–524.

Sumner, W. (1996), *Welfare, Happiness, and Ethics* (Oxford University Press).

—— (2002), "Happiness Now and Then," *Apeiron* 35:4, pp. 21–40.

Swann, W.B., Wenzlaff, R.M., Krull, D.S., and Pelham, B.W. (1992), "Allure of Negative Feedback: Self-Verification Strivings Among Depressed Persons," *Journal of Abnormal Psychology* 101:2, pp. 293–306.

Swanton, C. (2003), *Virtue Ethics: A Pluralistic View* (Oxford University Press).

Sweeny, K., Carroll, P.K., and Shepperd, J.A. (2006), "Is Optimism Always Best?," *Current Directions in Psychological Science* 15:6, pp. 302–6.

Taylor, S.E. (1989), *Positive Illusions: Creative Self-Deception and the Healthy Mind* (Harper Collins).

—— (1991), "The Asymmetrical Impact of Positive and Negative Events: The Mobilization-Minimization Hypothesis," *Psychological Bulletin* 110:1, pp. 67–85.

Taylor, S.E., and Brown, J.D., (1988), "Illusion and Well-Being: A Social Psychological Perspective on Mental Health," *Psychological Bulletin* 103:2, pp. 193–210.

—— (1994), "Positive Illusions and Well-Being Revisited: Separating Fact from Fiction," *Psychological Bulletin* 116:1, 21–7.

Taylor, S.E., Collins, R.L., Skokan, L.A., and Aspinwall, L.G. (1989), "Maintaining Positive Illusions in the Face of Negative Information: Getting the Facts without Letting them Get You," *Journal of Social and Clinical Psychology* 8, pp. 114–29.

Taylor, S.E., and Gollwitzer, P.M. (1993), "The Effects of Mindset on Positive Illusions," *Journal of Personality and Social Psychology* 69, pp. 213–36.

Taylor, S.E., Lerner, J.S., Sherman, D.K., Sage, R.M., and McDowell, N.K. (2003), "Are Self-Enhancing Cognitions Associated with Healthy or Unhealthy Biological Profiles?," *Journal of Personality and Social Psychology* 85:4, pp. 605–15.

Taylor, S.E., Lichtman, R.R., and Wood, J.V. (1984), "Attributions, Beliefs about Control, and Adjustment to Breast Cancer," *Journal of Personality and Social Psychology* 46:3, pp. 489–502.

Taylor, S.E., and Lobel, M. (1989), "Social Comparison Activity Under Threat: Downward Evaluation and Upward Contacts," *Psychological Review* 96:4, pp. 569–75.

Taylor, S.E., Neter, E., and Wayment, H.A. (1995), "Self-Evaluation Processes," *Personality and Social Psychology Bulletin* 21:12, pp. 1278–87.

Taylor, S.E., Wood, J.V., and Lichtman, R.R. (1983), "It Could Be Worse: Selective Evaluation as a Response to Victimization," *Journal of Social Issues* 39:2, pp. 19–40.

Tesser, A. (1988), "Toward a Self-Evaluation Maintenance Model of Social Behavior," in L. Berkowitz (ed.), *Advances in Experimental Social Psychology* 21 (Academic Press), pp. 181, 227.

Tesser, A., and Campbell, J. (1983), "Self-Definition and Self-Evaluation Maintenance," in J. Suls and A.G. Greenwald (eds.), *Psychological Perspectives on the Self*, volume 2 (Psychology Press), pp. 1–31.

Thompson, S.C. (1981), "Will It Hurt Less If I Can Control It? A Complex Answer to a Simple Question," *Psychological Bulletin* 90:1, pp. 89–101.

Thompson, S.C., Sobolew-Shubin, A., Galbraith, M.E., Schwankovsky, L. and Cruzen, D. (1993), "Maintaining Perceptions of Control: Finding Perceived Control in Low-Control Circumstances," *Journal of Personality and Social Psychology* 64:2, pp. 293–304.

Tiberius, V. (2006), "Well-Being: Psychological Research for Philosophers," *Philosophy Compass*, pp. 493–505.

—— (2008), *The Reflective Life: Living Wisely with our Limits* (Oxford University Press).

Tiberius, V. and Plakias, A. (2010), "Well-Being," in J. Doris and the Moral Psychology Research Group (eds.), *The Moral Psychology Handbook* (Oxford University Press).

Trafimow, D., Armendariz, M.L., and Madson, L. (2004), "A Test of Whether Attributions Provide for Self-Enhancement or Self-Defense," *Journal of Social Psychology* 144:5, pp. 453–63.

Treanor, N. (forthcoming a), "The Measure of Knowledge," *Noûs*.

—— (forthcoming b), "Trivial Truths and the Aim of Inquiry," *Philosophy and Phenomenological Research*.

Turner, R., Scheier, M., Carver, C., and Ickes, W. (1978), "Correlates of Self-Consciousness," *Journal of Personality Assessment* 42, pp. 285–9.

Unger, P. (1975), *Ignorance: A Case for Skepticism* (Oxford University Press).

Urmson, J.O. (1988), *Aristotle's Ethics* (Blackwell).

van Inwagen, P. (1990), *Material Beings* (Cornell University Press).

Vasquez, C.V. (1987), "Judgment of Contingency: Cognitive Biases in Depressed and Non-Depressed Subjects," *Journal of Personality and Social Psychology* 52, pp. 419–31.

Vazire, S. (2010), "Who Knows What About a Person? The Self-Other Knowledge Asymmetry (SOKA) Model," *Journal of Personality and Social Psychology* 98:2, pp. 281–300.

Vazire, S., and Carlson, E.N. (2010), "Self-Knowledge of Personality: Do People Know Themselves?," *Social and Personality Psychology Compass* 4/8, pp. 605–20.

Velleman, J.D. (2000), *The Possibility of Practical Reason* (Oxford University Press).

Wallace, D.F. (2009), *This is Water: Some Thought, Delivered on a Significant Occasion, about Living a Compassionate Life* (Little, Brown, and Company).

Walton, K. (1994), "Morals in Fiction and Fictional Morality," *Proceedings of the Aristotelian Society, Supplementary Volume* 68, pp. 27–66.

Wedgwood, R. (2002), "The Aim of Belief," *Philosophical Perspectives* 16, pp. 265–97.

—— (2007), *The Nature of Normativity* (Oxford University Press).

Weiner, M. (2005), "Must We Know What We Say?," *Philosophical Review* 114:2, pp. 227–51.

Weinstein, N.D. (1980), "Unrealistic Optimism About Future Life Events," *Journal of Personality and Social Psychology* 39:5, pp. 806–20.

Weinstein, N.D. (1987), "Unrealistic Optimism about Susceptibility to Health Problems: Conclusions from a Community-wide Sample," *Journal of Behavioral Medicine* 10(5), pp. 481–500.

White, R. (2007), "Epistemic Subjectivism," *Episteme* 4:1, pp. 115–29.

Williams, B. (1973), "Deciding to Believe," in his *Problems of the Self* (Cambridge University Press), pp. 136–51.

—— (1976), "Persons, Character, and Morality," in A.O. Rorty (ed.), *The Identities of Persons* (University of California Press), pp. 197–216, reprinted in B. Williams, *Moral Luck* (Cambridge University Press 1981), pp. 1–19.

—— (1980), "Internal and External Reasons," in T.R. Harrison (ed.), *Rational Action* (Cambridge University Press), pp. 17–28, reprinted in B. Williams, *Moral Luck* (Cambridge University Press, 1981), pp. 101–13.

—— (1995), "Internal Reasons and The Obscurity of Blame," in B. Williams, *Making Sense of Humanity: And Other Philosophcial Papers* (Cambridge University Press), pp. 35–45.

—— (2002), *Truth and Truthfulness: An Essay in Genealogy* (Princeton University Press).

Williams, J.T. (2004), "Moore's Paradoxes, Evans's Principle and Self-Knowledge," *Analysis* 64:4, pp. 348–53.

Williamson, T. (1996), "Knowing and Asserting," *Philosophical Review* 105:4, pp. 489–523.

Wills, T.A. (1987), "Downward Comparison as a Coping Mechanism," in C.R. Snyder and C.E. Ford (eds.), *Coping with Negative Life Events: Clinical and Social Psychological Perspectives* (Plenum Press), pp. 243–68.

—— (2000), *Knowledge and Its Limits* (Oxford University Press).

Wilson, D.S., and Lynn, S.J. (2009), "Adaptive Misbeliefs are Pervasive, but the Case for Positive Illusions is Weak," *Behavioral and Brain Sciences* 32, pp. 539–40.

Wilson, T.D., and Dunn, E.W. (2004), "Self-Knowledge: Its Limits, Value, and Potential for Improvement," *Annual Review of Psychology* 55, pp. 17.1–17.26.

Wright, L. (1973), "Functions," *Philosophical Review* 82, pp. 139–68.

Yablo, S. (1992), "Mental Causation," *Philosophical Review* 101, pp. 245–80

Zagzebski, L. (1996), *Virtues of the Mind: An Inquiry into the Nature of Virtue and the Ethical Foundations of Knowledge* (Cambridge University Press).

—— (2001), "Recovering Understanding," in M. Steup (ed.), *Knowledge, Truth, and Duty: Essays on Epistemic Justification, Responsibility, and Virtue* (Oxford University Press), pp. 235–51.

—— (2003a), "Intellectual Motivation and the Good of Truth," in M. DePaul and L. Zagzebski (eds.), *Intellectual Virtue: Perspectives from Ethics and Epistemology* (Oxford University Press), pp. 135–54.

—— (2003b), "The Search for the Source of Epistemic Good," *Metaphilosophy* 34:1/2, pp. 12–28.

—— (2004), "Epistemic Value and the Primacy of What We Care About," *Philosophical Papers* 33:3, pp. 353–77.

Zuckerman, M. (1979), "Attributions of Success and Failure Revisited, Or: The Motivational Bias is Alive and Well in Attribution Theory," *Journal of Personality* 47, pp. 245–87.

Index

Locations of definitions are in **bold**.